MW00628636

Transnational Media

Transnational Media

Concepts and Cases

Edited by Suman Mishra and Rebecca Kern-Stone

WILEY Blackwell

This edition first published 2019
© 2019 John Wiley & Sons, Inc.

All rights reserved. No part of this publication may be reproduced, stored in a retrieval system, or transmitted, in any form or by any means, electronic, mechanical, photocopying, recording or otherwise, except as permitted by law. Advice on how to obtain permission to reuse material from this title is available at http://www.wiley.com/go/permissions.

The right of Suman Mishra and Rebecca Kern-Stone to be identified as the authors of the editorial material in this work has been asserted in accordance with law.

Registered Office(s)
John Wiley & Sons, Inc., 111 River Street, Hoboken, NJ 07030, USA

Editorial Office
101 Station Landing, Medford, MA 02155, USA

For details of our global editorial offices, customer services, and more information about Wiley products visit us at www.wiley.com.

Wiley also publishes its books in a variety of electronic formats and by print-on-demand. Some content that appears in standard print versions of this book may not be available in other formats.

Limit of Liability/Disclaimer of Warranty
While the publisher and authors have used their best efforts in preparing this work, they make no representations or warranties with respect to the accuracy or completeness of the contents of this work and specifically disclaim all warranties, including without limitation any implied warranties of merchantability or fitness for a particular purpose. No warranty may be created or extended by sales representatives, written sales materials or promotional statements for this work. The fact that an organization, website, or product is referred to in this work as a citation and/or potential source of further information does not mean that the publisher and authors endorse the information or services the organization, website, or product may provide or recommendations it may make. This work is sold with the understanding that the publisher is not engaged in rendering professional services. The advice and strategies contained herein may not be suitable for your situation. You should consult with a specialist where appropriate. Further, readers should be aware that websites listed in this work may have changed or disappeared between when this work was written and when it is read. Neither the publisher nor authors shall be liable for any loss of profit or any other commercial damages, including but not limited to special, incidental, consequential, or other damages.

Library of Congress Cataloging-in-Publication Data

Names: Mishra, Suman, editor. | Kern-Stone, Rebecca, editor.
Title: Transnational media : concepts and cases / edited by Suman Mishra and Rebecca Kern-Stone.
Description: Hoboken, NJ : Wiley-Blackwell, 2019. | Includes bibliographical references and index. |
Identifiers: LCCN 2018061446 (print) | LCCN 2019008093 (ebook) | ISBN 9781119394563
   (Adobe PDF) | ISBN 9781119394570 (ePub) | ISBN 9781119394594 (hardcover) |
   ISBN 9781119394600 (paperback)
Subjects: LCSH: Mass media. | Journalism. | International broadcasting.
Classification: LCC P90 (ebook) | LCC P90 .T686 2019 (print) | DDC 384–dc23
LC record available at https://lccn.loc.gov/2018061446

Cover Design: Wiley
Cover Image: © derrrek / Getty Images

Set in 10/12pt Warnock by SPi Global, Pondicherry, India

10 9 8 7 6 5 4 3 2 1

Contents

Contributor Biographies

Alejandro Ocampo (aocampo@itesm.mx) is a scholar from the Monterrey Institute of Technology and Higher Education (State of Mexico Campus). Currently he is the Chair of the Department of Creative Industries. His lines of research are education, ethics, and their relationship with technology. Furthermore, he was the editor of *Razón y Palabra*, the most important online journal specializing in communication in Latin America. He studied communication, education, and philosophy.

Saba Bebawi (Saba.Bebawi@uts.edu.au) is Associate Professor in Journalism at the University of Technology Sydney (UTS). She has published on the role of media in democracy-building in conflict and post-conflict regions. She is author of *Media Power and Global Television News: The role of Al Jazeera English* and *Investigative Journalism in the Arab World: Issues and Challenges*.

O. Hugo Benavides (benavides@fordham.edu) is Chair and Professor of Anthropology at Fordham University. He has published three books: *Making Ecuadorian Histories: Four Centuries of Defining the Past*, (2004); *The Politics of Sentiment: Remembering and Imagining Guayaquil* (2006); and *Drugs, Thugs and Divas: Latin American Telenovelas and Narco-Dramas* (2008), as well as over 50 articles.

Isaac Abeku Blankson (abekublankson1@yahoo.com) is the Vice President of Ghana Technology University College (GTUC). His research focuses on social media and electronic communication applications, crisis communication, media studies, and public relations in developing countries. He has authored several publications and is co-editor of *Negotiating Democracy: Media Transformations in Emerging Democracies* published by SUNY press.

Glenda Daniels (Glenda.Daniels@wits.ac.za) is Associate Professor in Media Studies at Wits University, Johannesburg, South Africa. She is also a writer and media freedom activist. She is the author of the book *Fight for Democracy: The ANC and the media in South Africa* (Wits Press, 2012) and has spent around 20 years as a print journalist. She serves on the council of the South African National Editors' Forum (Sanef) as chair of the diversity and ethics committee. Daniels is also on the board of the Institute for the Advancement of Journalism based in Johannesburg, South Africa.

Karen Donders (karen.donders@vub.be) is a lecturer in Policy Analysis, Political Economy of Journalism, and European Media Markets at the Vrije Universiteit Brussel. She heads the MEDIA unit of research center imec-SMIT, hosting 30 PhD and senior researchers. She specializes in public service media policies across Europe, the interplay between media economics and policies, and competition law and media.

Scott Fitzgerald (s.fitzgerald@curtin.edu.au) is a Senior Lecturer at Curtin University, Australia. His research interests cover cultural industry corporations, creative work, public services (especially education), and new public management. He has published several chapters in international collections on the media industries and the book *Corporations and Cultural Industries* (Rowman & Littlefield).

Martin Fredriksson (martin.fredriksson@liu.se) is Associate Professor at the Department for Culture and Society, Linköping University. He has, among other things, published extensively on issues concerning the theory and history of piracy, commons, property rights, and the history of copyright. He is currently finalizing a project on the commodification of commons.

Thom Gencarelli (thom.gencarelli@manhattan.edu) (PhD, NYU) is Professor and Founding Chair of the Communication Department at Manhattan College. His research spans media ecology, media education/media literacy, popular media and culture, and popular music, and he is co-Editor of the recent *Baby Boomers and Popular Culture: An Inquiry into America's Most Powerful Generation.*

Fernando Gutiérrez (fgutierr@itesm.mx) is the Head of the Division of Humanities and Education at the Monterrey Institute of Technology and Higher Education (State of Mexico Campus). He earned a PhD in Design and Data Visualization from The Metropolitan Autonomous University (UAM). He is the author of several titles about media.

Grant Hannis (g.d.hannis@massey.ac.nz) is Associate Professor of Journalism at Massey University in Wellington, New Zealand. His research interests include media history and economics. He lives near to where Peter Jackson grew up and has closely followed the film-maker's career, after attending the New Zealand premiere of *Bad Taste* in 1988.

Rebecca Kern-Stone (rebecca.kern@manhattan.edu) is Associate Professor of Communication, Media, and Advertising at Manhattan College. Her research focuses on community and identity discourse and practice, critical/cultural studies, and digital culture. She has published in a number of journals including: *Sexualities, Information, Communication, and Society, Telematics and Informatics,* and *First Monday.*

Shin Dong Kim (kimsd@hallym.ac.kr) is Professor of Media and Communication at Hallym University, South Korea. His research and teaching cover global communication, media and cultural industries, and Asian cinema. He has traveled and taught widely in Asia, Europe, and North America, and currently work on a multi-year research project on the development of the Korean ICTs on a national funding.

Michael Lewis (lewism@msu.edu) is Professor of History, Emeritus, at Michigan State University. He has written widely on modern Japanese social, political, and cultural history and Japan's influence on its East Asian neighbors. His most recent study is *"History Wars" and Reconciliation in Japan and Korea* (Palgrave, 2017).

Suman Mishra (smishra@siue.edu) is Associate Professor and Graduate Program Director at the Department of Mass Communication, Southern Illinois University Edwardsville. Her research focuses on globalization, transnational media, consumer culture, and identities.

Onookome Okome (ookome@ualberta.ca) studied at the University of Ibadan, Nigeria, and is currently Professor of Anglophone African Literature and Cinema at the University of Alberta, Canada. His recent publications include *Global Nollywood: An African Video Film Industry* (with Matthias Krings, Indiana University Press, 2013), and *Popular Culture in Africa: The Episteme of Everyday Life* (with Stephanie Newell, Routledge, New York, 2014). "Islam et

Cinema en Afrique de l'ouest" (*Tresor de Islam en Afrique*. Paris: Silvania Editoriale, 2017) is his most recent essay. He is a Humboldt Scholar and was a Fellow of the Salzburg Seminar.

Humphrey A. Regis (hummuh@att.net) is Professor in the School of Communication at Texas Southern University in Houston, Texas, USA. He studies mass communication and culture, reference group orientation, and location in global social space; and won the Saint Lucia Medal of Merit (Gold) for "long and meritorious service in Education and Journalism."

Liudmila Voronova (lusyandrik@gmail.com) is Senior Lecturer at the Department of Journalism, School of Social Sciences, Södertörn University (Sweden). Her research interests are comparative studies of journalism cultures, political communication research, and gender media studies. In her studies, she focuses particularly on the media in Russia, Ukraine, and the Baltic Sea region.

D. Ndirangu Wachanga (wachangd@uww.edu) is Professor of Media Studies and Information Science at the University of Wisconsin. His research interests include memory, communication technologies, global media, and information ethics. He is the authorized documentary biographer of Professor Ngugi wa Thiong'o, and Professor Micere Mugo. His documentary, *Ali Mazrui: A Walking Triple Heritage*, won the 2015 New York African Studies Book Award. He is widely published and has presented his work internationally and is also a commentator for British Broadcasting Corporation Television.

Lisa Waller (lisa.waller@deakin.edu.au) is Associate Professor of Communication in the School of Communication and Creative Arts, Deakin University, Australia. She is the co-author of two recent books: *The Dynamics of News and Indigenous Policy in Australia* (Intellect, 2017) and *Local Journalism in a Digital World* (Palgrave, 2017).

Xinyuan Wang (xinyuan.wang.11@ucl.ac.uk) is a post-doc researcher from the UCL Department of Anthropology and received her PhD and MSc degrees from the same department. Her current publications are *How the World Changed Social Media* (co-author, 2016, UCL Press) and *Social Media in Industrial China* (2016, UCL Press).

Andreas Widholm (andreas.widholm@ims.su.se) is Associate Professor of Journalism in the Department of Media Studies (IMS) at Stockholm University, Sweden. His research addresses the relationship between media, politics, and culture with a particular focus on journalism, digital political communication, and social media.

1

Introduction

Rebecca Kern-Stone and Suman Mishra

This edited book is designed to meet the introductory needs of undergraduate and graduate courses in international media, international mass communication, global media transnational media, comparative media analysis, and the like. More broadly, it aims to fulfill the needs of colleges and universities who are internationalizing their curriculum to meet the needs of an increasingly globalized world through introduction of international-oriented courses. Books that exist on the subject tend to be highly theoretical and often focus on journalism or entertainment media or specific regions of the world. In this book we have provided a broader perspective on national and transnational media in an easy to read accessible form and covered different media forms from Africa, Asia (including the Middle East), the Americas, Europe, and Oceania.

In media studies, concepts such as global communication, transnational communication, international communication, trans-border communication, world communication, intercultural communication, and so on have been used to highlight the communication and flow of information across boundaries. Each of these terms has its own dimension and complexity (Kamalipour 2007). We use the term "transnational" to recognize media's role in communication and relevance both within a nation and also across the transnational arena.

Thus, this book provides a country-based perspective along with a transnational perspective. It is important to note that it is impossible to cover every region of the world and every country within a region; nevertheless, the book covers media from a wide array of countries from around the globe and highlights its national and transnational dimensions.

Chapters are arranged so that important foundation material is presented at the beginning of the book with regional and country discussions in the remaining chapters. The following two chapters introduce and discuss key transnational media concepts and theories and media systems. The first introduces concepts like globalization and the historical development of transnational media and communication theories in the area, also referred to in general as theories of international communication. It highlights the major strengths and weaknesses of these theories and changes over time. Last, it addresses the many complexities of today's world to provoke thought and discussion for future theories in this area. The chapter on media systems introduces how media is directly integrated with political, economic, and cultural conditions. These discussions are meant to be introductory and are presented not as highly theoretical models, but as background information to understand how media function around the world.

The book is then divided by regions of the world, namely: Africa, the Americas, Asia (including the Middle East), Europe, and Oceania. These regions have been defined based on the UN's Standard Country and Area Codes Classifications, revised October 2013 (UN Stats). In each

Transnational Media: Concepts and Cases, First Edition. Edited by Suman Mishra and Rebecca Kern-Stone.
© 2019 John Wiley & Sons, Inc. Published 2019 by John Wiley & Sons, Inc.

regional section of the book, we have first provided some basic information about selected countries from the region, including a brief description of their media, and then provided more in-depth country-specific media cases as well as transnational influences of media from that country.

We have invited international scholars to write essays or case studies on specific countries as we wanted to include more international voices in this book. The essays and case studies offer country-specific examples of media trends in television, radio, films, journalism, social media, and music, among others. As a whole, this book explores and answer the following questions:

1) How can media be understood on a global scale within and between nations?
2) How do changing global conditions – including economic, political, and cultural – impact media and how are they impacted by media in transnational information flow?
3) What are some of the primary centers of transnational media activities, both new and old?

1.1 Understanding Transnationalism and Related Trends

Transnationalism engages in political, cultural, social, and economic initiatives that extend beyond the borders of nation-states. A *nation-state* is a geographic locale that has defined borders where people share similar identities. These identities may be cultural in that they involve religion, food, traditions, clothing, history, or other factors that bring groups of people together. The identities may also be nationalistic or have *nationalism,* in that the people of the nation see themselves as part of a geographic place where they live, work, raise families, and engage with government affairs. As a result, there evolves a sense of allegiance with place. While not necessarily politically motivated, people of a nation-state feel a belonging to the place they call home. Nation-states, however, usually have fluid borders. Citizens, in most cases, are able to come and go from their home country and travel. Their view of the world expands beyond their local geography and culture, resulting in new curiosities about global understandings. Under transnationalism, global movement and interactions are what create a more integrated global society.

For transnationalism to occur a few additional factors need to exist. First, there needs to be "regular and sustained social contacts over time across national borders" (Portes et al. 1999, p. 219). In other words, regular trips across borders – whether business or pleasure – that involve activity and transaction, facilitate the concept of transnationalism. The trend of transnationalism is not new. While the term might be, transnationalism has existed since people have crossed borders to engage in political, cultural, social, or economic transactions. It can be tied to the history of globalization, which will be discussed in Chapter 2. Essentially, it could be argued that transnationalism is a long-established trend that only recently was given a name. Second, as Portes et al. (1999) note, transnationalism began with the individual. It is at the local level that individuals sought opportunities across borders, whether for political motivations – as a need to escape government policies or regimes, or economic motivations – as a way to obtain goods or connections for business, for example. Displays of nationalism in sport, music, art, and traditional dress are all presented by the individual. Transnationalism does not only exist at the level of the individual: it begins with the individual but works to embolden larger institutions. These institutions may be government, corporation, education, religion, or of course mass media. Mass media can function on both the local and public level, which would be considered more nationalistic, or on the transnational level. Both are important to how people gain information about the world around them.

Examples of transnationalism can be seen at a macro level through global statistics; for example, in population changes, economic changes, immigration flows, global travel, and technology. All these changes are intrinsically linked with growth, production and consumption of media, global flow of information, patterns of media adoptions, cultural influences and changes, and so on. For example, many leading media companies from America and Europe today, for example Bertelsmann, are investing in the media markets of developing countries like India, China, Brazil, and Nigeria because of their size, and this provides a growth opportunity for these companies as well as growth of international media reach in these countries. Further understanding of the international reach and investment of a large European conglomerate in growing markets is discussed in Chapter 19. Similarly, economic changes in China have helped Chinese businesses immensely; these businesses are now investing in the established media markets of America and Europe and are helping to boost them. Chinese investment in the American movie-theater chain AMC Entertainment Holdings Inc., Hollywood studio Legendary Entertainment, and India-based Reliance Entertainment's investment in Hollywood director Spielberg's DreamWorks studio, are just a few examples of global changes and the impact they have had on media business. US-based Hollywood's, Australia-based Wellywood's, India-based Bollywood's, and Nigeria-based Nollywood's contributions and connections to global media and markets are further discussed in Chapters 7, 10, 14, and 22, respectively. Other examples include the enormous transnational growth of several Latin American media companies, which has expanded the reach of telenovelas around the globe. For more on Latin American media conglomerates as well as the global impact of telenovelas, see Chapters 8 and 9. Transnational media has impacted news and journalism as much as entertainment. A number of news channels, such as BBC, CNN, Al Jazeera, and Russia Today (RT), are broadcast via satellite around the world, are available online, and have offices and reporters based in major cities around the world. This adds to differing perspectives on global events. The news systems and global reach of Al Jazeera and RT are discussed in Chapters 16 and 20 respectively.

1.2   Population Trends

Population changes can tell us a lot about clusters of growth, media opportunities, employment and capital, infrastructure needs, and other necessities. The population of the world currently is over 7.6 billion (UN DESA 2017). The United Nations Department of Economic and Social Affairs (2017), expects the population to reach 8.6 billion in 2030, 9.8 billion by 2050 and 11.2 billion by 2100. That is an increase of 14% by 2030, 12% by 2050, and 13% by 2100. The largest countries in terms of population size are China and India, representing 19% (1.4 billion inhabitants) and 18% (1.3 billion inhabitants) of the world's population (UN DESA 2017). However, India is set to overtake China's population within five years. Of the 10 largest countries in the world by population, see Figure 1.1, Nigeria and India are growing most rapidly.

1.3   Economic Trends

Overall, the world economy is projected to double by 2050 (PWC 2017). By 2050, China, India, the United States, Indonesia, and Brazil are projected to be the world's top five economies (PWC 2017). Vietnam, the Philippines, and Nigeria are expected to make the biggest leap upward in the ranking (PWC 2017). On average, the emerging markets (E7: China, India, Indonesia, Brazil, Russia, Mexico, and Turkey) are expected to grow twice as fast as the advanced economies (G7: US, UK, France, Germany, Japan, Canada, and Italy) (PWC 2017).

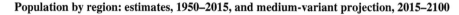

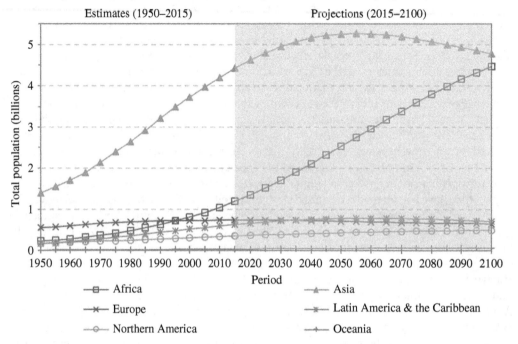

Population by region: estimates, 1950–2015, and medium-variant projection, 2015–2100

Figure 1.1 Population trends. *Source:* United Nations, Department of Economic and Social Affairs, Population Division (2017). *World Population Prospects: The 2017 Revision.* New York: United Nations.

The GDP (Gross Domestic Product) – a measure of economic output, growth, and development – for many countries is changing under overall transnational growth (World Bank 2018). That means a larger labor market, global connectivity, growing opportunities, and greater purchasing power for many. Higher GDP allows for an increase in infrastructure spending which then can be used to bring in media opportunities, such as local radio, internet, and newspaper, as well as education opportunities. It can also boost current media in developing as well as established economies. Overall, the GDP of most countries has been growing. Developing countries have been growing faster than developed regions (World Bank 2018) (see Figure 1.2).

While the economies of countries have been growing, poverty levels on a global basis have been dropping (UN DESA 2015; World Bank 2018). The global poverty line is set at US$1.90 PPP (purchasing power parity) a day, and since 1990 poverty has dropped by over 20%. However, as the United Nations notes, those in low-income countries – a GNI (gross national income) per capita below US$1025 or less, such as many in sub-Saharan Africa and southern areas of Asia – are more likely to be caught in the poverty coverage gaps. Poverty in high income countries – a GNI per capita of $12 476 or more – is often overlooked in poverty measurements as wealthier countries are not considered to have any extreme poverty (World Bank 2017). Yet, wealthier nations with extreme poverty gaps have similar problems to poorer nations when it comes to media access. Poverty level and inequity affect people's access to goods and services including access to technology and the communication infrastructure. This also means citizens have less opportunity to create their own stories, whether socio-political or cultural, or engage with transnational voices.

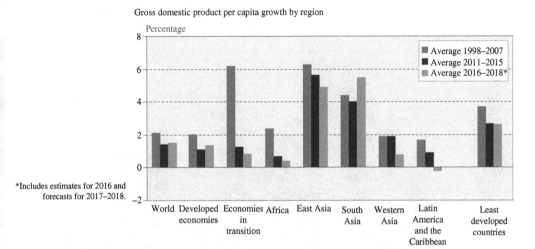

Figure 1.2 Gross Domestic Product (GDP) per capita growth by region. *Source:* UN/DESA, based on United Nations Statistics Division National Accounts Main Aggregates Database, United Nations Population Division World Population Prospects and UN/DESA forecasts.

1.4 Immigration Trends

Higher labor productivity may be to some extent a by-product of immigration flows. Transnationalism partially involves the movement of peoples across borders. As previously stated, this may be for travel, but under sociological definitions it also means sustained contact, often for business. This means people cross borders seeking work, or other forms of sustained political, economic, cultural, or social interaction. According to the United Nations, in 2017 approximately 257 million immigrants lived outside their country of birth. Asians, Central Europeans, and East Africans have made up the largest segments of immigrants by destination. In addition, as of 2017, Asia, Western Europe, and North America have hosted the greatest number of immigrants. Refugees account for less than 10% of the immigrant population worldwide, according to the Organisation for Economic Cooperation and Development (OECD 2017).

Immigration growth under transnationalism can be a positive occurrence. As the OECD (2017) note, when monitored, immigration can do a great deal to spur economic growth in a country. This is because the incoming workers, for example, fill necessary jobs, build businesses, and invest in the local economy. However, there are not always incentives to stay, especially if political, legal, or social entrapments make it difficult for the immigrant to stay in their host country.

Immigration and changes in population diversity also spur changes in media. As people cross borders and establish themselves in new places, they bring with them new languages, cultures, and traditions. In some cases, popular culture and media gain a global foothold, such as in the case studies from Asia, Chapters 13 and 15, where immigration and marketing efforts influenced worldwide interest. Or as in the case study from the Caribbean in Chapter 11, where media is created by immigrants who were brought there, along with indigenous peoples. Sometimes, governments see a need to expand media offerings to immigrants and indigenous groups in native languages. Chapters 17 and 21 explore this type of media expansion on two different continents (Figure 1.3).

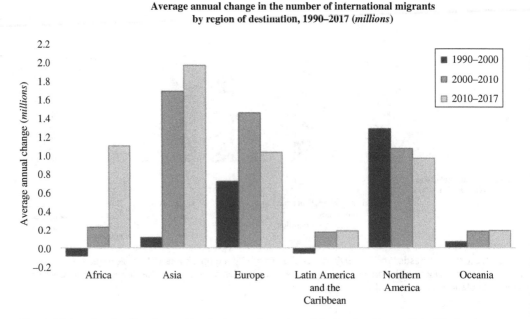

Figure 1.3 Immigration flow: international migrants by region of destination. *Source: United Nations' International Migration Report 2017.*

1.5   Global Travel: Trends

Besides immigration as a major component of transnationalism, global travel is important as it promotes economic growth, cultural curiosity, and increased cultural knowledge. Over the last several decades, global travel has become easier and faster. This is due to changes in mass transportation – airplanes, trains, ships – that can carry more people longer distances at greater speeds. To give some idea of how much this has impacted tourist arrivals globally, according to the United Nations World Tourism Organization (UNWTO) in 1950 world tourism arrivals were 25 million, by 2000 they were up to 674 million, and were 1235 million in 2016. The UNWTO (2017) also notes that tourism accounts for "10% of the global GDP and one in 10 jobs worldwide" (p. 3). Research has also shown that South Asia and Southeast Asia have seen the greatest growth in 2017: between 6.5 and 7%. South Asia is expected to be the frontrunner in the coming decade, with the rest of Asia close behind. These regions are followed by Saharan and sub-Saharan Africa, the Middle East, Latin America, and the Caribbean, all of which are expected to grow between 3.5 and 5% over the next decade. North America, Europe, and Oceania are expected to see the smallest increases, which is a significant reversal from years past.

1.6   Technology Trends

Technology has always impacted human lives in significant ways. Communication and the digital technologies of today have significantly increased the pace at which we send and receive information. Satellites, internet, wireless technologies, and social media are all aiding greater global interactions, global flow of local news and information, and entertainment media around the world. Google, Facebook, and Twitter have become major players in global news and information dissemination. Their worldwide use and popularity make them very powerful transnational players. For example, Facebook and Twitter have played a role in various protests around the world such as Egypt's "Arab Spring," Iran's "Green Revolution," and the United States' "Black lives matter." Their power crosses national boundaries and influences local populations, but also makes them targets for censorship and control in autocratic countries. China, for example, has developed its own social media ecosystem and search engines, and controls websites that its citizens can access (see Chapter 12). Cell phones, wearable technologies, voice driven assistants, and artificial intelligence (AI) are bringing significant changes to the world of media and local lives. The Reuters Institute's 2018 report notes, "China and India become a key focus for digital growth with innovations around payment, online identity, and artificial intelligence" (Reuters 2018, p. 6). Today, more than four billion people, that is more than half of the world's population, are online, a number that is only likely to grow. In July 2018, there were 4.1 billion active internet users, 3.8 billion unique mobile internet users, 3.3 billion active social media users, and 3.1 billion active mobile social media users (Statista 2018), so the world is even more digitally connected today than ever before.

According to The World Bank (2016), Canada, Western Europe, Australia, and Japan have the highest rates of internet usage as a percentage of the population, followed by the United States, Argentina, Saudi Arabia, and the Russian Federation, among others. The countries with the lowest usage include many countries in Africa – namely the Central African Republic, Niger, and Chad – as well as in central Asia, such as Iraq, and south Asia, such as Indonesia (Poushter 2016; World Bank 2016). However, as Poushter (2016) notes, significant increases in internet use have occurred in developing economies, in particular Brazil, Malaysia, and China. Regionally, internet users have grown more significantly in Asia and Africa than any other part of the world between 2009 and 2017 (see Figure 1.4).

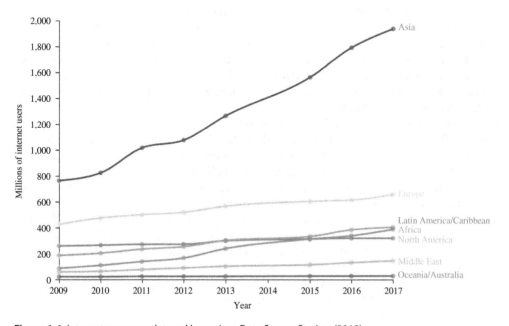

Figure 1.4 Internet user growth trend by region. *Data Source:* Statista (2018).

The *Economist* (2016) notes that while many in Africa do not have fixed broadband access, they do use internet on their mobile phones, which has allowed for increased trade, need for information, and opportunities to connect when other media outlets are unavailable or hindered due to government intervention. However, even within a continent where internet and other media growth has increased, infrastructure impedes growth on many levels and hides poverty in non-urban centers (*Economist* 2016) where many cannot afford basic communication technologies. The use of internet and mobile technologies in different contexts and in different types of economies is further discussed in Chapters 6, 12, and 18.

1.7 Transnational Media

Media are channels through which communication takes place. *Transnational media* is media consumed and constructed globally as well as by those who engage in transnational initiatives. *National media* is media of a nation-state. It is created locally, although it may be part of a larger network of media entities. In some cases, it may be community media or hyper-local media, created and funded by individuals or by the government. In other cases, national mass media may be more corporatized and funded through advertising. Transnational mass media crosses nation-state borders. This may happen because of the proximity of two countries, where radio and television signals reach farther than the countries' borders. It can also happen because media is imported and exported. This varies widely globally, as not all countries or regions import and export media equally.

Marshall McLuhan first described an early version of transnational mass media in his seminal book, *The Gutenberg Galaxy: The Making of Typographic Man and the Understanding of Media*. Here he discusses the idea of a *Global Village*, one that is made possible because of electric and electronic communication. He saw a future where mass media would shrink the distance between people globally and would increase cross-cultural understanding. His ideas about a Global Village have since been criticized by some as being romanticized because they do not account for global power imbalances regarding information access, infrastructure, and geopolitics, and because a Global Village would increase the homogeneity of individual cultures. So, it could be argued that transnational mass media is both positive and negative. Positive because information can be shared across long distances and could increase cross-cultural understandings. Negative because globally political and economic situations are not equal and this leaves some without opportunity to engage with global media formats and content.

The United Nations is working hard to promote information and communication technologies (ICTs) as they believe that this will help foster global development. As a part of their 2030 Sustainable Development Agenda, one goal includes developing infrastructure, particularly in emerging economies. One point in Goal 9 specifically states, "Significantly increase access to information and communications technology and strive to provide universal and affordable access to the Internet in least developed countries by 2020" (United Nations 2017, Sustainable Development Goal 9). This is because around 2.6 billion people in the world do not have consistent access to electricity, and nearly 1.5 billion do not have dependable phone access (United Nations 2017, Sustainable Development Goal 9). These are important initiatives to increase global access to communication, particularly electronic communication. These, paired with initiatives on literacy, poverty, and skills training – among others – can help to shift the power imbalances of information societies globally.

References

Kamalipour, Y. (2007). *Global Communication*. New York: Thompson Wadsworth.

Organisation for Economic Co-operation and Development (2017). *Perspectives on Global Development 2017*. OECD Retrieved from: http://www.oecd.org/dev/perspectives-on-global-development-22224475.htm.

Portes, A., Guarnizo, L., and Landolt, P. (1999). The study of transnationalism: pitfalls and promise of an emergent research field. *Ethnic and Racial Studies* 22 (2): 217–237.

Poushter, J. (2016). Smartphone ownership and internet usage continues to climb in emerging economies. *Pew Research Center*. Retrieved from: http://www.pewglobal.org/2016/02/22/smartphone-ownership-and-internet-usage-continues-to-climb-in-emerging-economies.

PWC (2017). The long view: How will the global economic order change by 2050. Retrieved from: https://www.pwc.com/gx/en/issues/economy/the-world-in-2050.html.

Reuters (2018). Digital news project. Retrieved from: https://reutersinstitute.politics.ox.ac.uk/sites/default/files/2018-01/RISJ%20Trends%20and%20Predictions%202018%20NN.pdf.

Statista (2018). Global digital population as of July 2018 (in millions). Retrieved from: https://www.statista.com/statistics/617136/digital-population-worldwide.

The Economist (2016). Mobile phones are transforming Africa. *The Economist*. Retrieved from: https://www.economist.com/middle-east-and-africa/2016/12/10/mobile-phones-are-transforming-africa.

United Nations (2017). Goal 9: Build resilient infrastructure, promote sustainable industrialization and foster innovation. Retrieved from: http://www.un.org/sustainabledevelopment/infrastructure-industrialization.

United Nations Department of Economic and Social Affairs (2015). Population report. *UNDESA*. Retrieved from: http://www.un.org/en/development/desa/news/population/2015-report.html.

United Nations Department of Economic and Social Affairs (2017). World population prospects: The 2017 revision. UNDESA. Retrieved from: https://population.un.org/wpp/.

United Nations Statistics Division (2018). Countries or areas / geographical regions. *UNSD*. Retrieved from: https://unstats.un.org/unsd/methodology/m49.

United Nations World Tourism Organization (UNWTO) (2017). UNWTO Tourism Highlights 2017 Edition. *UNWTO*. Retrieved from: https://www.e-unwto.org/doi/pdf/10.18111/9789284419029.

World Bank (2016). Fixed broadband subscriptions. World Bank. Retrieved from: https://data.worldbank.org/indicator/IT.NET.BBND.

World Bank (2017). Monitoring global poverty. Retrieved from: http://documents.worldbank.org/curated/en/353781479304286720/pdf/110040-REVISED-PUBLIC.pdf.

World Bank (2018). World development indicators. Retrieved from: http://databank.worldbank.org/data/source/world-development-indicators.

Part I

Setting the Foundations

Key Concepts

2

Transnational Media: Key Concepts and Theories

Suman Mishra

Media are one of the ways through which information and global culture flow around the world. Over the years, several theories and concepts have been developed to understand, explain, and predict how media operate in the transnational arena. These include globalization and various associated macro-level theories of international communication. These theories go beyond the national and connect the local to the global.

Theories and concepts are developed in a particular social, political, technological, and economic context, and hence they address the needs and concerns of the times in which they are developed. As the context and conditions change, new theories and ways of understanding the world are developed or needed. In the transnational arena, most early theories raised concerns regarding speed, reach, and control of communication by the developed nations of the Global North (e.g. the United States, the United Kingdom, France) and its economic, political, and cultural impact on the less-developed nations of the Global South (many Latin American, African, and Asian countries). Newer theories in this area, however, tend to focus on the complexities of global–local interactions, and the role communities and national audiences play in adoption of foreign content that is circulated through transnational media corporations.

2.1 Understanding Globalization

Globalization is not a new phenomenon; migration of people, goods, and ideas has taken place throughout human history. However, use of the term "globalization" began around the 1930s, and became a buzzword in the 1980s, when journalists, academics, and others started frequently to use the term to describe the integration of international markets (James and Steger 2014).

Even though the term globalization has been popularly used, scholars have differed in their conceptualization of its fundamental meaning. Consequently, today there are more than 100 definitions of globalization (Al-Rodhan and Stoudmann 2006). Most definitions underscore the dynamic and complex nature of globalization, and the many interconnections and inter-dependencies it creates across social, political, and economic boundaries. Al-Rodhan and Stoudmann (2006, p. 2) provide a good baseline definition in assessing globalization as "a process that encompasses the causes, course, and consequences of transnational and transcultural integration of human and non-human activities."

Globalization today has its supporters and critics, but few deny its effect on countries and cultures. It is a complex, multidimensional phenomenon that has been categorized into *economic globalization, political globalization,* and *cultural globalization.* These three areas are often discussed separately, but in fact they are interlinked. For example, globalization of

Transnational Media: Concepts and Cases, First Edition. Edited by Suman Mishra and Rebecca Kern-Stone.
© 2019 John Wiley & Sons, Inc. Published 2019 by John Wiley & Sons, Inc.

finance not only integrates world economies through spread of global capital, it also directly and indirectly affects the social and political spheres by influencing wages, income distribution, and employment, all of which have significant political implications for a nation. Similarly, cultural exchanges among nations – for example, through films, television programs, music, and so on – affect and are affected by the global flow of capital.

Globalization has been occurring for centuries, but three distinct phases of *modern* globalization are discussed below to provide historical context and background to its development and its relationship to theories of international communication. In each phase of globalization, media and communication technologies have played a significant role in connecting the world and facilitating inter-cultural exchanges, and hence their role and impacts have been theorized by scholars. The first phase of modern globalization occurred between 1870 and 1913, the second from 1945 to 1991, and the third from 1992 up to today (Verde 2017).

2.2   The First Phase of Globalization

The first phase of modern globalization began in the 1870s with the expansion of transportation (e.g. railways) and communication technologies (e.g. telephone, phonograph, wireless telegraph). All of these innovations helped to bring the world closer. They also helped to expand international trade among the colonies of Great Britain and other imperial powers and helped shift wealth and resources from the Global South to the Global North. Schmidt and Hersh (2000, p. 3) refer to this period as "the age of discovery and conquest characterized as the epoch of mercantilism and primitive accumulation." Colonization also helped to spread the cultural, economic, and the political ideologies[1] of the colonial powers to the colonized regions.

In 1914, World War I caused a slowdown in globalization as nations became involved in war. This global slowdown lasted for nearly 25 years until the end of World War II. This was also a period when many of the world's advanced countries experienced the Great Depression (1929–1932) and looked inwards to address their domestic problems.

2.3   The Second Phase of Globalization

Following World War II, the second phase of globalization began. Global cooperation and trade flourished as nations came together after the war in nation-rebuilding efforts and also in aid of the development of "third world" countries, many of whom had fought for independence from colonial rule and had become sovereign nation-states. Global financial organizations like the International Monetary Fund (IMF) and the World Bank (WB) were set up for reconstruction and to facilitate the developmental needs of nations. However, this was also the period of the Cold War when tensions between the two world superpowers, the United States and the Soviet Union and their allies, were at a highpoint. US and British concerns over the spread of communism and Soviet dominance in the political and economic arena of Eastern European countries and their political influence in Western European democracies led to closer political, economic, and strategic links between their allies, and also led to the formation of the North Atlantic Treaty Organization (NATO), a unified military command to contain the Soviet Union. NATO was made up of the United States and its European allies, many of whom had benefited from the US aid provided to them under the Marshall Plan (officially the European Recovery Program ERP). The United States then and now continues to hold tremendous power in NATO.

This period, the second phase of globalization, saw an accelerated growth in international communication because of advances in communication technologies including television, computers, and satellites. Major international communications organizations, such as the International Telecommunications Satellite Consortium (INTELSAT) and the International Maritime Satellite Organization (INMARSAT), were also established at this time to facilitate communication among nations. Entertainment media, particularly in the Western nations, flourished, and Western nations began to expand and provide their media content to other countries through import–export. Since many developing countries of the Global South did not have the advanced technologies or the resources to produce a lot of media content for their domestic consumption, they ended up importing American and European content.

International communication research took off after World War II, as debates around the role of the government in controlling the media, free flow of information across national boundaries, international relations and building coalitions, counteracting propaganda, and free speech and free press grew globally. At this time, nations of the Global South also became concerned over the imbalance in the flow of information from the Global North to the Global South. They began to ask for a more just and more efficient two-way flow of information between developed and developing countries to reduce the imbalance in international relations. This led to a decade-long debate through the 1970s and early 1980s on some of the major issues in international communication under the New World Information and Communication Order (NWICO) facilitated by the United Nations Educational, Scientific and Cultural Organization (UNESCO). UNESCO (1980) produced a report after this debate called the "Many Voices. One World" (also known as the MacBride report) outlining the many problems in international communication, such as the flow of information and market dominance, and also providing recommendations to democratize international communication systems, strengthening independence and self-reliance in domestic communication policies.

In this context, several theories developed; prominent among them were the free flow of information theory (FFI), world system theory, modernization theory, dependency theory, structural imperialism, media imperialism, and cultural imperialism, which are described in the following paragraphs.

2.3.1 Free Flow of Information Theory

The FFI (Lerner 1958) came out of Western traditions, and was rooted in the ideas of the First Amendment and US antipathy to government control of media, censorship, and the use of media for propaganda by its communist opponents. This was also the time when free market discourse and market capitalism[2] was pitched against state socialism[3] in the new world order after World War II. Free flow of information across national borders was considered important for promoting democracy and for selling products (including media products) across borders. The push for the free flow of information was controversial, and critics contend that it helped information and entertainment products that championed an American/Western way of life and its values of capitalism and individualism spread throughout the world, further serving the economic and political interests of the United States and contributing to its greater dominance.

2.3.2 Modernization Theory

Modernization theory came out of Lerner's (1958) *The Passing of Modernity* and Schramm's (1964) *Mass Media and National Development: The Role of Information in the Developing Countries* and is complementary to the doctrine of FFI. It was developed to understand the influence of American media, such as *Voice of America* radio broadcasting – which was once used for counteracting Nazi propaganda – in transforming traditional societies of the Middle East into modern societies though dissemination of Western ideas and values. According to this theory, media are a "mobility multiplier," i.e. exposure to Western media content can help postcolonial countries transition from "traditional" societies to "modern" ones by gaining experience of far off and more advanced places. This can further encourage people in these societies to question old ways of being, challenge hierarchies within their societies, and aspire to a modern way of life through participation in the economic and political realm; in essence, move toward a more modern, capitalistic, and democratic life.

Critics of the modernization theory (see Fangjun 2009; Martínez-Vela 2001; Strelitz 2005; Thussu 2006) have pointed to its many weaknesses. These include: its top-down and one-direction approach to international communication, not accounting for the historical past or the transnational structures that constrained local and national development of many countries; the assumption that all countries follow similar paths of development; and the assumption that media are a neutral force in the development as they are tied to the interests of specific nations. The theory also tends to ignore the fact that modern and traditional ways of living are not mutually exclusive. Modernity and tradition can coexist; for example, in the Islamic traditions that continue to define Muslim regions and in many cases have become even stronger despite modern communication technologies and exposure to the Western world through media.

Even though modernization theory has been found to have many weaknesses, echoes of it have resurfaced in recent years. There is a recurrence of a belief that information exchanges through internet communication technologies (ICTs) can help advance and solve problems of the developing countries (Castells 1998; Thussu 2006).

2.3.3 Dependency Theory

In the 1960s and 1970s, several theories originating primarily from Latin America challenged Western approaches to understanding social, economic, and political developments. These theories highlighted the *causes* of imbalances in power in the world. Dependency theory, world system theory, and structural imperialism theory, were some of most prominent that highlighted underlying structural problems in development. These theories, though different, also have significant overlap with each other.

Scholars from Latin America (Raul Prebisch and Fernando Henrique Cardoso), the United States (Paul Baran and Baran and Frank Frank), Africa (Samir Amin), and Europe (Dieter Senghass and Ulrich Menzel) (Nulens 2003) are known for their work related to dependency theory. Dependency theory focuses on the causes it deems unjust that helped create an asymmetrical relationship between first-world developed nations of the world, referred to as the *centre nations*, and third-world developing nations, referred to as the *periphery nations* by dependency theorists. Dependency theorists place great emphasis on *external causes*, particularly economic causes, for poor conditions in the periphery nations.

Dependency theorists explain that there are tremendous interactions between the centre (developed nations) on the political and economic front, and between the centre and the periphery (underdeveloped nations), but there are significantly fewer interactions among the periphery nations. This results in a strong and united centre and a weak periphery. Centre nations maintain their dominance in the world through transnational corporations (TNCs), international commodity markets, communication, and other means. TNCs, mostly based in the Global North, exercise control with support of their respective governments over setting the terms for global trade – dominating markets, resources, production, and labor, resulting in conditions that increase the dominance of centre nations and maintain the dependence of the periphery nations on the centre nations. Dependency theorists also argue that because periphery nations rely on investment and media technologies from the centre, they are dependent on sponsors and advertisers from centre nations who want to sell them Western goods and a consumer lifestyle to increase their profits; and hence media end up focusing on promoting goods instead of promoting community values. They also introduced the terms "media imperialism" and "cultural imperialism" to explain this, which were later elaborated upon by other scholars.

Dependency theory, like modernization theory, highlights a one-way flow of communication, but it also focuses on who is sending and controlling that flow. It highlights the imbalance in the flow of information at the international level but ignores the impact of media ownership and communication at the nation and local levels. In addition, it does not consider the role of a free media system or the role of the national elites in changing the conditions in periphery nations. It does not focus on internal domestic causes for inequality in the periphery nations, as domestic politics and contestation of power, corruption, poor policies, and other such factors affect the pace of growth and development in the periphery nations.

Dependency theorists provide solutions to mitigate the causes of inequality in the periphery nations by forming trading blocs consisting of periphery nations. These groupings can thereby gain better leverage from the core nations. They can also convince national elites in the periphery nations to use wealth for national developmental purposes.

2.3.4 World System Theory

Immanuel Wallerstein developed the world system theory as a reaction to the criticism of modernization theory. Wallerstein laid its foundation through his work: *The Rise and Future Demise of the World Capitalist System: Concepts for Comparative Analysis* (1974) and *The Modern World System I: Capitalist Agriculture and the Origins of the European World-Economy in the Sixteenth Century* (1976). He conceptualized that modern nation-states existed within a larger economic, political, and legal framework, and thus individual societies and nations could not be understood in isolation and without reference to the world system. Wallerstein theorized that under capitalism a larger division of labor takes place nationally, regionally, and internationally among nation-states of the world. In the world system, there are *core nations* (e.g. the United States, the United Kingdom, and France), nations with political, economic, and military might, *semi-periphery* (e.g. India, Brazil, China, and South Africa) and *periphery nations* (most African countries). The core nations promote accumulation of wealth by providing technology, capital knowledge, finished goods, and services to other zones; while the semi-periphery and periphery nations engage with the core through the supply of cheap low-skill labor and raw materials. These roles are mutually beneficial for the nations-states and are dynamic, so the roles of nations can change over time. World system theory acknowledges the exploitative nature of capitalism and the dominance of the core nations, but also notes the dynamic nature of the relationships between various nations of the world.

Wallerstein's initial focus in development of this theory was on economic globalization under global capitalism and economic interactions, but over time world system theory has been stretched beyond its original conception to include political, cultural, informational, and technological forms of interaction. It has been used as a framework for research ranging from international flow of information and international news to global governance. The world system theory falls into the dependency school of thought; therefore, many of the criticisms of dependency theory also apply to world system theory, including hierarchy in flow of information, separation of countries into only three categories – core, semi-periphery, and periphery – when lot of other variation in countries are possible, and the need for more fluid movements of countries in and out of the capitalist structure.

2.3.5 Cultural Imperialism, Media Imperialism, and Structural Imperialism

Schiller and Tunstall through their works *Communication and Cultural Domination* (Schiller 1976) and *The Media are American: Anglo-American Media in the World* (Tunstall 1977) popularized the cultural imperialism theory. Cultural imperialism focuses on the imbalance in cultural flow in the specific areas of news, television, internet, and other forms of entertainment. It argues that the imbalance and dominance of Western cultural products through Western media result in the destruction of domestic cultures and ways of life. Tunstall (1977, p. 57) writes, "authentic traditional, local culture … is being battered out of existence by the indiscriminate dumping of large quantities of slick commercial and media products, mainly from the United States." Schiller also argues that former European colonial empires, such as Great Britain, France, and the Netherlands, have largely been replaced by the American empire through USA-based TNCs, which yield tremendous economic and informational power in the world.

Media imperialism was developed within the broader analysis of cultural imperialism and dependency theories. It focuses on global media structures, transnational media industries and corporations, and the flow of media products and advertising across borders. Boyd-Barret (1977, p. 117) defined media imperialism as

> the process whereby the ownership, structure, distribution of content of the media in any one country are singly or together subject to substantial external pressures from the media interests of any other country or countries without proportionate reciprocation of influence by the country so affected.

He also noted the direction of media flow and imbalance: "While there is a heavy flow of exported media products from the US to, say, Asian countries, there is only a very slight trickle of Asian media products to the US," and even though there is a flow of media from the periphery nations, it is small and controlled by a handful of centre nations. Boyd-Barret explains that periphery nations and their audiences do have agency; nations can reduce the amount of foreign content in their television programming and audiences can watch less of them.

Boyd-Barret, however, refers to media content only in terms of import and export and ignores media form, type of content, local adaptations of foreign content, and local media regulation. Thus, one of the main criticisms of both media and cultural imperialism theory has been that it ignores the role of the audience in interpreting media texts which are "polysemic," that is, subject to multiple interpretations. Audiences take what suits them from foreign media and adapt them to suit their current lives. In addition, the imperialism thesis does not adequately consider national media policies and regulations that force foreign media to adapt to local context. Today, even though media and information flow from the core remains strong, counter media flow has also been observed. For example, in the flow of Anime and Manga from Japan, flow of telenovelas from Brazil and Mexico, flow of Bollywood films from India, and flow of news from Doha, Qatar through Al Jazeera's network.

Media imperialism, however, remains at the center of concern among international communication scholars, especially today with the rise of transnational media giants such as Google, Walt Disney, News Corp. International, Facebook, and others. In 2015, among the top 15 transnational media corporations by revenue, 12 were from the United States (Figure 2.1), and out of the top 100, the United States' proportion of the revenue was 67%, approximately 588.4 billion Euros (Institute of Media and Communication Policy 2018). Thus, the United States media have tremendous economic power, and do have an influence on national and international politics, economics, and culture. There are also some major regional media powerhouses, like

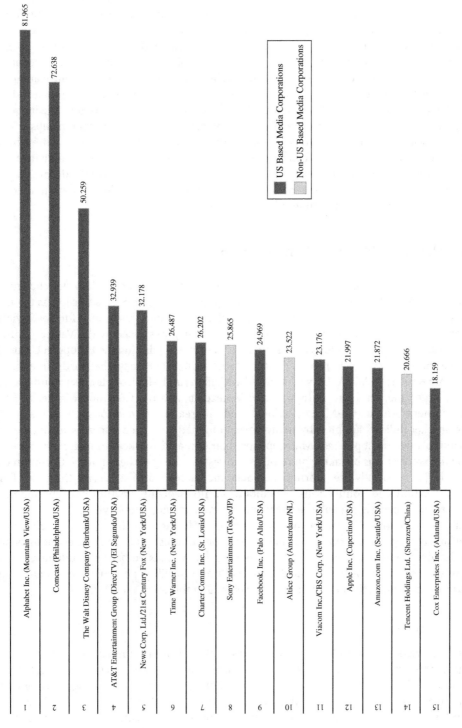

Figure 2.1 Leading transnational media corporations. *Source:* Institute of Media and Communication Policy. https://www.mediadb.eu/en.html.

the Altice Group (Amsterdam/NL) and Bertelsmann SE & Co. KGaA (Gütersloh/GER) in Europe (covered in Chapter 19), The Naspers Group (Cape Town/ZA) in Africa, Globo Communicação e Participações SA (Rio de Janeiro/BRA) (covered in Chapter 9) in Latin America, and Sony Entertainment (Tokyo/JP) and Tencent Holdings Ltd. (Shenzen/China) in Asia.

Galtung introduced the theory of structural imperialism through his work *A Structural Theory of Imperialism* (1979). This theory tries to explain the inequalities and dependency *between* nations, however it also includes inequalities *within* nations of the centre and periphery. It argues that there is tremendous inequality between centre nations (developed and highly developed nations) and periphery nations (less-developed nations). It explains the inequalities by highlighting a harmony of interest between the cores (elites or dominant groups who hold power) of the centre and periphery nations, and that the centre–periphery relationships are maintained and reinforced by information flow and reproduction of economic activities involving the cores. These create institutional linkages that serve the interests of the dominant groups in both the centre and periphery nations. Structural imperialism also shares the theoretical weaknesses apparent in other imperialism theories.

2.4 The Third Phase of Globalization

The third phase of globalization began in the early 1990s, when the world order changed with the collapse of the Soviet Union. With the USSR gone, the United States was left as the world's only superpower. New political realignments took place around this time as former Soviet bloc countries broke away to become independent nation-states allied with Western European countries. Various trading blocs were formed in the 1990s, including the European Union (EU), a single market of various European countries with a single currency; the North American Free Trade Agreement (NAFTA) between the USA, Canada, and Mexico; Mercosur, a union among Brazil, Argentina, Uruguay, Paraguay, and Venezuela; and the Common Market of Eastern and Southern Africa (COMESA). Global trade increased tremendously as a result of the open-market policies adopted by many developing nations which had now abandoned their previous protectionist policies. Many opened their domestic market because of pressures from the IMF to repay loans by taking on reforms and restructuring of their market. Communication technologies, especially the internet and social media, helped to accelerate the pace of global communication and connections. Instantaneous flows of information and communication from around the world shrunk the world into an even smaller "global village."

International communication theories developed during this third phase of globalization have largely focused on globalization's influence on cultures rather than on economics, which was the focus of earlier theories. One also notices a new focus on national audiences and their reasons for adoption of foreign media and culture. Hybridity, network society, and cultural proximity are among the newer theories developed in this area.

2.4.1 Hybridity

Many theorists since Schiller have focused on globalization's impact on culture and have proposed theories contrary to cultural imperialism. These theories do not exclusively focus on the notion of dominance and erasure of local cultures or even the homogeneity of cultures encapsulated in such terms as "McDonaldization" (Ritzer 1993) as a result of interactions between the dominant cultures of the West and the less-dominant cultures of the East. They describe the process and outcomes of the interactions as *hybridity* and *glocalization*. Hybridity scholars emphasize that "international communication practices are continuously negotiated in interactions of differential powers" (Kraidy 2002, p. 317), giving rise to a unique third space, a hybrid, where there is continuous mixing, appropriating, and cultural interdependence without a fixed or privileged position for any one culture (Bhabha 1994). Cultural hybridity recognizes the complex, fluid, and dynamic nature of globalization and its resulting unstable cultural hybrids.

Glocalization is a term that is related to the broader issue of cultural hybridity. It is defined as "the interpenetration of the global and the local resulting in unique outcomes in different geographic areas" (Ritzer and Atalay 2010, p. 319). Ritzer and Atalay (2010, p. 319) summarize Ronald Robertson's (1992) and other scholars' conception of glocalization which addresses the changes in the world. They note:

> ... the world is growing pluralistic (glocalization theorist is exceptionally alert to differences within and between areas of the world); individuals and local groups have great power to adapt, innovate, and maneuver within a glocalized world (glocalization theory sees individual and local groups as important and creative agents); social processes are relational and contingent (globalization provokes a variety of reactions – ranging from nationalist entrenchment to cosmopolitan embrace – that produce glocalization); and commodities and the media are seen not as (totally) coercive, but rather as providing material to be used in individual and group creation throughout the glocalized areas of the world.

Cultural hybridity and glocalization, like other theories, have been criticized for not adequately dealing with the issue of power, oversimplification of the process, and overuse of the concept to describe any and all interactions. Pieterse (2010) also points out that hybridity only makes sense if one assumes a difference, purity, and fixed boundaries in relation to cultures. Most cultures of the world have been perpetually mixing with other cultures, hence they are already hybrids.

2.4.2 Network Society

Jan van Dijk (1999) and Castells (1996, 1998, 2000) are known for their work on the network society. The theory's key ideas rest on the pervasive role of information and communication technologies (ICT). Castells argues that ICTs are adopted and integrated by individuals and organizations through use and "networking logic," which helps to create a *network society*. Castells' network society theory has four dimensions: a new technological paradigm, globalization, cultural manifestations, and the demise of sovereign nation-states. According to Castells (2000), the *networks* are made up of open and dynamic interconnected nodes (social structures and activities; for van Dijk these units are individuals, groups, organizations, and communities) which are capable of unlimited expansion without disturbing the whole system. In this global system of nodes, money rather than production dominates, managers of the network play a more important role than the capitalists themselves, there is an impact of globalization on institutions, organizations, and communication systems, and the occupational structure is reconfigured to create interaction among three dimensions of production relations: value making, relation making, and decision making. In the network society, culture is created and exchanged through hypertext. Castells (2010, p. 247) explains, "This hypertext constitutes the backbone of a new culture, the culture of real virtuality, in which virtuality becomes a fundamental component of our symbolic environment, and thus of our experience as communicating beings." Nation-states have very little power in a network society.

This macro-level theory has provided a new way of looking at the flow of information and values through networks; however, it been criticized for its lack of clarity, technological determinism, eradication of human agency, a heavy focus on process and relationships of the network, and insufficient focus on real actors (Marcuse 2010).

2.4.3 Cultural Proximity

Macro level theories of international communication have largely focused on economics or culture; however, audience-focused studies are gaining ground. Theories in this area largely focus on adoption and adaptation of foreign media for national audiences. Straubhaar (1991) introduced the concept of *cultural proximity* that explains that local audiences turn to media content produced in some other country only when the choices for that content are limited, unavailable, or obsolete (Rohn 2011; Straubhaar 2007). Foreign media content that does not resonate with the audience or fulfill some need in the domestic market is less likely to be adopted by national audiences and hence is not likely to be successful (Iwabuchi 2002; Rohn 2011; Straubhaar 2007).

Building on the concept of cultural proximity, Rohn (2009, 2011) has more recently developed a more complex analytical model called the *Lacuna and the Universal Model* to explain the adoption of foreign content among national audiences. Rohn (2011) argues that for imported media content to be successful it should *avoid the Lacunae* and *have the Universals. Lacunae*, according to Rohn (2011, p. 633), refer to the "gaps or mismatches between the cultural baggage of the media producers, which influences the topics and the style of the content, and the cultural baggage of the audiences, which influences the kind of media content they select, how they understand it, and to what extent they enjoy it." *Universals*, on the other hand, focus on aspects which help in better acceptability of the product in international markets (Rohn 2011).

Content Universal, Audience-created Universal, and *Company-created Universal* are three subsets of the general Universals. *Content Universal* refers to the content attribute that is popular outside a culture because it satisfies a demand that is not met by the domestic media, involves high quality media production, targets an international niche audience, and/or "does not imprint a particular culture or country" (Iwabuchi 2002, p. 28). Media content that provides fantasy or escapism (e.g. *Harry Potter*), arouses emotions (*Titanic*), and does not resemble a particular ethnicity (*Dora the Explorer*), tends to be popular across cultures. *Audience-created Universal* refers to the enjoyment of an imported content because of the meaning-making by the audience (the relationship of the audience with the text) and perceived cultural proximity. Audiences project their own experiences, hopes, and fears onto the media content they are consuming. *In The Da Vinci Code*, Indian audiences focused on the topic of sacred feminine which plays an important role in the culture. *Company-created Universal* refers to the resources put out by the foreign media in the marketing of its content. Media products that are easily available and omnipresent find it easier to transcend cultures. Disney's *Lion King*, for example, owed its success in India largely to its extensive promotion. Media planning, positioning, time, and cost for promotion can all affect audience enjoyment and popularity of the imported content.

2.5 Complexities of the Future

This chapter has introduced several key theories of international communication, both old and contemporary, and the context of their development. We are now living in a much more complex and hyperconnected globalized world that is driven by sophisticated technologies. Hence, today there is a need to develop newer theories of transnational media and communication.

In order to begin thinking about newer theories, it is important to look at a few ways in which the world is changing and perhaps entering the fourth phase of globalization.

At this time, we are seeing the world order shift. Countries like Great Britain and France, even though still very powerful, do not have same kind of economic, political, or cultural power and influence that they once did. On the other hand, countries like China and India are on the rise with their fast-growing economies and are beginning to flex their power on the world stage.

Even though globalization has helped in the overall growth of the middle class in the world and has made global goods available at a cheaper price, it is seen as a source of problems experienced by many, both nationally and internationally. Protests related to exploitative working conditions in the developing countries (e.g. garment factory fire and collapse in Bangladesh, suicides and labor condition in Foxconn factories in China) can be juxtaposed with protests related to unemployment, squeeze in income, and income inequality witnessed in the "occupy" movement in developed countries. Issues such as immigration, financial integration, income inequality, pollution and environmental degradation, social conflict, and global trade have once again become intensely debated within and among nations as people feel their impacts. Politically, at this time, one sees a wave of nationalist leaders come to power – for example in the United States, Hungary, and Poland – by making a case for and enacting protectionist policies that retract from globalization.

Communication technologies are shaping the world in significant ways. Communication and digital technologies such as smart phones, cameras, social media, and others have become ubiquitous and quite central to people's lives all over the world, allowing them to participate both locally and globally and be a part of a network society while remaining physically present within a nation's boundary. One can sit at home in any country and buy and send products to many parts of the world through websites like Amazon. One can also support and participate in social and political issues of other nations through hashtag activism such as #BringBackOurGirls, #BlackLivesMatter, #IStandWithAhmed, #MarriageEquality, and #JeSuisCharlie. One can also see how nation-states as well as deterritorialized non-state actors like terrorist groups ISIS, Taliban, and Al-Qaeda are using communication technologies to fuel hatred and discontent, recruit terrorists, and even influence elections in other countries. Communication technologies are also allowing people around the world to create alternative realities for themselves through filters and selective exposure to information. Algorithmic logic and feeds as well as deliberate misinformation are helping create information bubbles in which we are now living our lives. People can also live real and virtual lives through participation in virtual communities.

In addition, today, through global movement of people and technologies, world cultures are accessible to many, who are learning, adopting, and changing how they live their local lives. This is changing nations and cultures at an even faster pace than before. To some groups within nations these changes are a threat to their traditional way of being and a loss of power. As a result, the fight to preserve cultural and national identities has intensified in many countries. There is no doubt that today we are living in a more complex world which is showing convergence and divergence at the same time. These complexities will require development of newer theories of media and communication in the transnational arena.

Notes

1 The theory of ideology is rooted in the Marxist tradition. Karl Marx described it as a means by which the ideas of the ruling classes become accepted and normalized throughout society. Ideology is the organized beliefs or system of beliefs characteristic of a particular class or group. Capitalism, communism, socialism, liberalism, and so on are a few examples of ideology.

2 Capitalism is: "an economic system characterized by private or corporate ownership of capital goods, by investments that are determined by private decision, and by prices, production, and the distribution of goods that are determined mainly by competition in a free market" (*Merriam Webster Dictionary*).

3 Socialism is: (a) "a system of society or group living in which there is no private property"; (b): "a system or condition of society in which the means of production are owned and controlled by the state" (*Merriam Webster Dictionary*).

References

Al-Rodhan, N.R.F. and Stoudmann, G. (2006). Definitions of Globalization: A comprehensive overview and a proposed definition. Retrieved from: http://citeseerx.ist.psu.edu/viewdoc/download?doi=10.1.1.472.4772&rep=rep1&type=pdf.

Bhabha, H. (1994). *The Location of Culture*. New York: Routledge.

Boyd-Barrett, O. (1977). Media imperialism: towards an international framework for the analysis of media systems. In: *Mass Communication and Society* (ed. J. Curran, M. Gurevitch and J. Woollacott), 116–135. London: Edward Arnold.

Castells, M. (1996). *The Rise of Network Society*. Malden, MS: Blackwell.

Castells, M. (1998). *The Information Age: Economy, Society and Culture, Volume 3: End of Millennium*. Oxford: Blackwell.

Castells, M. (2000). Towards a sociology of the network society. *Contemporary Society* 29 (5): 693–699.

Castells, M. (2010). Toward a sociology of the network society. In: *Readings in Globalization: Key Concepts and Major Debates* (ed. G. Ritzer and Z. Atalay), 246–252. West Sussex, UK: Wiley-Blackwell.

Fangjun, C. (2009). Modernization theory and China's road to modernization. *Chinese Studies in History* 43 (1): 7–16.

Institute of Media and Communication Policy (2018). Media Data Base – International Media Corporations 2015. Retrieved from: https://www.mediadb.eu/en.html.

Iwabuchi, K. (2002). *Recentering Globalization: Popular Culture and Japanese Transnationalism*. Durham, NC: Duke University Press.

James, P. and Steger, M.B. (2014). A genealogy of 'globalization': the career of a concept. *Globalizations* 11 (4): 417–434. https://doi.org/10.1080/14747731.2014.951186.

Kraidy, M. (2002). Hybridity in cultural globalization. *Communication Theory* 12 (3): 316–339.

Lerner, D. (1958). *The Passing of Traditional Society: Modernizing the Middle East*. New York: Free Press.

Marcuse, P. (2010). Depoliticing globalization: from neo-Marxism to network society of manuel castells. In: *Readings in Globalization: Key Concepts and Major Debates* (ed. G. Ritzer and Z. Atalay), 252–259. West Sussex, UK: Wiley-Blackwell.

Martínez Vela, C. A. (2001) World Systems Theory. Retrieved from: http://web.mit.edu/esd.83/www/notebook/WorldSystem.pdf.

Nulens, G. (2003). The digital divide and development communication theory. *Communicatio: South African Journal for Communication Theory and Research* 29 (1–2): 68–78.

Pieterse, J.N. (2010, 351). Hybridity, so what? The anti-hybridity backlash and riddles of recognition. In: *Readings in Globalization: Key Concepts and Major Debates* (ed. G. Ritzer and Z. Atalay), 347. West Sussex, UK: Wiley-Blackwell.

Ritzer, G. (1993). *The McDonaldization of Society*. Thousand Oaks, CA: Sage.

Ritzer, G. and Atalay, Z. (eds.) (2010). *Readings in Globalization: Key Concepts and Major Debates.* West Sussex, UK: Wiley-Blackwell.

Robertson, R. (1992). *Globalization: Social Theory and Global Culture.* London: Sage.

Rohn, U. (2009). *Cultural Barriers to the Success of Foreign Media Content: Western Media in China, India, and Japan.* Frankfurt: Peter Lang.

Rohn, U. (2011). Lacuna or universal? Introducing a new model for understanding cross-cultural audience demand. *Media, Culture and Society* 33 (4): 631–641.

Schiller, H. (1976). *Communication and cultural domination.* New York: International Arts and Science Press.

Schmidt, J.D. and Hersh, J. (eds.) (2000). Introduction. In: *Globalization and Social Change,* 1–16. London: Routledge.

Straubhaar, J.D. (1991). Beyond media imperialism: Asymmetrical interdependence and cultural proximity. *Critical Studies in Mass Communication* 8 (1): 39–59.

Straubhaar, J.D. (2007). *World Television: From Global to Local.* Thousand Oaks, CA: Sage.

Strelitz, L. (2005). *Mixed Reception: South African Youth and Their Experience of Global Media.* Pretoria: Unisa.

Thussu, D.K. (2006). *International Communication: Continuity and Change,* 2e. London: Arnold.

Tunstall, J. (1977). *The Media Are American: Anglo-American Media in the World.* London: Constable.

UNESCO (1980). Many Voices. One World. Retrieved from: http://unesdoc.unesco.org/images/0004/000400/040066eb.pdf.

Van Dijk, J. (1999). *The Network Society: Social Aspects of New Media* (trans. Leontine Spoorenberg). London: Sage.

Verde, A. (2017). *Is Globalisation Doomed?: The Economic and Political Threats to the Future of Globalization.* Viterbo, Italy: Palgrave Macmillan.

Wallerstein, I. (1974). The rise and future demise of the world capitalist system: concepts for comparative analysis. *Comparative Studies in Society and History* 16 (4): 387–415.

Wallerstein, I. (1976). *The Modern World-System: Capitalist Agriculture and the Origins of the European World-Economy in the Sixteenth Century.* New York: Academic Press.

3

Introducing Media Systems

Rebecca Kern-Stone

Media systems are models that provide historical, philosophical, political, and economic information about the ways in which media is or could be constructed. They tend to appear rather polarized, where certain countries seem to fit neatly into one model. However, that is rarely the case. Media systems are always tied to particular sets of conditions – political, economic, and cultural – so different aspects of a country's or region's media may cross systems.

3.1   Elements of a Media System

In order to compare and contrast media systems in different countries and regions, it is necessary to understand the elements that comprise the system itself. The approach needs to be systematic so that the same elements are being compared and contrasted in each system equally. It is only in this way that each country can be viewed on the same level, and it can be best determined which media system fits the current conditions. By current conditions, again we do not mean that only one system fits one country or region, rather that varying aspects of one or more media systems may apply at different points in time, in different cultural contexts, as well as across different media platforms.

There are a series of interrelated elements that are pertinent to the understanding of any media system. The ways in which these are discussed or named may vary by scholar, but they essentially amount to the same fundamental categories. These include, but are not limited to: media access, media regulation, economic policies, political ideology, types and flow of content, news/information bias, global imports/exports, and audience involvement. Each of the elements directly and indirectly effects the others. Thus, to ignore one element, such as media access, is also to ignore how media content flows and how audiences are able to interact. As a result, this creates greater global information inequities.

Each media system was born from some political ideology or from scholarly ideas about how media and its policies could be improved. Some of these political ideologies are situated in historical contexts such that when translated into current media considerations, they lose original meaning. A good example of this is Siebert, Petersen, and Schramm's Soviet Communist model which has its philosophical underpinnings in Marxism. This is further discussed below. Others are contemporary models that are situated in relation to current transnational trends. Regardless, all of the models are temporally and culturally constructed, meaning they were established in a specific time and place. As such, they reflect political situations at a historical point in history and show the interplay of government intervention with media and audiences.

Transnational Media: Concepts and Cases, First Edition. Edited by Suman Mishra and Rebecca Kern-Stone.
© 2019 John Wiley & Sons, Inc. Published 2019 by John Wiley & Sons, Inc.

This includes who gets to produce media, what political and economic controls are in place regarding content and regulation, and whether ownership is public or private.

3.2 The (Contested) Media Systems

Many media studies scholars have discussed types of media systems, but there are some that became the initial established models in the field. The first four were introduced by Fredrick Siebert, Theodore Petersen, and Wilbur Schramm in 1956 in their seminal book *The Four Theories of the Press*. Their initial four theories – authoritarian, libertarian, social responsibility, and Soviet Communist – were deemed the *normative theories of the press*. They were given this distinction primarily because they were developed by the three scholars in the United States during the Cold War and were therefore created to match social and political systems during that period. In Siebert, Peterson, and Schramm's (1965) words "The press always takes on the form and coloration of the social and political structures within which it operates. Especially, it reflects the system of social control whereby the relations of individuals of these aspects of society is basic to any systematic understanding of the press" (p. 1–2). These four theories have since been deemed too simplistic as they did not take into account changing political and economic landscapes, nor the ways in which media, namely the press, was an institution which ultimately answered to the government or to the people. In other words, the press was always seen as emblematic of a democratic society and from a democratic perspective.

Other theories have since been proposed about how media models should be understood, in particular tackling the initial four theories. Nerone (1995), for example, does not see the value of the four theories in post-Cold War analyses. In addition, he argues that it favors the liberal tradition of the press over the other models, but the press is no longer about individual naturalized rights, as suggested by Siebert et al. (1965). Rather, the press is an institution, and needs to be discussed collectively and in political and economic terms. McQuail (2005), made a similar argument, but noted that it was imperative to include issues relating to commercialism, professionalism, liberalism, and democratization. As a result, he proposed four new normative models: the market model, social responsibility model, professional model, and alternative media model. These models were in response to the original four theories as well as the additional two he proposed in an earlier book: the developmental model and democratic participatory model. Other models and approaches have been offered by de Smaele (1999) and Hallin and Mancini (2004), among others. Some scholars, noting the Western bent in analyzing media, have proposed more globalized models. Blum (2005) in particular offered six models: an Atlantic-Pacific liberal model, a Southern European clientalism model, a Northern European public service model, an Eastern European shock model, an Arab-Asian patriot model, and an Asian-Caribbean model. Other scholars from Asia and Latin/South America have examined, and resisted, media models that are too focused on Eurocentric histories (Christians et al. 2009; Yin 2008).

However, the initial four theories do have their place as they were written in a particular time and place. Less useful in understanding the complex nature of media contexts, they do inform later models as well as provide comparison. The following offers brief examinations of many media models proposed by different scholars. It begins with the original four normative theories as presented by Siebert et al. (1965) and adds the two by McQuail (1994). Then the three Western models by Hallin and Mancini (2004) as well as McQuail's (2000) later models are offered as reinterpretations of the original four theories. Last, it discusses the six models as proposed by Blum (2005). In no way are the models presented here meant to be exhaustive, but they do note the progression of media models and offer a foundation for understanding how media is integrated with political, economic, and cultural forces. Each model is paired with a country that is a potential representation of at least part of that model. In addition to the explanation provided, it may be helpful to refer to the World Press Freedom Index map, which shows which countries have free media versus which countries do not (Figure 3.1).

3.3 The Original Four Normative Theories of the Press

3.3.1 Authoritarian

The authoritarian model has its historical beginnings in sixteenth and seventeenth-century Europe during a period when monarchies and the Catholic and Protestant churches had absolute rule over their constituents. The individual in the authoritarian model is not celebrated as they are valued as a member of society over all else (Siebert 1956, pp. 10–11). Adherence to the monarchy and to the churches, discussed as "the State," were the only opportunities for an individual to gain full potential within society. The model is based on the philosophical underpinnings of Plato and Hobbes, who argue that an organized society is an ideal and, as such, there should be "rigorous control of opinion and discussion" (p. 12), as well as Hegel who maintained that "The State is embodied morality" (p. 13). This top-down model focuses on collectivity, but power is derived through following State mandates. Individual opinion has no place in the collective, as the only voice that matters is that of the State.

In order to promote control, particularly over the press and other potential places for information to be distributed, strict measures are enforced. Not just anyone has the right to produce media, this is reserved for those with State approval through licensing and is subject to State surveillance. The press is heavily aligned with the ruling political party, and parallelism is high. Censorship is heavy, especially of those media outlets who choose to criticize the political and cultural ideologies of those in power. As a result, there is strong institutionalized self-regulation. Hence, the goal of media in an authoritarian system is to serve the State and its interests, particularly as it pertains to implementing government policy.

Despite all of this, and often with limited media outlets, media access and interest varies by region. In some places, such as Turkey, an authoritarian media system has not deterred the public from engaging with the press. Also, many have found a way around the heavy censoring of media and have established a public voice using digital platforms.

3.3.2 Libertarian

The libertarian model is the response to the authoritarian model of absolute power. Begun in seventeenth and eighteenth-century England and North America, its goal was freedom from government and absolute power. Born primarily out of the philosophy of the Enlightenment, it strongly believes in the free will of the people and their inherent rights as citizens. A great deal of importance is placed on the search for truth and knowledge, and it follows Milton's belief that the truth will always be found (Siebert 1956). J. S. Mills and John Locke were also influential in the creation of libertarian ideals. Mills believed that silence equaled a lack of search for the truth, and that one's liberty was a given right so long as no one else was harmed in the procuring of said liberty. Locke argued that the government exists to serve the people, and in the "will of the people" there is power (Siebert 1956, p. 43). Hence, the goal of this model is to promote free expression and freedom of press; however, these were not to be absolutes.

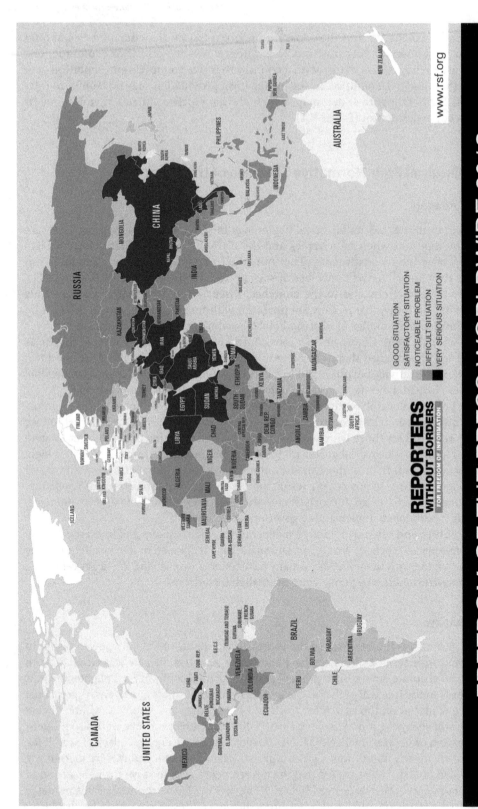

FREEDOM OF THE PRESS WORLDWIDE 2018

www.rsf.org

REPORTERS WITHOUT BORDERS
FOR FREEDOM OF INFORMATION

GOOD SITUATION
SATISFACTORY SITUATION
NOTICEABLE PROBLEM
DIFFICULT SITUATION
VERY SERIOUS SITUATION

Figure 3.1 World Press Freedom Index map.

Instead, measures were put in place to curb rampant speech and abuses of power. The first amendment, enacted in the United States in 1792 (later revised), was the initial such measure. It stated that,

> Congress shall make no law respecting an establishment of religion, or prohibiting the free exercise thereof; or abridging the freedom of speech, or of the press; or the right of the people peaceably to assemble, and to petition the Government for a redress of grievances.

Essentially, this was meant as a control on the government. Other measures include: libel protections, which ensured that citizens could not be defamed in the press; control of obscene or profane material, or that which is deemed immoral; treason, or any information which might threaten the security of the nation; and licensing of media outlets. The first amendment was left broad and open to interpretation, while the later measures have changed, some significantly, over time. There is an expectation that print media will self-regulate, while broadcast is subject to regulation from government bodies.

While anyone may own or produce media in the libertarian model, it is usually those with monetary means. Hence, ownership of media is private as opposed to owned and monetized by the government. Advertising helps media outlets earn money to continue running. There is also low parallelism, as media outlets are encouraged to remain free from bias, and mid to high professionalization. A primary example of a country with a history of a libertarian system is the United States, as the system was born out of the country's independence. However, it is less aligned with the current state of media in the United States, as media has begun to lose its professionalization, and new laws and government intervention continue to curb speech.

3.3.3 Social Responsibility

Social responsibility also grew out of the United States, but in the early twentieth century. This system can best be described as an expansion of libertarianism and a need to increase social discourse. This was primarily in reaction to social morality concerns relating to health and labor breaches, and the idea that the government has a responsibility to the people to keep them safe, and the press a responsibility to provide them with knowledge. Following Hocking, who developed the Commission on the Freedom of the Press, discourse promotes knowledge and personal growth, but the press is there to sort out the truth for the public (Peterson 1956). Under the social responsibility model, the press has the same functions as in the libertarian model (Peterson 1956); but the press has not always followed through on the tasks with which it was endowed. For example, the press may be financially stabilized through advertising, but it should not then privilege those advertisers above the truth.

As such, anyone with or without means should be able to have a voice. As a result, and with the expansion of media platforms, more individuals are given a voice. While most of the media is still privatized under this model, it calls for public options as well. Media has a responsibility to the public and will be checked on through public legislation. This is namely through consumer action groups, regulatory agencies and the courts, public opinion, and ethical codes. Professionalization is mid to high, and there is low parallelism. A prime example of a country partially operating under this model is Canada, which has a historical footprint of the social responsibility model and is now looking to advance a more financially stable and diverse media environment after losing press outlets in 2017 (House of Commons 2017).

3.3.4 Soviet Communist

The final of the four original models by Siebert et al. (1965), is the Soviet Communist model. Conceived in the former Soviet Union in the nineteenth century, it has its foundations in the teachings of Marx, Lenin, and Hegel. Power in this model is gained through organized social action, and as a result media must be in the hands of the people. Also at the root of this model are the Marxist concepts of a society that is unified, and one that is classless as is necessary in order to achieve equality. For Marx, borrowing from Hegel, change happens in economic struggle, where the thesis (the worker) and the antithesis (the owners/buyers) merge in synthesis (Schramm 1956). As Schramm (1956) notes, the press could not operate "as a forum for free discussion" (p. 110) under Marxist ideals, as it would be used as a tool of power; one that would act as a mouthpiece for the people and an outlet for criticism of the government. This is not, however, the way in which the model grows. According to Schramm (1956), Marxist idealizations were overshadowed by various dictatorships, namely that of Stalin, which left power in the hands of the few. Stalin argued that in a country impacted by outside capitalist forces, the State had to step in and promote national unity. As a result, media became owned and run by party members, with approval from the State. Its goal was to teach party doctrine and improve the overall esthetics of the country. Media would also be heavily surveilled, and those who spoke out against government policies or Soviet party ideologies would be censored. With heavy political parallelism to one party, media became an arm of the State.

Currently, it is hard to determine if any country truly follows a Soviet Communist system, especially after the fall of the Soviet Union in 1991. At the time, the Soviet Union was moving to a more democratized government and free market economy, which was to open media opportunities. In what is now the Russian Federation, there is a mixture of private and public media, but self-censorship remains high as do adherence to political ideologies.

3.4 Extensions on the First Four Normative Theories

3.4.1 Development

This is an additional model offered by McQuail (1987, 1994, 2005) to further expand upon what Siebert et al. (1965) had originally proposed. Development theory tries to acknowledge the "development" of countries as they move from colonial rule to independence as well as the changing economic landscape of developing nations. The model acknowledges lack of infrastructure, access, and monetary power, as well as a skilled media body, literacy issues, and audience growth (McQuail 2005). As such, development theory looks to help impoverished nations grow socially and economically.

The model also has its beginnings with UNESCO (the United Nations Educational, Scientific, and Cultural Organization) which works to build global partnerships for citizens. Their efforts include promoting free expression and democracy, giving access to education and science, and providing media access through infrastructure improvements (UNESCO 2017). Through these efforts, UNESCO encourages the building of national unity and promotes media freedom through information access and improved discourse. Everyone with means has the opportunity to produce media, much like in the libertarian theory. However, many receive funding from NGOs (non-governmental organizations), which allows for many more voices to have the opportunity to create and produce media. While these opportunities do promote open discourse, if the discourse impedes social development it will be shut down. As a result, media freedoms may be curbed, including press freedom, if the government deems the speech to impede national and social growth. In this way, at times, development theory in practice may seem closer to the authoritarian model (McQuail 2005).

With reference to issues of politicization, this varies by country and region. Nations that might correspond with a development media model are themselves at different stages of development politically and economically. As a result, parallelism of the press with the government might be high in some circumstances and low in others. The level of State intervention in terms of what national rhetoric is expected will often determine the level of parallelism. As far as economic State intervention goes, it tends to be rather high as governments are often required to help media outlets thrive, even where advertising has been an accepted form of media economic stability. Professionalization, on the other hand, tends to run low to intermediate as audiences gain access to new media platforms. As access grows, so does the need to train professionals

Nigeria is a good example of a country that has a development media model. As a whole, Nigeria has a partly free media environment, where there are many media outlets and government criticism is allowed (Freedom House 2017d). However, despite having opportunities to criticize government, journalists are often pressured to monitor their speech when it applies to national security and national growth (Freedom House 2017d). Despite this, media has grown substantially over the years, especially television. But as with many nations with a development model, media is financially insecure as it often relies upon taxes and licensing fees to survive, even when advertising is accepted.

3.4.2 Democratic Participatory

This is the second additional model proposed by McQuail (1987, 1994, 2005) as an extension of the original four press models. This late twentieth-century-based model is heavily media platform-based as it is in direct relation to new platforms available and global availability of information. This model can best be described as an answer to the ways in which participants in a democratic society interact with media and the public sphere.

The democratic participatory model was created primarily academically by the likes of Rosen and McChesney, and encourages civic participation, transformation, and a plurality of voices (UNESCO 2013). The plurality also tries to give a voice to the voiceless, such as underrepresented and marginalized groups in society. It promotes representation of cultural identity. As a result, the concept that anyone with means can create media is less about money and more about desire for expression. It shares similarities with the libertarian model (free expression) and the social responsibility model (debates on public affairs). Parallelism in the model may be low, but pluralism may be higher as many voices have access to media. Professionalization still exists, but fewer people have formal training in this model overall, especially with newer interactive platforms. For example, social media, blogs, and other online forums do not necessarily have professionally trained voices, rather they are citizens with opinions and knowledge.

A good example of a country that follows this model might be Estonia. This democratized media market has made great strides since the fall of the Soviet Union in the early 1990s. Media in Estonia has been established both for ethnic Estonians as well as Russians who remained in Estonia. Along with national newspapers, local municipalities frequently publish their own newspaper or newsletter. While the national papers strive for political independence, the local papers fall toward the political bias of the region (Loit 2018). There is also a relatively large public broadcasting system. With a free media system and limited regulatory authority, Estonia has encouraged growth in various media outlets and a plurality of voices.

3.5 New Media Models

3.5.1 Liberal

Hallin and Mancini (2004) proposed three media models that are primarily aimed at European media markets but can have applicability beyond those borders. The liberal model, also called the North Atlantic model, developed in the mid to late 1800s in North America and the United Kingdom. Heavily influenced by Protestantism and the growth of literacy (Hallin and Mancini 2004), the model finds its roots in industrialized capitalism at the turn of the nineteenth century. Much like the libertarian model, the liberal model touts individualism and the growth of knowledge, and its goal is to inform the public through open discourse.

Media ownership is primarily private and commercialized; however, there is some public and government funded media. It is a very fact-based system (Chalaby 1996), and as a result political parallelism tends to be low and professionalization high. The state tends to have low intervention as this system is reliant on capitalist growth and private ownership; however, in some of the countries that embody the liberal tradition, namely Canada, Ireland, and Britain, there is a moderately strong public broadcasting sector that exists next to a rapidly growing commercial sector.

Opinion has no place within the journalism of this model, yet a strong tabloid press and moderate pluralism, particularly in Britain, have marked that nation's media. It is in this country, unlike others in the liberal model where parallelism has remained higher, that the party press has a foothold (Hallin and Mancini 2004). The printed press, as a result, does not have the trust of the public and newspaper circulation is low.

3.5.2 Polarized Pluralist

The polarized pluralist model is heavily grounded in the political history of the primarily Mediterranean regions of Europe. In particular, media was dependent on the Catholic Church, State entities, and the associated political parties (Hallin and Mancini 2004, p. 90). Philosophically, it began under the auspices of political regimes and religious doctrine and grew under fascism.

This model is highly associated with politics, where media serves to represent the wide range of political influences (Hallin and Mancini 2004). As such, journalistic market growth has been slow, and commercial presses have had low circulation. This also does not encourage high professionalization of journalistic practice, as politics tends to sway journalistic integrity; however, this has been changing. As Hallin and Mancini (2004) note, secularization as well as the influence of the American and British media have altered the media landscape. There has been a growing public broadcasting sector as well as commercial broadcasting that is not tied to political influence as the press had been formerly.

While fewer countries in recent years could be said to have a truly polarized pluralist model, Italy may still be the closest. For years, Italy has tied its media closely to political parties, and perhaps no more so than with Berlusconi. Berlusconi served as prime minister of Italy until 2001 and continues to remain a part of Italian politics. In addition to his role in Italian government, he still owns the largest share of Italian media through his company Mediaset. Italy continues to have many political parties, and political parallelism is still prevalent (Mancini and Gerli 2017). While press circulation remains low in Italy, television is highly consumed and as a result takes the main share of commercial advertising revenues (Mancini and Gerli 2017).

3.5.3 Democratic Corporatist

The last model proposed by Hallin and Mancini looks to countries in Northern and Central Europe that have been influenced by Protestantism and the desire for increased literacy across Europe. It stems from Martin Luther's desire to "create a common culture and common public sphere," and because of the printing press new political and religious discussions began (Hallin and Mancini 2004, p. 143). Countries within this model involve consensus politics, have strong welfare states, and encourage free expression.

Due to these elements, newspaper readership is high and many voices are heard. Pluralism exists here as well, but it is segmented, meaning that media tends toward subgroups, especially as pertains to politics, religion, and social concerns. This is also true within the public broadcasting environment. There has, however, been in recent years fast growth of a commercial media sector. Regardless of ownership, public or private, press freedom and freedom of expression are highly protected. Professionalization among journalists is also highly valued. The government provides subsidies for media, and media access is generally quite high.

Norway is a country that embodies this model. It has the highest press freedom index of any country according to Freedom House (2017a), as press freedom and freedom of expression continue to be supported. Internet access is at nearly 100% and is currently the most used and generally trusted medium for news (Østbye 2017). While much of the printed commercial news sector has diminished in recent years due to internet usage and online papers, local newspapers and national opinion papers continue to flourish (Østbye 2017). Overall, media is owned privately and by the government. The government continues to license media outlets and provides some regulation regarding advertising and the offering of subsidies; however, there is little regulation about content.

3.5.4 Market Model

McQuail (2005) offered four new normative models (in addition to the two previously discussed), as a re-evaluation and a summary of the original four theories. He states, "These models are what media ought to do rather than what they actually do" (p. 185). This is why they are deemed normative models, and why they are simply re-imagined and updated from the models offered by Siebert et al. (1965).

The market model is really a redefined libertarian model, where media should be free from government control and should encourage a "free marketplace of ideas" (p. 184). Advertising is the primary economic source as media is primarily privately owned. As a result, media is created to appeal to what will bring in the largest audiences and the largest profit margins. This frequently includes more entertainment and sports genres. Despite being free from government control, some regulation of media is through government agencies that ensure a free market economy of media outlets, primarily for broadcast entities.

Japan is perhaps a country that has embodied the market model in recent years. As Iwabuchi (2010) notes, "The spread of Japanese cultural products in the world reflects the fact that Japanese media industries and cultural forms are playing a substantial role in global cultural flows" (p. 410). Their press is relatively homogenous and press clubs abound, which keep news from disrupting the "status-quo" (Press-reference, Japan 2017), but they do have a strong history of press freedom and professionalization. What really marks Japan as having a market model is the increase of commercialized television and other entertainment media, as well as the capitalistic endeavors of exporting their media to other Asian nations and Western markets.

3.5.5 Public Interest Model

This model is also known as the social responsibility model. It is not that dissimilar to the social responsibility model proposed by Siebert et al. (1965). Responsibility to a wider public and their self-interests is seen as necessary, as opposed to the self-interests of the media outlet owners (McQuail 2003). Media in this model should serve the public interest and should inform using varying viewpoints. Public broadcasting is supported by this model, although it is not necessarily extensive.

Professionalization runs high in this model, and journalists of all types are encouraged to self-regulate. Government regulation is in place for broadcast outlets, but internet and other digital spaces have little to no regulation. However, public interest groups and professional organizations do regulate media in this model and can put pressure on media institutions relating to content. In other words, the public sphere as envisioned by Habermas becomes a place for active civic discourse. In places where media economies may be lacking, and infrastructure and access is poor, NGOs may play an important role and contribute to "good governance" (Buckley et al. 2008, p. 15).

Evidence of the incorporation of the public interest model has been apparent in many places where democratic values have entered the consciousness of citizens. As a result, media is used as a platform to fight corruption, provide platforms for many voices, and increase civic dialog. Media in Argentina have been increasingly an example of this model. In 2017, Argentina's press score rose again from a 50 to 46. While the country remains partly free, new political leadership in 2015 reversed many restrictive policies and opened up many more media outlets and opportunities. As stated by Freedom House (2017b), "professional groups are free to support journalists' rights and interests," and citizens and journalists use media to openly discuss political and economic issues the country faces.

3.5.6 Professional Model

This model is concretely focused on the journalist, the press, and the need for complete autonomy from interference. This model, as its name suggests, insists on high professionalization and ethical standards. Perhaps most closely tied to the libertarian ideals of the press as proposed by Siebert et al. (1965), it really only works as an idealized theoretical model. There is low pluralism as the model encourages free expression and pushes democratic values (McQuail 2010). The libertarian media model, as noted by Nerone (1995) and McQuail (2010), focuses primarily on ownership of media which is problematic, they argue, when ensuring free expression and press freedom. It also centers on the printed press and fails to acknowledge broadcast or digital platforms. The professional model aims to include all media platforms, as well as varying levels of ownership where concentration of ownership does not lie with a few.

As a result, indicating a country that exemplifies this media model is difficult. While countries have very open and democratic press systems, they still have concentrated ownership. In some cases, Germany embodies this system. It has a diverse print media, with many independent publishers, and readers have options of over "1,528 different dailies with a run of about 16m copies per day" (Thomaß and Horz 2017). However, it also has a very concentrated publishing industry, the fifth largest in the world. The commercial television industry has similar broad diversity, but again is concentrated within a small percentage of owners. Public broadcasting rounds out Germany's offerings, and other channels offered are inclusive of immigrant populations, as is digital media.

3.5.7 Alternative Media Model

The last model suggested by McQuail (2010) is the alternative media model, which focuses on grassroots and independent media or non-mainstream media as well as alternative modes of distribution, such as via digital channels. Community participation is encouraged and there is a rejection of concentrated ownership. This is a particularly important part of this model as members of each media community play a role in shaping the overall organization and its governance. Just as with the democratic participatory model, while there is a focus on professionalization of journalists, citizen journalists are emboldened. Content in this model does not simply focus on what will garner advertising funding; rather, content is both mainstream ideologically as well as oppositional to the mainstream (Fuchs 2010).

As it stands globally, no country or region would be a good example of such a model; rather, some incorporate this model to certain media organizations. For instance, public media in the United States uses this model, as their public media is primarily funded by readers and listeners and strives to present all perspectives on a variety of issues. Professionalization is highly valued, but individual media creators and curators are also given a space to voice viewpoints and interests.

3.5.8 Blum's Models

Blum (2005) went further with his analysis of media systems by not only engaging with the political and economic condition, but also the cultural. His criteria for analysis included those of Hallin and Mancini (2004) as well as examinations of media freedom, media culture, and ownership and funding (Jakubowicz 2010). The first three of Blum's (2005) models, the Atlantic–Pacific liberal model, the Southern European clientalism model, and the Northern European public service model are based on Hallin and Mancini's (2004) Western media models. He also proposed three additional models: the Eastern European shock model, the Arab–Asian patriot model, and the Asian–Caribbean model.

The Eastern European shock model is based around very strong state intervention – including funding, content, and ownership – yet media is guaranteed freedom of press and expression (Jakubowicz 2010). Not all Eastern European countries can be placed in this model, however, as much of media in these countries works very hard to support a free press and free expression. This will be made evident in the chapters on Europe. A country that is closely tied to this model would be Turkey, as many media outlets were closed or greatly curbed after the failed coup in 2016, this included jailing journalists (BBC News, Turkey 2017).

The Arab–Asian patriot model, seen frequently in Middle East/North African countries, suggests that authoritarian governments keep media from developing. The political structures of these countries often support the ways in which the governments control media. For example, in Egypt, despite citizen desire to expand media expression – as was evident during the 2011 uprisings and continued advocacy – the recent government has continued to constrain media outlets. Egypt has jailed numerous journalists and media operators over content concerns as well as creating three supervisory departments to control content, funding, and licensing (Freedom House 2017c).

Lastly, in the Asian–Caribbean model, media is wholly in the hands of the government, but the funding of media is partially market driven (Jakubowicz 2010). The goal of media here is to spread state or special interest ideologies through very limited media outlets. Funding may be from the state or through private organizations and advertising as supported and controlled via the state. An example would be Vietnam, where the ruling Communist Party uses media as a mouthpiece for state-serving interests. While much of the media is owned and funded by the state, private outlets may have print options which are financially self-sufficient (Freedom House 2015).

Media should be evaluated based on many factors. This means not examining only broadcast media or print media within a country, for example, but also how both are regulated, owned, and operated. In addition, consider funding sources and the financial stability of media organizations as well as political forces that may shape content and structure. Elements of infrastructure and access, journalistic integrity, and legal environments are also important indicators.

As noted at the beginning of this chapter, there is no singular model that applies equally to any one region or country. In addition, the models presented here are by no means exhaustive. Instead, the models presented offer perspectives, and show where certain models and perspectives may be focused too heavily on Western media landscapes. As such, it is important to consider the elements involved in each model and look at their applicability in global contexts.

References

BBC News (2017). Turkey profile – Media. *BBC News*. Retrieved from: http://www.bbc.com/news/world-europe-17992011.

Blum, R. (2005). Bausteine zu einer Theorie der Mediensysteme. *Medienwissenschaft Shweiz* 2 (2): 5–11.

Buckley, S., Duer, K., Mendel, T., and Siochrú, S. (2008). *Broadcasting, Voice, and Accountability: A Public Interest Approach to Policy, Law, and Regulation*. Ann Arbor: University of Michigan Press Retrieved from: https://quod.lib.umich.edu/n/nmw/5661153.0001.001/1:2/--broadcasting-voice-and-accountability-a-public-interest?g=dculture;rgn=div1;view=fulltext;xc=1.

Chalaby, J. (1996). Journalism as an Anglo-American invention: a comparison of the development of French and Anglo-American journalism 1830s–1920s. *European Journal of Communication* 11 (3): 303–326.

Christians, C., Glasser, T., McQuail, D. et al. (2009). *Normative Theories of the Media: Journalism in Democratic Societies*. Urbana: University of Illinois Press.

deSmaele, H. (1999). The applicability of Western media models on the Russian media system. *European Journal of Communication* 14 (2): 173–189.

Freedom House (2015). Vietnam. Retrieved from: https://freedomhouse.org/report/freedom-press/2015/vietnam.

Freedom House (2017a). Freedom of the press. Retrieved from: https://freedomhouse.org/report/freedom-press/freedom-press-2017.

Freedom House (2017b). Argentina. Retrieved from: https://freedomhouse.org/report/freedom-press/2017/argentina

Freedom House (2017c). Egypt. Retrieved from: https://freedomhouse.org/report/freedom-press/2017/egypt.

Freedom House (2017d). Nigeria. Retrieved from: https://freedomhouse.org/report/freedom-press/2017/nigeria.

Fuchs, C. (2010). Alternative media as critical media. *European Journal of Social Theory* 13 (2): 173–192.

Hallin, D. and Mancini, P. (2004). *Comparing Media Systems: Three Models of Media and Politics*. Cambridge: Cambridge University Press.

House of Commons, Canada (June 2017). Disruption: Change and churning in Canada's media landscape. Retrieved from: https://www.ourcommons.ca/DocumentViewer/en/42-1/CHPC/report-6.

Iwabuchi, K. (2010). Taking "Japanization" seriously: cultural globalization revisited. In: *International Communication: A Reader* (ed. D. Thussu), 410–433. London: Routledge.

Jakubowicz, K. (2010). Media systems research: an overview. In: *Comparative Media Systems: European and Global Perspectives* (ed. B. Dobek-Ostrowska, M. Glowacki, K. Jakubowicz and M. Sukosd), 1–21. New York: Central European University Press.

Loit, U. (2018). Estonia. *European Media Landscapes*. Retrieved from: http://ejc.net/media_landscapes/estonia.

Mancini, P. and Gerli, M. (2017). Italy. *Media Landscapes*. Retrieved from: https://medialandscapes.org/country/italy.

McQuail, D. (1987). *McQuail's Mass Communication Theory*. Los Angeles: Sage.

McQuail, D. (1994). *McQuail's Mass Communication Theory*. Los Angeles: Sage.

McQuail, D. (2000). *McQuail's Mass Communication Theory*. Los Angeles: Sage.

McQuail, D. (2005). *McQuail's Mass Communication Theory*. Los Angeles: Sage.

McQuail, D. (2010). *McQuail's Mass Communication Theory*. Los Angeles: Sage.

Nerone, J. (1995). *Last Rights: Revisiting Four Theories of the Press*. Urbana: University of Illinois Press.

Østbye, H. (2017). Norway. *Media Landscapes*. Retrieved from: https://medialandscapes.org/country/norway.

Peterson, T. (1956). The social responsibility theory. In: *The Four Theories of the Press: The Authoritarian, Libertarian, Social Responsibility, and Soviet Communist Concepts of What the Press Should Be and Do* (ed. F. Siebert, T. Peterson and W. Schramm), 73–104. Urbana: University of Illinois Press.

Press Reference (2017). Japan. *Press Reference*. Retrieved from: http://www.pressreference.com/Gu-Ku/Japan.html.

Schramm, W. (1956). The soviet communist theory. In: *The Four Theories of the Press: The Authoritarian, Libertarian, Social Responsibility, and Soviet Communist Concepts of What the Press Should Be and Do* (ed. F. Siebert, T. Peterson and W. Schramm), 105–146. Urbana: University of Illinois Press.

Siebert, F. (1956). The authoritarian theory and the libertarian theory. In: *The Four Theories of the Press: The Authoritarian, Libertarian, Social Responsibility, and Soviet Communist Concepts of What the Press Should Be and Do* (ed. F. Siebert, T. Peterson and W. Schramm), 9–71. Urbana: University of Illinois Press.

Siebert, F., Peterson, T., and Schramm, W. (eds.) (1965). *The Four Theories of the Press: The Authoritarian, Libertarian, Social Responsibility, and Soviet Communist Concepts of What the Press Should Be and Do*. Urbana: University of Illinois Press.

Thomaß, B. and Horz, C. (2017). Germany. *Media Landscapes*. Retrieved from: https://medialandscapes.org/country/germany.

United Nations Educational, Scientific, and Cultural Organization (UNESCO) (2013). Beyond 2015: Media as democracy and development. Retrieved from: http://www.unesco.org/new/fileadmin/MULTIMEDIA/HQ/post2015/pdf/UNESCO_Media_Democracy_Development.pdf.

United Nations Educational, Scientific, and Cultural Organization (UNESCO) (2017). About us. *UNESCO*. Retrieved from: https://en.unesco.org/about-us/introducing-unesco

Yin, J. (2008). Beyond the four theories of the press: a new model for the Asian & world press. *Journalism and Communication Monographs* 10 (1): 3–62.

Part II

Africa

Transnational Media: Concepts and Cases, First Edition. Edited by Suman Mishra and Rebecca Kern-Stone.
© 2019 John Wiley & Sons, Inc. Published 2019 by John Wiley & Sons, Inc.

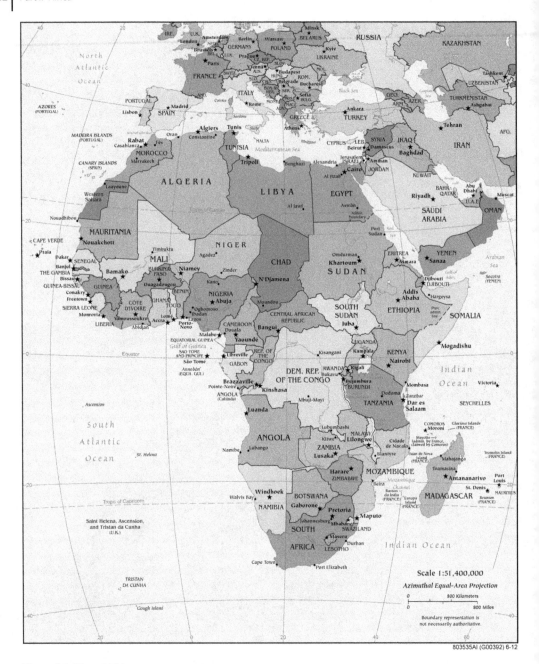

Figure II.1 Map of Africa.

The continent of Africa (Figure II.1) had just over 1.2 billion people as of 2016, with approximately 40% of the population living in urban areas. It has the lowest number of international migrants compared to other continents, and as of 2017 they made up just 2% of the total population (UN DESA 2017a). However, since 2000, the percentage of international migrants has increased by 67%, which was the largest global increase. In 2017, Africa also hosted the second largest refugee population (UN DESA 2017a).

Access to electricity and internet services varies widely, but on the whole there has been growth over the past decade. Mobile technology is thriving in Africa, with mobile penetration at around 82% of the population. Internet penetration is just over 35%. The countries in Northern and Western Africa have much higher penetration rates than Eastern, Central, and Southern Africa, with South Africa as a notable exception (African Economic Outlook 2017).

Africa is best described geographically, as each area is influenced very differently by its political, economic, geographic, and cultural surroundings. In addition, each region is affected by colonialism from the nineteenth and early twentieth centuries, where some media in individual countries is still owned and operated by outside European conglomerates, and European languages – particularly English, French, and German – still abound alongside local dialects.

Colonialism has had an impact on African nations and how media have developed in African countries. As Fisher (2012) notes, borders were drawn based on colonialist designations of the region, not on the tribal and other historic land designations. This has, however, posed interesting challenges as countries in Africa continue to grow politically and economically. Africa has had political and economic turmoil, particularly since many countries gained independence from the 1950s onward, but the goal of its people is one of growth, peace, and democracy (Fisher 2012). Countries and particular media trends are detailed in the coming chapters, which focus on Kenya, Ghana, South Africa, and Nigeria. To provide a general media background for each, however, the following offers some key media insights and statistics.

PII.1 Kenya

Kenya is one of 20 countries in Eastern Africa, which are all along the Indian Ocean, including the Horn of Africa. It has a population of just over 50.6 million, and most people live in the capital, Nairobi, in major cities, such as Mombassa, along the coast, and along Lake Victoria (Internet World Stats 2018). Kenya continues to have a fast-growing economy, one of the fastest in sub-Saharan Africa, with a GDP of 70.88 billion in USD (World Bank 2016a). The country has also seen GDP growth from 5.5% in 2017 to 5.8% in 2018, with an expectation of growth in 2019 to 6.1% (World Bank 2018a).

As a republic, Kenya has a president; however, recent elections of its current president, Uhuru Kenyatta, have been disputed as not adhering to a fair election process. Historically, this region of Africa was colonized by Belgium, Germany, France, Britain, and Portugal, and media from these countries still thrives there, as do the languages. As Kenya gained its independence from Britain in 1963, English is the primary language in Kenya next to Kiswahili. In addition, Christianity dominates, as most of the population practices this religion, with the next most prominent being Islam.

Media in Kenya is primarily owned by two commercial corporations, the Nation Media Group and Standard Media, and uses advertising as its primary source of funding. Both have print and broadcast entities, which are available in English and Kiswahili. In major cities, television is the primary source of news, but in rural areas radio is very important (BBC News 2017c). This is likely due to electricity access, infrastructure, and literacy. Additional digital television programming is available through transnational media groups, South Africa's DStv, Kenyan-owned Zuku TV, and the Chinese-owned StarTimes, and radio is available via England's BBC World Service. There is state-owned media, such as the Kenyan Broadcasting Corporation (KBC), which is funded through advertising and government sources.

Press freedom has shrunk in recent years, and currently Kenya ranks 96/180 on the 2018 World Press Freedom index. This is due to concerns over the political climate, which restricts information gathering among journalists as well as any coverage that goes against the current government of Prime Minister Kenyatta, and as a result of the commercial domination of two media companies (Reporters Without Borders 2018c). It does, however, have the most competitive press in the region.

The country also has an 85% internet penetration rate, the highest in Africa (Internet World Stats 2018). They have a mobile subscriber penetration at 86% of the total population. This is among the highest in Africa. Facebook is by far the most used social media site at 66%. WhatsApp is also an important tool for communication, both local and global. Chapter 6 discusses not only the importance of mobile usage in Kenya, but more importantly how it has been used as a platform for reporting and survival.

PII.2   Ghana

Ghana is a part of Western Africa, which includes 16 countries that sit just below Western Sahara Africa, and along the Atlantic Coast and the Gulf of Guinea. The country has a population of 29.5 million, with most of the population living along the Atlantic coast in the cities of Accra, Takoradi, and Cape Coast. More than half of the population is under the age of 25 (Internet World Stats 2018). Another country with a fast-growing economy, they have a GDP of 42.8 billion in USD, with a growth of 8.5% driven by oil production (World Bank 2016b, 2018b). It is also the first country in sub-Saharan Africa to halve poverty according to The United Nations Development Programme (2018).

Ghana was colonized by Britain until 1957, when it gained independence, the first to do so in sub-Saharan Africa. Many of the countries in this region were colonized by France and England and have only gained independence within the past 80 years. English is the official language in Ghana, with local dialects such as Asante and Ewe also spoken. Christianity is practiced by a majority of the population, and Islam by nearly a quarter. Ghana is a democratic republic, and its president, Nana Akufo-Addo, has continually upheld the constitution and democratic process.

Ghanaian newspaper and radio have historically been, and continue to be, important in the growth of the nation. Newspaper was an important platform as the country strove for independence in the 1950s. Radio was brought in by British colonists, and the BBC continues to broadcast here; local radio flourished in the period after deregulation in the 1990s (Reporters Without Borders 2018a). Radio continues to be the most popular medium as access and infrastructure have added to its growth. Television has seen recent growth as access has increased across the country (BBC 2017b). Currently, there are both commercial and government run stations. Ghana Broadcasting Corporation operates many radio stations, both national and local, as well as a number of terrestrial and digital television stations. Commercial stations are also available, such as Metro TV and TV3 Ghana, the latter of which is owned by Media General. Multi Media Group operates MultiTV as well as both a digital and satellite stations.

Pluralism and independence are guaranteed in Ghana's constitution, yet news media coverage in Ghana is often lacking on television and radio due to government ownership or private ownership among only three corporations (Reporters Without Borders 2018a). In addition, pluralism has been weakened by a lax regulatory system. Criticism of the government has been generally tolerated after the removal of strict libel laws in 2001, and journalists are rarely harassed. Ghana ranked 23/180, above many developed democratic countries like United

States, on the 2018 World Press Freedom Index (Reporters Without Borders 2018b). It had a third peaceful transfer of power in 2017, putting it on an even stronger democratic path and in top among the African nations. Chapter 4 further illustrates the history and political conflicts of media in Ghana.

Ghana has an internet penetration rate of just 38%, but this is up over 33 000% from 2000, which indicates that the country has increased digital infrastructure and digital access (Internet World Stats 2017). Of those using internet, most are doing so on mobile devices (67%) and 19% are actively using social media (Business Ghana 2018). WhatsApp and Facebook are the two most widely used social media sites.

PII.3 Nigeria

Nigeria is also located in Western Africa, but further east. The most populated country in all of Africa, it has a population of 190.6 million people, which is comprised of over 250 ethnic groups. The majority of the population lives along the Atlantic Coast (Internet World Stats 2018). Much of the population is under 14, primarily due to high birth rates. It has a slow growing economy: the country has a GDP of 404.7 billion in USD and is expected to show growth of 2.8% (World Bank 2016c, 2018c).

Gaining its independence from Britain in 1960, Nigeria's official language is English. However, Hausa and Yoruba as well as over 500 indigenous languages are also spoken. While Christianity is practiced by 40% of the population, 50% practice Islam. In the northern part of the country, fundamentalist Islam is growing. Nigeria is a federal republic, and the current president, Muhammadu Buhari, has made promises to support democracy, and to help deal with militant Boko Haram; however, corruption still exists.

Nigeria is one of the largest media markets in Africa. They have a similar press landscape to Ghana, as ownership is both private and public, but not fully independent as government agencies play a strong role in censoring editorial content – although this has lessened considerably in recent years. However, their rank on the 2018 World Press Freedom index is 119/180, primarily for their treatment of journalists who are threatened and denied access to information and government restrictions on news content (Reporters Without Borders 2018d). Bloggers are also at risk after the recent passing of a cyber-crimes law.

Newspaper and radio continue to do relatively well, and there are hundreds of media outlets throughout Nigeria. Radio and internet are the most used mediums for information. As English is the official language, a few international broadcasts are popular, namely the BBC and CNN (BBC 2017a). Television is both state owned as well as having some private ownership. OGTV is public, state-owned channel that was established to preserve the Yoruba language. ONTV, a privately-owned station, offers local programming as well as Hollywood movies from the United States, and telenovelas from Columbia, the Philippines, and Venezuela.

Nigeria has an internet penetration rate of nearly 48%, which is up over 45 500% since 2000 and is the fifth largest in Africa (Internet World Stats 2018). As a result, younger Nigerians are using the internet and social media as a means of gaining news and entertainment. Facebook is the most widely used social media site.

Nigeria is of particular note among the discussed countries, as it currently has the world's fastest growing and one of most productive film industries: Nollywood. Producing more than 1500 films a year, Nollywood films have gained global popularity on streaming platforms such as Netflix. More discussion on the introduction and growth of Nollywood, both domestically as well as internationally, is discussed in Chapter 7.

PII.4   South Africa

South Africa is one of 10 countries in Southern Africa. It has a population of 57.4 million people, with most of the population living in urban areas (Internet World Stats, 2018). Many live along the southern coast, or inland near Johannesburg and Pretoria (Tshwane). The country has a GDP of 295.7 billion in USD; however, growth has been stagnant and expected growth is about 1.4% (World Bank, 2016d, 2018d).

South Africa was first colonized by the Dutch and then later by the British. It gained its independence in 1934 from Britain, but this ushered in a white, minority government, and years of apartheid measures. Apartheid ended in the early 1990s. Today, South Africa is a constitutional democracy, and its president, Cyril Ramaphosa, recently took office after his predecessor, Jacob Zuma, stepped down among corruption allegations.

Much of this region has media in English as that is the official language of most of the countries. In South Africa, however, there are a number of official languages, most predominantly isiZulu, isiXhosa, and Afrikaans. Less than half of the country practices Christianity.

Some media is state-owned and it is modeled on the British Broadcasting Corporation, and historically British rule. They offer a few television stations as well as many national and regional radio stations that broadcast not only in English, but also in Afrikaans, Sethoso – one of the official languages of Lesotho, and isiZulu (BBC, 2017d). South Africa has more private ownership, but also houses a very large transnational media organization, Naspers, which has media holdings in print, broadcast, and internet around the globe. In South Africa, they own DStv and Multichoice – which imports media from the Americas and India as well as producing and offering local content – and broadcasts throughout sub-Saharan Africa.

Their press sector still sees harassment of journalists and political involvement in media ownership. Despite this, South Africa has seen press freedom growth, and currently ranks 28/180 in the 2018 World Press Freedom index. (Reporters Without Borders, 2018d). Chapter 5 further discusses the challenges and growth of press freedom in South Africa.

In addition to a healthy press sector, South Africa also has the third largest internet penetration rate in Africa at 54% (Internet World Stats, 2017), as there have been increased initiatives to grow this sector, particularly for underserved audiences (Shapshak, 2017; South Africa Media Innovation Program, 2018). In 2017, there were 30.8 million internet users (Internet World Stats, 2018), and there were approximately 18.5 million smart phone users, which represents 60% of the population (Statista, 2018). This is expected to grow by 73% by 2020 to 83% of the population. Less than half of the population accesses the internet via their phones, which could indicate that data costs are too high. WhatsApp and Facebook are the most widely used social media sites.

Media models in Africa are best described as developmental; however, many appear to be authoritarian. The democratization of media in some countries may indicate the struggle to be democratic participatory, such as in Ghana and South Africa. The majority of the countries in Africa do not have a free press, according to Freedom House (2017) and Reporters Without Borders (2018b). There are exceptions, of course, as many countries in Western Africa are free or partly free and are pushing for more democratic systems of media. Overall, both Saharan and sub-Saharan African media struggle to provide safe spaces for journalists, particularly due to political and social unrest, repressive leaders, and increased tightening of media regulations.

References

African Economic Outlook (2017). African Economic Outlook 2017. Retrieved from: http://www.africaneconomicoutlook.org/sites/.../2017.../African_Economic_Outlook_2017.pdf.

British Broadcasting Corporation (2017a). Nigeria profile – Media. Retrieved from: https://www.bbc.com/news/world-africa-13949549.

British Broadcasting Corporation (2017b). Ghana profile – Media. Retrieved from: https://www.bbc.com/news/world-africa-13433793.

British Broadcasting Corporation (2017c). Kenya profile – Media. Retrieved from: https://www.bbc.com/news/world-africa-13681344.

British Broadcasting Corporation (2017d). South Africa profile – Media. Retrieved from: https://www.bbc.com/news/world-africa-14094861.

Business Ghana (2018). Over 10 million Ghanaians use the internet – Report. Retrieved from: https://www.businessghana.com/site/news/general/159800/Over-10-million-Ghanaians-use-the-internet-Report.

Fisher, M. (2012). The dividing of a continent: Africa's separatist problem. *The Atlantic*. Retrieved from: http://www.the http://atlantic.com/international/archive/2012/09/the – dividing-of-a-continent-africas-separatist-problem/262171.

Freedom House (2017). *Freedom of press* 2017. Retrieved from: https://freedomhouse.org/report/freedom-press/freedom-press-2017.

Internet World Stats (2017). Internet penetration in Africa. Retrieved from: https://www.internetworldstats.com/stats1.htm.

Internet World Stats (2018). Internet user statistics for Africa. Retrieved from: http://www.internetworldstats.com/stats1.htm.

Reporters Without Borders (2018a). Media ownership monitor: Ghana. Retrieved from: https://ghana.mom-rsf.org/en/context/history.

Reporters Without Borders (2018b). Media pluralism but not enough independence. Retrieved from: https://rsf.org/en/ghana.

Reporters Without Borders (2018c). Kenya. Retrieved from: https://rsf.org/en/kenya.

Reporters Without Borders (2018d). South Africa. Retrieved from: https://rsf.org/en/south-africa.

Shapshak, T. (2017). South Africa has 21 million internet users, mostly on mobile. *Forbes*. Retrieved from: https://www.forbes.com/sites/tobyshapshak/2017/07/19/south-africa-has-21m-internet-users-mostly-on-mobile/2/#50af243f36d8.

South Africa Media Innovation Program (2018). Retrieved from: https://samip.mdif.org.

Statista (2018). Number of Smartphone users in South Africa from 2014 to 2022. Retrieved from: https://www.statista.com/statistics/488376/forecast-of-smartphone-users-in-south-africa.

United Nations (2017a). Population facts. Retrieved on 2 January 2018 from: http://www.un.org/en/development/desa/population/migration/publications/populationfacts/docs/MigrationPopFacts20175.pdf.

United Nations (2017b). International migrant stock [graph]. Retrieved on 2 January 2018 from: http://www.un.org/en/development/desa/population/migration/data/estimates2/estimatesgraphs.shtml?0g0.

United Nations Development Programme (2018). About Ghana. Retrieved from: http://www.gh.undp.org/content/ghana/en/home/countryinfo.html.

World Bank (2016a). Country profile – Kenya. Retrieved from: http://databank.worldbank.org/data/views/reports/reportwidget.aspx?Report_Name=CountryProfile&Id=b450fd57&tbar=y&dd=y&inf=n&zm=n&country=KEN.

World Bank (2016b). Country profile – Ghana. Retrieved from: http://databank.worldbank.org/data/views/reports/reportwidget.aspx?Report_Name=CountryProfile&Id=b450fd57&tbar=y&dd=y&inf=n&zm=n&country=GHA.

World Bank (2016c). Country profile – Nigeria. Retrieved from: http://databank.worldbank.org/data/views/reports/reportwidget.aspx?Report_Name=CountryProfile&Id=b450fd57&tbar=y&dd=y&inf=n&zm=n&country=NGA.

World Bank (2016d). Country profile – South Africa. Retrieved from: http://databank.worldbank.org/data/views/reports/reportwidget.aspx?Report_Name=CountryProfile&Id=b450fd57&tbar=y&dd=y&inf=n&zm=n&country=ZAF.

World Bank (2018a). World Bank in Kenya – Overview. Retrieved from: http://www.worldbank.org/en/country/kenya/overview.

World Bank (2018b). World Bank in Ghana – Overview. Retrieved from: http://www.worldbank.org/en/country/ghana/overview.

World Bank (2018c). World Bank in Nigeria – Overview. Retrieved from:https://www.worldbank.org/en/country/nigeria/overview.

World Bank (2018d). World Bank in South Africa – Overview. Retrieved from:https://www.worldbank.org/en/country/southafrica/overview.

4

Broadcasting in Ghana

Opportunities and Challenges of a Plural Media in an Evolving African Democracy

Isaac Abeku Blankson

The Republic of Ghana is located on the Gulf of Guinea in West Africa. It was the first country in sub-Saharan Africa to gain independence from the British in 1957. In 2018, Ghana had an estimated population of about 29.46 million (World Population Review 2018). Ghana is a model for African democracy as the country has experienced decades of relative stability and has good governance and an entrenched democratic tradition. Its economy is one of the strongest and most diversified in West Africa. Ghana is a multicultural nation with a variety of ethnic and religious groups. It is a member of a number of regional and international bodies including the African Union (AU), the Economic Community of West African States (ECOWAS), the United Nations (UN), and the Commonwealth of Nations.

Ghana has one of the most vibrant media landscapes in Africa. This is evidenced by the many and diverse media. As of September of 2017, there were 367 FM radio stations operating in Ghana compared to the 75 television stations that were operating in 2016 (National Communications Authority [NCA] 2018a). Ghana's media has historically been shaped by alternating policies of libertarian tolerance and revolutionary control based on the ideologies of successive governments. Presently, the country's media operates in the most liberal environment. Not only does Ghana's Constitution guarantee media freedom and independence, mass participation and technology are also unrestricted.

4.1   History of Radio and Television Broadcasting

Broadcasting was introduced to Ghana (then known as the Gold Coast) in 1935 by the British colonial administration as an instrument of colonial policy. The colonial administration, under Sir Arnold Hodson, set up a small wired radio station in Accra known as Radio ZOY to transmit BBC programs to British residents and Ghanaian elites. The service was later extended to Kumasi, Sekondi, Koforidua, and Cape Coast. In 1954, Radio ZOY became known as the Gold Coast Broadcasting Service (GCBS). After independence in 1957 it was renamed the Ghana Broadcasting Corporation (GBC). It has since remained under government control. Its programming policies continue to be closely linked to the priorities of the state.

During the 1960s, the administration of the country was transferred to local Ghanaians. The new Nkrumah Convention Peoples Party (CPP) administration retained ownership of broadcasting in the state and continued to use it as a top-down communication tool to forge a common sense of national identity. In 1961, the government launched the External Service of Radio Ghana to transmit information, propaganda, and solidarity messages to promote

Transnational Media: Concepts and Cases, First Edition. Edited by Suman Mishra and Rebecca Kern-Stone.
© 2019 John Wiley & Sons, Inc. Published 2019 by John Wiley & Sons, Inc.

freedom and self-determination among Africans on the continent and in the diaspora. The service also reached North America, Europe, Japan, and Australia. Programs were broadcast in Arabic, English, French, Hausa, Portuguese, and Swahili. The External Service was discontinued in 1979 by the military government under Jerry Rawlings. The service was restored in 1987. GBC provides two domestic radio services: Radio 1 and Radio 2. The former transmits in six local-languages, namely Akan, Ga, Ewe, Nzema, Dagbani, and Hausa, and English. Radio 2 only transmits in English.

By the 1980s, state monopoly of mass media was beginning to diminish. Many, including Ansah (1988), argued that opening up the airwaves could stimulate development and create more jobs. In 1986, GBC, with assistance from the German government, began broadcasting a VHF-FM service in the Accra-Tema metropolitan area. In the late 1980s and early 1990s, GBC opened new FM stations in the regions and districts of Ghana, namely Radio GAR in Accra, Garden City Radio in Kumasi, Twin City FM in Sekondi-Takoradi, and Volta Star Radio in Ho.

Unlike radio, television broadcasting was established in Ghana in 1965 by the CPP government in collaboration with Sanyo of Japan, which had a television assembly plant in Tema. President Nkrumah saw television as a tool for education and a platform for promoting his socialist ideals. In his inaugural speech, Nkrumah stressed:

> Ghana's Television will be used to supplement our educational programme and foster a lively interest in the world around us. It will not cater for cheap entertainment nor commercialism. Its paramount object will be education in the broadest and purest sense. Television must assist in the socialist transformation of Ghana. (Nkrumah Info Bank 1965)

Like radio, television broadcasting was the monopoly of the state-owned GBC (GBC-TV) until 1997. Currently, GBC-TV, or simply GTV, broadcasts from its central studios in Accra to transmitters at Ajankote near Accra, Kissi in the Central Region, Jamasi in the Ashanti Region, and a relay station in Tamale in the Northern Region. In 1986, another transmitter was added in Bolgatanga in the Upper East Region and since then others have been added in Sunyani in the Brong Ahafo Region, Han in Upper West Region, Amajofe and Akatsi, both in the Volta Region. Transposers or boosters operate at Ho, Akosombo, Prestea, Sunyani, Oda, Tarkwa, Dunkwa, and Mpraeso. The Ghana television transmission standard is PAL B-5 with five low-power relays. Through these transmitters, 95% of Ghana has access to GTV broadcasts.

4.2 Growth of Independent Private Broadcasting

Ghana's broadcasting landscape was monopolized by the state broadcasting network, GBC, until the early 1990s. The 1992 Constitution of Ghana paved the way for establishing private media and the constitutional protection necessary to operate it. Article 162(3) states:

> There shall be no impediments to the establishment of private press or media; and in particular, there shall be no law requiring any person to obtain a license as a prerequisite to the establishment or operation of a newspaper, journal or other media for the mass communication or information. (Republic of Ghana 1992)

Though the constitution made provision for the ownership of private broadcasting, it was not until 1993 that intellectuals began to talk openly about the need for the government to free the airwaves. During a three-day international seminar on broadcasting in Africa held in Accra in 1993, many of the participants pointed at the immense contribution private radio had made to the developmental efforts of countries in Asia and Latin America and recommended that African governments should use the national frequencies to stimulate development (Ansu-Kyeremeh and Karikari 1998; Blankson 2007). Although the Constitution provided for liberalization of the airwaves, the democratically elected National Democratic Convention (NDC) government that was inaugurated in January 1993 refused to grant licenses or allocate frequencies to private broadcasters. In 1994, opposition politician Charles Wereko-Brobby started a series of pirate broadcasts, *Radio Eye*, in protest of this policy. The government confiscated his equipment and pressed for his criminal prosecution. However, his provocative action sparked pressure on the government to allow private broadcasting.

Under pressure from Ghanaian civil society and other external agencies such as the World Bank, the NDC government reluctantly liberalized the airwaves in 1995 (Blankson 2007; Karikari 1998). It began allocating licenses and frequencies through the Ghana Frequency Registration and Control Board (GFRCB), currently the NCA. In July 1995, 10 commercial radio services were issued frequencies to operate in Accra, Kumasi, and Sekondi-Takoradi. The first FM license was granted to Radio Univers, a station operated from the University of Ghana. Others that followed included Joy FM, Vibe FM, Radio Gold, Groove FM, and Peace FM. A further 10 frequencies were assigned in May 1996 for rural areas, including three community radio services. The government gave approval for the allocation of frequencies to private television stations as well. Two private channels went on the air in 1997, with the first being Metro TV followed by TV3 (Blankson 2007).

In 1996, GFRCB became known as the National Communications Authority, which continues to assign frequencies to private commercial broadcasting services to date. As of the second quarter of 2018, the total number of television operators authorized by the NCA in Ghana was 129. These include 3 Analogue Terrestrial Television, 1 Digital Terrestrial Pay Television (Service only), 5 Digital Terrestrial Pay Television (Service and Frequency), 31 Digital Terrestrial Free-To-Air Television Programme Channel (Nationwide Coverage), and 7 Digital Terrestrial Radio Service on TV Multiplex. The others are 4 Digital Terrestrial Free-To-Air Television Programme Channel (Regional Coverage), 8 Satellite Television Broadcasting (Pay TV Direct-To-Home Bouquet), 11 Satellite Television Broadcasting (Free-To-Air Direct-To-Home Bouquet), 58 Satellite Television Broadcasting (Free-To-Air Direct-To-Home Single Channel), and 1 Digital Cable Television (National Communications Authority 2018a).

Similarly, as of September 2017, the NCA has given frequency authorizations to 471 FM Radio Broadcasting Stations in Ghana. Out of the total number of authorized FM Broadcasting Stations, 367 stations were operational. These included 31 public radio stations, 5 public (foreign) radio stations, 74 community radio stations, 21 campus radio stations, and 340 commercial radio stations (National Communications Authority 2018a).

The process of obtaining a broadcasting license is costly. As of April 2018, licenses are awarded for an initial fee of approximately US$8600 for radio broadcasting and US$43 000 for television operation (National Communications Authority 2018b). In addition, an annual broadcast fee is collected and distributed to the Copyright Society of Ghana to remunerate artists and musicians. Critics argue that the cost prohibits ordinary Ghanaians from establishing radio or television stations. On the contrary, it has favored a small group of people with the money to establish as many radio and television stations as possible. The entire process is controlled by the government through the NCA and licenses are often issued to ruling party sympathizers.

4.3   Interplay of Politics and Media

Media and politics have been intertwined throughout Ghana's history. Since the late 1960s, the country has been ruled by interchanges of military regimes and democratic republics with corresponding media policies of authoritarian control and libertarian tolerance (Gadzekpo 2008). In 1966, the Nkrumah CPP government was overthrown through a military coup by the National Liberation Council (NLC). In contrast to state domination under Nkrumah, the NLC took a more libertarian approach to media. It released independent journalists from prison, closed down instruments of state propaganda, and lifted forms of censorship and bans on foreign journalists.

Various regimes have applied a variety of techniques of official and unofficial censorship, repressive laws, public intimidation and harassment, bans on oppositional publications, and arrest and detention of media practitioners and journalists. In 1981, the Provisional National Defence Council (PNDC, later NDC) of Rawlings government seized power from a democratically elected government. Following in the footsteps of Nkrumah, Rawlings used media to actively promote the revolutionary ideals of his military regime. The editorial staff of the state media were reshuffled or dismissed. The editorial policies were strategically shaped to suit the government's interests. In 1992, Ghana returned to democratic rule with the ratification of a new constitution. Rawlings and the NDC government was twice elected into power, first in 1992 and then again in 1996. After 19 years of the NDC and its denunciations of the private media, the New Patriotic Party (NPP), under Agyekum Kuffour, was elected into power in December 2000. The NPP government urged media to be responsible and advocated free expression, political pluralism, and an independent media as important elements of liberal democracy. Since then, successive democratically elected governments have allowed media freedom and independence to varying degrees.

4.4   Broadcasting Language

English is the official language of Ghana. In the early days of private media, none of the radio and television stations broadcast in any of Ghana's vernacular languages (Blankson 2005a). In fact, all of the new FM stations chose to broadcast exclusively in English. Critics raised concern over the exclusive use of English language by the stations to the neglect of vernacular languages. They argued that the practice did not encourage the development of Ghanaian cultural artifacts and talents. In response, Peace FM began the drive to establish vernacular radio stations broadcasting in the various local languages. The station became the first private radio station to fully broadcast in Twi, a dominant vernacular language. Several other FM radio stations have introduced very popular local-language programs, including news and newspaper review programs in local languages. Particularly popular are the call-in programs, where disc jockeys and callers alternate between local languages and English in discussions of local, national, and global events. Similarly, some television stations such as Adom TV and UTV broadcast most of their programs including news segments in Twi.

This linguistic pluralism has ushered in a diversity of content and styles as the various private and public radio and television stations target specific classes of people with specific needs. For example, Joy FM targets elite and middle-class listeners while Peace FM targets the lower class. Similarly, Adom TV and UTV appear to cater for the lower class. Their programming content and style reflect their target audiences. Religious broadcasting media have also increased dramatically, with almost every church in Ghana establishing a digital television station. The majority broadcast in the Twi language.

4.5   Legal and Regulatory Framework for Broadcasting

Ghana's broadcasting landscape has within the last two decades undergone radical transformation, from state monopoly to private liberal broadcasting. Yet, the legislation and regulatory framework to guide the development of radio and television broadcasting has lagged behind. The policy and regulatory context to guide broadcasting is unclear and weak. According to Philipatawura (2017), these have contributed to the weaknesses seen in the provision of broadcasting services.

The 1992 Constitution of Ghana provided the most important and fundamental legal framework for broadcasting. Chapter 12 guarantees media freedom and independence. Article 162 clause 3 states that there shall be no impediments to the establishment of private press or media; and in particular, there shall be no law requiring any person to obtain a license as a prerequisite to the establishment or operation of a newspaper, journal or other media for mass communication or information (Afari-Gyan 1998; Apenteng 2014).

Apart from the Constitution, a number of pieces of legislation on broadcasting have also been created over the years. These include the Ghana Broadcasting Corporation Act 1968 (NLCD 226), the National Media Commission Act 1993 (Act 449) established in accordance with articles 166 and 167 of the Constitution, the National Communications Authority Act 2008 (Act 769) established as the central body to license and regulate communications activities and services, and the Electronic Communications Act 2008 (Act 775), plus subsidiary legislation enacted under these laws. Other media regulatory bodies include the National Media Commission, the National Media Policy of 2000 which provides for a three-tier system of public, community, and commercial radio and television stations, the Ghana Journalists Association, the Electronic Communications Act of 2008, the Ghana Broadcasting Standards, the Ghana Guidelines for Fair and Equitable Coverage, Ghana Guidelines for Political Journalism, and the Ghana Guidelines for Print Journalism. These bodies help to promote professionalism in the Ghanaian media environment.

Despite these regulatory and legislative instruments, Ghana does not have a clear, transparent, and uniformly applied legal criteria for broadcasting operations. Similarly, there is no strong regulatory oversight of the content of programs. Even though the Ghana Media Commission was established to, among other things, maintain sanity within media, its weaknesses in enforcement has enabled some media outlets to occasionally broadcast inflammatory messages, use personal insults and attacks, and use vulgar language on air. Critics have charged that the present regulatory arrangements are not sufficient guarantee of constitutional commitments to freedom of expression and to media independence, and thus cannot enable the effective development of broadcasting in the public interest (Philipatawura 2017). They have called for a broadcasting law to provide the legal and regulatory framework for broadcasting. This is yet to be achieved.

4.6   Media Freedom, Censorship, and Legal Issues

Presently, Ghana's media operate in an environment of unprecedented freedom. Most of the repressive laws against the media and journalist have been repealed. Apart from the Rawlings NDC government, which used controversial laws of libel and sedition to crack down on media, successive governments have respected free expression and media independence. For example, the Kuffour NPP government demonstrated its commitment to freedom of expression and independent media by repealing the seditious criminal libel law in 2001. The NDC governments of Atta-Mills and Mahama also respected the rule of law and media freedom. Unfortunately, no government has been bold enough to pass the Right to Information Bill into law. The right to information, also known as freedom of information, is an internationally recognized fundamental human right to access information held by government bodies. The bill was presented to parliament in 2007 but it has still not passed into a law. Successive governments have failed to pass the bill and, on certain attempts, opposition members have declined to participate in its passage. For example, in December 2016, the minority in parliament threatened to walk out over the passage of the bill, on the grounds that due process and consultations be made by the majority in Parliament and the Presidential Transitional Act be respected. If passed, this Right to Information Bill will help journalists and media practitioners easily access information, especially information held by government agencies.

Despite the repeal of repressive laws, many journalists and media houses continue to face challenges. Incidents of violence and attacks against media practitioners and journalists continue to be reported. Most of these violations were perpetrated by the state agencies, particularly the police and officials of the Bureau of National Investigation, and individuals who have influence in the ruling governments. For example, during the Kuffour NPP era, two cameramen of the TV3 network were assaulted by police officers who were providing security at the special delegates' congress of the New Patriotic Party at the University of Ghana campus on 22 December 2007. The police officers claimed they were controlling the crowd. In another incident, on 25 May 2008, a regional correspondent of the *Daily Graphic* newspaper and a reporter at GBC were allegedly assaulted by security guards on the orders of a member of parliament. On 22 April 2009, three journalists were attacked for photographing the private residence of ex-president Kuffuor without permission. Similarly, during the Atta-Mills NDC tenure, some ex-presidential guards attacked journalists and destroyed their equipment in the process. Under the Mahama NDC administration, a Kumasi-based Fox FM presenter and his panelists were attacked by people reported to be supporters of the opposition NPP during a live program on 25 April 2016. As recently as March 2017, a freelance journalist was beaten up and his phone smashed by soldiers of the Ghana Armed Forces when he attempted to film an assault on a civilian by the military officers during Ghana's 60th Anniversary Independence Day Celebration at the Black Star Square in Accra.

Some government officials have publicly condemned the media for doing their job. For instance, the Chairman of the Defense Committee of Parliament warned journalists in Ghana against retorting to military officers or risk being beaten. He boldly declared on GH One TV's State of Affairs program on Tuesday, 21 March 2017 that "Officers will continue to beat up journalists who are loud-mouths." Additionally, there are several reported cases of media owners terminating their employee contracts without applying the national labor laws, cases of slander and libel, cases that are troubling on ethics, corruption, and professionalism. Coupled with these challenges is the National Media Commission's (NMC) inability to sanction offending media organizations, thereby negatively impacting broadcasting and the journalism profession in Ghana.

Cases of libel and slander are occasionally brought up against journalists. This has created a system of self-censorship among media owners and broadcasters. With the exception of a few identified media who have leanings toward the ideology of some political parties, most media houses censor internally to avoid conflict with the government. According to Asante (1996), some editors refuse to broadcast critical comments against government decisions and programs or direct criticism of the political leadership. Unfortunately, incidents of hate speech and harassment against journalists and their media organizations continue to be part of Ghana's media landscape.

Ethical concerns have been raised against media practitioners and journalists, especially because media practitioners have lowered their professional standards drastically in terms of following regulations on the practice of journalism. Some sections of the Ghanaian public have cautioned about the abuse of the freedom given to journalists. Others have doubted the media's ability to promote good governance and democracy and to uphold the rule of law that would translate into accelerated development and economic growth (Amoakohene 2007). A case that sparked national debate was that of the Accra-based Montie FM saga under the Mahama administration. Reportedly, the radio host and two panelists made derogatory and sexually threatening remarks about the courts and the Chief Justice, Georgina Theodore Wood. The comments were condemned by many Ghanaians leading to the three, together with the owners of the media house, pleading guilty to the charges of contempt. They were sentenced on 27 July 2016 but granted a presidential pardon by President Mahama after serving a few days.

4.7 Emerging Trends

Ghana's broadcasting and media landscape is experiencing new trends, mostly following Western popular culture, especially from the United States. There is a drastic shift from programming that focuses on public services and the public good toward commercialized programming. Public service broadcasting is rapidly giving way to the development of various forms of "pay" television. In Ghana, most people subscribe to the services of the South African Company, DSTV, and other distribution companies like Multimedia's MultiTv.

As media companies have expanded, new lines of business are being added in a process of diversification. Media groups in Ghana, such as the GBC, Multimedia, Global Media Alliance, Despite Group of Companies, and the Graphic Communications Group have all shifted from one media form of production to several forms of production. For example, some of these media corporations have grown larger, more profitable, and have added companies that are in the same line of business, thus integrating horizontally. Most of these groups have been able to move from core media functions to organizing fairs, producing Ghanaian movies, and providing other services that increase their profit-making margins.

Another new trend is the growing potential for media houses and businesses to work together to more effectively market their products and services, thus producing a synergy that maximizes profits. Some media organizations are able to promote programs of their sister organizations without paying for advertisements. For instance, the Adom Habitat fair is promoted on all multimedia stations and sister stations across the country. Similarly, the Happy FM Bridal fair and Mass Weddings are promoted on Global Media Alliance networks.

As the Ghanaian broadcasting scene has drastically changed, a new popular culture has evolved around radio and television, consisting of media personalities, Radio and Television (RTV) awards, review magazines, and live shows. Similarly, a plethora of religious broadcasting both on radio and television has emerged. Interestingly, the television channels appear to have been taken over by religious programming because the mega churches seem to have the money to establish a station or pay for program slots.

Finally, some forms of journalism, particularly investigative journalism, have assumed an important role in the democratic dispensation. Some private media houses have consistently been critical of the government, demanded accountability from public officials, and exposed the ills of the society. The most popular case involved investigative journalist, Anas Aremeyaw Anas, who brought to light serious corruption in the justice delivery system by exposing the biggest judicial scandal in Ghana. Previously, his contemporary with the Multimedia Group, Manasseh Azure Awuni, had exposed several shady deals and contracts gone bad under the ruling NDC government.

4.8   Conclusion

A free and vibrant media is critical to the survival and progress of any nation. Ghanaians continue to enjoy liberalization of their media landscape. Despite a few incidents of attacks on the media, practitioners and journalists have generally enjoyed freedom of expression and media independence. They continue to experience more freedom, cooperation, and respect in their dealings with the state. Ghanaians are hopeful that the political liberalism will continue to develop a foundation for a more permanent maintenance of press freedom and broadcast professionalism in the future. Despite these positive developments, there is widespread concern about the economic viability of the private media. There is also concern about the passage of the Content Standards Regulation 2015 (LI 2224) by parliament on 9 December 2015. This law allows the NMC to establish and maintain standards in the distribution of content of public electronic communication and broadcasting services. It also empowers the NMC to grant content authorization to an operator or revoke the same if an operator contravenes the regulations. Finally, lack of access to official information remains a big hindrance to media practice. The hope is that the Freedom of Information Bill becomes law because of its potential to enhance media practice and liberalization.

References

Afari-Gyan, K. (1998). *The Ghanaian Constitution: An Introduction*. Bonn: Friedrich Ebert Foundation.

Amoakohene, I. M. (2007). Ghana: Media and Democracy in 50 Years of Independence. Retrieved from: https://www.ucalgary.ca/tettey/files/tettey/ghana_media_democracy.pdf.

Ansah, P.A.V. (1988). In search of a role for the African media in the democratic process. *African Media Review* 2 (2): 1–16.

Ansu-Kyeremeh, K. and Karikari, K. (1998). *Media Ghana: Ghanaian Media Overview, Practitioners and Institutions*. Legon, Ghana: School of Communication Studies Printing Press.

Apenteng, B. (2014). *Revised Broadcasting Bill, Post Forum Review*. Ghana: Ministry of Communications.

Asante, C.E. (1996). *The Press in Ghana: Problems and Prospects*. Maryland: University Press, Inc.

Blankson, I.A. (2005). Negotiating the use of native languages in emerging independent broadcast systems in Africa. *Africa Media Review*, 13 (1): 1–32.

Blankson, I.A. (2007). Media independence and pluralism in Africa: opportunities and challenges of democratization and liberalization. In: *Negotiating Democracy: Media Transformations in Emerging Democracies* (ed. I.A. Blankson and P. Murphy), 15–35. New York: SUNY.

Gadzekpo, A. (2008). *Communication Policies in Civilian and Military Regimes: The Case of Ghana*. Michigan: Michigan State University Library.

Karikari, K. (1998). *The Press and the Transition to Multi-Party Democracy in Ghana. Ghana: Transition to Democracy*. Accra: Freedom Publications.

National Communications Authority (2018a). *List of Authorized VHF-FM Radio and Television Broadcasting Stations in Ghana, 2nd Quarter Report*. Ghana: Accra.

National Communications Authority (2018b). *Revised Schedule of Fees*. Ghana: Accra.

Nkrumah Info Bank (1965). Ghana Television Service Ceremony of Inauguration. Retrieved from: http://www.nkrumahinfobank.org/article.php?id=447&c=51.

Philipatawura (2017). Regulatory framework of the media in Ghana. Retrieved from: https://philipatawura.wordpress.com/2017/05/02/regulatory-framework-of-the-media-in-ghana.

Republic of Ghana (1992). *Constitution of the Republic of Ghana, 1992*. Accra: Ghana Publishing Company Limited.

World Population Review (2018). Ghana population 2018. Retrieved from: http://worldpopulationreview.com/countries/ghana-population.

5

The State of Press Freedom in South Africa

Robust Despite the Intimidation

Glenda Daniels

While a robust press exists in South Africa,[1] especially in the form of investigative journalism, there are disparate forces of power which press down upon this freedom to attempt more ideological closures and hegemony. This means that the ruling party, the African National Congress, would prefer more unity with the press and thus attempts various interventions to shut down their dissenting voices.

First, in an optimistic section, the chapter delineates the enormous contribution that investigative journalism made in relation to the now infamous #Guptaleaks – which caused international ripples in complicit companies such as Mckinsey and KPMG. In tandem with this theme on corruption exposure, the chapter turns to the charges against a journalist Jacques Pauw for writing a book – *The Presidents Keepers: Those Keeping Zuma in Power and out of Prison* (2017) – in which he exposes state capture by an Indian business family close to the former president of South Africa, Jacob Zuma. In February 2018, Cyril Ramaphosa replaced Zuma.

Second, the constitutional legal landscape – or the supreme or overarching laws of the land – and then the regulatory framework within which journalists work are outlined. The constitution clearly stipulates the free flow of information, but there looms what can be called ideological and hegemonic impediments: impending legislation such as the Protection of State Information Bill (Secrecy Bill), and a Media Appeals Tribunal which could shut down the robust voices of dissent in an unfolding democracy such as South Africa's. These robust voices and noises are necessary for a radical democracy which encapsulates plurality, as Mouffe has argued (2000, 2006).

Third, this chapter discusses attacks on journalists and, finally, it reaches some conclusions on the state of press freedom in South Africa. The analysis and reflections will be framed within theories of radical democracy, which argue for more fights and contestations and more voices from the margins in order to deepen democracy, rather than a rational consensus which closes the spaces for greater plurality.

As part of this introduction, an important development to note is that the National Press Club in South Africa, which every year reveals their newsmaker of the year, named "the Gupta Leaks" their newsmaker in 2017. These leaks consisted of over 100 000 emails that revealed the state of corruption at the nexus between the government and particularly the then head of the state, President Jacob Zuma, and his close friendship with an immigrant family from India named "the Guptas." Among the many bombshell revelations was the fact that the Guptas were running the country by making decisions about who went into cabinet from their homestead compound in Johannesburg. There were kickbacks through tenders worth billions of rands and state entities were robbed; for example, R30 million (or approx. 3 million USD) which was

Transnational Media: Concepts and Cases, First Edition. Edited by Suman Mishra and Rebecca Kern-Stone.
© 2019 John Wiley & Sons, Inc. Published 2019 by John Wiley & Sons, Inc.

meant to kick-start projects for poor black farmers in the Free State province was siphoned off into a Bollywood-style wedding for a Gupta family member. The leaks exposed vast money laundering and bribery. An article by the Nieman Lab Harvard (2018) stated that the leaks powered the possibility of President Zuma's controversial leadership of the country coming to an end – as indeed it did in February 2018.

The Gupta Leaks were part of an investigation that dug deeply into political network patronage by amaBhungane (which means "dung beetles" in isiZulu, one of South Africa's official languages), a non-profit investigative organization, together with other investigative units in the country, such as Scorpio from the *Daily Maverick* as well as teams in the *Sunday Times* and News24 outlets.

Besides the Gupta Leaks, Pauw's brilliant and brave piece of work – *The President's Keepers: Those Keeping Zuma in Power and out of Prison* – revealed explosive details of corruption of the same ilk as those of amaBhungane.

5.1 Intimidation Tactics and Unfolding Democracy to Come

The South African Revenue Service (SARS) filed charges against Pauw in December 2017. His book, which became an overnight bestseller nationally, revealed the tax affairs of the president, including that he was paid a R1-million a month salary from a business man after he became president in 2009. The charge is based on a declaratory order that Pauw contravened confidentiality clauses in the Tax Admin Act. However, this is an issue in the public interest given that it's the president that is involved and, two, civil society has widely condemned the charge as being intimidation tactics, stifling the free flow of information, freedom of expression, and the rights of journalists. Media Monitoring Africa (MMA), a non-governmental organization, began a crowd-sourcing funding mechanism in January 2018 through social media to raise the legal costs for Pauw's case. Thousands of rands have already been collected.

The group, MMA, is one of many robust civil society advocacy groups in the country all dedicated to protecting the free flow of information and freedom of expression that is so intrinsic to a democracy. Some others include: Right2Know, Save our South African Broadcasting Corporation (SABC), South African National Editor's Forum (Sanef),[2] and the Freedom of Expression Institute, among others. It is commonly noted that the high number of bodies devoted to this kind of advocacy and watchdog role in South Africa is rare among most countries in the world. It must be noted that the South African press, although far from one united whole, professes to play a vital role in entrenching the articles of the constitution by ensuring a transparent democracy, which holds public officials accountable for their decisions and actions, and exposes the abuse of power and corruption by ruling elites. It plays a watchdog role.

5.2 The SA Constitution Supports the Free Flow of Information but then "The Secrecy Bill" Does the Opposite

The supreme law that governs the country is the Constitution of South Africa, which provides for freedom of expression and the right to information. It protects human dignity and does not allow hate speech or racism, among other undesirables in a progressive society and it contains important protections for press freedom. The right to freedom of expression is protected by the clauses in Section 16 (1). Everyone has the right to freedom of expression. This includes:

a) freedom of the press and other media
b) freedom to receive or impart information or ideas
c) freedom of artistic creativity
d) academic freedom and freedom of scientific research.

Just over 10 years ago, the Freedom of Expression Institute (FXI) pointed out that even though press freedom is constitutionally protected and the country has one of the freest media in Africa, "however, as the honeymoon phase of our new democracy fades, so it becomes clear that attacks on media freedom are increasing," (FXI 2007, p. 1). This has become evident with the trajectory of the Protection of State Information Bill (dubbed the Secrecy Bill),3 which would impede a democracy to come, to use Derrida's conception. In the *Last of the Rogue States,* Derrida explains how no democracy is fully realized, it is always evolving and becoming but needs certain conditions to deepen.

The Secrecy Bill, which was first mooted in Parliament in 2008 to ostensibly protect national security, has received widespread attention over the past decade. The bill contradicts the right to information contained in the Promotion of Access to Information Act (Paia) of 2000, having a chilling effect on citizens' rights to information, as well as journalists' abilities to access information, be in possession of certain documents, and impart information (Daniels 2014). The aim of the bill was to repeal the apartheid era information /classification legislation of 1992, after several drafts and re-drafts the amended bill that was re-introduced in Parliament in 2011 was passed by the majority of members in the National Assembly in 2012. However, it was passed without an adequate public interest defense clause: it did not protect whistleblowers and journalists from disclosing or being in possession of information which could be classified or state secret.

At the time of writing in 2018, the bill awaited the President's signature before it became law – but this will be challenged in the Constitutional Court, and civil society organizations are poised for action – with hundreds of thousands of signatures collected, including many marches and demonstrations over the past decade.

The R2K campaign (launched in 2010 as coalition of organizations as a direct result of antipathy toward the bill), the Congress of South African Trade Unions (Cosatu), the official opposition party, the Democratic Alliance, and the South African National Editors' Forum (Sanef) are among some of the bodies opposed to the bill and they intend to challenge it in the Constitutional Court. The bodies made various interventions in parliament for amendments and were successful; for instance, the limited public interest defense. The organizations opposed to the bill, even in its amended form,[4] argue that it still impedes the free flow of information stipulated in the constitution via Paia. If this bill is passed, it would become an act which would create a society of secrets and result in self-censorship for journalists, discourage whistle-blowers from passing on damning and indicting information, and, most of all, hinder the public's right to information. The most controversial part of the Secrecy Bill is the fact that you could go to jail for disclosure of information that may be deemed to be anti the national interest – in other words, journalists and whistleblowers could go to jail.

5.3 The Secrecy Bill has Jail Terms for Journalists

The parameters of what constitutes the national interest have not been narrowed down sufficiently, and the now partial limited interest defense still criminalizes some activities of investigative journalism. There are still wide-ranging powers given to the security cluster/ agency, which could slant the country toward a security state.

The classifier of information may classify categories of documents without interrogating whether each specific document poses a threat to national security. This issue is exacerbated by the fact that according to media rights lawyer, Dario Milo, there is no imperative in the bill for a classifier to sever from a document the material which does not harm national security and make that available. "These twin flaws may well result in over-classification and hence censorship" (Milo 2013, para 8).

There are jail sentences of between 15 and 25 years for disclosures which could be deemed against the national interest and therefore considered espionage. Journalists and whistleblowers could fall into this bracket.

The Secrecy Bill views media and civil society as "outsiders" to the democracy; as enemies, so to speak. However, enemies do not share a common symbolic space, whereas friends do (Mouffe 2005). In this case, media and civil society argue for more transparency and accountability through the free flow of information, which would deepen democracy rather than impede it. We must accept difference and agonistic differences, rather than treating those with different views as enemies (jailing journalists and whistleblowers would be the ultimate in "othering" or making an enemy of players in a democracy). Treating others (who clearly share symbolic spaces but with different views and voices) as legitimate adversaries rather than enemies would instead constitute the support and development of pluralism in society, deepening democracy in the process. The rational consensus dream of total mastery over everything (in this case the Secrecy Bill as the weapon or master of closure) must be given up. Instead, democracy should be viewed as a process encompassing agonism and difference. The next section discusses a further possible closure: a resolution of the ruling party, the African National Congress (ANC), for a Media Appeals Tribunal (MAT).

5.4 Media Appeals Tribunal (MAT): From Robust to Doormats?

Since the start of democracy in 1994, South Africa's press has been governed through self-regulation. Under pressure from the ruling party, the ANC, the press agreed to re-examine its governing system. In 2012, the press appointed the Press Freedom Commission (PFC) to conduct public hearings, carry out research on best practices around the world, and advise on an appropriate system of governance/accountability system for the press.

The decision after these processes was to change the press regulatory system from self-regulation to "independent co-regulation."[5] Essentially this means that the press does not regulate itself completely, but there is an equal number of members from the public which sit on the Press Council to adjudicate disputes. The decision came after a series of public hearings involving, for example, members of the ANC, South African Communist Party (SACP), individuals, representatives from non-governmental organizations (NGOs), editors, and academics. In addition, the PFC conducted research in Tanzania, India, the United Kingdom, and Denmark.

As already stated, the media conducted this process because it was under "pressure"; it was wary of the ANC's proposal for a MAT, made at its national policy conference in December 2007. It is not completely clear what a MAT might entail, but it would mean that regulation of the press would ultimately lie in the hands of parliament, the majority of whose members belong to the ruling party, the ANC.

Despite this change to co-regulation, and despite research showing that the system is working well, the ANC still held onto the idea of a MAT in a resolution that was first mooted at its policy conference in Polokwane in 2007, again at the next policy conference in Mangaung in 2012 (ANC 2013), and then again at the most recent policy conference in Johannesburg in December 2017. It resolved that there was a need "for Parliament to conduct an inquiry on the desirability and feasibility of a MAT within the framework of the country's constitution that is empowered to impose sanctions without the loss of any constitutional rights."[6] It appears that as the ANC loses some of its power (some major cities went to the opposition party in the last local municipal election in 2016), it becomes more insecure and committed to gaining some form of political control of the media. Theoretically, this ties in directly with the "ideological closures and hegemony" mentioned in the introduction to this chapter, because as the ANC becomes more insecure it desires more unity with the press – and this is evidenced in its idea for a MAT.

5.5   A MAT Would Also Be Anti-Constitutional

If a MAT was instituted, freedom and independence of the press would be crushed. Journalists would probably be required to register and acquire "licenses" as they do in many parts of the world, such as some South American countries, many Middle Eastern countries and Eastern European and African countries, beside the main offender, China. Who would then be the arbiter of whether a journalist could practice or not? Journalists would probably self-censor for fear of being hauled in front of parliament for particular stories they had written which could be considered to be not in the "national interest" as they are embarrassing for the government, the president, or the ANC. The aim of the ANC is to create a society with more consensus, rather than to accept the society which exists at present – one that is full of fights and contestations, where corruption scandals are laid bare on the front pages of the newspapers. A MAT would close down the space of the multiplicity of voices, the plurality that is struggling to assert itself in the public sphere through the press. Through its desire for a MAT, the ANC clearly wants a society in which it could hegemonize further by closing down open spaces. If journalists had to register to acquire licenses to write and the ruling party decided who could and who could not get a license, critical voices in media would surely be lost. Journalists would be viewed as enemies rather than legitimate adversaries in a democracy.

5.6   Physically Attacking Journalists

The chapter now turns to attacks against journalists in post-apartheid or democratic South Africa. There are regular attacks on journalists by the state, such as the police, but sometimes also private security guards who do not understand the role of the press in a democracy. The most recent attack or assault took place at the ANC's 54th elective conference in December 2017, ironically enough against Sanef's media freedom chairperson Sam Mkokeli. He was apparently muttering under his breath about the bad state of the organization of the conference, when he was grabbed, manhandled, and roughed up by ANC security personnel and his phone was confiscated. Sanef released a statement on 19 December 2017 which stated that this was one incident among many others. The chairperson of Sanef Mahlatse Mahlase held a meeting with the ANC, and reported back (Mahlase 2017):

> Since this afternoon's incident, Sanef has received complaints from reporters. These include pictures which have been deleted, a journalist was punched in the stomach, another was pushed down and women journalists have reported being inappropriately touched by marshals inside the Plenary Hall. The meeting was very productive and the ANC has apologised for what happened today. They will now try and get Mkokeli's accreditation back, after he handed it over to avoid being further manhandled. ... As Sanef we will continue to ask for the ANC to be more transparent and allow a free flow of information. (Mahlase 2017).

The ANC was contrite and said the right things, but its actions (and proposals for future policies) speak otherwise. The South African authorities' attack on journalists appears to be part of a world-wide trend if one considers the research of the Committee to Protect Journalists (CPJ), which in 2018 reported a record number of journalists in jail: 262 in 2018, up from 259 the year before. The worst offenders were Turkey, China, and Egypt. The CJP statement in 2018 also named its global press oppressors of press freedom (the USA's Donald Trump, Recep Tayyip Erdoğan, Turkey, President Abdel Fattah el-Sisi, Egypt, President Xi Jinping, China, and President Vladimir Putin, Russia) who use rhetoric (and fake news), legal action, and censorship to silence their critics.

Journalists in South Africa do not appear to be in danger to the same extent; for instance, there are no journalists in jail. However, as discussed so far, there are worrying trends developing. Over the past decade in South Africa, photojournalists have been targeted most often when covering demonstrations by the police and sometimes by protestors. Sue Valentine, the CPJ's then Africa program director in 2014, observed: "They are targeted because of the power of images – photographs can provide incontrovertible proof of events. Anyone with a camera in their cellphone can be a target of police hostility as we have already seen this year" (Valentine 2014). There appears to be little evidence that police are adequately trained to understand the role of the media.

5.7 Conclusions: A Robust Press in a Robust Democracy

In radical democracy theory, voices, dissent, fights, and contestations and noises are an essential and intrinsic component of democracy. In the theory of "democracy to come," democracy can never be fully realized – it is always becoming. However, it will never have a chance of "becoming" if there are as many foreclosures as we have seen recently in the South African media freedom landscape: the impending Secrecy Bill (Daniels 2012), the MAT which would probably make journalists accountable to parliament, the charging of journalist Pauw over his book, and physical attacks on journalists. These selected examples have been used to reach some conclusions about the press freedom landscape in South Africa's transitional democracy. This is a young democracy indeed, but one in which the deepening of democracy is constantly under the tug of war or push and pull.

The space of democracy is symbolically occupied by both the ANC and the press. Unfortunately, the press is viewed as a symbolic outsider, an enemy, and not a friendly and legitimate adversary within the unfolding democracy. With enemies there are no common symbolic spaces. Yet in South Africa, the press are not enemies to a democracy – quite the reverse – they try to keep information flowing and they shine the spotlight on corruption (Daniels 2012).

Closure of voice results in the homogenization of society and requires unity of the press and the ruling party. This contradicts the role of the press in a democracy. The unity and ideological homogenization of the press with the ruling party is not good news for the public or democracy. Ultimately, if the free flow of the press is impeded, both the public and democracy suffer. It is a generally accepted fact that secrecy obstructs democracy by keeping the public ignorant of information. Beyond the normative role of media to provide information, it should contribute to the creation of agonistic public spaces in which there is the possibility for dissensus to be expressed or alternatives to be put forward to enable the democracy to become. The press cannot contribute toward this radical democracy project if these impediments persist. However, presently, the investigative press shows no sign of abating its commitment to uncovering corruption, shining a spotlight on the powerful and holding them to account.

South Africans draw enormous strength from the growth of investigative journalism and how this has contributed to exposing corruption and state capture. It is the robust press freedom that South Africa has that is probably the biggest contributor to bringing about the end of the reign of a corrupt president. Despite the intimidation from the state, legal impediments pressing down as threats, charges against journalists, and even physical fights, South Africa can be proud of its vociferous and muscular civil society which the press is an intrinsic part of. There is enormous press freedom in South Africa, with strong voices of dissent and criticism over corruption, an independent judiciary, and a constitution which protects the press's rights to report freely. There is an amazing spirit of activism, but ever-present vigilance could not be more important.

Notes

1 Especially in numbers: there are over 400 newspapers if you include community newspapers together with commercial, even more radio stations, a bouquet of television stations, online news outlets, all among growing social media usage.
2 It must be disclosed that the author of this chapter is the chairperson of the Diversity and Ethics sub-committee at Sanef.
3 In 2012, and as a direct result of the bill, Reporters without Borders downgraded South Africa's ranking by 10 notches in terms of freedom of information: it went from 42nd in the world to 52nd. The reason cited was that the bill would threaten investigative journalism.
4 *Mail & Guardian* 28 November 2012, Concourt action will be secrecy bill activists' last resort: http://mg.co.za/article/2012-11-28-00-info-bill-will-go-to-concourt-say-experts.
5 Press Council 9 October 2012, South Africa's Press – a new start for old values. *A revamped Press Council* www.presscouncil.org.za/News/View/south-africas-press--a-new-start-for-old-values-72
6 Ibid.

References

ANC (2013). The battle for ideas. Communications and the battle for ideas: 53rd National Conference. Retrieved from: www.anc.org.za/docs/res/2013/resolutions53r.pdf.
Daniels, G. (2012). *Fight for Democracy: The ANC and the Media in South Africa*. Johannesburg: Wits Press.
Daniels, G. (2014). *State of the Newsroom, South Africa, 2014: Disruptions Accelerated*. Johannesburg: Wits Journalism.
Freedom of Expression Institute (FXI) (2007). *The Media and the Law: A Handbook for Community Journalists*. Johannesburg: Freedom of Expression Institute (FXI).
Mahlase, M. (2017). Sanef statement on the treatment of journalists at the 54th ANC elective conference.
Milo, D. (2013) Protection of State Information bill- Looser Muzzle. Retrieved from: www.leader.co.za/article.aspx?s=6&f=1&a=4484.
Mouffe, C. (2000). *The Democratic Paradox*. London: Verso.
Mouffe, C. (2005). *The Return of the Political*. London: Verso.
Mouffe, C. (2006). *On the Political: Thinking in Action*. London and New York: Routledge.
Nieman Journalism Lab at Harvard (2018). Digging for Dung. Retrieved from: https://www.google.com/url?rct=j&sa=t&url=http://www.niemanlab.org/2018/01/digging-for-dung-unearthing-corruption-this-south-african-investigative-nonprofit-could-help-take-down-the-president.
Valentine, S. (2014) Email interview on press freedom situation in SA: 24 February.

6

Here is our Ushahidi

Participatory Communication Culture in Kenya

D. Ndirangu Wachanga

Driving most innovations in the field of communication technologies is often the need to advance the way societies exchange messages without being present. The invention of the telegraph, for example, allowed communication with others without being physically present. And whenever communication changes, society is transformed, particularly because communication technologies have always allowed people to share.

Communication technologies, however, do not generate human behavior; rather, by offering a novel platform, they create requisite and conducive conditions for existing human behavior to be exercised in new and diverse ways. For example, information shared online can serve many functions, including unintended ones: "It can spread shared grievances, draw international attention to domestic plights, broaden the appeal of social movements, and facilitate new connections between people and organizations" (Baym 2015, p. 108). In other words, users can harness online sharing to do public good, perpetuate self-aggrandizement, or enhance evil and predatory acts. As Papacharissi and Oliveira (2012, p. 280) note, communication technologies "provide a form of emotional release that simultaneously invigorates and exhausts tension ... depending on context, these affective attachments create feelings of community that may either reflexively drive a movement, and/or capture users in a state of engaged passivity." These technologies are not enough to cause change; instead, they serve as a conduit that is necessary to express existing motivations among users, creating new capacity and means to overcome challenges.

As such, it is important to examine the participatory culture among users; a culture that is produced by complex integration of "existing socio-material infrastructures with novel technical capabilities," while simultaneously combining "historical conditions, local contingencies and process dynamics" (Boczkowski 2004, p. 12). To have a better understanding of participatory culture, this discussion focuses on Ushahidi, a personal blog started in Kenya by Ory Okolloh in 2008 during a moment of national crisis that evolved into a "non-profit tech company that develops free and open source software for information collection and interactive mapping" (ushahidi.com). Ushahidi is an insightful case because it validates the efficacy of participatory culture as practiced by ordinary people and debunks the assumption that "the purpose of the media is to allow ordinary people to consume professionally created material" (Shirky 2010, p. 19), a postulation that anchored the media industry in the nineteenth and twentieth centuries.

Transnational Media: Concepts and Cases, First Edition. Edited by Suman Mishra and Rebecca Kern-Stone.
© 2019 John Wiley & Sons, Inc. Published 2019 by John Wiley & Sons, Inc.

6.1   Testimonies, Witnesses' Accounts, and Ushahidi

Ushahidi was conceived at a moment of collective crisis in Kenya. Kenya degenerated into violence in 2007 after conducting a contentious presidential election. More vulnerable than ever before, the country hung on a genocidal precipice. By the time a peace deal was brokered in February 2008, an estimated 1133 people had died and 350 000 had been internally displaced (Commission of Inquiry into Post-Election Violence – CIPEV 2008). As the violence escalated, the Kenyan government banned live reporting and blatantly censored some of the mainstream media, accusing them of broadcasting caustic and ethnically dividing narratives that fanned the violence. In its report, CIPEV (2008, p. 306) also highlighted, among other reasons, the offensive messages that were shared through media as instigation:

> [M]any (witnesses who appeared before the Commission) recalled with horror, fear, and disgust the negative and inflammatory role of vernacular radio stations in their testimony and statements to the Commission. In particular, they singled out KASS FM as having contributed to a climate of hate, negative ethnicity, and having incited violence in the Rift Valley region. However, there were also similar complaints in other parts of the country. These included the vernacular music and negative ethnicity allegedly coming from Kikuyu FM stations including Kameme, Inooro, Coro, and others in other different parts of the country.

During this crisis, however, a US-educated Kenyan lawyer and activist, Ory Okolloh, started Ushahidi as a personal blog, hoping to document the violence. On this blog, she requested ordinary people to send their testimonies of violence as they witnessed them. These testimonies were in form of audio, pictures, e-mails, blog entries, or a combination of these formats. Okolloh would then mash up the testimonies and mark the locations on a map where the reported incidents were taking place. She traces the cradle of this platform from her:

> collaboration *with* Kenyan citizen journalists during a time of crisis. The original website was used to map incidents of violence and peace efforts throughout the country based on reports submitted via the web and mobile phones. This website had 45,000 users in Kenya, and was the catalyst for us realizing there was a need for a platform based on it, which could be used by others around the world. Since early 2008 we have grown from an ad hoc group of volunteers to a focused organization. (Ushahidi 2018)

Prior to this crisis, cellular phones were an already existing platform among ordinary citizens in Kenya. According to a Communication Commission of Kenya report, over 80% of Kenyans were already using cellular phones (Pew Research Centre 2015), allowing citizens to create, disseminate, and circulate text messages to multiple recipients. This capacity allowed them to alter or edit received SMS before sharing with others, making circulation of SMS a process rather than a product.

   The availability and embrace of mobile telephony among ordinary citizens creates indispensable tools for daily activities (Jenkins 2006; Mudhai, Tettey, and Banda 2009; Shirky 2008), especially in sub-Saharan countries. Kenya is among the four leading cellular phone markets in Africa; in the same league as Nigeria, South Africa, and Ghana. By the beginning of 2013, more than half a billion people in the continent were connected via cellular phone. By their nature, cellular phones have reduced the cost and simplified the process of forming groups. This does not imply that a participatory communication culture is merely a product of an expansive technological infrastructure, even as these infrastructures continue to play critical role in enabling complex communication shifts. But it is the nature of this architecture of participation that allowed ordinary Kenyan citizens to frame SMS in ways that conformed to their political position during this moment that was defined by ethno-political crisis. Ushahidi, therefore, thrived because of two main reasons:

a) the existence of a population that was already using cellular phones, and
b) a violent ethnic-political crisis that had muted spaces for exchanging information, precisely because the mainstream broadcasting houses had been blocked from covering the escalating violence.

Ushahidi, therefore, served as a resourceful site that provided information about the unfolding crisis. The efficacy of Ushahidi was in serving as a forum that glued together disparate testimonies by and about dispersed ordinary Kenyans into a cohesive nationwide picture. Importantly, it provided a space to share acts of violence as they unfolded as opposed to reporting after the fact. Involvement of ordinary people allowed for reports from far and wide, including far-flung rural districts. Within a very short period, Okolloh had received overwhelming volumes of messages, prompting her to ask for help from IT volunteers. On her blog, Okolloh explained the significance of initiative as she requested technical assistance:

> Google Earth supposedly shows in great detail where the damage is being done on the ground. It occurs to me that it will be useful to keep a record of this, if one is thinking long-term. For the reconciliation process to occur at the local level the truth of what happened will first have to come out. Guys looking to do something – any techies out there willing to do a mashup of where the violence and destruction is occurring using Google Maps?

Volunteers, led by David Kobia and Erick Hersman, joined Okolloh to design a website that allowed people to post their messages anonymously using SMS – a popular way to communicate in Kenya because they are affordable (5 Ksh or 0.16 USD per text), dependable, and immediate – changing the communication landscape in the country. They named the website Ushahidi. The success of this partnership sprang from the availability, affordability, and accessibility of phones that had SMS capability, and the willingness users who were witnessing atrocities to testify about them. As scholarship in mobile communication indicates, cellular phones serve an integral role in connecting audiences to survivors of traumatic experiences.

During moments of national crises, differences in multi-ethnic societies tend to wane, uniting communities that are ordinarily in opposition – especially when the suffering of the "other" is brought to our proximity. Along these lines, Jenkins, Ford, and Green (2013, p. 2) define such a mode of participatory communication as one "which sees the public not as simply consumers of reconstructed messages but as people who are shaping, sharing, reframing, and remixing media content in ways which might not have been previously possible." In the case of Ushahidi, participation was aided by communication technologies that facilitated the horizontal flow of information across disjunctive spheres of social and political life. Importantly, the platforms allowed for media spreadability across multiple platforms in a nonlinear fashion. I use the term spreadable as it is defined by Jenkins, Ford, and Green (2013, p. xv) in their proposal for "an approach to media production, promotion, and circulation, which encourages a greater respect for the agency of grassroots participants, calling attention to the clashes occurring as media texts move between commercial and noncommercial spheres." Informing media spreadability is a complex form of participation, which has transformed ordinary people from mere consumers of information to producers and collaborators with the potential to review a story as it develops, edit it creatively, modify it critically, and respond to it spontaneously, almost immediately after consuming it. Beneath this architecture of participation is users' "collective intelligence" – a consciousness among users that one cannot know everything, prompting the necessity of entering in a network where "each of us knows something [and we can therefore] put the pieces together if we pool our resources and combine our skills" (Jenkins 2006, p. 4). This architecture of participation allowed ordinary people to share violence-related incidents no matter how small they were and no matter where they were happening; whether in urban centers or in rural and remote hamlets.

As information continued to stream in, Okolloh developed a verification mechanism that was shared on her site. Where reporters were identified, volunteers at Ushahidi would contact them as part of the fact-checking process. When information was sent anonymously, its veracity was evaluated using its consonance with other similar reports (Okolloh 2009). Unverified reports were appropriately labeled thus. Within a very short period of time, Ushahidi's popularity had reached thousands of users across the globe and was it visited by international organizations and mentioned in the international media. The site used open source software and was based on Google Maps and Frontline SMS. What Okolloh started as a personal blog had become a major information-sharing site within a very short period of time. Ushahidi was so popular that some established media stations started using it (Goldstein and Rotich 2008).

Since its launch in 2008, the Ushahidi platform has been transformed in powerful ways, particularly because of its success. Importantly, it offered the promise of incorporating features that would enhance data gathering processes, information sharing, mapping capabilities, effective means of information verification, and user friendly and interactive capabilities. Beside Ushahidi's technological sophistication, equally compelling is its ability to offer ordinary citizens the chance to self-report their experiences, which are then aggregated in ways that powerfully influence policy makers. Because of its capacity to be indigenized to solve local problems, Ushahidi has been deployed in different contexts: from mapping earthquakes in Chile, Haiti, and Japan, to monitoring elections in several countries across the globe; from tracking acts of violence in Atlanta, Georgia, to mapping corruption in Macedonia or traffic in Washington DC (see, for example, Fildes 2010; Giridaharadas 2010). It was used in 2008 in the Democratic Republic of Congo to map acts of violence in the war-torn country. Victims of violence were able to report the incidents by logging into the Ushahidi platform or by sending an SMS. According to Marsden (2013, p. 62),

> The reasons for the success of Ushahidi lie precisely in its raison d'etre: it was conceived as a way for people to give testimony to the world about a crisis they were experiencing. Although the aphorism: Necessity is the mother of invention is apropos, there is more to Ushahidi's inception than simple necessity. Ushahidi was meant to empower, to give voice, and was specifically designed to do so, but a host of underlying technologies were necessary before Ushahidi's "spontaneous" development could occur.

The use of the Ushahidi platform to help crises in the Global North, for instance, shows the disruption of the linear and traditional North–South flow of ideas, just as it offers novel vistas to challenge the assumption that media in Africa thirstily drink from the fountain of Western models. It challenges the long-held notion that media in Africa indiscriminately emulate Western media templates. Also contested is the assumption that information has always flowed from the Western capital. Ushahidi offers important lessons on the disruption of information directionality, with Kenyans telling their stories to themselves; sharing them with the world just as they are receiving, editing, contesting, and indigenizing stories from other global communities.

Owing to Ushahidi's promises, Humanity United, a non-profit organization committed to battling contemporaneous acts of slavery, funded it. This marked a new phase in Ushahidi's transformation, particularly when users outside Kenya adopted it to solve their localized needs. The funds provided by Humanity United facilitated further developments and the transformation of Ushahidi from its original design into a complex but easily accessible non-profit technology company that develops free and open source software. Its main focus is to facilitate effective and convenient collection and visualization of information using interactive maps. As a company, Ushahidi is committed to developing technological tools that support democratization of information, augmented transparency, and reduction of obstacles for individuals to share their testimonies.

Currently, Ushahidi has three free open source products: the Ushahidi platform, the SwiftRiver platform, and the CrowdMap application. The Ushahidi platform allows for crowd-sourcing information. Anyone with a cellular phone, email or who has access to the internet is able to share information on this platform, which then maps events by utilizing OpenStreet Maps or Google Maps, and creates geographically coded archives of covered incidents. Like the Ushahidi platform, the SwiftRiver platform is also downloadable and is made up of instantaneous information programming interfaces. The SwiftRiver platform expedites the swift management of information, particularly during the early hours of a disaster when the information streaming in is not only intense but also messy. Like the course of a river, SwiftRiver ensures that there is no data overflow. By using artificial intelligence processing, SwiftRiver organizes the unorganized data in real-time and contextualizes content by providing the location of the incidents reported. It is also powered by the capacity to mine SMS and Twitter data while verifying the source of the information provided on Ushahidi. By storing the CrowdMap application in the cloud, there is access efficiency without the necessity of a server.

As a company, Ushahidi is a "disruptive organization that is willing to fail in the pursuit of changing the traditional way that information flows" (Ushahidi 2018). Beneath this disruption of information flow lies insightful discovery of new ways to gather, share, and organize data. The use of Ushahidi in the aftermath of the earthquake in Haiti is instructive because it raised unprecedented question of translation. After messages in Haitian Creole started streaming in on the Ushahidi platform, there was need to find volunteers who could translate Creole into English, French, and to other multiple languages that were spoken by the emergency relief workers. On its platform, Ushahidi requested translators to volunteer and within a very short time it was possible to translate a message in Creole, map it, and efficiently communicate back to the responders. According to Munro (2010), there were more than 100 volunteer translators online within the first week. Following its services in the wake of this tragedy, various international organizations, including the UN, credited Ushahidi with helping thousands of relief workers who saved hundreds of lives. A report by the Knight Foundation noted that the noteworthy innovations to emerge from the Haiti crises were: the translation of crowd-sourced data to actionable information; the use of SMS message broadcasting in a crisis; and crowd-sourcing of open maps for humanitarian application. During the Haiti crisis, for instance, Ushahidi-Haiti was able to map incoming text messages that were urgent and actionable in near real-time. By having almost 300 volunteers from Boston to London, Montreal to Geneva, from Washington DC to Portland, Ushahidi-Haiti was able to operate around the clock. If volunteers in Boston, for instance, needed to get some rest, they were able to seamlessly hand over to a group of volunteers in Geneva, without any hitches. The impact of Ushahidi-Haiti was huge, to the extent that rescue workers depended on information provided on the Ushahidi site, as demonstrated by an official with the US Marine Corps:

> I cannot overemphasize to you what the work of the Ushahidi-Haiti has provided. It is saving lives every day. I wish I had time to document to you every example, but there are too many and our operation is moving too fast. [...] I say with confidence that there are 100s of these kinds of [success] stories. The Marine Corps is using your project every

second of the day to get aid and assistance to the people that need it most. [...] Keep up the good work! You are making the biggest difference of anything I have seen out there in the open source world. (knightfoundation.org)

Communication technology scholars are still exploring the reasons that motivate users to share information online by borrowing theoretical frameworks from other disciplines, including cognitive sciences. Keller's (1987, 2008) ARCS model of intrinsic motivation and instructional design might be useful in offering insights regarding what motivates ordinary citizens to share their testimonies on Ushahidi. This model consists of four factors with an ordered relationship: Attention, Relevance, Confidence, and Satisfaction. In order to act, people must know that something exists; attention is, therefore, integral to this model. The use of Ushahidi in Kenya as in other parts of the world is predicated on that factor: users are aware of its existence. After recognizing its presence, users evaluate its value in relation to their needs. Attention toward Ushahidi in Kenya resulted from the need to know what was happening in the country at a moment of political turmoil. The discontinued transmission of live broadcast by the mainstream

---

Technical factors

- Telepresence:
  - An environment created by means of an electronic communication medium that provides a mediated environment for shared activities.
- Technology scaffolding:
  - A training method based on engaging trainees in a task above their skill level with demonstration and help when necessary.
- Accessibility
  - The ability to provide access to information, resources and other people to a geographically distributed group.
- Digital literacy
  - An individual's ability to recognize when information is needed and to locate, evaluate, and use it effectively via digital technology.

Social factors

- Culture
  - The collective programming of the mind common among groups of people that facilitates communication and knowledge sharing, and which distinguishes one group or category of people from another.
- Motivation
  - Factors leading people to engage in a particular behavior.
- Trust
  - The willingness of a party to be vulnerable to the actions of another party irrespective of the ability to monitor or control that other party
- Leadership
  - The ability of a person or persons to promote and engage in practices that establish team norms, facilitate relationship building and develop trust. Collaborative learning
  - The ability of a group to engage actively in a discovery process and collaboratively construct meaningful and worthwhile knowledge
- Social system
  - The way in which individual members within an organization relate to each other and to the organization as a whole

Figure 6.1 VOSS model. *Source:* (Cogburn et al. 2011).

media only encouraged the search for alternative sources of information, and Ushahidi filled this role in a prominent and credible way.

The Relevance factor is evaluated on the basis of presence of the system and its ability to solve users' needs when they need it. Still, users must have the Confidence that they are able to use the system when they need to, and this leads to the Satisfaction that users derive after using the system and undertaking their task. Ushahidi addresses these four factors: users are aware of its existence (Attention); they understand its significance (Relevance); they trust it to deliver desired results (Confidence); and they are content with the feedback (Satisfaction).

Cogburn et al.'s (2011) Virtual Organizations as Socio-Technical System (VOSS) model is helpful in showing the convergence of technical and social factors in determining the success of a virtual organization (Figure 6.1).

Ushahidi satisfies the 10 socio-technical factors as identified by Cogburn et al. (2011) and this explains its success globally. Accompanying this celebratory narrative that defines Ushahidi, however, is a reminder by Jenkins, Ford, and Green (2013, p. 194) that any kind of participation on a digital platform is complicated because "our capacity to participation" can be problematized "by issues of who owns the platforms through which communication occurs and how their agendas shape how those tools can be deployed." Meaningful participation, these scholars argue, will require a continued quest to understand "the social and institutional factors that shape the nature of circulation," because this will enable users to become "effective at putting alternative messages into circulation" (Jenkins, Ford, and Green 2013, p. 194).

Media in Africa departs from and is not tied to the traditional Manichean paradigm of opposition, where the peripheral position of Africa in global circles is portrayed as emulative and imitative of the center. Ushahidi is an instructive case study, especially because its very structure sheds light on ordinary people's information-seeking behavior, information gathering, and information sharing. The participatory nature of the users makes the information shared on Ushahidi a process rather than a product because it is open to verification and contestation.

References

Baym, N. (2015). *Personal Connections in the Digital Age*. Malden: Polity Press.

Boczkowski, P.J. (2004). *Digitizing the News*. New Baskerville: MIT Press.

Cogburn, D.L., Santuzzi, A., and Espinoza, F. (2011). Developing and validating a socio-technical model for geographically distributed collaboration in global virtual teams. 44th Hawaii International International Conference on Systems Science (HICSS-44 2011), Proceedings, 4–7 January 2011, Koloa, Kauai, HI, USA.

Commission of Inquiry into Post-Election Violence (CIPEV). (2008). Report of the Commission of Inquiry Into Post-election Violence. Retrieved from: http://www.khrc.org.ke/documents/Waki_Report_08.pdf.

Fildes, J. (1 March 2010). Net puts Kenya at centre of Chile rescue efforts. *BBC News*. Retrieved from: http://news.bbc.co.uk/2/hi/technology/8543671.stm.

Giridaharadas, A. (13 March 2010). Africa's gift to Silicon Valley: How to track a crisis. *The New York Times*. Retrieved from: http://www.nytimes.com/2010/03/14/weekinreview/14giridharadas.html?scp=1&sq=ushahidi&st=cse&_r=0.

Goldstein, J. and Rotich, J. (2008). Digitally networked technology in Kenya's 2007–2008 post-election crisis. Berkman Center at Harvard University Research Publication No. 2008–09. Internet & Democracy Case Study Series, September 2008, 1–10.

Jenkins, H. (2006). *Fans, Bloggers, and Gamers: Exploring Participatory Culture*. New York: New York University Press.

Jenkins, H., Ford, S., and Green, J. (2013). *Spreadable Media: Creating Value and Meaning in a Networked Culture*. New York: New York University Press.

Keller, J.M. (1987). Strategies for stimulating the motivation to learn. *Performance Instruction* 26 (8): 1–7.

Keller, J.M. (2008). An integrative theory of motivation, volition, and performance. *Technology, Instruction, Cognition, and Learning* 6 (2): 79–104.

Marsden, J. (2013). Stigmergic self-organization and improvisation of Ushahidi. *Cognitive Systems Research* 21: 52–64.

Mudhai, O., Tettey, W., and Banda, F. (2009). *African Media and the Digital Public Sphere*. New York: Palgrave – MacMillan.

Munro, R. (2010). Crowdsourced translation for emergency response in Haiti: The global collaboration of local knowledge. In Ninth conference of the association for machine translation in the Americas: amta2010. Retrieved from: http://amtaweb.org.

Okolloh, O. (2009). Ushahidi, or "testimony": web 2.0 tools for crowdsourcing crisis information. *Participatory Learning and Action* 59: 59–70.

Papacharissi, Z. and Oliveira, M. (2012). Affective news and networked publics: the rhythms of news storytelling in # Egypt. *Journal of Communication* 62 (2): 266–282.

Pew Research Centre (2015). Report: Global Attitudes and Trends. Retrieved from: http://www.pewglobal.org/2015/04/15/cell-phones-in-africa-communication-lifeline/.

Shirky, C. (2008). *Here Comes Everybody: The Power of Organizing Without Organizations*. New York: Penguin Press.

Shirky, C. (2010). *Cognitive Surplus: How Technology Makes Consumers into Collaborators*. New York: Penguin Press.

Ushahidi home page. Retrieved from: http://ushahidi.com Accessed January 2018.

7

Nollywood

A Cinema of Stories
Onookome Okome

Recent studies on Nollywood are beginning to clear up common assumptions about the industry, and the field of Nollywood studies is showing obvious signs of serious scholarship. Since the pioneer essay, "Evolving Popular Media The Nigerian Video Film (1998)," published just five years after the release of *Living in Bondage* (1992/1993), the body of scholarly texts has grown by leaps and bounds and they chart a clear path that defines the future of scholarly enterprise on Nollywood and the debates that are likely to emerge in the future. Scholarly debates about Nollywood have improved tremendously, and the movement away from mere affirmation of the affiliation of this cinematic form to the overwhelming and overstated influence of the Yoruba traveling theater tradition is also beginning to wane. Bringing a deeper and nuanced understanding of the roots of this cinematic practice, these essays and books have gone beyond the clichés associated with the scholarship on the subject. Writing about Nollywood is no longer an all-comers' game, and mere curiosity no longer a good reason for being part of the discussion; the text of the Nollywood film is not construed as a curio anymore. Firmly moving away from the clichéd reading of the industry and its text, the body of texts that has emerged over the last 10 or so years has mined the field and made clear the social instigators of this popular art form, providing reasonable discussion along the lines of the social and cultural influences that have given Nollywood its distinctive mark as a local media that has gone global on its own terms.

Recognition that Nollywood began as a popular local grassroots medium instigated a new way of thinking about media history in Nigeria, and indeed in the whole of Africa. Providing a distinct epistemic synthesis from its peculiar way of articulating social life, these scholarly texts also understand that reading Nollywood with a new vocabulary is one of the surer ways of getting to the crux of the alternative episteme which it produces. To achieve this, the authors of these texts had to move away from the comparatist mode of reading that ties Nollywood to global cinematic practices. "Evolving Popular Media: The Nigerian Video Film" has a lot to do with the framing of the discourse of the new Nigerian film industry that was later christened Nollywood by the intrepid journalist Norimitsu Onishi (2002). Several essays and books were published between 1992 when the first major film, *Living in Bondage*, was released and 2018, but none has the same breadth and analytical consistency that Jonathan Haynes' *Nollywood Genre* (2016) brings to the subject. It is currently the most seminal of the books on the subject and will be for some time to come. In its encyclopedic and analytical scope, this book brings some stability to the longstanding clichéd criticism that initially attended the emergence of the Nollywood film. What this brief chapter hopes to do, then, is to frame the discourse of the Nollywood film as a popular expression with influences from within and across a number of

Transnational Media: Concepts and Cases, First Edition. Edited by Suman Mishra and Rebecca Kern-Stone.
© 2019 John Wiley & Sons, Inc. Published 2019 by John Wiley & Sons, Inc.

cultural histories and texts, and in so doing isolate and discuss the essential marker of the Nollywood film: the Nollywood story. My contention is that it is prudent to do this by restating and discussing some of the clichés in the writing about this industry and the Nollywood film. Additionally, this emphasis on the Nollywood story as the essential item of this film culture will refocus the essence of the industry and the culture it promotes. It will bring to the debate the larger significance of story and storytelling in Nollywood. It is important to make the point that the clichéd readings that I refer to have traveled into, and helped shape, the presentation of Nollywood in many "overseas" documentary films. The list of such documentaries is long, but some of the most popular in Europe and America are *This is Nollywood* and *Nollywood Babylon*.

Defining the Nollywood film is a tricky business. It may not even be productive to engage in such an enterprise. In this regard, it seems to me that the prudent thing to do is to reiterate the fundamental aspect of the Nollywood film: that which constitutes its permanent marker as a cultural product. Jonathan Haynes' (2016) book has done some of this work. It provides an extensive reading of this industry, foregrounding the way that the fragmentary narrative of Nollywood's primary city, Lagos, influences the content of the Nollywood film. This is central to the character of Nollywood, a theme which it shares it with the other notable low-budget filming tradition in Africa, the Ghanaian video film industry; like the Ghanaian industry, Nollywood "reconstitutes, even as it is complicit with the grand narrative of modernity and globalization" (Garittano 2013, p. 9).

Nollywood films are all about this local modernity defined by and in the Nigerian city. But it is a modernity that is yet to give up the tangible and irreconcilable claims of the past, nor of the rural past which is always lurking under the surface of the performances of this modernity. In this sense, the films express the global in a peculiarly Nigerian way, even if they work within distinguishable links to this global modernity in an unguarded – if not reckless – consumption of the global. Distilled from years of careful research and reinforced by sheer love for the subject, Haynes' (2016) perspective gives the city its capricious place in the making of Nollywood. It gives the reader eloquent descriptions of how the city defines the artisanal workings of the industry. Finally, the book gives the discipline of Nollywood studies a discursive stability that removes discussions outside the framework of Euro-American critical language about cinema. The city is important to the study of Nollywood, so too is the story about and around the city. Nollywood's first city is, no doubt, Lagos. It was here that it all began in the early 1990s.

The release of *Living in Bondage*, one of the most referenced films in Nollywood scholarship, marked a significant point in both the artistic and infrastructural histories of the industry. This film is intricately tied to Lagos and to the technology which it appropriated, domesticated, and compelled to yield to the values of the narrative story. The history of this appropriation is connected to the merchant, Kenneth Nnebue, who was said to be the first to give the industry a taste of glory. *Living in Bondage*, the first major blockbuster of the industry was his brain child. There are controversies around who directed this film, but what is not debated is that it was key to defining the story of the Nollywood film and the melodramatic style which Nollywood came to adopt. Even the most casual observer of the workings of this industry knows the story of Kenneth Nnebue and the beginning of the industry – it is a common item in Nollywood studies. Unsure of what to do with a cargo of VHS tapes, which came from Taiwan, he used them to record live theater performances. According to Pierre Barrot (2008, p. 121), he was led to this path when "he heard about the profit people were making selling pre-recorded video tapes in Ghana." His experiment began with one of the local Yoruba language theater companies. One of the myths in the industry is that these recordings, shot straight on VHS, were such a great success that in 1992, with the help of Chris Obi Rapu, he was able to make *Living in Bondage* – first in Igbo and then dubbed in English following huge success with the local audience. A second part of this story was made and the rest is history.

Living in Bondage became an instant hit with local audiences for a number of reasons, and chief among them was that it hit on what was already the huge question in the minds of Lagosians at the time of its release. This was the basic question about the unconfirmed source of the wealth of the nouveau rich in the city. This film provided an answer to this question and offered a way out of the moral quagmire which the source of the so-called blood money generated. It was the first time that Pentecostal Christianity was introduced into the narrative of the Nollywood film as a way of resolving this moral problem. It quickly caught on as a narrative device to ward off the evil of blood money, which accrues from ritual activities associated with human sacrifice. The success of this film saw a slew of so-called "ritual" films, many of them providing gory details of beheadings and organ harvesting for ritual purposes. *Ritual* (1997) is a good case in point. In *Living in Bondage*, Andy Okeke kills his wife in a ritual sacrifice and becomes instantly rich, but when he tries to remarry, the ghost of his wife appears to him, scuttling his desire and then sending him mad. This was the real beginning of Nollywood and the structure of the Nollywood story. The story of the so-called new Nollywood film, which is made for cinema release and with better esthetic value, is not so far from this formula; and before we run away with the idea that the industry has left behind the ritual basis of the old Nollywood film, we only have to look at films that have been recently released. A sizeable number of them still follow in the footsteps of *Living in Bondage*. Two cases in point are *African Ritual* 1&2 (2017) and *Blood and Money: The Oath Brother* (Season 1 and 2, 2018).

The initial successes of the industry blossomed further after the release of *Living in Bondage*, facilitated in part by intrepid Nigerian travelers who made physical copies of Nollywood VHS tapes part of the items of their baggage. Ironically, this was also a process that encouraged piracy as more and more people were drawn to the new world of the Nigerian video film in new locations, some out of curiosity and some for other reasons. This interest soon led to unauthorized copying, and this was naturally followed by the creation of the new cultural "publics" that soon formed around the Nollywood film in Nigeria and around the world, especially in Africa. In no time audiences emerged from these publics. Moradewun Adejunmobi (2007) contends that this means of transportation of VHS tapes was one of the factors that made the regional character of the Nollywood film possible. It was this mobile character of Nigerian travelers and the portability of VHS technology that expanded the consumption base of this cultural practice in the early phases of the industry. It was also through engagement in this process of exchange between travelers and consumers that Nollywood managed to create a distinct cultural integrity across Africa and in the African diasporas as a cinematic practice.

At home, the inauguration of this public began something novel: the close connection between filmmakers and audience. Nollywood filmmakers realized quite early that forging an abiding and sustained relationship with the local audience was good for business, and they spared no chance to make this happen. Part of the reason for this was the need to maximize profit. One of the positive outcomes of this alliance was that early in the history of the Nollywood film, content was framed mostly, but not always, from the perspective of its audience. From the beginning, what might seem to outsiders as a mere reiteration of everyday banalities was in fact part of the mystique of Nollywood. Although this audience is still internally differentiated, it was clearly formed around the desire to experience a new way of screening Nigeria. Identification with the drama of the socially distinct modernity of characters whose primary quest was to move up in the social ladder quickly became the essential, if not the main, ingredient of the Nollywood narrative. Illegal distribution, piracy, and unauthorized public exhibitions in sites such as street corners, gendered zones of the city, video parlors, and long-haul busses (Okome 2007) were also crucial to the expansion of this audience and the culture that these films promoted. Barely 10 years after the first major Nollywood film was released, these travelers made the Nollywood film available to the world, inviting outsiders to see Nigeria as Nigerians see themselves, but in all the ambiguity of the symbolic reiteration of everyday Nigeria. However, as Moradewun argues,

> "global corporation may indeed offer more opportunities than previously for small scale producers," but the attachment to local audiences is still crucial in defining the content of the Nollywood film. Indeed, while Nollywood producers "circulate content on their network, their ability to shape the type of content is constrained by the fact that they do not generally remit significant profits to such producer" (Adejunmobi 2014, p. 75).

Piracy was a big part of the distribution infrastructure in Nollywood early in the development of the industry. It still is to some extent. The boom in the consumption of the Nollywood film exacerbated this problem, prompting new calls for government intervention in the late 1990s. This headache has not gone away. Lancelot Imasuen, one of the most prolific filmmakers in the industry, experienced this first hand. He spoke of his fears in an informal conversation we had on the occasion of his visit to the School of Media and Communication at the Pan Atlantic University, located in Victoria Island, Lagos. He was agitated about this because he was about to release his latest film, *1884* – based on a story about the British expeditionary massacre in 1884 during which the British sacked the ancient Kingdom of the Edo people in Nigeria and subsequently looted valuable artifacts. Just before he gave the assigned monthly talk at the School, his fears were realized when we found out that *Half of Yellow Sun* was already in the streets of Lagos. Just as he feared, this film had been pirated a couple of weeks before it was due to be officially released. Among pirated copies of films from Hollywood and Bollywood, the vendor we encountered as we stepped out of the university building proudly displayed copies of *Half of A Yellow Sun* – completely oblivious to the fact that they were pirated versions for which he could have been arrested. I am not sure whether this was also the fate of the film *1884*, but Imasuen's fear was palpable at the time.

Problems of piracy have been a longstanding headache in Nigerian cinema history. It was an intractable problem during the celluloid era as it is now with the Nollywood era. Moses Olaiya, also known as Baba Sala, was the hardest hit during the era of celluloid filmmaking, which began in 1970 with the release of *Kong's Harvest* and continued all the way to the release of Baba Sala's *Mosebolatan* (1986). Olaiya's film was pirated even before he had the chance to travel around with the reels – as was the practice with the Yoruba filmmakers who transitioned into the craft in the early 1980s. This landed the ace-comedian in trouble with the bank that provided the money for the film. Problems of piracy were exacerbated with the emergence of Nollywood as cinematic force, especially from the 1990s, and a new dimension was added with the success of films such as *Ritual* (1997), *Karishika* (1996), *Highway to the Grave* (2002), *Nneka: the Pretty Serpent* (1992), and *Osuofia in London* (2003/2004).

Piracy took on a transnational dimension in the early 2000s partly because of the rapid expansion in the global consumption of Nollywood on the internet and through cable broadcasting. Broadcasting on satellite and cable television distribution outlets, such as the South African-based MNet Cable Company, made this cultural product susceptible to the activities of unscrupulous characters looking to make fast money. These DVD pirates had no problem finding ingenious ways to copy and redistribute Nollywood content ad infinitum. Nollywood filmmakers were now faced with a new problem. In addition to the bad deals they were subjected to in their dealing with operators of internet platforms and cable stations, they now had to contend with piracy on the internet and with the cable operators' backhanded contracts. This is only the more recent phase of the problem. Phillip Cartelli's (2007) report on the booming underground trade in Nollywood films in the island nation of St Lucia is quite telling in this regard. Topping the piracy chart, demand for Nollywood films far outstripped the demand for pirated American and Bollywood films. Alessandro Jedlowski (2013) gives a fascinating account of his experience in Naples, Italy. Noting that "Nollywood films … travelled largely under the regime of piracy," he goes on to describe his chance meeting with a Senegalese video vendor "selling what I thought were Francophone films" (p. 33). It turned out that the vendor actually had "a copy of the copy" of a Nollywood film, which came all the way from Lagos, Nigeria, via a television station in Ivory Coast. Ironically, this example and the example of digital bootlegging from internet platforms have been useful vehicles for the spread of the culture of the Nollywood. They fostered the insertion of this film culture and filmmaking practices into the corporate global network of content distribution like never before. But Nollywood did not give up its cultural integrity for this or any other reason.

The thriving informal transnational transactions in Nollywood films are just one aspect of the stunningly lucrative business of bootlegging that has helped push Nollywood into the world market. Ingenious "businessmen and women" are now making huge profits from copying Nollywood films from online platforms and reselling them on optical disks. At the national level, marketers/producers in the industry accuse directors, who are mostly university-educated graduates, of being part of the piracy chain. For their part, Nollywood directors, who are marginal in the chain of exchange between the marketers/producers and the audience, point their fingers at the marketers/producers, accusing them of orchestrating the "piracy" of their own films in order to cook the books. This drama of accusation and counter-accusation is one of the best-known discursive items in the industry and is not likely to go away soon. When I interviewed the charismatic evangelist, Helen Ukpabio, in 2006, the story making the rounds at the time was that she compelled her video jacket designers to take an oath of loyalty not to sell the jackets to pirates. She is no ordinary preacher. She was one of the first to see the use of videoed stories for preaching and converting potential believers – the other prominent actor in this arena being the owner of the Ibadan-based Mount Zion Ministries. If the gossip were true, all she was doing at the time was simply trying to prevent the pirates from swooping in on her films. She had good reasons do this. Her films were runaway successes, especially among members of her congregation who often paid upfront for their production. Tunde Kelani was also a victim. In 2015, Tunde Kelani told me in an informal conversation that he was at some point forced to "pirate himself." He "volunteered" to do this so as to ward off the real pirates before they found ingenious means of doing their shady business. His tactics only worked partially. During this meeting with him, he showed me pirated copies of his film and the original which he "pirated." There was hardly any difference between the two versions. Fragmentary and unorganized as it was in the early 2000s, piracy and other forms of bootlegging in Nollywood accounted for more than a third of the accrued income in the industry. Much of this illicit gain came from sales of the Nollywood films outside Nigeria.

Indeed, as Moradewun Adejunmobi (2007) argues eloquently in "Nigerian Home Video Film as A Minor Transnational Practice," local forms of the practices of unauthorized distribution and exhibition were an integral part of this industry from the very beginning and claims of piracy were rampant at this time. Not a lot has changed in this regard. The popularity that accrued from these activities may not have been consciously courted by the filmmakers, but it created what Karin Barber (1997) describes as new publics, which later transformed into new local and international "audiences" for Nollywood films. Over the last 10 years or so, a number of documentary films have been made about Nollywood by foreign film companies, all trying to understand why this industry is what it is: locally successful. Although not stated explicitly in these films, the real question they're asking is obvious to the trained mind. They all want to know why Nollywood is outdoing major film nations in sales in Nigeria. While the new audiences created in the 2000s were no doubt internally differentiated, they were mostly formed around the desire to understand notions of economic mobility in the increasingly "de-cultured" and socially fragmented urban milieus of Lagos and other big cities in Nigeria. These new audiences congregated in locations that included the domestic arena, street corners, and video parlors (Okome 2007).

So, what drives the popularity of the Nollywood film? The answer to this question, unlike answers to other matters related to Nollywood, is simple. It is the Nollywood story. Simple, heartfelt, often stark, melodramatic, and stylistically unencumbered, the Nollywood story shocks and awes local and transnational audiences alike. It is not based on just the unmediated imagination of one director, but rather is the play of the filmmaker's reading of questions emerging from the communal quest to find answers to the extraordinary events in contemporary Nigerian society. It is true that the Nollywood story "reflects and produces, in ways that are perhaps exceeds any other cultural medium or movement, the contradictions of the state and society in their encounter with global capitalist modernity" (Jeyifo 2014, p. 524). But it is hard to believe that the Nollywood story is merely full of "bluster and verve, but for the most part breathtakingly underdeveloped" (p. 590). The contention that the Nollywood film, which is often a reference to the Nollywood story, is "… often poor in quality," is in direct opposition to the assertion that Nollywood films "constitute the repertoire of the most preferred and most popular tradition in Africa" (p. 595). If the Nollywood story is important, it is because it matters to the target audience and to all those who consume it and continue to do so for different reasons. In fact, the basis for the popularity of the Nollywood story across the nation and in the continent is partly because of the simplicity of the *retelling* of what is already a common narrative property. The story as well as the retelling can be therapeutic for those who see in it different forms of social therapies. Retelling what is already a communal event most surely instigates and reinvents the making of new meaning.

The Nollywood story can be unnecessarily expansive and often digressional, but that too is hardly a drawback for this audience if we go by the mass patronage. Complaints about the acting may have some grounds, but not that of the "originality of the story idea" (Jeyifo 2014, p. 596). As a social and cultural form, acting for the stage or film is culturally specific. The audience of Nollywood, I would argue, is culturally specific. It is the product of its time and place. My point here, which is still tentative one, is that this audience may have some familiarity with Nollywood's method of telling a story and, until it is rejected, we should be humble enough to acknowledge the significant relationship between the two. Nollywood's story is often communal, plucked from the belly of the street and given back to audiences who already know something about it. Much of the popularity of the different subgenres of the Nollywood film across the African continent is based on this fact. This is the point made by Dominica Dipio (2008) about Ugandan viewers of Nollywood films. Based on personal interviews with viewers, she writes that Ugandan "viewers are entertained by the (Nollywood) film because most of what is represented is recognizable in their own social-cultural set-up; and it is fun to see the everyday enacted out and fictionalized" (p. 58). For the Ugandan audience, Nollywood's "stories are often experienced as part of [one's] reality" (p. 58). In the section of Pierre Barrot's edited book, *Nollywood: The Video Phenomenon in Nigeria* (2005) appropriately subtitled "Nollywood and Its Conquest of Africa," three of the four essays give vivid, even tantalizing, accounts of the magic of the Nollywood film in Niger, Congo (Kinshasa), and Kenya. Not surprisingly, Barrot closes this section with his rhetorical article "Is the Nigerian Model Fit For Export?" making the point that "The Nigerian model offers some undeniable assets" (p. 126). This is typical of the reception of Nollywood films all over Africa and elsewhere in the so-called developing world. Faced with peculiar economic problems – but insisting on the need to keep the narrative of social life vibrant – several developing countries outside Africa have embraced some of the methods employed in Nollywood. When the chief executive of Saudi Arabia's General Authority for Culture, Ahmed Almaziad, sought to seek inspiration for the Kingdom's quest for a national cinema, it was to Nollywood that he turned. Such is the power of the Nollywood film across developing nations. There have been moments of disquiet about the content of Nollywood films in many parts of the world, especially in Africa, but these were moments when cultural policy makers sought to censor Nollywood for its openness and vibrant discussion of sex and sexuality. Nollywood has also provoked cultural unrest in some African nations, Ghana and Tanzania being cases in point. But this has not stopped the thriving cooperation between filmmakers from Ghanaia and Nigeria over the last 10 or so years, leading to a form of grass-roots pan-Africanism that is new to the definition of this philosophical ideology.

A lot has happened over the last 20 years in Nollywood, and some of the innovations are disruptive to the very notion of what we know as African film and filmmaking in Africa. Observers of the industry, like Pierre Barrot, may put the emphasis on the disruptiveness in the domestication of digital filmmaking – first by converting the VHS cassette from its reportage use into a means of telling stories. Others may account for this disruptive presence in the recognition of Nollywood's reconfiguration of existing cinema institutions – such as film scholarship, exhibition, distribution, production – and in the methods of promoting newly released films locally and globally. These are important points to note about the ways in which Nollywood disrupts the study of African cinema, filmmaking, and consumption in Africa, but the point ought to be emphatically made that there is nothing as ingenious as hawking Nollywood VCDs and DVDs on wheelbarrows in the street of Ilorin, Lagos, and Port Harcourt, a distribution feat that is grassroots and mobile. This is the act that cuts out the power of local and international corporate capital. It redefines a new way of democratizing the "newsy" story of Nollywood film.

It is equally important to acknowledge the point that Nollywood producers/marketers make their films with local audiences in mind and are not unduly bothered with audiences outside the immediate frame of cultural reference. Even the most vociferous critics of Nollywood admit and acknowledge the strategic practicality of its low-budget filmmaking option, which has served the industry very well. These are obvious and reasonable readings of an industry that became, in a very short order, the largest cinema industry in the world in terms of the number of films produced annually. Yet, I argue that the essential and irreplaceable aspect of the practice of Nollywood in the last 30 years is its strong connection to the local audience, and at the heart of this symbiotic relationship is the Nollywood story. The argument I make is that it is not the way the story is told, but the story itself that is the essential core of what "constitute[s] the repertoire of the most preferred and most popular cinema tradition in Africa" (Okome 2014, p. 159). Understanding this film practice requires a thorough understanding of its popular base. It requires an approach that recognizes it as a popular art form. Audience attachment to the story is a significant element in this equation. Nollywood has produced its own *classics* or its own *evergreens* to quote Emmanuel Obie China's use of the word to reference the classics of the Onitsha market pamphlets (1971). It is the story that makes the film of new Nollywood new in the world. From Kenneth Nnebue's *Living in Bondage* (1992/1993), through Kingsley Ogoro's *Osuofia in London* (1993), to Fred Amata's *Amazing Grace* (2006), the element of story trumps all else. It is at the heart of Nollywood.

References

Adejunmobi, M. (2007). Nigerian video film as a minor transnational practice. *Postcolonial Text* 3 (2): 1–16.

Adejunmobi, M. (2014). Close-up: Nollywood – a worldly creative practice: evolving Nollywood templates for minor transnational film. *Black Camera, An International Film Journal* 5 (2): 74–94.

Barber, K. (1997). Preliminary notes on audiences in Africa. *Africa: Journal of the International Institute*, 67/3, 347–362.

Barrot, P. (ed.) (2008). Is the Nigerian model fit for export? In: *Nollywood: The Video Phenomenon in Nigeria*, 121–130. Oxford: James Currey.

Cartelli, P. (2007). Nollywood comes to the Caribbean. *Film International* 5 (4): 112–114.

Dipio, D. (2008). Uganda viewership of Nigerian movies. In: *Africa Through the Eye of the Video Camera* (ed. F. Ogunleye), 52–73. Swaziland: Academy Press.

Garittano, C. (2013). *African Video Movies and Global Desires: A Ghanaian History*. Ohio: Ohio Research in International Studies.

Haynes, J. (2016). *Nollywood: The Creation of Nigerian Film Genre*. Chicago: University of Chicago Press.

Haynes, J. and Okome, O. (1998). Evolving popular media: the Nigerian video film. *Research in African Literatures*, 29 (3): 108–129.

Jedlowski, A. (2013). From Nollywood to Nollyworld: processes of transnationalization in the Nigerian video film industry. In: *Global Nollywood: The Transnational Dimensions of An African Video Film Industry* (ed. M. Krings and O. Okome), 35–45. Bloomington/Indiana: Indiana University Press.

Jeyifo, B. (2014). Will Nollywood get better? (did Hollywood and Bollywood get better?). In: *Drama and Theatre in Nigeria: A Critical Source Book* (ed. Y. Ogunbiyi), 589–621. Lagos: Tanus Books.

Obiechina, E. (1971). *Literature for the Masses: An Analytical Study of Popular Pamphleteering in Nigeria*. Enugu, Nigeria: Nwamife Publishers.

Okome, O. (2007). Nollywood spectatorship, audience and the sites of consumption. *Postcolonial Text*, 3 (2): 52–73.

Okome, O. (2014). A Nollywood classic: *Living in Bondage* (Kenneth Nnebue, 1992/1993). In: *Africa's Lost Classics: New Histories of African Cinema* (ed. L. Bisschoff and D. Murphy), 152–160. London: Legenda.

Onishi, N. (16 December 2002) Step aside, L.A and Bombay, for Nollywood. *The New York Times*, Retrieved from: https://www.nytimes.com/2002/09/16/world/step-aside-la-and-bombay-for-nollywood.html.

Part III

The Americas and the Caribbean

Transnational Media: Concepts and Cases, First Edition. Edited by Suman Mishra and Rebecca Kern-Stone.
© 2019 John Wiley & Sons, Inc. Published 2019 by John Wiley & Sons, Inc.

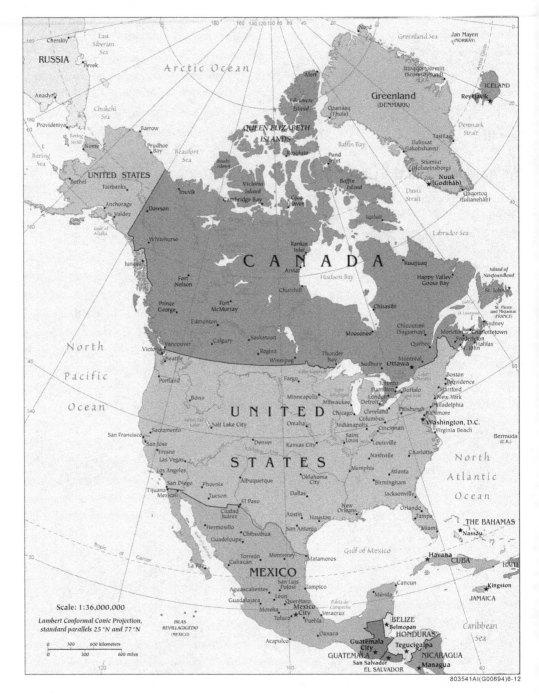

Figure III.1 (a) Map of North America.

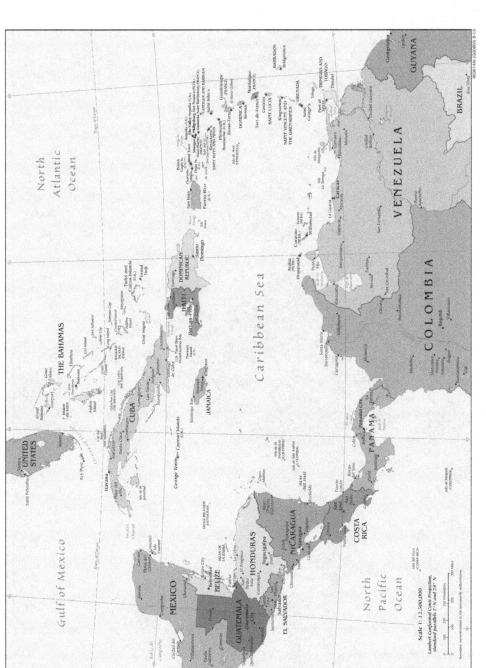

Figure III.1 (b) Map of Central America and Caribbean.

Figure III.1 (c) Map of South America.

The Americas consist of two continents – North and South America – connected by Central America, and many nations of the Caribbean (Figure III.1). In this region, the northern countries (United States Canada) are well-developed while the countries of the south are still developing or are underdeveloped. The United States is undoubtedly one of the most dominant countries of this region as well as the world. Its economic, political, military, and technological might is comparable to none other in the region. However, it too is facing many domestic and international challenges. In terms of media, many of the world's largest transnational media conglomerates are centered in this region: the United States, Mexico, Brazil, Venezuela, and Argentina. Many argue these countries have the most concentrated media in the world (Podesta 2016).

From a regional perspective, while media in the Americas is thriving, that does not mean that press and internet freedom is. While North America as well as much of the Caribbean currently has a free press, only a few countries in Central and South America enjoy the same. Canada and countries in the Caribbean have some of the highest press freedom in the world, primarily because they guarantee either freedom of press and/or expression and have legal and political systems in place to ensure these freedoms. These include editorial independence, diversity of views, opportunities for private enterprise, and little to moderate government intervention and regulation (Reporters Without Borders 2016). Much of Central and South America, or Latin America, are only partly free, as press freedom may be constitutionally guaranteed but there are few legal supports for such a guarantee. In addition, there is still much government intervention, including ownership, and journalists face harsh penalties for criticizing government entities (Reporters Without Borders 2016). Media system models throughout the Americas range from authoritarian, to social responsibility, to market driven.

In this section, a brief country profile and overview of the media landscapes of Brazil, Mexico, the United States, and Jamaica are discussed. They are intended to provide a snapshot of these countries as well as a broader diverse perspective of the region.

PIII.1   Brazil

Brazil is the largest South America country. In terms of the demographics, Brazil has a population of about 207 million (World Bank 2018). There is a high concentration of people who live in one of its largest cities, Sao Paulo, which has over 11.9 million inhabitants. The majority of Brazilians speak Portuguese and a majority of Brazilians identify themselves as Christians. According to Brazil's 2010 census, 50.7% of Brazilians identified themselves as black or mixed race and 47.7% as white (Phillips 2011).

Brazil is a developing country which is rich in natural resources. It is a country that has enjoyed economic booms and busts throughout the twentieth century. Between 2000 and 2012, it was one of the fastest growing economies of the world. However, after more than a decade of boom, the country entered a long recession. Political scandals, the impeachment of former president Dilma Rousseff, and corruption resulted in instability and economic crisis. Brazil had a negative annual growth rate of −3.6% in 2016, but in 2017 the economy started to pick up and grew slightly at 1%. Brazil's GDP, which is an important indicator of a country's economic power, stands at 1.8 trillion USD in 2017 (World Bank 2017).

Brazil has had waves of dramatic political changes and crises. Brazilians experienced dicta-torship for nearly four decades, from 1964 to 1985, when the Brazilian military took control after overthrowing the reformist government of President João Goulart. Various military heads ruled during this time and used heavy-handed measures to maintain power. Media were censored, human rights were ignored, dissidents were killed or jailed, many simply vanished, and propaganda was used to control the masses. The military rule eventually collapsed after the economic woes of the country became too great and opposition grew stronger. Subsequently, a new civilian leader was elected, and Brazil was set on a democratic path.

Brazil has a large media market estimated to be 35.7 billion USD, which is projected to grow to 48.7 billion USD by 2020 (Statista, 2018a). Brazilian media have played an important role in entertainment and politics. Media conglomerate Globo Communicação e Participações S.A., located in Rio de Janeiro, has a considerable influence on people and politicians as it controls much of the country's television and radio stations, newspapers, and pay TV and other outlets. Today, Globo is particularly known for its production of Brazilian soaps, also known as the telenovelas, which are extremely popular in the country. Globo also exports programming via satellite, focusing on Portuguese speakers in Europe, the Middle East, Africa, and Japan. Telenovela production and its meaning in South America and Mexico and are covered in more detail in Chapter 8. Globo played a significant role in propaganda during the dictatorship period (Coehlo 2013) and continues to have significant influence in Brazilian politics and elections, which is further discussed in Chapter 9.

Brazil is a democratic country which supports free press; however, Reporters Without Borders ranks Brazil 102/180 in press freedom and notes, "Brazil continues to be one of Latin America's most violent countries for journalists. Their difficulties are compounded by the lack of a national mechanism for their protection and a climate of impunity fuelled by ubiquitous corruption" (RSF 2018a).

Internet and mobile media are a fast-growing sector in Brazil. Nearly 70% about 149 million Brazilians use the internet, though significant difference in usage exists based on region and class. Mobile phones and apps like Facebook and WhatsApp are extremely popular for communication. There are 257 million mobile phone subscriptions, which means many individuals own more than one mobile phone (Internet World Stats 2018a).

PIII.2   Mexico

Located in the southern part of North America, Mexico shares more similarities with Central and Southern American countries than with its northern neighbors of the United States and Canada. Mexico's population in 2017 was around 129 million (World Bank 2018). Demographically it is made up of 62% Mestizo (Amerindian-Spanish), 21% predominately Amerindian, 7% Amerindian, and 10% Other (mostly European) (Statista 2012). The majority of Mexicans identify themselves as Christians. Spanish is the main language spoken in the country.

Mexico's economy is sizeable, with a GDP of 1.15 trillion USD and an annual growth of 2% respectively (World Bank 2017). Economically, Mexico is better situated than most Latin American countries, but it has its own challenges with political corruption, organized crime and drug cartels, and killing of politicians, all of which impacts the economic and political climate of the country. In 2018, Mexicans elected a new leftist populist president, Andrés Manuel López Obrador, who has promised many reforms.

Mexico has a large media market, and Grupo Televisa in Mexico City is one of Mexico's largest media conglomerates. Televisa in Mexico is an interesting case as this conglomerate is the owner of Telemundo, which is carried only in the United States, the Telenovela channel, which is broadcast solely in the Philippines, TLN which broadcasts Portuguese programs in countries in Africa, Europe, and Brazil, and Canal des Estrellas, which is primarily available in

Europe and Oceania. Televisa also produces music and a number of print publications, and helps to import programming from the BBC (British Broadcasting Corporation).

Mexico, which does not have a free media system, is one of the most dangerous places in the world for journalists who are frequent targets for intimidation, physical violence, and killings when they cover organized crime or corruption (Reporters Without Borders 2018a). Reporters Without Borders ranks Mexico 147/180 countries in press freedom (Reporters Without Borders 2018a). Journalists also face possible fines and other penalties if they report on public officials in a manner that the official disagrees with. The government routinely impacts freedom of expression in both commercial and independent media organizations, and additionally uses bribery to influence content and economic stability through advertising (Freedom House 2017a). However, as previously mentioned, Mexico does have a number of media outlets, though many are facing reduction. Their internet is only partly free, yet internet access penetration has increased over the last few years to 53.7%, where the majority of usage is in urban areas (Internet World Stats 2017). While this has been a positive, the internet is also used as a surveillance tool against journalists (Freedom House 2017b). Chapters 8 and 9 discuss more about media in Mexico.

PIII.3   United States

The United States is the most populated country in the region with approximately 328 million inhabitants (US Census 2018). The United States population constitutes 76.6% whites, 18.1% Hispanic or Latino, 13.4% Backs or African-Americans, 5.8% Asians, 1.3% American Indian and Alaska Natives, and mixed and other races making up the rest of the population (US Census 2018). Nearly 70.6% of the US population identifies themselves as Christians (PEW Research 2018). Like many countries, the demographic of the United States has been changing because of both legal and illegal immigration particularly from Mexico and Central American countries. Immigration has become a very politically charged issue in the US in recent years, as it has been in Europe, where immigrants from worn torn countries of the Middle East and African countries as well as economic migrants from other parts of the world are seeking homes and refuge.

In terms of the economy, the United States has the largest economy in the world with a GDP of approximately 19.4 trillion USD and an annual growth rate of approximately 2.3% (World Bank 2017). In comparison, its neighbors, Canada and Mexico, have a smaller economy. Thus, the United States wields considerable economic power in the region.

The United States is federal republic where the President, Congress, and federal courts share powers. In 2016, Donald Trump was elected the US president amid a populist wave that swept many Western nations who elected nationalist leaders in many parts of the world. Trump's election domestically as well as globally has been marred by controversies; particularly noteworthy are his attacks on the press and his frequent use of the term "fake news" and the press as the "enemy of the American people" to discredit media – the latter was used by dictators such as Stalin and Hitler who also called the press the "enemies of the people" (Kalb 2018; Smith 2018). In spite of these attacks, media in the US remains robust. The First Amendment in the US Constitution guarantees freedom of speech and press. The United States, even though it has a free press, has been dropping on the World's Press Freedom Index, where it was ranked 45/180 in 2018 (Reporters Without Borders 2018a). This is partly due to increased government intervention, lack of sweeping protections for journalists – such as shield laws, and significant economic conglomeration. According to Freedom House (2017c), additional recent problems have begun to show with the new administration, including berating and harassment of journalists covering the president and the covering of protests. News media is also becoming increasingly polarized between the left and the right. Despite these negative measures, the economic environment for private media is strong and diverse and continues to be primarily funded through advertising. Professionalization is still valued, although the increase of online media platforms has introduced more opinion-based media. Internet penetration in the United States is 88%, but only 42% of web traffic is from mobile devices, which is low for such an economically developed country (Internet World Stats 2018b; Statista 2018c). However, internet freedom is among the highest in the world as the United States ranks fourth (Freedom House 2017d).

The United States has dominated the media industry. Google, Comcast, the Walt Disney Company, Newscorp/21st Century Fox, and Time Warner are among the top media companies that dominate the US and global media landscape. Currently, the United States accounts for a third of the global media and entertainment industry and is expected to bring in $771 billion by 2019 (Department of Commerce 2015). One of the most popular media exports from the United States is its Hollywood films. Hollywood does not produce the highest number of films, but its universal storylines, wide distribution, and marketing helps it earn the highest revenue. For example, Walt Disney's 2017 film *Star Wars: The Last Jedi* made $1.33 billion at the global box office, which included $700 million from overseas markets (Box Office Mojo 2018; Mendelson 2018). Chapter 10 examines the transnational Hollywood behemoth in more detail.

PIII.4   Jamaica

Jamaica is a constitutional monarchy and a parliamentary democracy. Its governance system is based on the British model. Jamaica gained its independence from the British in 1962 after a long period of colonial rule. Jamaica is one of 25 independent Caribbean countries with a population of approximately 2.9 million, and a GDP of 14 billion USD (World Bank 2017). A majority (90.9%) of Jamaicans are black, 1.3% are East Indian, 7.3% are of mixed ethnicities, and the rest are of other ethnicities (Oxford 2018). The majority of Jamaicans practice some form of Christianity.

Countries in the Caribbean have shown significant media growth in recent years. Today many, like Jamaica, have a well-developed print and broadcast media. Jamaica enjoys a vibrant free press. It is ranked 6/180 on the press freedom index (Reporters Without Borders 2018a), just below the Scandinavian countries which top the list for press freedom. Media in Jamaica grew primarily due to the deregulation and liberalization of state-owned media that paved way for the development of private media (Storr 2014). However, due to lack of media anti-trust laws, media in Jamaica are concentrated in just a few hands (Storr 2014). Internet penetration in Jamaica is 56%, which is just below the average for islands in the Caribbean (Internet World Stats 2018c). The internet has given rise to citizen journalists who gather and share information. This increase in citizen journalism and conglomeration has actually led to decreased professionalization as media outlets focus more on profit than expertise (Storr 2014). Furthermore, the regulatory structure that has been left from the British colonial rule has impacted libel and defamation laws and the ways in which journalists can criticize the government.

Jamaica is known to the world as the home of Bob Marley, a prominent Reggae musician. Bob Marley's music has traveled the world and inspired many within and outside the country to fight for peace and justice. In Chapter 11, the Reggae "Revolution" is covered in detail.

References

Box Office Mojo (2018). Yearly box office. Retrieved from: http://www.boxofficemojo.com/yearly/?view2=worldwide&view=releasedate&p=.htm.

Coehlo, J.T. (2 September 2013).Globo media organisation apologises for supporting Brazil's dictatorship. Retrieved from: www.independent.co.uk/news/world/americas/globo-media-organisation-apologises-for-supporting-brazil-s-dictatorship-8795277.html.

Freedom House (2017a). Freedom of the press. Retrieved from: https://freedomhouse.org/report/freedom-press/2017/mexico.

Freedom House (2017b). Freedom on the net. Retrieved from: https://freedomhouse.org/report/freedom-net/2016/mexico.

Freedom House (2017c). Freedom of the press. Retrieved from: https://freedomhouse.org/report/freedom-press/2017/united-states.

Freedom House (2017d). Freedom on the net. Retrieved from: https://freedomhouse.org/report/freedom-net/2016/united-states.

Internet World Stats (2017). Mexico and Central America. Retrieved from: http://www.internetworldstats.com/central.htm#mx.

Internet World Stats (2018a). Brazil. Retrieved from: https://www.internetworldstats.com/south.htm.

Internet World Stats (2018b). United States. Retrieved from: https://www.internetworldstats.com/america.htm#us.

Internet World Stats (2018c). Jamaica. Retrieved from: https://www.internetworldstats.com/carib.htm#jm.

Kalb, M. (2018). Enemy of the People: Trump's War on the Press. Retrieved from: https://www.brookings.edu/book/enemy-of-the-people.

Mendelson, S. (28 January 2018). Box Office: Why 'Star Wars: The Last Jedi' Is Still A Big Win for Disney. *Forbes*. Retrieved from: https://www.forbes.com/sites/scottmendelson/2018/01/28/why-star-wars-the-last-jedi-with-just-1-3b-worldwide-is-still-a-win-for-disney/#41fd0f8ef2d3.

Oxford (2018). Jamaica. Retrieved from: http://www.oxfordaasc.com/public/samples/sample_country.jsp.

PEW Research (2018). Religious landscape study. Retrieved from: http://www.pewforum.org/religious-landscape-study.

Phillips, T. (2011). Brazil census shows African-Brazilians in the majority for the first time. Retrieved from: https://www.theguardian.com/world/2011/nov/17/brazil-census-african-brazilians-majority.

Podesta, D. (2016). Media in Latin America. *Center for International Media Assistance*. Retrieved from: http://www.cima.ned.org/wp-content/uploads/2016/01/CIMA-Media-in-Latin-America_the-Path-Forward.pdf.

Reporters Without Borders (2016). World press freedom ranking. Retrieved from: https://rsf.org/en/ranking.

Reporters Without Borders (2018a). More insecure than ever: Retrieved from: https://rsf.org/en/brazil.

Reporters Without Borders (RSF). (2018b). Press Freedom. Retrieved from: https://rsf.org/en/ranking.

Smith, D. (17 January 2018). Republican senator Jeff Flake: Trump's attacks on media reminiscent of Stalin. *The Guardian* Retrieved from: https://www.theguardian.com/us-news/2018/jan/17/jeff-flake-donald-trump-fake-news-stalin-senate-speech.

Statista (2012). Mexico: Proportion of ethnic groups as of 2012. Retrieved from: https://www.statista.com/statistics/275439/ethnic-groups-in-mexico.

Statista (2018a). Media in Brazil - Statistics & Facts. Retrieved from: https://www.statista.com/topics/3962/media-in-brazil.

Statista (2018c). Percentage of mobile website traffic in the United States from 1st quarter 2015 to 2nd quarter 2018. Retrieved from: https://www.statista.com/statistics/683082/share-of-website-traffic-coming-from-mobile-devices-usa.

Storr, J. (2014). Caribbean journalism's media economy: advancing democracy and the common good? *The International Communication Gazette* 76 (2): 177–196.

United States Department of Commerce (2015). 2016 Top markets report: Media and Entertainment. http://Trade.gov. Retrieved from: https://www.trade.gov/topmarkets/pdf/Media_and_Entertainment_Executive_Summary.pdf.

US Census (2018). Population. Retrieved from: https://www.census.gov/topics/population.html.

World Bank (2017). GDP current US $. *WorldBank*. Retrieved from: https://data.worldbank.org/indicator/NY.GDP.MKTP.CD.

World Bank (2018). Population total. Retrieved from: https://data.worldbank.org/indicator/SP.POP.TOTL.

8

What Do They Know of Telenovela Who Only Telenovela Know?

Melodrama, Passion, and Latin America's Modern Identity

O. Hugo Benavides

The title of this chapter purposely paraphrases Rudyard Kipling's original question relating power and cricket. I do so to underline the powerful cultural and political elements that are intertwined with, and inherent in, the melodramatic production of telenovelas in Latin America (Benavides 2008). Despite the fact that telenovelas have had such a massive audience, not only in Latin America but all over the world, academics and scholars in general have been slow to assess the enormous cultural potential expressed in them. What, without a doubt, was an original Latin American cultural artifact, is now a pervasive product in the global media market (García Canclini 1999). Latin American telenovelas are no longer the only ones privy to global consumption; other national productions, such as South Korean, Nigerian, and Turkish productions come to mind. Quite justly, it is many of these foreign telenovelas that are now the rage throughout the Americas.

Of course, this melodramatic phenomenon begs several questions, not the least of which is why intellectuals have been so slow, almost unwilling, to recognize telenovelas' broad cultural impact. The flipside of that question is to also wonder why national audiences have, from Mexico to Argentina, engaged so powerfully with telenovelas from the very beginning. Perhaps this is what media scholar, Jesús Martín-Barbero (1993), most succinctly assesses in his paradigmatic text, *Communication, Culture and Hegemony: From the Media to Mediations.*

For Martín-Barbero (1993), melodrama in general and telenovelas in particular came to express a kind of media revolution. They express a kind of revenge on the senses that the popular classes have exercised upon the rich and powerful throughout Latin America. Latin America, as part of its colonial and neo-colonial legacies, inherited an oppressive social structure that allowed an elite and ideologically white (either European or North American inspired) minority to claim control over the political and intellectual establishment of its national government and educational systems. It was only in the arts, whether this be literature, painting, music, film, etc., where one could see a greater opening and a critical questioning of this colonial historical legacy.

8.1 Melodramatic Representation

Melodramatic productions such as telenovelas, but also narco-dramas, were quick to celebrate the everyday lives and situations of the local populace and to elevate their national drama (Stavans 2010). In a way, they allow common people to see themselves reflected on the screen and express that their emotions, lives, and conflicts are socially valid and of national importance.

Transnational Media: Concepts and Cases, First Edition. Edited by Suman Mishra and Rebecca Kern-Stone.
© 2019 John Wiley & Sons, Inc. Published 2019 by John Wiley & Sons, Inc.

Of course, this has made telenovelas very popular, to the extent of to work schedules being shifted in order to make sure people wouldn't miss episodes, and ultimately affecting whole cities that seemed to stop when the last episodes of certain telenovelas were aired. In Latin America, only the World Cup (which occurs every four years) has a similar popular impact. And one could argue that the World Cup is the more patriarchal and masculine globalized melodramatic brethren of telenovelas.

Telenovelas also allowed the poor to take center stage in the drama. It did not matter how fantastical or stereotypical their representations were, working-class contributions and feelings were taken into account for the stories' denouement. This new melodramatic reality, which most importantly was always also about big business and commercial consumption, also incorporated two essential characteristics from the films of Mexico's Golden Age (1940–1970).

Key in this transition from film to televised melodrama was the central role that emotions and feelings would almost exclusively take. No longer was high drama defined by European notions of rational civilizing behavior and reified intellectual plot lines, but rather by the raw emotional reactions to life's injustices, of which there were many. Rather than seeing emotional reaction as a backward reaction to modernity, emotions were used as the cue to signal plot movements (always highlighted by musical undertones) and express the complexity of the human heart.

One could argue that after centuries of rational oppression from the West, Latin American melodrama, initially through Mexican (and Argentinian) films but more robustly through telenovelas, highlighted the counterpart role that feelings play in the Latin American social landscape. And it was the radio-novelas that most probably enabled this bold move. It was these radio melodramas that initially enthralled national audiences, allowing media television companies in the 1950s to start investing on televised melodrama.

This is most succinctly captured by Martín-Barbero's (1993) anecdote of laughing at one of these stereotypical melodramatic productions, only to have an older gentleman, who had been crying throughout, tell him that he should have more respect for his feelings. It was this moment that in a way, for Martín-Barbero (1993), crystallized the enormous social power that emotions have. It also enables us to assess how emotions are fiercely policed and checked by neo-colonial forms of political and cultural governance.

8.2 Stock Characters or Stereotypical Representations

However, melodramas did not (and still do not) explicitly acknowledge this paradigmatic shift. Because it is precisely their use of stereotypical representations that allows for an even more complex form of cultural (which in a neo-liberal context is always also commercial) consumption. The use of stereotypical archetypes of good versus bad, ugly versus beautiful, etc., allows a simplistic reading of what everybody knows – particularly the viewers – are more complex social situations. However, the stereotypical representations allow for several things to occur at the same time.

In this succinct economic representation, for example, you are able to highlight the most important characteristics implicated in many thorny social situations. Of course, one never, or at least very rarely, finds exclusively evil or good people, but highlighting these characteristics isolates what in many ways might be the most important quality that ultimately drives the situation. At the same time, it is this stereotypical recourse that allows telenovelas to escape national and international censors. Because who could take these melodramas seriously when they are representing such stereotypical portrayals of reality? And yet, it is telenovelas that have gained access to a multimillion-dollar market and put minority characters (Afro-Latin women, homosexuals, etc.) and sensitive social situations (i.e. single mothers, incest, etc.) on the national television screens.

One of the main arguments against telenovelas is precisely this supposedly simplistic stereotypical portrayal of social reality. However, this initial shortcoming, not surprisingly, is more complex than would be originally assumed. The stereotypical portrayals are imbued with desirous elements of love and transgression, both in the personal and social arenas, that are also a central tenet in the civilizing discourse regulating Latin America since colonial times.

The stereotypes at first would seem to be missing the point, but at a second glance the enormous popularity of telenovelas along transnational lines as well as class ones belies a different understanding. Clearly, these over-the-top characters are hitting a particular truth point, even if it is one of fantasy and escape. It allows the viewer to enjoy a reality that they know not to be theirs, and yet allows for varied forms of representation and different solution to the daily malaise of one's life.

However, fantasy and escape work to a point, and telenovelas such as *Maria de nadie, Dos mujeres un camino, Los ricos también lloran, Doña Beija, Xica, Pasión de gavilanes*, etc., allow audiences to also self-identify with the melodramatic reality. It is this self-identification that provides a more effective form of viewing and commodification. After all, it might be the rags to riches story, or the succeeding under terrible odds plot line, that is attractive, but it is ultimately knowing that this does not happen in real life that allows for the pleasurable consumption.

8.3 Imagined Realities

Instead of denying or distorting reality, telenovelas have reminded Latin American viewers for several decades now that their reality is complex and full of hardships, precisely because it is so different from what is presented to them on the melodramatic screen. As the Italian director Michelangelo Antonioni commented when asked on his first visit to the United States if he knew the country, he said he did; after all, it would be nothing like the Hollywood films produced and consumed.

Telenovelas, like Hollywood, Bollywood, and all other successful media productions, are in the business of representing social reality in a meaningful and commercially viable way. And telenovelas do this quite successfully by reminding viewers not only of what could be, but, most importantly, what their lives are not and never will be like.

So, unlike the myriad of cultural critics that have described telenovela audiences as incompetent or stupid, it might be the exact opposite. The viewers are the savvy ones who know that social reality is a game of attrition and struggle, and that without unethical odds there really is no chance of winning one's hand. Rather than believing patronizing stories of violent revolutions and heroic social transformations it is much better to take in sobering stories about one's limited social (and personal) reality (Guillermoprieto 2001). These stories do the exact opposite to what one would think: provide personal solace and give social meaning to one's daily struggle.

It is also important to recognize that telenovelas are always about big business and making a profit. Telenovelas like *Xica* in Brazil and *Yo soy Betty, la fea* in Colombia allowed two giant media conglomerates, Rede Machete (not Rede TV) and RCN (Radio Cadena Nacional), respectively, to survive hard times and become major national and transnational media corporations. How both companies accomplished this is quite telling since neither telenovela was initially or strategically situated to be a major commercial success.

Yo soy Betty, la fea was such a surprise hit that the plotline had to be continuously extended, both making a profit and satisfying a growing audience that demanded more of this cultural product. Likewise, a telenovela dealing with slavery – set within the seventeenth-century plantation period of Mina Gerais in Brazil and making an Afro-Brazilian woman the main character of the film – *Xica* seemed more likely to challenge and upset the racist and racialized discourses of the nation, rather than provide easy profit-making escapist reality.

Therefore, telenovelas provide a particular entry into understanding not only the manner in which capital and colonial resource extraction continues to work in the globalized world, but also how culture is an essential element of commodification. In a Western world, inheritors of slavery and market values, the price of the body and its representation is far from a historical or past matter. Rather, the commodification of the human body, particularly that of the native one, is still at the center of not only capitalist production but also very much cultural reproduction in general.

Who we are? Who do we want to be? And how we get to be those things? are all central questions that are embedded within larger constraints of unequal access to resources, particularly the most fundamental one of all: desire. As Jacques Lacan (1971) pointed out several decades ago, the role of desire is to keep desiring, and telenovelas do that incredibly well. Telenovelas allow us to keep desiring, making us more aware of what we desire, almost unapologetically so, but also in a way that reminds us of culturally viable ways of being who we always wanted (and in a way continue) to be.

8.4   Mexican Telenovela Production

It is this kind of desirous business in which passions, sexual and otherwise, take center stage. It is what has allowed Mexican transnational corporations such as Televisa and Azteca TV to become large media monopolies – although that begs the question of whether they are the enforcers or the servants of the national discourses produced on a whole by the Mexican nation. It would be in the late 1960s and early 1970s that the big Mexican telenovela production company, Televisa, came into greater control of the production and distribution of telenovelas.

For many, the development of this media conglomerate marked the transition into a media-controlled political hegemony for Mexico; one where media control and popular culture went hand in hand in terms of refueling (and limiting) Mexico's political imagination. It is not a farfetched hypothesis to suggest that telenovelas very much contributed to the financial success of the large Mexican media conglomerates and furthered legitimized the one-party rule of the PRI (Partido Revolucionario Institucional) until 2000.

It was Telesistema Mexicano that produced the first telenovelas in 1958 – including *Sendas prohibidas*, *Gutierritos* (which would be redone in 1966), and *Más allá de la angustia*. And it also would be the new conglomerate of Televisa (which Telesistema Mexicano would merge with) that would produce most of the iconic telenovelas that would not only achieve national recognition but would also greatly influence the telenovelas market in other Latin American countries, like Venezuela, Argentina, and Brazil. It would not be until 1993 that another multimedia conglomerate, Azteca TV, owned by Grupo Salinas, would provide some competition. Only in 2016 does a third media company enter into the competitive foray with the name of Imagen Televisión.

For many, telenovelas are partly to be blamed for the cultural apathy within Mexican society; while others would argue the contrary that it was precisely in these repressed melodramatic expressions that deep-seated feelings of resentment and lack of agency had an actual outlet and were successfully expressed in a daily fashion. Either way, telenovelas have become the staple of Mexican television and in so doing have very much revolutionized the life of the three biggest multimedia conglomerates of the country: Telesistema Mexicano, Televisa, and TV Azteca. The issues raised and represented within telenovelas hit a core of Mexican identity and continue to be a vehicle for many of the nation's population, especially for those with less access to political power and intellectual elite resources.

8.5   Conclusion: Transgressive Desire

This commercial transgressive desire as a motor for self-fulfillment also manages to critique a pervasive market economy that entitles the privileged, exposing both the hollowness of elite behavior but also reinforcing the revenge of the common folks. The poor may be desirous of the rich other, but similarly the rich cannot be complete without the poor. This is a reformulation of the logic of capital in an extremely succinct and modern (even postmodern) fashion.

There is no doubt that desire is exactly what telenovelas do best. They provide an endless mirror image to reflect our endless selves as they are redefined by a new form of capital that no longer destroys difference but rather looks to engage and be fulfilled by it (Hall 1997). It is in this reformulation of exotic identities that Latin American telenovelas are able to most successfully survive and thrive.

Again, what makes the telenovela seductive for global audiences is that we know that this is not par for the course. On the contrary, our daily lives and our global existence shows us that the good guys seldom, if ever, win. Rather, those that are deemed underdeveloped (or from the Global South) seldom get a chance to show themselves to be otherwise. The telenovela inverts our represented reality and cohesively presents a visual image primed for global consumption. In this melodramatic representation the truly good and beautiful are not only recognized but actually beat the superficial monsters of the market at their own corrupt game.

Of course, the viewers know that is only a telenovela and not reality, not even reality television. Yet, the hope is still so pervasive and powerful. What is being sold, in a way, is another particular market dream, one encased in a particular Latin American guise. Our hope for authenticity and emotional truth is so powerful that it is actually commodified, sold, and exported to the world in melodramatic form.

This globalization of melodramatic images then becomes a powerful moment which we currently inhabit. The fact is that our hopes for equality, democracy, and fair play have been so enormously betrayed that even this hope becomes a vehicle of commodification and submitted to the value of the marketplace – particularly in a world that is still so heavily invested in forms of modern capital that must incorporate, reproduce, and engage difference rather than deny or simply repress it as in colonial times. The key is that today developed countries exploit in a more democratic manner, recognizing and celebrating difference instead of simply trying to destroy and repress it (Hall 1997). Ultimately, telenovelas allow people the world over to ponder, even unconsciously, their complicity in a global market that exploits the majority of the world, ourselves included.

References

Benavides, O.H. (2008). *Drugs, Thugs, and Divas: Telenovelas and Narco-Dramas in Latin America*. Austin, TX: University of Texas Press.
García Canclini, N. (1999). *La Globalización Imaginada*. Buenos Aires: Editorial Paidós.

Guillermoprieto, A. (2001). *Looking for History*. New York: Vintage Books.

Hall, S. (1997). The local and the global: globalization and ethnicity. In: *Culture, Globalization and the World-System: Contemporary Conditions for the Representation of Identity* (ed. A.D. King), 19–39. Minneapolis: University of Minnesota Press.

Lacan, J. (1971). *Ecrits; A Selection*. New York: W.W. Norton & Company.

Martín-Barbero, J. (1993). *Communication Culture and Hegemony: From the Media to Mediations*. New York City: Sage Publications.

Stavans, I. (ed.) (2010). *Telenovelas (Ilan Stavans Library of Latino Civilization)*. Santa Barbara: Greenwood.

9

Latin America: From Media Censorship to Media Ownership

New Forms of Communication Hegemony Across the Continent

Fernando Gutiérrez and Alejandro Ocampo

Media's impact has been decisive for the development of many societies, and Latin America is no exception. The main features that characterize Latin American media are the concentration of media property in the hands of a few, the privatization of public broadcasting, and the deregulation of the whole industry.

This chapter will generally review the situation of media in Mexico, Central America, and South America in the first two decades of the twenty-first century. Specifically, the symbiotic relationship between media and the government will be analyzed, highlighting some prominent cases, and the main problems and challenges that the region has in this area. As the Mexican media analyst Raúl Trejo Delarbre (2011, p. 56) says "We have no news of any developed or developing country, where the political function of media is not being discussed."

9.1 Mexico, the Perfect Dictatorship? An Incestuous Relationship Between Politics and Media

In 2014, the Mexican director and producer Luis Estrada premiered the movie *The Perfect Dictatorship* – a critical film in the form of a political satire about the Mexican government of President Enrique Peña Nieto and the role of commercial media. This work exposed specifically the morbid relationship that the filmmaker perceives between the political class (governors, senators, deputies ...) and Mexican television. It follows the thematic line that Estrada has used in other films such as *Herod's Law*, *A Wonderful World*, and *Hell*. A line that could very well describe the appreciation of many Mexicans of the history of their environment, and of media, at the end of the twentieth century and the beginning of the twenty-first century.

In September of 1990, the Peruvian writer and Nobel laureate, Mario Vargas Llosa, made the analogy between the experience of the Latin American dictatorships and the political hegemony of the PRI, the largest political party in Mexico – which he called the perfect dictatorship. This dictatorship used the power and domination of media to ensure the continuity of a single political party (Vargas Llosa 1990 writing in *El País*).

The control and sway of media that began at the time of the Mexican Revolution still continued in the last decade of the twentieth century. As Oscar Müller (2015) points out, political power tends toward the control of media. In a totalitarian country, this is achieved through prior censorship, which the state carries out before the publication of information; but in countries where there is relative media freedom, the public power will look for other means, such as official advertising, to control the information that is transmitted to the community. Such is the

Transnational Media: Concepts and Cases, First Edition. Edited by Suman Mishra and Rebecca Kern-Stone.
© 2019 John Wiley & Sons, Inc. Published 2019 by John Wiley & Sons, Inc.

case of Mexico, where the state is one of the main consumers of media publicity, and the state can become selective in the acquisition of advertising spaces through a marked preference to those media that cause it the least discomfort.

During the government of President Ernesto Zedillo (1994–2000), media structure in Mexico continued to be highly concentrated and centralized. In the mid 1990s, when the internet became an alternative form of communication, many organizations took advantage of it – as was the case with the Zapatista Army of National Liberation (EZLN). However, Televisa, one of the only two commercial television stations in the country at that time, controlled between 85 and 90% of the market. As Enrique Krauze suggests, the control wielded by the PRI governments upon media during the twentieth century was almost absolute, and this was crucial for that party's 70-year tenure in power (Krauze 2016). The relationship between Televisa and the PRI was always close. Mexicans do not forget that in 1990, Emilio Azcárraga Milmo, CEO of the firm, defined himself as "a soldier of the PRI" (Villamil 2002).

By the beginning of the new millennium, there were two famous phrases in Mexico in the political scene: "I do not pay to be hit" by José López Portillo and "I do not read because they hit me" by Vicente Fox. The first sentence is attributed to the former president of Mexico, José López Portillo, and allegedly derives from the constant accusations of corruption in the government, which were published in the weekly magazine *Proceso* directed by the journalist Julio Scherer García. According to this magazine, in April 1982, the head of the General Coordination of Social Communication of the Presidency, Francisco Galindo Ochoa, gave the order to cancel all advertising contracts with *Proceso*. Federal government agencies, state governments, and the PRI had to withdraw their advertising investments, but only with this magazine (*Proceso* 2004). The aforementioned statement was a retaliation for the critical line that Julio Scherer García stated in the periodical publication.

The second sentence, "I do not read because they hit me," was highlighted by Jenaro Villamil (2002), paraphrasing José López Portillo, because the anti-politics of the social communication manifested during the Fox era had been expensive to the president in the field of popularity. President Vicente Fox made an unfortunate mistake when he acknowledged that he did not read the newspapers anymore because he felt that they did not reflect the truths and realities that he perceived. Perhaps for that reason, Fox's government operated politically against the journalist José Gutiérrez Vivó, whom he considered close to Andrés Manuel López Obrador. Finally, in March 2004 and with the support of the Aguirre family (owners of Radio Centro Group), the "government of change" achieved the departure of the journalist who, by that time, had one of the largest audiences on the radio. Gutiérrez Vivó was one of the most influential journalists in the history of radio in Mexico, but just as it was with Pedro Ferriz de Con and Carmen Aristegui, he was removed from the microphone due to his informative work that was uncomfortable for those who exercised power. For Gabriel Sosa Plata (2017), it was incredible that none of these three journalists operated in any of the 1700 radio stations in the country, but this is explained due to the great concentration that prevails in the industry as well as to the political and economic interests that still strongly influence it. Today, just 11 families control the news that most Mexicans receive (Tourliere 2018).

During the administration of President Felipe Calderón, who succeeded Vicente Fox, the relationship with media changed dramatically due to the increase in violence of organized crime that left 50 000 dead (Univisión 2012). Calderón declared war on drug trafficking and launched a military offensive against the organized crime cartels on 11 December 2006 – 10 days after he assumed the presidency. For the National Front of Journalists for the Freedom of Expression, Calderón's administration was the worst in the history of the Mexican press because it cost the lives of 48 journalists. The censorship and self-censorship were the most severe threats to the freedom of expression during the Calderonist period (*Animal Político* 2011). The press were forced into silence after the murder of journalists by Cartels.

However, on 1 July 2012, what some thought impossible happened: the PRI returned to the government of Mexico. Enrique Peña Nieto, former governor of the State of Mexico, won the federal elections with a significant margin, and although he offered assurances that there would be no return to the past, the communication arena of the new government continued with the policy of high advertising expenditure that was exercised previously. From 2012 to 2016, the publicity expenditure of Peña Nieto's new government was 38 billion pesos (Castaño 2017). The national newspapers, such as *Excélsior, La Jornada, Milenio, El Universal, Reforma / El Norte, El Financiero, La Crónica, El Economista, Notimusa,* and *Capital News,* received 88% of the official budget allocated to newspapers. On the other hand, Televisa, Azteca, Excélsior, and Imagen Television took the entire official budget allocated to broadcast television. Additionally, censorship and self-censorship continued during Peña Nieto's administration, as the government demonstrated with the untimely rescission of the journalist Carmen Aristegui's contract. This operation was carried out as retaliation for the investigation and dissemination of the case of the luxurious "white house" acquired by the wife of the president from a government contractor (*Animal Político* 2017). According to Article 19 (2017), in Mexico there is a perverse relationship between information and public money that enters media and causes society to receive biased information.

9.2 Chaos and Control in Central America

For Andrea Cristancho (2014), the political and legal framework that dominates in Central America is favorable to the large commercial media oligopolies. This has led to strong and constant pressure from the market against the free exercise of journalism, favoring censorship and self-censorship due to the lack of legal protection for reporters of the region and due to the organized crime that plagues media. In addition, as in the case of Mexico, there is no secondary regulation that controls official advertising. Governments use discretion in the delivery of official budgets for the media, and if the government does not like the editorial line of the media, it can simply withdraw advertising (and therefore revenue).

In Nicaragua, for example, the family of President Daniel Ortega, in office for the fifth time, controls the country's media. The main broadcast television channels are directed by Tino and Daniel Edmundo Ortega Murillo (channel 4), Juan Carlos Ortega Murillo (channel 8), and Camila, Luciana, and Maurice Ortega Murillo (channel 13). The Mexican Ángel González owns the other channels (2, 9, 10, and 11). For the journalist Josué Bravo (2015), in Nicaragua, the second poorest country in the continent after Haiti, there are only three major media with independence: the newspaper *La Prensa,* Radio Corporación, and Channel 12.

In Honduras, there is great media coverage that constantly strives to reach a good percentage of the audience in order to secure the official budget to strengthen its business model. According to the National Telecommunications Commission in Honduras, there are 657 operators of broadcasting services (CONATEL 2017). However, the control exercised by the government, headed by Juan Orlando Hernández Alvarado, is notorious, through instruments such as the law of the voluntary program of rescue, promotion, and development of the communications sector. This law allows protected contracts with the presidency of the republic and with the institutions that the presidency designates beneficiaries of publicity in exchange for any financial obligation that the companies operating media may have with the state, with no limit.

A few families of the economic elite, close to the ruling power and with a strictly commercial vision, have traditionally owned the media in Panama and Costa Rica. For this reason, the representation of the multiplicity of opinions and interests that exist in the societies of these two countries is almost nil. In this case there is no public intervention in the production and distribution of content, nor an effective regulatory function of the state that ensures a balance of voices (Luna 2014).

In general, for the Central American countries, the dynamics of the press oscillate between prior censorship and working at their own risk. In Guatemala, for example, "even the coverage of beauty contests or of football issues has become risky for journalists," says Claudia Samayoa, director of the Unit for the Protection of Human Rights Defenders of Guatemala (cited in Nájera 2013). The cartels have sought to control the various media in the region, exerting strong pressure through threats against journalists and editorial directors.

In summary, the advances in the area of freedom of expression in the region are embryonic, and for this reason it is necessary to implement clear policies that facilitate conditions in which the media can develop.

9.3   An Overview of Some Media Systems in South America

The South American countries have formed large multimedia groups that, as in other regions, control both the production and distribution of content. Given this scenario, some governments have entered into the competition for information by putting up television channels and radio stations financed with public money and with a specific orientation. Such is the case of teleSUR, a television station founded in 2005 by the governments of Venezuela, Cuba, Ecuador, Bolivia, Nicaragua, and Uruguay, whose mission seeks to promote Simon Bolivar's antique idea of uniting all of Latin America as one powerful country, as well as building a new communication order (teleSUR 2017). Initiated by the Venezuelan government of Hugo Chávez, teleSUR can be seen openly in the partner countries of the system, as well as in a large number of South American countries and some European through the pay television systems (cable and satellite).

It is worth noting that although South American policy has been extremely restrictive regarding foreign investment in communication and telecommunications media, the Spanish group PRISA has managed to get radio stations in Argentina (Radio Continental and Los 40), Chile (Iberoamericana Radio Chile), and Colombia (Radio Caracol), (PRISA 2017). In countries such as Ecuador (Los 40) and Paraguay (Los 40), where legislation prevents it from becoming a shareholder due to its foreign status, the PRISA Group has a presence through the production and distribution of content through agreements with local partners.

Although each country has its own internal structure, the large media groups in South America are characterized by being unipersonal or family businesses. In Colombia, for example, there are 10 media families that control the majority of the television channels, radio, press, magazines, and digital media. The four largest of these groups have business interests in other types of companies, which allows the media themselves to become a kind of spokesperson for the activities of these groups in other areas (Reporteros sin fronteras and FECOLPER 2015). For detailed information about this in other countries, see Table 9.1.

In the case of Ecuador, although at the beginning of the twenty-first century there were 11 fully identified groups, media share has been decentralized due to the left-oriented legislation promoted by President Rafael Correa (2007–2017). Due to the fact that more than 90% of media ownership was in private hands, and that media consolidation might restrict or manipulate news coverage, the Ecuadorian government in 2007 founded a national television and a radio network, a print media, and a news agency. Some other Latin American governments have initiated very similar policies, arguing for the necessity of stopping the tremendous power accruing to media tycoons.

Table 9.1 Media concentration in Latin America.

Countries	Media Concentration
Argentina	Héctor Magnetto, Jorge Rendo, José Aranda, Lucio Rafael Pagliaro (Clarin) Luis María Casero, Daniel Vila, José Luis Manzano (America Group)
Belize	Evan X Hyde (Kremandala Group)
Bolivia	Episcopal Conference Daher Family, Rivero Family (Lider Group) Monasterio Family (Unitel) Kuljis Family (Red Uno)
Brazil	Marihno Family (The Globo Group /Organizações Globo) Silivio Santos (Brazilian System of Television / Sistema Brasileiro de Televisão) Victor Civita (Abril) Joao Jorge Saad (Bandeirantes) Octavio Frías de Oliveira (Folha Group)
Chile	Edwards Family (Edwards Group) Álvaro Saieh (COPESA)
Colombia	Julio Mario Santo Domingo (Santo Domingo Group) Luis Carlos Sarmiento Angulo (*El Tiempo* & CEETTV) Carlos Ardila Lülle (Ardila Lülle Organisation)
Costa Rica	Alfredo Echandi Jiménez (Nación Group) Remigio Ángel González (Albavisión: Repretel Group) René Picado and Olga Cozza (Picado-Cozza Group)
Ecuador	Pérez Barriga Family (El Universo Group) Fidel Egas Grijalva (Teleamazonas) Alvarado Roca Family (Alvarado Roca Group) Remigio Ángel González (Albavisión: RTS)
El Salvador	Boris Eserski (Telecorporación Salvadoreña TCS) Elias Antonio Saca (SAMIX Group) José Luis Saca Meléndez (Corporación FM) Flores Barrera Family (Corporación Radio Estérero) Monterrosa Family (Corporación KL)
Guatemala	Remigio Ángel González (Albavisión: Radio and Televisión of Guatemala) Edgar Archila Marroquín (Emisoras Unidas Group) Minerva Solís de Alcázar (Radio Corporación Nacional)
Honduras	Ferrari-Villeda Family (Televicentro) Rosenthal Oliva Family (*Tiempo*) Andonie Family (Radio América) Flores Facussé Family (Diario *Tribuna*) Canahuati-Larach Family (OPSA)
Mexico	Azcárraga Family (Televisa) Salinas Family (Salinas Group / TV Azteca)
Nicaragua	Ortega-Murillo Family (Channel 4, 8, 13) Remigio Ángel González (Albavisión: Channel 2, 9, 10 and 11)
Panama	González Revilla (Medcom) Alberto Eskenazi and Henry Mizrachi (EPASA) Diego Quijano (Corprensa: *La Prensa*)

(*Continued*)

Table 9.1 (Continued)

Countries	Media Concentration
Paraguay	Antonio Vierci (Vierci Group)
	Remigio Ángel González (Albavisión: Channel 5, 9, 10 and 12)
	Cristian Chena (Chena Group)
	Aldo Zucolillo (Zucolillo Group)
	Sarah Cartes (Nación de Comunicaciones Group)
Peru	Gustavo Mohme Seminario (La República)
	Manuel Delgado Parker (RPP)
	Miro Quesada-Garcia Miro (El Comercio)
Uruguay	Hugo Romay Salvo (Romay)
	Fontaina and De Feo Families (Fontaina-De Feo)
	Luis Eduardo Cardoso and Daniel Scheck Families (Cardoso-Pombo-Scjeck)
Venezuela	Cisneros Family (Cisneros Group)

Note: Data about media concentration in Latin America from Apertura (2015), from Bravo (2015), from IFJ (2016), from Luna (2014), Reporteros sin fronteras & FECOLPER (2015), and from Santos (2014).

Bolivia deserves special attention for two reasons: the first is its topography, which makes it a country with deeply isolated regions and difficult access, and the other is that it is the least developed country in Latin America. Both have contributed to the fact that until the end of the 1980s, the only national media group was the Catholic Church. Today, the Catholic Church continues to be the largest group controlling Bolivian media, but the openness to foreign investment and multi-ownership has had an impact on the formation of other groups.

Argentina also requires a more in-depth review, since the relationship between media and government has always been extremely tense. The Clarín Group is the largest media group. Its business interests range from newspapers and periodical publications, publishing houses, television channels, radio stations, and pay television providers nationwide. Founded in 1945 by Roberto Noble, whose family still owns most of the shares, the Clarín Group is also a 49% shareholder of the Papel Prensa SA, the only company producing newspapers in Argentina since 1971, which reveals the tense relationship between the media and the government. The Clarín Group has also been able to exercise control over the sale of papers to the rest of media and its competition (Apertura 2015; Clarín Group 2017).

Due to its size, language, and culture, Brazil's unique circumstances make it more like an entirely different continent, not just a different country. It is the fifth largest country in the world of 8.5 million square kilometers; as well as the sixth most populated with 212 million inhabitants; for these reasons the Brazilian market is extremely important for any industry. Due to the size of the territory, in Brazil the local media are very strong in terms of audience and coverage, such that several groups do not have national broadcasts, just regional ones (Santos 2014). However, there are two important national groups: the Globo Group (Organizações Globo) leading the media conglomerates, whose networks include broadcast, pay television, radio stations, print media, music and film production companies, as well as digital platforms and also banks and other companies in various sectors. Another important group is the Brazilian Television System (Sistema Brasileiro de Televisão), whose business interests are essentially in the production and distribution of television content.

We close this brief review with Venezuela, which at present is going through a complicated situation in terms of serious social, political, and economic issues, from which the media is not immune. The hegemonic group in the Venezuelan industry is the Cisneros Organization, founded in 1929 in Caracas by Diego Cisneros, who in 1961 officially commenced his story in media by buying the bankrupt Televisa channel. Currently, the Cisneros Group owns the largest television network in Venezuela (Venevisión), as well as pay television channels, music, and television production companies. The Cisneros Group also has business interests in media companies outside Venezuela (it is a shareholder of Univisión in the United States, as well as of other media in some other South American countries). Venezuela's government also operates the VTV channels, the ViVe Television (founded by Hugo Chávez), as well as the National Radio of Venezuela. Finally, it is necessary to mention 1 BC Enterprises, a company founded in 1920 by William Phelps, who in 1953 also started the station Radio Caracas Television (RCTV). However, in 2006 Hugo Chávez's government decided not to renew the concession to RCTV, thus causing its exit from the airwaves and initiating the seizure of its facilities by the National Communications Commission (Chirinos 2007).

Even though every South American constitution guarantees freedom of the press, the governments do regulate some media activities to control impact on culture. Critics constantly point to these regulations as the origin of pressure to keep them aligned with the official discourse. In certain periods, some media have benefited from their relations with the government, while in others they have been harmed to the point of even disappearing.

9.4 Conclusions

Even though all the Latin American nations were inspired by democratic ideals for the constitution of their countries, no Spanish or Portuguese-speaking country in the region has enjoyed democratic normality through the twentieth century, at least not nearly to the extent that its North American neighbors have. In the last 50 years, the South American region has been in constant oscillation between authoritarian nationalist governments – in many cases emanating from coups d'etat – both right-wing and left-wing, and liberal governments whose policies could be considered neo-liberal.

However, something that all countries have shared is the vision of media as the great strategic asset for the maintenance of power and the established order. The ideological orientation of the official authorities and distrust have been common problems in the relationship between media and government Additionally, the fact that the form of government of all countries – when there has been no dictatorship – has been the Presidential Republic has allowed the exercise of power to fall on a single person without equally strong institutional counterweights.

Advances in the freedom of the press and expression are still embryonic in these countries. It is necessary to improve the conditions in which the communication takes place in the region, which in turn makes it necessary to change and adjust the legal frameworks in force and the specific regulations that govern the role of media in each country. It is also necessary to end the serious problem of media concentration as it contributes to unwelcome scenarios that facilitate censorship, self-censorship, and interferes with the free dissemination of ideas; and a proliferation of media that serve and represent only the interests of the political or economic elites.

References

Animal Político (2011). *Calderon's six-year period, the worst for the Mexican press: Journalists.* Retrieved from: http://www.animalpolitico.com/2011/05/sexenio-de-calderon-el-peor-para-la-prensa-mexicana-periodistas.

Animal Político (2017). *Carmen Aristegui's air outing was illegal, declares judge; MVS will not pay compensation.* Retrieved from: http://www.animalpolitico.com/2017/07/salida-del-aire-carmen-aristegui-fue-ilegal-declara-juez-mvs-no-pagara-indemnizacion.

Apertura (2015). *Map of media 2015: who are media in Argentina?* Retrieved from: http://www.apertura.com/negocios/Mapa-de-medios-2015-quienes-son-los-duenos-de-la-comunicacion-en-la-Argentina-20150713-0002.

Article 19 (2017). *Historic decision of the Supreme Court obliges Congress to regulate official publicity*. Retrieved from: https://articulo19.org/fallo-historico-de-la-suprema-corte-obliga-al-congreso-a-regular-publicidad-oficial.

Bravo, J. (February2015). *The Ortega Family monopolizes media in Nicaragua*. Retrieved from: https://www.diariolasamericas.com/familia-ortega-monopoliza-medios-comunicacion-nicaragua-n2965310.

Castaño, P. (2017). Counting "good things cost a lot" the official advertising expenditure of the federal government from 2013 to 2016. *Fundar*. Retrieved from: http://fundar.org.mx/mexico/pdf/P.O.2013-2016oK2.pdf.

Chirinos, C. (2007). *RCTV without signal and without antennas*. Retrieved from: http://news.bbc.co.uk/hi/spanish/latin_america/newsid_6694000/6694213.stm.

Clarín Group (2017). *Us*. Retrieved from: https://grupoclarin.com/institucional/institucional.

CONATEL (2017). *Performance of the Telecommunications Sector in Honduras. First quarter report of 2017*. Retrieved from: http://www.conatel.gob.hn/doc/indicadores/2017/Desempe%C3%B1o_del_Sector_De_Telecomunicaciones_1T2017.pdf.

Cristancho, A. (2014). Regulation of media in Central America: opportunities and challenges. *ALACIP*. Retrieved from: http://files.pucp.edu.pe/sistema-ponencias/wp-content/uploads/2014/12/Ponecia-ALACIP.pdf.

IFJ (2016). The concentration of media in Latin America. Retrieved from: https://www.ifj.org/fileadmin/user_upload/Concentracio__n_de_medios_Nov_2016.pdf.

Krauze, E. (2016). *For a Democracy Without Adjectives (Liberal Essayist 4)*. Debate.

Luna, C. (2014). Concentration of media system in Panama and its relations with economic and political power. *Comunicación y Sociedad*, 22. Retrieved from: www.scielo.org.mx/scielo.php?script=sci_arttext&pid=S0188-252X2014000200008#nota.

Müller, O. (2015). Media and its control by the State. *Chicago Tribune*. Retrieved from: http://www.chicagotribune.com/hoy/ct-hoy-8429446-los-medios-de-comunicacion-y-su-control-por-el-estado-story.html.

Nájera, A. (2013). *What is silent for fear in Central America*. Retrieved from: http://www.bbc.com/mundo/noticias/2013/07/130716_periodistas_centroamerica_narcotrafico_infernal_tarea_barrow_honduras_guatemala_an.

PRISA (2017). *Who we are?* Retrieved from: http://www.prisa.com/es/info/un-grupo-global.

Proceso (2004). *He wanted, he could not ... and he rotted*. Retrieved from: www.proceso.com.mx/231363/quiso-no-pudo-y-se-pudrio.

Reporteros sin fronteras & FECOLPER (2015). *Who owns media?* Retrieved from: http://www.monitoreodemedios.co.

Santos, B. (2014). The concentration of media in Brazil and the actions of social movements. *Pueblos*. Retrieved from: http://www.revistapueblos.org/blog/2014/08/16/la-concentracion-de-los-medios-de-comunicacion-en-brasil-y-la-actuacion-de-los-movimientos-sociales.

Sosa Plata, G. (2017). José Gutiérrez Vivó. Retrieved from: http://www.sinembargo.mx/04-04-2017/3185014.

TeleSUR (2017). *About teleSUR*. Retrieved from: https://www.telesurtv.net/pages/sobrenosotros.html.

Tourliere, M. (2018). *Eleven families control the news that most Mexicans receive*. Retrieved from: www.proceso.com.mx/526937/once-familias-controlan-las-noticias-que-recibe-la-mayoria-de-los-mexicanos.

Trejo Delarbre, R. (2011). *Mediocracy Without Mediations. Press, Television and Elections.* Mexico: Cal & Arena.

Univisión (2012). *What marked the government of Felipe Calderón?* Retrieved from: http://www.univision.com/noticias/noticias-de-mexico/que-marco-al-gobierno-de-felipe-calderon.

Vargas Llosa, M. (1 September 1990). México is the perfect dictatorship. *El País.* Retrieved from: https://elpais.com/diario/1990/09/01/cultura/652140001_850215.html.

Villamil, J. (2002). *Republic of the screen.* Retrieved from: http://www.jornada.unam.mx/2002/12/01/008a1pol.php?printver=1.

10

Hollywood, the Global Media Market, and a Time of Transition for the American Media Empire

Thom Gencarelli

The roots of Hollywood, the world's first motion picture industry, began with the dreams and life's work of a group of Jewish immigrants to the United States. Men like Samuel Goldwyn and Louis B. Mayer (co-founders of Metro-Goldwyn-Mayer, or MGM), the Warner Brothers (Harry, Albert, Sam, and Jack), and Adolph Zukor (founder of Paramount Pictures) conceived their "dream machine" in Southern California in the early twentieth century. In doing so, given their original audience but also their experience as recent immigrants to the "land of opportunity," they laid the foundation for an American-centric approach to escapism, fantasy, and the ideal, elevated plane that in many ways still dominates entertainment fare on the big, two-dimensional screen.

With the entry point of the small screen, and the golden age of television in the post-World War II 1950s in the United States, a group of white male industry executives and producers placed their similar stamp on what they envisioned the mass American audience wanted in their screen-based entertainments: the white, suburban, white picket-fenced dream vignettes of such shows as *Father Knows Best, Leave it to Beaver,* and *Ozzie and Harriet.* Yet while it took until near the end of the century for the motion picture and television industries in the US to merge into a singular power – for the US Department of Justice to allow the parent companies of the major motion picture studios to own US television networks and vice-versa – the global selling of both big-screen and small-screen properties was well underway by the mid-1960s. This resulted in clarion calls of criticism, such as Herbert Schiller's in his book *Mass Communications and American Empire* (1969, 1971, 1992) and Jeremy Tunstall's in *The Media are American* (1979).

An important distinction between these two seminal works on the subject of media imperialism is that Schiller's concern was always the cultural consequences of content, while Tunstall's pre-occupation was the influence of media themselves. As Schiller wrote, as of the mid-1960s: "Made in America movies, TV programs, music, news, and popular culture in general constituted the imagery and message fare of most of the rest of the world" (1992, p. 3). Tunstall, in turn, argued the following:

> In most of the world's countries the media are only there at all, on the present scale, as a result of the imports in which the American media (with some British support) predominate. One major influence of American imported media lies in the styles and patterns which most other countries in the world have adopted and copied. This influence includes the very definition of what a *newspaper,* or a *feature film,* or a *television set* is. (1979, p. 17) (Emphases original)

Transnational Media: Concepts and Cases, First Edition. Edited by Suman Mishra and Rebecca Kern-Stone.
© 2019 John Wiley & Sons, Inc. Published 2019 by John Wiley & Sons, Inc.

In updating his work in 1992, Schiller revised his thesis in the face of a changed global arena, wherein globalization had already kicked into high gear and the neo-liberal ideology had begun to take shape and take hold. Within this new world order:

> American cultural imperialism is not dead, but it no longer adequately describes the global cultural condition. Today it is more useful to view *transnational* corporate culture as the central force, with a continuing flavor of U.S. media know-how, derived from long experience with marketing and entertainment skills and practices. (1992, pp. 14–15) (Emphasis added)

In 2007, Tunstall then added his own postscript in the face of the continued evolution of global media affairs – which he succinctly captured in the title to his follow-up book, *The Media Were American.*

Although these analyses and claims have lost a bit of currency now in the early years of the twenty-first century,[1] they remain a significant platform for the study of transnational media and mass media and the place of US media within this global context. My point, and the purpose of this chapter, then, is to continue their project, and to attempt to move our understanding forward into the present day. It is to ask two questions. The first question is: What has changed in the decade since the publication of Tunstall's *The Media Were American*? The second is: What has such change brought about with respect to the power and place of Hollywood's film and television within the present twenty-first century global hegemony of mass media and media systems?

To be clear, my allegiance and perspective are more with Tunstall than Schiller. The nature and variants of Hollywood-derived, screen-based content continue very much the same – with *one* salient exception I will eventually arrive at here – and any change has been driven more by media shifts than transcultural concerns and corrections, which is another way of pointing out McLuhan's axiom that "the medium is the message" (1964). Thus, my focus in this chapter is on the media part of the equation and the consequence of the same.

As a result, however, I am also guilty of minimizing the factors that are the political-economics of globalization and the forces of postcolonialism. In doing so, I do not mean to deny or ignore the fact that these are essential to understanding what has transpired over these past few decades. I simply acknowledge that no one analysis can be all things or provide all things to all readers. It is my hope, then, that this chapter might serve as a basis for future research that will synthesize the elements of globalization and postcolonialism into a more complete picture that includes from where we have come, how we got here, what we have come to, and where we might be headed.

The cultural imperialism of US mass media has always arisen chiefly from the power and attraction – and the deep pockets – of Hollywood's motion picture industry and its accompanying production of entertainment television programs. The cultural imperialism of US *and* UK mass media – which is to say Anglo-American, or white, Western European-based mass media – is and has always been a product of: (i) the creation and establishment of *prestige* newspapers, which the British created and the US borrowed – or copied – with great success; and (ii) the development of three influential news wire services: The Associated Press, Reuters, and United Press International.

Let us begin then, for the sake of chronology, with news.

The Times of London was first published in 1788, after beginning publication in 1785 as *The Daily Universal Register. The New York Times* began its life as *The New-York Daily Times* in 1851, shortened its name in 1857, and was taken over by Adolph Ochs, the former publisher of *The Chattanooga Times*, in 1896. Admittedly, a focus on just these two newspapers leaves out the entirety of the history of world newspapers. In addition, the prestige factor did not rear its head right away, and certainly not for *The New York Times* which did not truly become non-partisan and non-sensational until Ochs took control. However, it can be argued – and has been argued by Tunstall (1979, pp. 28–29) among others (e.g. Schudson 1981) – that these two newspapers set the tone for the creation of, and the need for, prestige newspapers in cities and countries across the globe – emblematized by *The New York Times* arguably taking its very name from *The Times* of London. Thus, the origins of non-partisanship and the aim toward objectivity and truth came first from these two models and, moving forward, shaped the very idea and ideal of what a newspaper is and should be – as well as, to paraphrase the title of Jay Rosen's (2001) book, "what a journalist is for."

The consequence of the three wire services for US and UK cultural imperialism (at the same time that the UK's on-the-ground influence as a colonial power was in decline) is different. It stems from the fact that once these services were in place and, in the case of Reuters and United Press International, were collecting and disseminating news on a global scale, many countries' media became subscribers out of necessity.[2] They could not compete with these services to collect international news because of the economies of scale, and so were relegated to relying upon and using Anglo-American sources and reporting to provide the news of the world to their citizens. Given that objectivity became the aim in journalism, but could not be the ends – we "cannot separate the knower from the known" – the importance of this latter point cannot be overstated. The result is that an Anglo-American worldview, spreading the doctrine and cause of liberal democracy, along with all other Anglo-American interests, including economic and corporate ones, became the implicit frame for the provision of international news.

Entertainment media are yet another story. The obvious point to begin from is that with narrative, objectivity is never an issue: stories are always told from a point of view. Stories always have a moral and/or an underlying message. Stories are, like all of our art, more subject to interpretation than our expository use of language, which, as a medium of communication, is as exacting as we can get in our attempts to communicate a message and not be misunderstood. Here, then, is where the US parts ways with its own former colonial occupiers from across the pond. For it is with the rise of our electric and electronic forms of mass media in the early twentieth century, and with the first-wave apex of our mass or popular culture, that the US extended its general approach to industrial practice by developing a commercial system of broadcasting, while the UK innovated what would become the *social* model of broadcasting in the West (Scannell and Cardiff 1991, pp. 6–10). In doing so, the UK assured that content would become the people's beneficent king: that the basis for what would be produced and distributed would be that which served the greater good. Conversely – and one might argue this reflects the system of representative democracy in the US, wherein the people are supposedly at the center of power – the commercial imperative of the US system resulted in radio and later the television industry producing and distributing mainly that which would attract and sustain people's attention.

In addition, while popular music is also a significant form of Anglo-American entertainment, it is clear that the transnational power of US film and television is based in the very nature of these media as forms of *visual* communication. The moving images of film and video can be fantastical: offering us ways of seeing, as well as things *to* see that we cannot and do not see in our travels through our "real world." They offer *spectacle* – on the big screen, in larger-than-life celebrities, via special effects. Most importantly, they offer us what is to date a form of storytelling and entertainment that is our media's closest analog to real life, save that we watch these fictionalized depictions on two-dimensional screens and from a distance.

As Hollywood's film and then television industries arose, beginning in the early twentieth century, and great sums of money were poured into this "dream factory" – including such extensions of the Lumière brothers' original invention as Technicolor and synchronized sound, and the studios' creation of a "star system" – the result was the creation of escapist fantasy that became wildly popular not just in the US but for people all over the world. As a result, it also became ripe for export as a means of expanding the market and bringing in greater revenue and profit. Of course, this also led to repercussions. In the UK, Australia, and Canada there has been a history of political and industrial response arising from the "need to protect indigenous production from foreign competition" (Head 1985, p. 198). Obviously, the UK and Australia are English-language countries, and Canada, while English and French-speaking depending upon the province, shares a 3897-mile border with the US that does not stop broadcast transmissions from crossing over from the south.[3] Thus, a clear factor in these countries' protectionist concerns is that they end up being the ideal secondary markets for movies and television programs from the US and Hollywood due simply to language. Likewise, France has also experienced ongoing protectionist concerns arising from distrust, if not an outright "hostility toward the Anglo world" (Stevenson 1994, p. 172), but which is also in great part the by-product of US and Hollywood imperialism (see Tunstall 2007, pp. 251–254).

What turned this cultural imperialism into a global matter was not simply the Hollywood machinery's voracious appetite for unlimited growth in revenue. As Hollywood's movie makers and executives became more and more enamored with the possibilities of special effects to create spectacle, budgets logically and simultaneously increased, meaning more money at risk. This led to the making of movies "by committee" – bringing in multiple producers and production companies, script doctors, marketing and promotion consultants, merchandising tie-ins, and the like – both in the attempt to minimize risk but also to spread it across multiple stakeholders and responsible parties. While I acknowledge that I am only telling a part of the story of this global shift in media by focusing on feature films, it is clear that what happened at this time resulted in an emphasis on formulaic action movies in which the good guy fights the stereotyped villain *du jour* (e.g. Russians during the Cold War, Middle Eastern "terrorists" after 9/11, etc.), or against nature, with all manner of explosive destruction of vehicles and buildings and, most importantly, *where dialogue takes a back seat to storytelling through action*. Not only did this bring about a domestic market in which teenage boys became the primary audience for the theatrical release of movies at the local cineplex, but also because dialog was no longer central or really even necessary to telling the story this eased entry for such movies into markets in non-English speaking countries. (I am reminded of the time I brushed elbows with Tom Cruise in Taipei as he was doing promotional work for *Mission Impossible III*. It might as well have been Harrison Ford or Arnold Schwarzenegger or Will Smith or any other similar action hero/celebrity.)

The developments in this direction led to a pinnacle of sorts in 2016 – and a question mark moving forward – with the release of *The Great Wall*.

It is clear that India, with its 1.3 billion people, and China, with its 1.4 billion people, represent such sizable media markets that they could never, and still cannot, be ignored by Hollywood. India, a democratic republic since 1947, is a relatively open society. It is also, however, across the great many cultures of people who live on the subcontinent, a relatively chaste society – a factor that has long been reflected in its entertainment media. This is one explanation for the creation and growth of its own quite substantial domestic motion picture industry, well known as "Bollywood," as opposed to the country and its people allowing themselves to continue to be culturally colonized by the Anglo-American industry since their independence. As a former British colony, and because of the resulting influence of the English language in India, we in the West are also familiar with Bollywood cinema because of the extent to which India exports its own English-language films.

China, on the other hand, also has its own vast and powerful domestic motion try. In fact, as of the first quarter of 2018, China's gross domestic box office for theatrical films surpassed that of the US for the first time, by $3.17 to the US's $2.89 billion (Frater 2018). China is not, however, a major exporter of films to the West because of the language barrier; with the exception of films exported from the country's "Special Administrative Region" of Hong Kong. At the same time, the country has relatively closed cultural borders and has been, to date, greatly restrictive with respect to the growth, development, and investment of US and other Western companies within those borders.

Nonetheless, China is and has been an importer of Hollywood's motion pictures. As a country intent on satisfying and distracting its people with the same kind of escapist entertainment enjoyed by so much of the rest of the world – in following the "bread and circuses" tradition that dates back to ancient Rome, and which Huxley (1932), Schiller (1969), Postman (1985), Adorno (2002), and others continue to point to as a means of distracting people from matters of politics and state – and because Hollywood's fare is widely pirated and available in China via the black market anyway – Hollywood's action-based films have long been popular in China. As I have noted, action-oriented stories and their spectacular visual effects cross, if not negate, the language barrier.

It is within this context that *The Great Wall* was produced as a collaborative effort between the Chinese and US film industries – not just as a mutually beneficial business proposition but as an attempt toward a kind of industrial and cultural *détente*. It represented Hollywood's effort to sustain its popularity among Chinese moviegoers in the face of concerns about market and industry restrictions, and at the same time it represented the Chinese motion picture industry's effort to forge its own path onto the global stage and into the lucrative, if not insatiable, US market for popular cultural entertainments (Tull et al. 2016).

The result, however, was a resounding "dud," particularly in the US. The film suffered from myriad issues. A centerpiece of the monster/war narrative was an unconsummated love story between Matt Damon's character and the character played by Chinese actress Jing Tian, who were never allowed to so much as kiss. Much of the film was shot in Qingdao (they were not allowed to actually shoot *on* the Great Wall), and the movie cost $150 million to make. The theatrical box office take in China was $171 million – much less than investors anticipated – and only $34.8 million in the US (McClintock and Galloway 2017). The film closed in the US just after its President's Day weekend opening, and it is estimated that the project will lose in excess of $75 million (McClintock and Galloway 2017).

This, then, is a telling example of where the US motion picture and television industry presently stands within the realm of transnational mass media markets and practices. However, perhaps the more interesting and important question is: Where and how might things move forward from here?

As I have written above, on a planet with 7.6 billion people, the US industry cannot possibly ignore the market value of two countries with a combined population of 2.7 billion people, or almost one-third of the global population. At the same time, nationalist film and television industries continue to rise and compound the problem of market competition: the "Nollywood" industry of Nigeria, on the African continent, is a salient, notable example. Short of discovering life on other planets, then, and exploiting those beings as media markets, it seems Hollywood has reached an end of sorts with respect to the potential to expand its audiences – with, of course, the exception of that one fortunate property that arises every now and again to become as vastly and globally popular, or as evergreen as, say, *Baywatch*.

In the meantime, if media and technological change are the harbinger of, or reason behind, changes to content, then developments in convergent media must be considered for the potentials they bring to the global table. Netflix, for instance, can be viewed (pun intended) as just another premium television channel, but one where the subscriber is no longer beholden to the channel's schedule; where we can watch what we want when we want. Meanwhile, Apple endeavors to grow its Apple TV service to compete with Google's attempts to turn YouTube into a new, must-watch television service in the twenty-first century. Amazon has entered the game not only through its Amazon Prime service, where it competes with Netflix and Hulu, but by developing its own Amazon Studios to produce films and television. Facebook has created – and entrepreneurial-minded users and exploiters of the social media service have attempted to program – "Facebook Live."

To my mind, however, it is virtual reality that will be the real game changer, once Hollywood takes VR technology beyond its current use in the gaming industry and toward a realm in which we replace our two-dimensional screen-based entertainments with practices and potentials for immersive entertainment. This is to say that if Hollywood originated with the creation of moving-image based entertainment, but on the flat and distanced screen, the next significant transition for our global media entertainments will be moving images that surround us, and which, in various ways and to various extents, we will be able to interact with, participate in, and influence as actors in our own right.

Notes

1 Schiller's revised edition of *Mass Communications and American Empire* (1992) was published around the same time Marc Andreessen developed Mosaic, the first web browser, at the University of Illinois Urbana-Champaign, which led directly to the first commercial web browser, Netscape Navigator, in 1994. Tunstall's *The Media Were American* (2007) came out soon after Facebook had begun expanding beyond college and university campuses and to the general public, but also some two years before the arrival of the smart phone.
2 A significant exception for the greater part of the twentieth century, as Siebert et al. (1963) pointed out, was the former Soviet Union.
3 It bears noting that these three countries – the UK, Australia, and Canada – along with New Zealand are the originators of and driving forces behind programs in media literacy and media education (e.g. the work of the UK's British Film Institute since the late 1970s, under David Buckingham since the early 1980s, and then later under Cary Bazalgette). I have argued that a primary reason these programs arose and became influential in these English language-speaking countries, for both children and citizens in general, is as a response to the cultural-colonial threat of the Hollywood juggernaut (Gencarelli, 2003).

References

Adorno, T. (2002). *The Dialectic of Enlightenment* (trans. E. Jephcott). Stanford: Stanford University Press (Original work published 1947).

Frater, P. (2 April 2018). China box office overtakes North America in first quarter of 2018. *Variety*. Retrieved from: http://variety.com/2018/film/asia/china-box-office-global-biggest-first-quarter-2018-1202742159.

Gencarelli, T. (November 2003). *The New York School of Media Ecology in the History of Media Education*. Paper presented at the National Communication Association Conference, Miami, FL.

Head, S. (1985). *World Broadcasting Systems: A Comparative Analysis*. Belmont: Wadsworth.

Huxley, A. (1932). *Brave New World*. London: Chatto and Windus.

McClintock, P. and Galloway, S. (2 March 2017). Matt Damon's 'The Great Wall' to lose $75 million; future US-China productions in doubt. *The Hollywood Reporter*. Retrieved from: https://www.hollywoodreporter.com/news/what-great-walls-box-office-flop-will-cost-studios-981602.

McLuhan, H.M. (1964). *Understanding Media: The Extensions of Man*. New York: McGraw- Hill.

Postman, N. (1985). *Amusing Ourselves to Death: Public Discourse in the Age of Show Business*. New York: Viking.

Rosen, J. (2001). *What Are Journalists for*. New Haven: Yale University Press.

Scannell, P. and Cardiff, D. (1991). *A Social History of British Broadcasting, Volume One 1922–1939: Serving the Nation*. Oxford: Basil Blackwell.

Schiller, H. (1969). *Mass Communications and American Empire*. New York: Augustus M. Kelley Publishers.

Schiller, H. (1971). *Mass Communications and American Empire*. Boston: Beacon Press.

Schiller, H. (1992). *Mass Communications and American Empire*, 2e. New York and London: Routledge.

Schudson, M. (1981). *Discovering the News*. New York: Basic Books.

Siebert, F.S., Peterson, T., and Schramm, W. (1963). *Four Theories of the Press: The Authoritarian, Libertarian, Social Responsibility, and Soviet Communist Concepts of What the Press Should Be and Do*. Urbana and Chicago: University of Illinois Press.

Stevenson, R.L. (1994). *Global Communication in the Twenty-First Century*. White Plains: Longman.

Tull, T., Roven, C., Jashni, J., and Loehr, P. (Producers), & Zhang, Y. (Director)(2016). *The Great Wall*. United States and China: Universal Pictures and China Film Group.

Tunstall, J. (1979). *The Media Are American: Anglo-American Media in the World*. New York: Columbia University Press.

Tunstall, J. (2007). *The Media Were American: U.S. Mass Media in Decline*. New York and Oxford: Oxford University Press.

11

The "Sanctioned" Reggae "Revolution," and Confrontations Between Cradles of Culture

Humphrey A. Regis

One framework for the elaboration of the "reggae revolution" of the 1970s might focus on its success, and as a result might lead to two conclusions. It was speedy, because although the ska grandparent of reggae started in the 1960s, the "revolution" was in full swing by the mid-1970s. It also seemed to represent the adoption of cultural values and cultural expression from the former colony of Jamaica by "superior" former and current colonial and neo-colonial dominators such as Britain and the United States.

Another framework for the assessment of the "revolution" views the world as including a Southern cradle of culture and a Northern cradle of culture. It views the confrontation between the two cradles in recent millennia as including the domination by the North of the South (Diop 1978; Finch 1991) by re-importation and re-exportation (Regis 2004, 2015a), as well as the current pre-eminence of the West (Finch 1991). The framework finds application in the examination of change in the conception of the ultimate state in the universe that we find among reggae and other Jamaican and Caribbean musicians, as well as in the histories of two of these musicians in the North and in the South.

11.1 Fundamentals on Cradles of Culture

Cheikh Anta Diop (1978) and Charles Finch (1991), in their interpretation of Diop's work, describe the world millennia ago as including two "cradles" of civilization. The Southern cradle included Africa and displayed such cultural tendencies as collectivism, xenophilia, cosmopolitanism, peace and justice, goodness and optimism, and the centrality of the female in the family and in transmission between generations. The Northern cradle included Greece and Rome and displayed such tendencies as individualism, xenophobia, internal patriotism, war and violence, crime and conquests, and the centrality of the male in the family and in transmission between generations. Even after millennia, these cradles have not lost their respective attributes completely (Diop 1991; Finch 1991).

In Kemet (Land of the Blacks), the most elaborated and most advanced ancient African civilization, the core enunciated philosophy was Maat, at the center of which was an ethical code that the Kemetu viewed as key to eternal life (Karenga 1993). To lay persons the "principles," but to scholars the "interpretations," of Maat include (Karenga 1993) Truth, Justice, Propriety, Harmony, Reciprocity, Balance, and Order. The philosophy and the related code seem to be at the foundation of thinking and living and being in many other African societies. For example, it seems consistent with three African attributes: the major propositions in traditional African constitutions (Williams 1976); the view of the major purpose of traditional African legal

Transnational Media: Concepts and Cases, First Edition. Edited by Suman Mishra and Rebecca Kern-Stone.
© 2019 John Wiley & Sons, Inc. Published 2019 by John Wiley & Sons, Inc.

process as the restoration of equilibrium in relations (see Smith 1972); and especially, the traditional African proposition that in the universe "coherence among persons and things accords" (Smith 1972, p. 368).

11.2 Maat in the Music of Caribbean PADs

For centuries, that "coherence" appears to have inspired, informed, and guided the ideational, lyrical, and structural attributes of the creations of Caribbean People of African Descent (PADs). This emerges from an analysis of the creative works of many Caribbean PADs, especially Jimmy Cliff and Sparrow, whose music received concurrent acclaim early in their careers, and especially in their islands – the Caribbean and Africa.

The first manifestation of the coherence is ideational – it is in the idea that undergirds the music and that may be in the names of songs. In the music of Cliff, it is in his call for an aspiration toward "love" and "oneness," his naming of his band Oneness, his staging at Reggae Sunsplash 1981 of a Night of African Oneness, and his use of the words "love" and "oneness" in the titles of his songs. In the music of Sparrow, it is in the call for the understanding of marginal entities, such as in Fat Man or in Sweet Man, or in the names of songs, such as Interdependence. Among other musicians, titles of songs include All Uh We Is Wan Famuhlay ("We Together Constitute One Family") from Lord Nelson.

The second manifestation of the coherence is lyrical – in words that affirm or elaborate or rationalize the coherence. In the work of Cliff, the affirmation is in My Love is Solid as a Rock ("It has got no age, no beginning, no end/Won't slip, won't slide, won't break, won't bend"); the elaboration is in Where There is Love ("Where there is love, there's harmony/And unity, comes naturally"); and the rationalization is in Love Is All ("Still I love the rich, because they're yet so lonely/And I love the poor, because there're still so many"). There also is the exhortation toward that coherence in Wonderful World, Beautiful People ("Instead of fussing and fighting, cheating, backbiting, scandalizing, hating/We could have a wonderful world, beautiful people"). And there is exhortation toward a decidedly special-interest-agnostic coherence in Universal Love – Beyond the Boundaries ("We don't need no new religion/We don't need no other savior/What we need is to understand/Our fellow man and our behavior/To live in love and unity/Universally! Universal Love!"). The affirmation and elaboration, and rationalization and exhortation, are also in works by kaisomasters: Interdependence from Sparrow, All Uh We Is Wan Famuhlay from Lord Nelson, and Caribbean Man from Stalin.

The third manifestation of the coherence is structural, and includes three aspects – call and response, multiple rhythms, and syncopation. In call and response, the lead singer, lead instrument, vocal accompaniment, or instrumental accompaniment takes the "lead" or "leading" role, one or more of the other participants assumes a "response" role, and one or more of the others may act as a "bridge." The execution of the whole song is akin to an exercise in give and take, in taking turns, and in complementarity among the parts, and the audience members who join by following any one and any combination of the parts may develop a sense of participation, immersion, and "communion." With the multiple rhythms, the song may have a principal rhythm that may well be as unaccentuated and metronomic as the heartbeat, there are faster and slower rhythms subsumed under the principal rhythm, and thus there is rhythmic diversity within the context of rhythmic unity, and audience members who follow any one or any combination of the rhythmic patterns develop the sense of participation and immersion and "communion." And in syncopation, performers do not play out all integral or obvious accents, members of the audience seem to receive an implicit invitation to provide these accents, and members who do so develop the sense of participation and immersion and "communion."

These structural elements are in Bongo Man, from Cliff. Here, in the last verse, the lead starts with "I hope you are prepared," the vocal accompaniment joins and responds as he sings "prepared," and the repeater drum serves as a reminder and as an emphasizer (thus as a responder) and forms a bridge. The lead continues, "The Bongo Man is here," the vocal accompaniment joins and responds at "here," and the repeater again provides a reminder and emphasizer (thus a responder) and another bridge. Then the lead and the vocal accompaniment proclaim "The Bongo Man has come," and the repeater once more serves as a reminder and emphasizer (and thus a responder) and bridge. Finally, the lead singer exclaims with "rapture" and vocal accompaniment exclaims in "unison," "Come! Come!" and the repeater provides a simultaneously calming and accentuating conclusion (and response). The bass drum lays out a metronomic reference; the funde drum weaves more "stepping stone" accents as it draws lead and vocal accompaniment and repeater onward; and the repeater teases even more accents as it joins the lead and vocal accompaniment and accentuates, reverberates, and extends their phrases and provides bridges between these phrases. The audience members receive an implicit invitation to fill out the spaces between the sparing accents of the bass drum; to fill out the spaces between the "stepping stone" accents from the funde drum; to join the vocal accompaniment in accentuating and/or responding to the phrases of the lead singer; to join the repeater drum in providing a second melody that is contrastive and in this way emphasizes the phrases of the lead singer and vocal accompaniment, and integrative in that it responds to these phrases and forms bridges between them. The performance of Bongo Man elicits a certain calm thanks to the communal assurance the lead singer and the vocal accompaniment evince and to the participation the structure (with the use of call and response, syncopation, and interwoven rhythms) ensures in the attainment of an ultimate that is a certain integration, coherence, immersion, communion, "oneness."

We find comparable weavings of structural elements in multiple other works of music from Caribbean PAD. One is the depiction of the animation of one work of art so that it comes to be at one with the celebrants in carnival – in The Statue from kaisomaster Sparrow. Another is the depiction of the solidarity that supporters of dancer Matilda display toward her during her performance at "bongo competition time" – in the song Bongo, from kaisomaster Sparrow (and virtually all of the works that Earl Rodney arranged for Sparrow). And yet another is the spirit of joy from interaction and immersion and communion and "oneness" in the popular Hot Hot Hot from kaisomaster Arrow (and, too, virtually all of the works that Leston Paul arranged for Arrow).

The idea that one of the objectives of the music of Caribbean PAD is to cultivate a certain coming together, coherence, or communion also seems to arise from analyses of the reasons they volunteer for wanting their music to become popular. They would like the music to become popular in the Caribbean because they perceive that this popularity would indicate the Caribbean valuation of Caribbean creativity and would help the integration of the region (see Regis 1995). They would like it to become popular in Africa because they perceive that this popularity would indicate that People of the African Continent (PACs) are aware of the Caribbean solidarity with them (Regis 1995). They would like it to become popular among people in countries in Europe and North America because they anticipate that with this popularity these people would visit the Caribbean and the economies of the entire Caribbean – not the "pockets" of individual musicians or the economies of individual islands – would reap benefits from these visits (Regis 1995). With these rationales, the Caribbean PADs seem to reveal that observers may view their music as one of the indicators of their sense of membership in a whole, as a resource they may utilize in their realization of their membership in a whole, or as a resource they may employ in the realization of the whole of which they are members. These rationales seem to reveal the presence in these Caribbean PADs of an aspiration toward solidarity, toward coherence, toward "communion," and toward "oneness."

We may use the ideational, lyrical, and structural elaborations of "oneness" to explain the popularity of at least two Caribbean musicians over decades. The kaisomaster and ethnomusicologist Chalkdust (Liverpool 2001) reports that Caribbean and European people exported samples, interpretations, and appreciations of the works of Sparrow and Kitchener and other kaisomasters from the Caribbean to Europe, and PAC exported them from Europe to Africa. Cliff also had many samples, interpretations, and appreciations of his works experience a comparable trajectory. But these works were not exceedingly popular in Europe, and this led to such reactive works by Cliff as No. 1 Rip-Of Man that focuses on betrayal and Going Back West that focuses on returning home. Thus, the music industry, PACs, and People of the European Continent (PECs) in Europe did not "export" the popularity of these works among the PECs to Africa, but the PACs in Europe exported their samples, and the interpretations and appreciations they had developed, of the works to Africa.

With these exportations, by the late 1960s, the works of Cliff and Sparrow had become very popular in Africa. Indeed, Nigerians almost universally have told the author that in Nigeria in the 1970s the Cliff song House of Exile from the album of the same name was like a second national anthem and that some Cliff vinyl albums may have outsold those of Fela Anikulapo Kuti; while Ibelema (2013) lists Cliff as the first among those Jamaican musicians whose popularity in Nigeria in the 1970s he discusses. Liverpool (2001) reports that the works of such kaisomasters as Sparrow and Kitchener were referents in the development of highlife in West Africa. Given the elaborations of "oneness" in the music of members of the World African Community, one thesis worthy of investigation is that the works of Jimmy Cliff have been popular in Jamaica, the Caribbean, Afro-Brazil, and Africa, and the works of Sparrow have been popular in Trinidad, the Caribbean, and Africa, in part because of the incorporation in these works of the ideational, lyrical, and structural expressions of solidarity, of coherence, of "communion," of "oneness."

That solidarity, coherence, communion, and oneness are consistent with the following point of view that Ka'bu Ma'at Kheru, a member of the committee that selected Cliff for the first IRIE FM Lifetime Achievement Award and the Program Director at IRIE FM's parent company Grove Broadcasting, says that Cliff maintains: "If the community does not benefit from what I do, then, I am not successful" (Meschino 2017).

11.3 Northern Cradle and Dichotomization

In the two-cradle thesis (Diop 1978; Finch 1991), the Northern cradle conceives of the universe as an arena for individualism and the associated dichotomization that spawns xenophobia, internal patriotism, war and violence, and crime and conquests. This appears to have found expression in the ideational, lyrical, and structural aspects of the reggae culture that the children of that cradle – PEC and People of European Descent (especially in North America) – conceived in the 1970s.

The first manifestation of the dichotomization and related conceptions was ideational – it was in the essential idea that undergirded the reggae culture of these children, and thus seemed to be captured in many of the songs they deemed definitive of the culture. These songs included The Harder They Come by Jimmy Cliff; I Shot the Sheriff by The Wailers; Get Up, Stand Up by The Wailers; and Stepping Razor by Peter Tosh.

The second manifestation of the dichotomization and related conceptions was lyrical – it was in the words that affirm or elaborate or rationalize the dichotomization and the related conceptions. The affirmations came in such lyrics as "We nuh know how we an dem ah go work dis out" ("We don't know how 'we' and 'them' are going to work this out") in the song We an

Dem by Bob Marley and the Wailers. The elaborations included the view of the essential dynamic in the world as Rasta vs. Baldhead, the system vs. the suffering, the righteous vs. the heathen, and the good vs. the bad. The rationalizations held that in the universe the lyricist's "side" is righteous, some other "side" or "sides" is or are heathen, problems are the works of that other "side" or "sides," and the solution to the problems is the triumph of the lyricist's "side" and demise of the other "side(s)."

This manifestation seemed to find expression in one of the popular "positive" songs of the reggae revolution, One Love by Bob Marley and the Wailers. In the song, Marley the lead singer advises and so exhorts, "Let's get together to fight this Holy Armagiddyon/So when the Man comes there will be no, no doom/Have pity on those whose chances grows t'inner/There ain't no hiding place from the Father of Creation/One love; one heart/Let's get together and feel all right!" Of course, the lyricist advocates an ultimate order that follows a certain Armageddon in which the lyricist and the related sectorial interest that The Man represents are victorious and thus assume a position in which they can impose that order. The lyrics seem to encode the Northern cradle or European ultimate state that centers on individualism, xenophobia, internal patriotism, war and violence, and crime and conquests. The call for that emphasis seems to be captured in the review by Lester Bangs (1978) in *Rolling Stone* of the Bob Marley and the Wailers vinyl album titled "Rastaman Vibration," and in the criticism by Laura Frost (1990) in the magazine *Caribbean Review* of the "slackness" in the reggae of after the 1970s.

The third manifestation of the dichotomization and related conceptions was structural – it was in the rhythmic accents in the songs. Early in the history of reggae, the accents sounded quite subtle or even incidental like those in calypso, they sounded quite "fluid" and akin to the crest of a sinusoidal wave, and performers executed them mainly with the organ or the guitar twang. But in the reggae that the children of the Northern cradle in the United States preferred in and after the mid-1970s, there were two tweaks in the execution of the accents. First, there was the greater use of "hiccuppy" rhythm guitar "licks" in the first and third beats the reggae genre emphasizes. Second, there was the foregrounding of the main rhythm (especially through the contrast between the rhythm guitar and the bass guitar) and/or backgrounding of the cross-rhythms, with the result being the overwhelming of the cross-rhythms by the main rhythm. That especially was the case with the "one-drop" rhythmic accents that were perfected by the accompanist duo of Sly Dunbar and Robbie Shakespeare (Sly and Robbie). These changes happened to meet the demands of the children of the Northern cradle in two ways: first, they met the needs of these children for the expression of the idea of the triumph of one over one or more others; second, they met the needs of these children for structural or rhythmic schemes that were less "confusing" than those in other genres from African peoples.

As Lashley (2001) reports, for the same reasons such simplifications in structure and accentuations in rhythm took place in the offshoot of calypso music – whose developers called it soca. And to this writer, for comparable reasons, the changes took place in the offshoot of cadence music – whose developers called it zouk.

These attributes of the reggae music culture of the children of the Northern cradle seem to have reflected the attributes of the cradle, related characteristics of the children, and conditions at the time of the development of the culture. They reflected the presence in the cradle of the idea of self or self-interest versus another or others, the emphasis in its children of the related idea of triumph of self or self-interest over another or others, and the expression of the presence and the emphasis in the "counterculture" movement of the 1960s and 1970s. They met the needs of the Northern children that sprang from the intersection of these three factors and elements in the film *They Harder They Come:* the resisting by the protagonist of the evils of the "system;" the capturing of this resisting in the song of the same name; and the validation in the film of the idea of replacements for the "system." In addition, the simplifications in structure and associated accentuations in rhythm addressed the needs of the children for structure and rhythm that were less "complicated" or less "confusing" to them than those in other music from the World African Community (WAC).

11.4   Reggae Music Trajectory in 1970s

Within the context of the relationships between cradles of culture that are of interest here, cultural domination by re-exportation or re-importation includes these processes: origination of cultural elements by a Southern society; the transmission of the elements to a Northern society; the modification(s) of these elements by the Northern society; the re-importation of these modifications by the Southern society from the Northern one, or re-exportation of these modifications by the Northern society to the Southern one; and the adoption of the modifications by the originating Southern society.

One may describe the trajectory of the works of music under study in this treatise using the cultural domination by re-importation or re-exportation framework. For millennia, children of the Southern cradle who have been members of the WAC have internalized the philosophy of Maat, have espoused the related ideals of coherence, communion, and oneness, and have created music that has an ideational, lyrical, and structural center in philosophy and ideals; and musicians from Jamaica recently have created their reggae music culture that reflects their philosophy and ideals (origination). The Jamaican musicians embedded their philosophy, ideals, and culture in the works they exported to the children of the Northern cradle in Europe and North America (exportation). These recipients then developed their own reggae music culture marked by the ideals of dichotomization and contestation, and conquest and triumph, and in their reggae culture and the Jamaican reggae culture they emphasized individual works and a high proportion of the aggregate of works with the ideational, lyrical, and structural elements that embed these ideals (modification). Then the children of the Southern cradle in Jamaica became aware of the attributes of individual works and the high proportion of the aggregate of works that the children of the Northern cradle stressed in the reggae cultures of both cradles (re-importation or re-exportation). The children of the South in Jamaica then adjusted their conception of, and their output in, reggae music, in keeping with the emphases of the children of the North (adoption).

In the late 1960s and early 1970s, before the exponential exportation of reggae to the children of the Northern cradle in Europe and in North America, Cliff won the hearts and minds of members of the WAC in Jamaica and other parts of the Caribbean, in Nigeria and other parts of Africa, and in Salvador de Bahia and other parts of Brazil, with many Maatian songs of coherence, communion, and oneness that included Wonderful World Beautiful People. In the mid-1970s, during the exponential exportation of reggae to children of the Northern cradle in Europe and North America, the members of the WAC received word of the endorsement of such dichotomization songs of contestation, conquest, and triumph, as One Love, as well as the elevation of Marley to the status of creator of works (such as albums Natty Dread and Rastaman Vibration) that represent the epitome of reggae. After receiving word of these developments, many members of the WAC, especially those in Jamaica and the English-speaking Eastern Caribbean, would not express for Universal Love an appreciation that was comparable to what they showed for Wonderful World Beautiful People. They also would not express this appreciation for other "Maatian" works that Cliff later created and that include Oneness, I am in All, We All are One, No Problems Only Solutions, I Walk with Love, People, Where There is Love, Love Comes, Precious Love, and the implicit guilt-inducing and sense-of-urgency-inducing plea for "love" for destitute children that is Lonely Streets. Indeed, in the late 1970s and early 1980s, when the writer was news director for Caribbeana on WPFW-FM in Washington, DC, and during the 1990s and early 2000s, when the writer visited to conduct research on the mass media and culture in the Eastern Caribbean, in remarks to the writer and remarks the writer overheard, many Caricommoners deemed these and comparable other works from Cliff too "soft" to be reflective of the "real" reggae. These remarks especially came from people who were aware of the preferences of the children of the Northern cradle and who served as gatekeepers with authority over music playlists.

One group of explanations for the adjustment may be what Comstock et al. (1978) call contextual conditions. They include financial gains the children of the Southern cradle stood to reap from the adjustment, and what Alleyne (1994) sees as the submission of Jamaican and other Caribbean PADs to the role of their former colonial and current neo-colonial dominators in Europe and in North America as interpreters of, and assigners of value to, their creative output. The submission appears to be captured in three observations the writer received in an interview in 1991 from Linda Walrond, a mass media professional, a mass media studies instructor, and one of the partners in the mass media services organization Ideas Management in Bridgetown, Barbados in the Eastern Caribbean: many Caricommoners praised the works of Marley largely on the basis of their perception of the interpretation and validation of the works in Europe and North America; they then rationalized the praise with the claim that the basis for it was the quality of the works; and, therefore, what Jamaica, the Caribbean, and the world saw in the 1970s was a "sanctioned" reggae "revolution." The submission in turn may be the result of two factors in the psyches of Caricommoners: their Corrective Automatic Reactions to Membership in the World African Community or CARMWAC (in Regis 2003) and related psychological distancing of themselves from members of that community; and their messianization of members of the World European Community or MASSAHIANISM (see Regis 2015b) and associated psychological orientation toward, and psychological disarming in the presence of, members of that community.

11.5 Review and Conclusion

The world over millennia has included two contrasting cradles of culture: the Southern cradle that has been characterized by the orientation toward collectivism, xenophilia, cosmopolitanism, peace and justice, and goodness and optimism; and the Northern cradle that has been characterized by the orientation toward individualism, xenophobia, internal patriotism, war and violence, and crime and conquests. The children of the Southern cradle who are PACs and PADs have created works that have included ideational, lyrical, and structural expressions of their orientation for millennia, and Jamaican or other Caribbean peoples have created such works in the calypso (for centuries) and reggae (for decades) genres. In the 1970s, the children of the Northern cradle in Europe and North America received works in reggae that reflected the Southern cradle orientation but developed a reggae culture that reflected their Northern cradle orientation. Then children of the Southern cradle in Jamaica and the Caribbean modified their conception of the ideal orientation, and incorporated ideational, lyrical, and structural expressions of that modification in their music in ways that made the new conception and expression consistent with the enunciations and preferences of the children of the Northern cradle. The change may be a result of at least three contextual conditions that probably affect PAC or PAD: the likelihood of financial gain from the change; the level of their orientation to each other that is related to their CARMWAC; and the level of their orientation to their colonial and neo-colonial dominators that is related to their "messianization" of members of the World European Community (MASSAHIANISM).

References

Alleyne, M. (1994). Positive vibration? Capitalist textual hegemony and Bob Marley. *Bulletin of Eastern Caribbean affairs* 19 (3): 76–84.

Bangs, L. (1 June 1978). Bob Marley aims high, misses big: tepid cliches and tourist bait. *Rolling Stone*, 56.

Comstock, G., Chaffee, S., Katzman, N. et al. (1978). *Television and Human Behavior*. New York: Columbia University Press.

Diop, C. (1978). *Cultural Unity of Black Africa*. Chicago: Third World Press.

Diop, C. (1991). *Civilization or Barbarism*. New York: Lawrence Hill Books.

Finch, C. (1991). *Echoes of the Old Dark Land: Themes from the African Eden*. Decatur, GA: Khenti, Inc.

Frost, L. (1990). DJ Reggae: slackness becomes standard. *Caribbean Review* 16 (3, 4): 6. 74.

Ibelema, M. (2013). Cultural relations and cultural change: reggae and knowledge of the Caribbean. In: *Liberated Academics in Studies of Caricommoners* (ed. H. Regis), 49–62. Vieux Fort, Saint Lucia: Vieux Fort Comprehensive Secondary School.

Karenga, M. (1993). *Introduction to Black Studies*. Los Angeles: The University of Sankore Press.

Lashley, L. (2001). Decades of change in calypso culture. In: *Culture and Mass Communication in the Caribbean: Domination, Dialogue, Dispersion* (ed. H. Regis), 83–93. Gainesville, FL: University Press of Florida.

Liverpool, H. (2001). Re-exportation and musical traditions surrounding the African masquerade. In: *Culture and Mass Communication in the Caribbean: Domination, Dialogue, Dispersion* (ed. H. Regis), 63–82. Gainesville, FL: University Press of Florida.

Meschino, M. (16 February 2017). Reggae legend Jimmy Cliff receives Lifetime Achievement Award, performs in his rural hometown. *Billboard.com*. Retrieved from: https://www.billboard.com/articles/events/7694065/jimmy-cliff-lifetime-achievement-award-irie-radio-jamaica.

Regis, H. (1995). Collectivism and the desire for popularity for Caribbean music. *Bulletin of Eastern Caribbean Affairs* 30 (1): 8–16.

Regis, H. (2003). *Africans Before CARICOM: Commencements and Continuations*. Vieux Fort, Saint Lucia: The S. Wayne Louis Foundation.

Regis, H. (2004). Mass communication and cultural domination: the re-importation/re-exportation framework. *The Journal of African Communications* 6 (2): 3–65.

Regis, H. (2015a). *How American Reggae Redefined Jamaican and Caribbean Reggae: A Theoretical Study of the Relationship Between Mass Communication and Cultural Domination*. New York: The Edwin Mellen Press.

Regis, H. (2015b). CARMWAC, MASSAHIANISM, and Caribbean creolism. In: *Envisioning the Greater Caribbean: Transgressing Geographical and Disciplinary Boundaries* (ed. Faraclas, R. Severing, C. Weijer and E. Echteld), 211–220. Willemstad, Curaçao: University of Curaçao and Fundashon pa Planifikashon di Idioma.

Smith, A. (1972). Markings of an African concept of rhetoric. In: *Language, Communication and Rhetoric in Black America* (ed. A. Smith), 363–374. New York: Harper and Row.

Williams, C. (1976). *The Destruction of Black Civilization: Great Issues of a Race from 4500 BC to 2000 AD*. Chicago: Third World Press.

Part IV

Asia

Transnational Media: Concepts and Cases, First Edition. Edited by Suman Mishra and Rebecca Kern-Stone.
© 2019 John Wiley & Sons, Inc. Published 2019 by John Wiley & Sons, Inc.

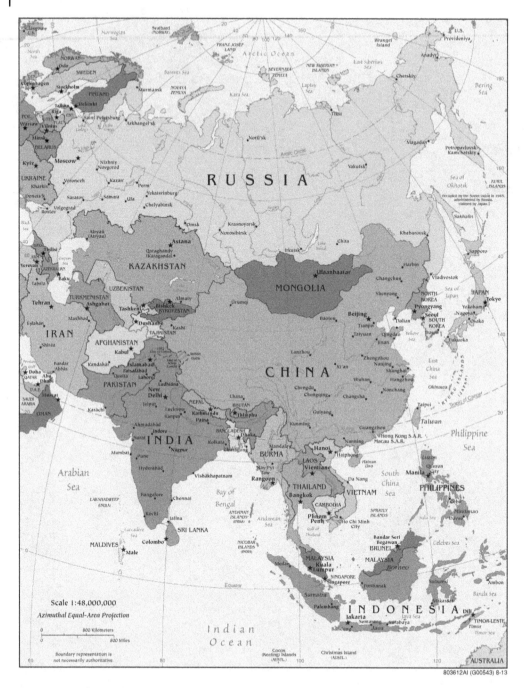

803612AI (G00543) 8-13

Figure IV.1 Map of Asia.

Asia is vast, diverse, and the most populated region of the world (Figure IV.1). It has seen tremendous growth in all sectors of its market, including media, over the last two decades. Countries like China, India, Japan, and South Korea – and even smaller countries like Qatar – have become major players in the transnational media market. These countries today are not only meeting the huge media demands of their domestic markets, they are also exporting media to other countries. They are beginning to challenge the Western dominance that still remains significant in the global flow of information and culture. Asian countries are swiftly building their media infrastructure for the information age, and thus in the coming decades one can expect many changes in the flow of communication and information from Asia to other parts of the world.

In this section, country profiles of China, India, Japan, South Korea, and Qatar are very briefly discussed, and the broader media landscapes in these countries are introduced.

PIV.1 China

China's rise on the world stage over the last couple of decades has been like none other. With a population of 1.38 billion, a GDP of 11.2 trillion USD, and an annual growth of 6.7%, China has become a major player in world politics and economics (Internet World Stats 2018; UN DESA 2017; World Bank 2016a, b). China has had a one-party system governed by the Chinese Communist Party (CCP) since 1949. Its current president, Xi Jinping, came to power in 2012 after being selected by his predecessor, Hu Jintao. In 2018, the Communist Party moved to allow him to stay in the office indefinitely, changing the convention of two-term limits for presidents in China, essentially giving him control and power for life.

China has one official language, Mandarin (*putonghua*), but many regional dialects and other languages are spoken in China. The Chinese government recognizes five religions: Buddhism, Taoism, Islam, Protestantism, and Catholicism. However, a large segment of the Chinese population is atheist. Confucianism, Taoism, and Buddhism have left a collective and lasting impression on Chinese culture and tradition, which is more than 4000 years old.

The Chinese media landscape is considered one of the largest in the world, but is also one which is tightly controlled by the Communist Party. Media in China generally enjoy commercial freedom, but have relatively little political freedom. Dissent is often seen as a threat to the Party and the social stability of the country. Thus, restrictions are imposed on journalists and other media professionals. News deemed "sensitive" is blocked. Jamming of broadcast waves, blocking websites, and keyword censoring are commonly employed. These extensive filtering measures have been dubbed as China's "Great Firewall." Journalists are also threatened and detained when they write about issues considered problematic by the Party. Thus, China has been ranked very low (176/180) on the 2018 World Press Freedom Index (Reporters Without Borders, 2018a). China, however, is not completely closed off from the world; foreign correspondents do work and report from within its borders albeit with many restrictions. News and information still flow through its borders as people travel outside the country and use various circumventing technologies to get outside information. Information and criticisms of the government flow through social media, in spite of surveillance, through direct voices, and through indirect means such as use of memes and metaphors, as in the recent case of the use of the Winnie the Pooh's love for "hunny" memes created after Xi Jinping became the permanent head of the CCP. The Chinese government censors blocked Winnie the Pooh on social media.

In China, there are "Party newspapers" and non-Party newspapers. The former carry the Communist Party's informational agenda and the non-Party newspapers are commercial newspapers. Both types of newspapers often exist under the same management structure, with the commercial newspapers supported by advertising revenue, and advertising and government funding financially supporting the Party newspapers. Television is a popular medium, and most Chinese households own a television. There are approximately 3300 local, regional, and national TV channels (BBC 2018). The largest media company in China is the state-owned Chinese Central TV (CCTV), which caters to the domestic market. State-run China Global TV

Network (CGTN) in recent years has begun to expand with the aim of influencing the international audience by creating a positive image of the country. The Chinese film industry is on a rise after decades of control and censorship. Today "China has more movie screens than the U.S. and is expected to exceed all of North America in box-office revenues and audiences by 2020" (NPR 2018). China has the world largest internet user base, roughly around 772 million (Internet World Stats 2018), and most access the internet through their smart phones. China has developed its own online media and social media ecosystem that is separate from the world and tightly controlled. World's major players like Google, YouTube, Twitter, and Facebook remain blocked in China. In the online market, there are three major players, collectively called the "BAT." Baidu is the top search engine; Alibaba is the e-commerce leader, which has allied with Sina, which operates the Weibo – a microblog platform like Twitter; and Tencent owns the extremely popular instant messenger WeChat which has more than 900 million active users worldwide (Internet World Stats 2018). The Chinese social media landscape is covered in more detail in Chapter 12.

PIV.2   Japan

Japan is one of the few "developed" nations in Asia. It has a population of about 127 million (Internet World Stats 2018; UN DESA 2017). Japan is currently facing a demographic crisis with low birth rates and an increasing number of older adults. Its GDP is the second highest in Asia, behind China, with 4.95 trillion USD and has an annual growth rate of 0.9% (Work Bank 2016a, b). It is a democratic country with a bicameral parliamentary system of governance. Japan's current prime minster, Shinzo Abe, came to power promising many economic reforms to revive Japan's stagnant and struggling economy. Under Prime Minster Abe, Japan's long standing post-war pacifist constitution is poised to be amended, which has geopolitical consequences.

Japanese (*nihongo*) is the official language, though different dialects and other Ryukyuan languages are spoken in many parts of Japan. Shinto and Buddhism are the two main religions that influence Japanese life.

In Japan, press freedom is constitutionally guaranteed, and Japan has a free and open press. Japan ranks 67/180 in the 2018 World Press Freedom Index (Reporters Without Borders 2018a). Japanese news media are, however, criticized for carrying similar stories that appear in big newspaper or television outlets. The Japanese Press Club (*kisha kurabu*) – located in most major governmental, political, and business organizations – tends to control the access to and presentation of news. It has been particularly criticized for not sufficiently challenging the government in their coverage of the Fukushima Daiichi nuclear plant meltdown that exposed many individuals to radiation and significantly affected local lives. In terms of broadcast, Japan has both a publicly (NHK) and privately owned commercial broadcasting system (TV Asahi, Fuji TV, Nippon TV, and Tokyo Broadcasting System (TBS); Inter FM, J-Wave, etc.). A wide variety of television programs can be seen on Japanese television ranging from sport to soaps. Many television programs are adaptations of popular manga (comics) series or novels. Japan is a technologically advanced country and internet usage is high among the public. In 2017, there were more than 118 million Japanese internet users (93.3% of the population) (Internet World Stats 2018). Facebook, Twitter, and Instagram are quite popular in Japan, but home-grown social media Line leads the pack with 76.9% usage reach in 2017 (Statista 2018a). Mixi is another popular national social media platform. The Japanese film market is the third largest in the world. Japan produces and exports a wide variety of films, particularly anime (animations). More recently, under the Japanese government's *Kūru Japan* (Cool Japan) initiative, export of

Japanese cultural products such as television programs, animation, fashion, and food has increased to Europe, America, and other regional East Asian countries. In Japan, anime and manga hold a special place both as an art form and as entertainment. They have also become very popular in other parts of the world. Chapter 13 provides more details about manga.

PIV.3 India

India is one of the fastest growing developing nations of the world. Its current GDP stands around 2.26 trillion USD and it has an annual growth rate of 7.1% (World Bank 2016a, b). It is the world's largest democracy with a population of 1.3 billion (Internet World Stats 2018; UN DESA 2017). It has a parliamentary system of government with multi-party elections. India's current prime minister, Narendra Modi, came to power promising to root out corruption and bring economic reform. He and his political party, Bharatiya Janata Party (BJP), have been criticized for a Hindu nationalist fervor in India.

Indian culture is very diverse with many regional variations. British colonialism and other invasions (e.g. Muslim, Mongol) have affected its history and culture. It has two official languages, Hindi and English, and more than 22 regional languages and many more dialects. It is a majority Hindu country, with close to 80% of its population practicing Hinduism. Islam is the second largest religion in India, with close to 14% (172 million) of the population. Christianity, Sikhism, Buddhism, and other religions are also practiced by many in India. Religion plays an important role in Indian life and culture.

India's diversity in language and culture gives rise to its multilingual media. Most states within India have their media (film, television and radio programming, newspapers, etc.) in the state language. Traditional media – such as newspapers, films, and television – enjoy tremendous popularity, but new media are gaining ground. In most countries of the world, newspapers are on a decline, but in India they are still on a growth trajectory. In India, media are both publicly and privately owned, but there are more privately-owned media today. This is partly because of the population size and growth in literacy. *Dainik Jagran*, a Hindi language newspaper, has the highest circulation. The highest circulated English newspaper is *The Times of India*. There are more than 12 000 newspaper titles published in India (BBC 2018b). Television is a popular medium. There are more than 180 million households with television sets and approximately 800 licensed satellite TV stations in India (BBC 2018b). On Indian television, one can see a wide variety of programs. Popular programs include broadcast of cricket and prime-time soaps. Many adaptations of American and British programs can also be seen, such as *American Idol* (*Indian Idol*), *Who Wants to be a Millionaire* (*Kaun Banega Crore Pati*), *Big Brother* (*Big Boss*), and so on. Broadcast news has grown over the years, and now there are many 24-hour news channels (e.g. Zee News, NDTV, DD News, ABP News). Commercialization and news-as-entertainment have become growing concerns with the rise of the 24-hour news networks. While India has a vibrant and growing press, threats to journalists through libel and sedition laws, intimidations, harassments, and even death, has placed India low on the World Press Freedom Index, where it currently ranks at 138/180 (Reporters Without Borders 2018a). There are many news- and music-based FM radio stations. All India Radio (AIR) stations reach more than 99% of the population (BBC 2018). Internet and mobile usage is growing substantially in India. Data from 2016 shows that there are 460 million internet users in India, and by 2021 this number is projected to grow to 635.8 million (Statista 2018b). The Indian internet market is considered the second largest after China. Social media usage is on the rise. There are more than 195 million Facebook users, making India Facebook's largest global user base (Statista 2018b). Phone apps like WhatsApp have become immensely popular as more people today are using mobile phones. Internet and mobile communication technologies are transforming Indian media and other businesses and affecting social life. Films in India have a huge following. The Indian film industry is vast and a source of lot of content for other media. Bollywood, India's Hindi film industry, is popular both nationally and internationally. It is discussed in detail in Chapter 14.

PIV.4   South Korea

South Korea has been referred to as one of the three "Asian Tigers" for its rapid industrialization and economic growth. This East Asian country has a population of 51 million and an economy of 1.41 trillion USD with an annual growth rate of 2.8% (Internet World Stats 2018; UN DESA 2017; World Bank 2016a, b). It is a democratic country with a presidential system of government. Its current president, Moon Jae-in, a human rights lawyer, replaced president Park Geu-hye after her impeachment following many scandals. Moon Jae-in has been steadily working toward reducing tensions in the Korean peninsula and involving North Korea in diplomatic talks over nuclear arms.

Korean (*hangul*) is the official language in South Korea, but many dialects are spoken. Buddhism, Confucianism, Christianity, Daoism, and Shamanism are practiced by South Koreans, but a large segment of the population is also atheist. South Korea is surrounded by Japan, North Korea, and China, all of whom have had an influence on its history and culture and share South Korea's tumultuous past and present.

In terms of media, South Korea ranks relatively high on the 2018 World Press Freedom Index (43/180) (Reporters Without Borders 2018a). However, defamation and security laws result in self-censorship among journalists. South Korea is one of the leaders in high-speed internet and wireless usage: 92.6% of its population (approximately 47 million) have access to high speed internet (Internet World Stats 2018). KakaoTalk or KaTalk is a popular messenger app among South Koreans, and online gaming is popular too. In South Korea, public and private broadcasting systems exist. For example, the Korea Broadcasting System (KBS) is publicly owned while Jeonju Television Corporation (JTV) is privately owned. South Korea is now competing with Japan in export of media and cultural products to the region and the world. The South Korean film industry has grown tremendously since its days of tight control and its use for propaganda during the Korean War. Today, South Korean films are collecting both awards and box office dollars in the domestic and international markets. South Korean TV soaps and pop music videos have also become very popular internationally, especially in the neighboring countries. This phenomenon has been referred to as the "Korean wave," and is discussed in Chapter 15.

PIV.5   Qatar

Qatar is a very small gulf nation which has transformed itself from being one of the poorest among the oil rich gulf countries to becoming one of the richest. It has a GDP of 152.5 billion USD and a growth rate of 2.2% annually (World Bank 2016a, b). It has a population of about 2.7 million, but less than 10% of the population are Qatari nationals, the rest are migrant workers who are dependent on Qatari employers/sponsors to work and stay in Qatar. Qatar is extremely dependent on these migrant workers for all types of jobs. Qatar's *kafala* system, which ties migrant workers to their employers, has recently drawn a lot of criticism from Human Rights organizations and other organizations for exploitative worker conditions. Qatar is a constitutional monarchy. Emir Sheikh Tamim bin Hamad al-Thani is currently the head of the state. In 2005, Qatar made several democratic reforms, but the country still remains tightly controlled by the ruling family. Qatari social life is influenced by Islam. Arabic is the official language of the country, but English is spoken by the Arab, European, and Asian communities who reside in Qatar.

In Qatar, media are both state run and privately run. Privately-owned media tend to be as pro-government as the state-run media. Media are available in English and Arabic languages. The internet infrastructure in Qatar is quite advanced, and there are 2.2 million internet users, roughly 97.4% of the population has internet access (Internet World Stats 2018). Qatari media caters to its domestic market through news sources like *Al-Watan* (The Homeland), *Al-Rayah* (The Banner), and others. Qatar ranks 125/180 in the 2018 World Press Freedom Index (Reporters Without Borders 2018a); freedom of press and expression is highly restricted. The country is known to block online content that it deems offensive to Islam, pornographic material, and those violating privacy. In 2014, Qatar adopted a controversial cyber-crime law which imposed additional restrictions on journalists and criminalized posting "false news" online (Reporters Without Borders 2018a). Qatar TV and Qatar Broadcasting Service (QBS) are state-run media for the domestic audience, and Al-Jazeera, covered in more detail in Chapter 16, is geared toward the pan-Arab and other international audiences. Reporters without Borders (Reporters Without Borders 2018b) criticizes Al Jazeera and Qatar; it notes:

> The outspoken Qatari TV broadcaster, Al Jazeera, has transformed the media landscape in the rest of the Arab world but ignores what happens in Qatar itself. The Doha News website continues to be blocked within Qatar. Journalists in this small emirate are left little leeway by the oppressive legislative arsenal and the draconian system of censorship.

References

BBC (2018). China profile – Media. Retrieved from: http://www.bbc.com/news/world-asia-pacific-13017881

BBC (2018b). India profile – Media. Retrieved from: http://www.bbc.com/news/world-south-asia-12557390.

Internet World Stats (2018). Top 20 countries with the highest number of internet users. Retrieved from: https://www.internetworldstats.com/top20.htm.

NPR (20 May 2018). China is a fast-growing presence in the world of cinema. Retrieved from: https://www.npr.org/2018/05/20/612747622/china-is-a-fast-growing-presence-in-the-world-of-cinema.

Reporters Without Borders (2018a). Reporters without Border's 2018 World Press Freedom Index. Retrieved from: https://rsf.org/en/ranking.

Reporters Without Borders (2018b). Media caught in the information war. Retrieved from: https://rsf.org/en/qatar.

Statista (2018a). Most popular social networks in Japan as of October 2017, ranked by audience reach. Retrieved from: https://www.statista.com/statistics/258849/most-popular-social-networks-in-japan-ranked-by-reach.

Statista (2018b). Internet usage in India - Statistics & Facts. Retrieved from: https://www.statista.com/topics/2157/internet-usage-in-india.

UN DESA (21 June 2017). World population prospects: The 2017 revision. Retrieved from: https://www.un.org/development/desa/publications/world-population-prospects-the-2017-revision.html.

World Bank (2016a). GDP. Retrieved from: https://data.worldbank.org/indicator/NY.GDP.MKTP.CD?end=2016&start=1960&view=map.

World Bank (18 May 2016b). GDP Growth. Retrieved from: https://data.worldbank.org/indicator/NY.GDP.MKTP.KD.ZG.

12

The Chinese Social Media Landscape

Xinyuan Wang

To this day, the world's four most visited websites – Google, Facebook, YouTube, and Twitter – are completely blocked in mainland China. Yet, most Chinese do not really notice the absence of the global internet because the "Chinese internet" satisfies them (Wang 2016). In many ways, mainland China has the world's most active social media environment. This chapter will first provide an introduction to the thriving social media landscape in China, focusing on the main social media platforms Tencent QQ and WeChat, and subsequently analyze how *guanxi* (social relationships) is maintained through social media. At the end, the cultural differences in social media use will be discussed.

12.1   Tencent QQ

QQ is the first and the biggest platform in terms of registered users. However, QQ is not a Chinese version of Facebook – not just because QQ started five years earlier (in 1999). It is also more than just a social media platform, as QQ offers a whole package of digital solutions, including instant message, video call, social media (Qzone), microblog (Tencent Weibo), email, games, music and video streaming, etc.

For many people in mainland China, QQ means their first email, social media profile, music player, and online game. Such a high media convergence at the beginning of Chinese digital development appears even more striking in the face of the relatively recent trend of "convergence culture" (Jenkins 2006) in the West where previously separate multiple media technologies have gradually merged into one. Chinese social media started with a high convergence approach. With the rise and popularity of smart phones, such high convergence has become even more intense.

Besides high media convergence, there are other striking features of QQ: (i) a high degree of anonymity; (ii) high customization; (iii) rich visuals; and (iv) a hierarchical structure. A QQ account is a string of figures randomly generated by the system, while a QQ name is what users pick for themselves. Real names are very rarely used as QQ names, and real photographs are not commonly used as QQ avatars (profile image) either. The high customization of QQ is well illustrated by the hundreds of personal webpage models, background pictures, and music.

The features of "high customization" and "strong visuals" are highly consequential. Unlike the white and blue minimal colors of Facebook, the Qzone interface appears much more colorful and visually rich. Chinese website design is known for its richer colors and more complicated, cluttered layouts compared to Western websites which value simplicity far more. The principle

Transnational Media: Concepts and Cases, First Edition. Edited by Suman Mishra and Rebecca Kern-Stone.
© 2019 John Wiley & Sons, Inc. Published 2019 by John Wiley & Sons, Inc.

Figure 12.1 A visual available on QQ.

of "the more, the merrier," frequently found on Chinese dining tables, also contributes to the "visual feast" available on QQ.

QQ's hierarchical structure manifests itself too in the hierarchical level system. Launched in 2004, the QQ level system is based on customers' usage time – the longer the usage, the higher the level. Users with a higher QQ level enjoy some extra functions, such as more decorative functions – including various models and themes from the online QQ shop shown in Figure 12.1. A while ago, to gain a higher QQ level, people used to log in to QQ for as long as possible. This common practice received complaints from the Chinese National Grid, who accused QQ of causing nationwide wastage of electricity. As a result, QQ applied a new algorithm which counts days of active usage, rather than hours, and two hours per day is counted as an active day. Besides the basic QQ level system calculated by time, users can also purchase different kinds of privileges or QQ VIP membership. Privileges include having one's QQ name highlighted and always listed on the top of others' contact lists, and advanced privacy settings such as "invisible visiting" (*yin shen fang wen*), which enables users to erase the evidence of their visits of others' profiles – which otherwise would be recorded and visible not only to the profile owners but also to all the visitors of their profiles.

"Recent visitors" (*zui jin fang ke*) is a defaulting section of Qzone, the social media profile of QQ, which displays information on who has visited the profile and when. Unlike on Facebook, where "digital stalking" is relatively straightforward as it is invisible, on QQ it is more difficult to secretly visit others' profiles. From research, it is evident that the privacy setting on QQ has allowed (though not caused) a whole range of negotiations and confrontations in relationships. For example, one would first purchase the "invisible visiting" function or set up a "fake" QQ account and then spend hours viewing the profiles of recent visitors of a partner's profile in order to spot any slightest trace of love affair. Or, as some reported, they would care a lot about how many persons visited their profiles, and make sure to pay a visit to these recent visitors' profiles in return, in order to maintain a good relationship. To make a visit to each other's profile following the principle of reciprocity is believed to be one of the important social norms of relationship maintenance and development among Chinese.

In retrospect, the early use of QQ marked the active digital engagement of ordinary Chinese more than a decade ago. China's commercial internet came into existence in 1995 in urban areas such as Beijing and Shanghai and was mainly used by urban elites. Due to the digital divide and other gaps in material life, urban lifestyles have long been considered superior and thus admired by the rural population. In such a context, QQ used to be regarded as a digital privilege enjoyed by the urban population in the eyes of the rural population. However, after more than a decade of popularity among Chinese people, and despite remaining the biggest social media platform, QQ has lost its association with the image of being modern. Nowadays a QQ number is regarded to be as normal as a telephone number and there is no obvious rural–urban difference in terms of the penetration rate of QQ. At the end of 2017, there were 772 million internet users in China (CNNIC 2018). According to the quarter one financial statement of Tencent company, QQ had 805.5 million monthly active users (MAU), which is even higher than the total number of Chinese internet users. Given one internet user may have more than one QQ account, the figure is possible and reflects the coverage of QQ among Chinese internet users. In the field of daily communication, QQ has become somewhat old-fashioned, however, because QQ provides many more applications than social media; other applications such as QQ email, QQ music, and QQ games remain major digital applications among Chinese.

12.2   WeChat

WeChat, a smart phone-based multi-purpose social media app launched in 2011 by the same company Tencent that owns QQ, has now become the most popular social media in China. WeChat provides text and audio messaging, audio and video calls, location sharing, multi-media sharing, a payment service, as well as a wide range of functions from taxi hailing to online shopping – no wonder it has been called "super app" or "app for everything." The growth of WeChat is impressive: by 2014, WeChat had become the most popular messaging app in the Asia-Pacific region.[1] By 2015, the penetration rate of WeChat in Chinese main cities had reached 93%.[2] By 2017, the total number of daily active WeChat users was 902 million. At the end of March 2018, the total of monthly active WeChat users was 1040 million.

   WeChat "moment" is the social media personal profile, and the WeChat public account is where users can subscribe to information from more than 10 million accounts on the platform – ranging from media outlets and various institutions to personal blogs and more. Information on WeChat is storable and searchable. Users can save postings to their built-in WeChat files, or search for postings and conversation logs by key word on WeChat. In 2015, a WeChat user on average read 5.86 articles per day, WeChat has also become a "reading app."

   There are seven features of WeChat: (i) smart phone-based; (ii) visually oriented; (iii) strong voice message function; (iv) a low degree of anonymity; (v) a relatively stricter privacy setting; (vi) a closed community; and (vii) a high monetization.

   Launched at the same time as the fast rise of the smart phone in China, WeChat leapfrogged over the PC era directly to smart phone. WeChat is designed to suit the "smart phone lifestyle" and has become an aggregator of mobile services. Compared to the "visual feast" on QQ, on WeChat the room for customization is limited. The layout of WeChat profiles is fixed, and one can only change the avatar and cover photograph, similar to Facebook. However, WeChat gives priority to the visual in a different way. Posting on WeChat is designed to be visually orientated. For each post, one needs to upload images before the text input area appears. As a result, it is effectively impossible to post anything on WeChat without an image. The WeChat "album" refers to a user's personal profile, where images are regarded as the main body of the post – something quite similar to Instagram.

   The visually orientated and mobile-based entry on WeChat encourages users to take more photographs with their smart phones to capture "on the go" occasions. The images on WeChat are not only shared with others, but also stored on WeChat for users' future access. It has been found that a timely mindful engagement with good or nice things in daily life, so called "savoring," can highlight the positive emotions, heighten and enhance the positive experience of daily life

(Bryant 2003). By posting a visual of those "moments" of daily life, WeChat users seem to maximize the positive experience of daily life. Besides visual orientation, voice messaging, another major function of WeChat, also enhances the platform's media richness. In 2015, the average daily amount of WeChat voice messaging was 280 million minutes – equivalent to 540 years of phone calls.[3]

Compared to QQ, real names are used more frequently on WeChat. Real names are required to register a WeChat account. Generally speaking, WeChat represents a closed community that mainly consists of offline networks (family, friends, and colleagues at work). Having said this, WeChat users can still add strangers by functions such as "people nearby" and "shake." The "People nearby" function facilitates users searching for strangers, listed by gender, who are allowed to be located just within one's vicinity; whereas "shake" allows the user to shake their device to find any random person who happens to be shaking their smart phone at the same time all around the world.

The default privacy setting on WeChat is stricter than on QQ and Facebook. For example, as mentioned above, the visiting record of QQ is recorded in most cases. Such high visibility makes "stalking" on QQ without being noticed by others complicated. In contrast, on WeChat, for ordinary users, there is no way to find visiting records. Also, WeChat users have no access at all to the list of contacts of their WeChat friends, whereas on Facebook, users' contact lists are visible under the default privacy setting. On top of this, in many cases users have no access to any interaction underneath others' posts. For example, both A and B are contacts of C, but A and B are not connected on WeChat. Then A cannot see B's comments or likes to C's posts. Moreover, one can only share posts from WeChat "public" accounts but not private accounts.

"High monetization" is another striking feature of WeChat. On 28 January 2014, WeChat launched "WeChat red envelop," which allowed users to send "digital red envelopes" of money to WeChat contacts online. Handing out red envelopes of cash as festival or ceremony gifts has long been part of Chinese tradition. WeChat red envelop applies this tradition online, and makes it more fun: the sender can either send a "fixed amount" red envelope to certain contacts or inform contacts that they can "grab" red envelops. For instance, A can decide to hand out 20 RMB to five of her WeChat contacts. The money could be divided into five digital red envelopes with a random amount assigned by the system. Once the recipients have been informed, they can "grab" their envelopes online and find out how much cash they received (Figure 12.2). The gambling-like red envelope grabbing soon went viral. On Chinese New Year Eve 2014, shortly after its introduction, already more than 5 million people had tried out the feature;[4] by New Year 2018, 688 million people used WeChat's red envelope to send money to relatives and friends.[5]

The popularity of red envelopes significantly fueled monetization of WeChat, as users had to link their bank account(s) to their WeChat accounts before they could hand out or withdraw money from red envelopes. This in turn paved the way for a whole range of applications facilitated by WeChat payment.

Besides business institutions, all the WeChat public accounts can sell products or services on WeChat. Through WeChat pay, service accounts are able to provide a direct in-app payment service to users. Customers are allowed either to pay for items or services on webpages inside the app or to pay in store by scanning WeChat QR codes. In 2015, WeChat launched the "City Services" project, further expanding the scope of services to pay utility bills, book a doctor's appointment, send money to friends, obtain geo-targeted coupons, etc. (Figure 12.3) Aside from stores and restaurants, WeChat payments are even the norm among vegetable markets and other small-scale vendors. Through such practices, WeChat has become an aggregator of the most frequently used and popular services available on mobile devices.

Figure 12.2 The WeChat red envelope.

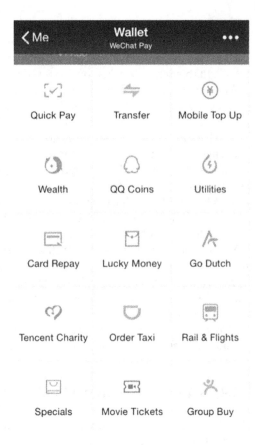

Figure 12.3 WeChat options.

12.3 A Focus on the WeChat Business

It is not rare to see people doing business via WeChat – so called WeChat stores. Many of them run their WeChat business part-time, selling products like homemade cakes and crafts or providing an overseas purchasing service. For small businesses, it is very common to see commercial posts blended with other personal posts on WeChat. Generally speaking, special/ local goods (local specialties) or products endorsed by friends sell best. Dee is a trader; her best-selling product on WeChat is organic chicken eggs.

At the end of 2013, the outbreak of bird flu turned hundreds of eggs in Dee's parents' chicken farm into an unmarketable product. Inspired by various commercial posts on WeChat that she encountered every day, Dee posted a photograph of a basket of eggs on her WeChat and urged her friends to spread the word.

All the eggs were sold within two weeks. A friend of Dee's, Yun, who ordered 50 eggs, commented "I think it is a good deal, I helped her out, but it's not that she owes me a big favor since I also benefit a lot from the good price of the quality eggs." Curiously, the interaction between Dee and Yun on WeChat became much more active after the egg purchase. "I think I owe her a favor (*renqing*), so maybe because of that I paid more attention to her updates on WeChat since then … and I do think we have a better relationship now," Dee explained.

Dee's egg sale on WeChat is more than "word-of-mouth marketing." It is important to acknowledge that *guanxi* has its fundamental impact on a whole range of social interactions, from business activities to public relations. Unlike Western societies, where business is supposed to take place in a professional context without personal touch, doing business and establishing personal relationships in China are usually the same approach, with slightly different fronts. In this sense, WeChat business seems to match with the very feature of *guanxi*.

Anthropologists of China have long noted the significance of the "gift economy" in Chinese society. It is argued that in the cycle of giving, receiving, and the reciprocity of gift exchange, *guanxi* is established and maintained (Yan 1996). Gift money given with the expectation of return has always been an integral part of personal relationships in China. In Dee's case, the gift exchange does not take place in the form of a physical gift, but through *renqing* (favor), which also follows the principle of reciprocity. *Renqing* referring to the feelings inherent in personal relationships and provides a moral sense of obligation toward others, which motivates further gift exchanges. In Dee's case, therefore, her return "gift" was positive interaction on WeChat. In the end, as Dee remarked, the relationship in question had become closer and more positive through the cycle of "gift exchange."

WeChat business along with WeChat red envelopes sheds light on the cultural difference of money. Philosopher Georg Simmel contended that money can never become an "adequate mediator of personal relationships" as it "distances and estranges the gift from the giver much more definitely" (Zelier 1997, p. 82). Conversely, in China money has long been used to express concern and love in social relations and is regarded as a perfect gift. The success of the monetization of WeChat is, to a large extent, the result of Chinese personal relationships which intrinsically include business elements; such forms of success cannot necessarily be copied by other societies.

12.4 Other Social Media Platforms

Popular social media platforms which are mainly used within mainland China also include Weibo, Douban, Zhihu, Youku Tudou, and Momo.

Weibo is the Chinese version of Twitter. In China, there are several Weibo platforms, such as Tencent Weibo and Sohu Weibo. As a public-facing social media, Weibo is the target of strict censorship in mainland China. Since 2013, the Chinese government has started to "clean" up the internet, targeting Weibo. Officials have clamped down on the spread of online rumors, and Weibo users can be jailed for up to three years for posting false information that is forwarded 500 times or viewed 5000 times. A large number of online public intellectuals had to give up their accounts as a result of this enforcement. Some of them began to shift toward the WeChat public account which works relatively less publicly than Weibo.

Douban, an "online community"-like platform, focuses on literature, art, travel, and lifestyle. It is most popular among the urban population with a higher educational background where users can connect with each other based on common tastes and interests. Strictly speaking, Douban is more like a Bulletin Board System (BBS) than a social media platform, as its strength lies in content sharing rather than interpersonal communication. It does not even require users to sign up to access content.

Similarly, Zhihu – which literally means "do you know?" – is a question-and-answer platform where an active user community is the name of the game. Popular Zhihu answerers are regarded as opinion leaders and can open their own column on Zhihu. It is also common to see users "tip" the authors of good answers or articles via WeChat payment.

Youku Tudou, a video-sharing platform, is equivalent to YouTube. MoMo, a dating app, is seen as the Chinese version of Tinder. Even though it's convenient to categorize these platforms as the Chinese versions of their Western counterparts, many of these Chinese social media are larger than their Western counterparts and have different/extra functions.

12.5 *Guanxi* and Social Media

The landscape of Chinese social media is impressive. Equally impressive are the ways in which people skillfully apply social media in their daily life to navigate their relationships online, and a whole set of social norms have emerged around the use of social media.

Chinese society has long been seen as a typical collective or "low-individualism" society – placing the needs, interests, and objectives of in-groups at a higher priority than those of individuals (Kim et al. 1994). Individuals are valued by their ability to live harmoniously with others and how they perceive themselves in interpersonal relations – so called *guanxi*.

The use of social media has thus become woven into the daily development and maintenance of *guanxi*. For instance, WeChat family groups have become popular in urban areas with more and more older people starting to use WeChat, efficiently connecting several families and generations together. Hundreds of sets of emoji which are available on WeChat seem to contribute to a more harmonious atmosphere. Traditionally, senior family members are supposed to be serious, yet since the seniors have started to use cute emojis in conversation, junior family members have started to see the funny side of their senior family members, thus narrowing the social distance.

In addition, social media provides possibilities for exploring new *guanxi* which did not necessarily exist before, such as online friendship. While in urban areas there is a high overlap between one's offline contacts and online contacts, such an overlap is not prevalent among all user groups as recent ethnographical evidence (Wang 2016) revealed: people even feel online friendship to be very "pure" without too many pragmatic concerns as compared to offline situations. For example, a successful business woman feels comfortable entering an anonymous WeChat group to share the frustrating experiences with her teenager and mother-in-law with her "WeChat friends," whereas in offline situations she either feels the pressure to "perform" as a perfect woman or fears people make friends with her only because of money. Also, low-income factory workers prefer to make friends on QQ with strangers whom they have never met face to face as they feel such an online-only relationship is free from the social discrimination they have suffer a lot in offline situations.

There is a constant discussion over the idea that increased technological mediation will lead to the loss of authenticity of social relationships. However, here we see that Chinese people appreciate social media mediation because in many ways it takes away the pressures of maintaining social hierarchies and relationships. Offline life has always been entirely mediated by factors such as social expectations, wealth, and social status. There is no relationship which is not mediated. The social media mediation provides us with a new lens to understand the complicated *guanxi* in China.

12.6 Conclusion

Hundreds of millions of people, who only a decade ago had limited experience of digital, now find themselves in possession of instruments that are as powerful as their Western equivalents and, as we have seen, are often used for a still greater range of purposes (Figure 12.4). The Chinese social media landscape has been formed as a result of a dynamic movement. It was cut off from the outside environment by the Great Firewall, carried forward by a vast domestic market demand, and accelerated by the booming growth of smart phones. In due course, it was this demand that collided with the traditional pattern of social relations and technological innovation. From visiting each other's social media profiles under the principle of reciprocity, to exploring friendship online and establishing friendship with strangers online, social media

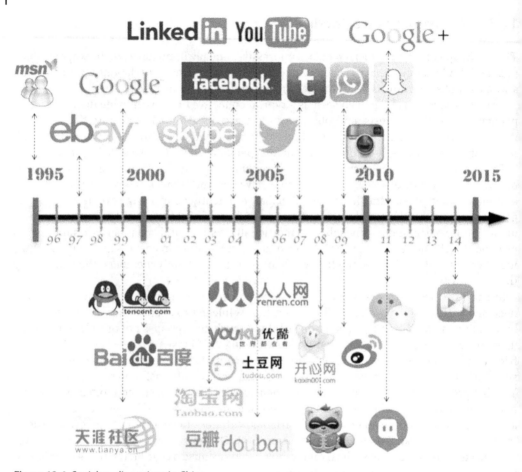

Figure 12.4 Social media options in China.

have become an integral part of everyday life in China and are providing people with an opportunity to develop and maintain *guanxi* – including those form of *guanxi* that are not yet fully developed, or do not even exist in prior offline situations. Coupled with the proliferation of digital applications and economic development, the continuous dynamism of Chinese social media will certainly be interesting to follow in a global context. With the growth of online users, surveillance on social media profiles has grown, and they are subject to greater scrutiny than most offline spaces. It is thus not rare to see people tailoring the privacy setting of individual posts. How this aspect of social media develops in the coming years will be interesting to follow.

Notes

1 http://www.chinainternetwatch.com/10939/wechat-dominates-apac-mobile-messaging-q3-2014.
2 "2015 WeChat Impact Report" http://www.199it.com/archives/398617.html.
3 http://www.chinainternetwatch.com/15287/wechat-users-insights-2015.
4 http://thenextweb.com/asia/2014/02/05/messaging-app-wechat-brings-chinese-new-year-traditions-into-the-mobile-era.
5 https://technode.com/2018/02/18/wechat-hongbao-2018.

References

Bryant, F.B. (2003). Savoring beliefs inventory (SBI): a scale for measuring beliefs about savoring. *Journal of Mental Health* 12 (2): 175–196.

CNNIC (2018). The 41th Statistical Report on China's Internet Development.

Jenkins, H. (2006). *Convergence Culture: Where Old and New Media Collide*. New York: New York University Press.

Kim, U., Triandis, H.C., Kagitcibasi, C. et al. (eds.) (1994). *Individualism and Collectivism: Theory, Method and Applications*. Newbury Park, CA: Sage.

Wang, X. (2016). *Social Media in Industrial China*. London: UCL Press.

Yan, Y. (1996). *The Flow of Gifts: Reciprocity and Social Networks in a Chinese Village*. Stanford: Stanford University Press.

Zelier, V. (1997). *The Social Meaning of Money*. Princeton: Princeton University Press.

13

Modern Manga
Michael Lewis

Cartoon art has been a feature of Japanese culture – elite and popular – since well before the advent of modern manga. Drawn representations dating from at least as early as the mid-twelfth century, sophisticated line drawings of bullfrogs, rabbits, and other animals in very human poses, have been preserved as Japanese national treasures. The *Chōjū jinbutsu giga* painting, for example, depicts frolicking beasts walking on two legs and speaking to one another.

Although the precise meaning of such images is unknown, the scenes suggest pointed social satire aimed at elites, a purpose also apparent in many modern manga. Over the centuries, the use of widely understood satirical caricatures with accompanying commentary rich with double entendre brought severe penalties, including imprisonment and mutilation of the artist. During the early modern period (c. 1600–1868) samurai governments meted out extreme punishments when woodblock print (*ukiyo-e*) artists aimed at powerful political figures such as regional lords or the central shōgun himself as targets for satire.

13.1   Modern Manga: Encountering the West and Early Twentieth Century Development

The long tradition of popular cartooning in Japan is undeniable, but the continuities connecting the modern manga that appeared in the second half of the nineteenth century to what preceded it are implicit and indirect. Instead of gradual liminal development from premodern cartooning forms to the modern manga, disruption best characterizes what actually occurred. The sharp discontinuity resulted from the intertwined factors of mid-nineteenth century Western cultural and political influence and accompanying technological transformation. The main roots of Japanese modern manga are therefore found more in the emulation of Western modernity than in ancient domestic precedent. This applies to form (e.g. Japanese adaptation of the single frame humorous cartoon, strips, comic books, and editorial cartoons) as well as content (e.g. jokes, silly situational humor, social satire, and political commentary). Bryce et al. (2008, para 2) distil the essential features of Japanese modern manga as: "story-driven narratives, exaggerated, deformed illustrations, flexible use of diverse and discursive frames, and linguistic (mostly spoken and onomatopoeic) text" and note that manga today can treat every conceivable subject.

Modern Japanese manga's hybrid origins can be seen in the joint efforts of late nineteenth-century European, American, and Australian expatriates who founded satirical magazines in newly opened trading ports such as Yokohama and Kobe, and the output of Japanese artists who worked on the novel publications. Kitazawa Rakuten (1876–1955), widely considered the

Transnational Media: Concepts and Cases, First Edition. Edited by Suman Mishra and Rebecca Kern-Stone.
© 2019 John Wiley & Sons, Inc. Published 2019 by John Wiley & Sons, Inc.

foremost originator of modern Japanese cartooning and credited with popularizing the very word "manga," followed just such a career trajectory in creating manga as a cultural hybrid. After studying Japanese traditional painting, Kitazawa joined the staff of *Box of Curios* in 1895, where he worked as a cartoonist under Australian Frank Nankivell's direction, and then moved on to independent publishing and a post as an artist employed by major Japanese newspapers and other periodicals. In this unique work environment, Kitazawa honed his surpassing drawing skills and ironic sensibility, expressed in manga distinguished by sharp visual and verbal artistry and satirical commentary on local and international issues. His burgeoning popularity enabled him to found his own, full-color, trilingual manga magazine, *Tokyo Puck*, in 1905 (Lewis 2016).

The work of Kitazawa's contemporary, Miyatake Gaikotsu (1867–1955), reveals fewer explicit ties to Western cartooning. Nevertheless, the content of manga created by this first generation of what came to be called *manga-ka* or "professional cartoonists" demonstrates an approach to humor rarely seen before the opening to the West. The work of both men and that of following generations of *manga-ka* influenced by them produced manga critical of internal corruption, economic and social unfairness, and supportive of Japan's expanding international role and rising status among powerful Western nations. At home, the cartoons also served as agitprop for suffrage expansion and for fostering nationalistic sentiments.

Manga artists – members of a profession that, depending on the *manga-ka* and his subject, straddled the worlds of both journalism and fine art – expressed their love of country during the 1930s and 1940s by contributing to the wartime national propaganda effort. This aimed at both whipping up the public's fighting spirit and depicting the corruption and weakness of the "America, Britain, China, and Dutch" (ABCD) political and military enemies. The vehicles for these wartime messages included editorial cartoons, comic strips, and even animated cartoons. As John Dower has explored in his research, the US mounted a parallel effort to dehumanize the enemy in graphic depictions that presented the Japanese as lice, apes, and murderous dwarfs (Dower 1986). The Japanese visual vocabulary differed somewhat in emphasizing the greed, cupidity, and cowardice of Western imperialists who blocked Japanese attempts to create a Greater East Asia Co-Prosperity Sphere. Such wartime propaganda efforts, intended more to inflame than inform, disappeared with Japanese surrender in 1945. Strict US Occupation Period (1945–1952) censorship now dictated "democracy." It was a policy full of contradictions in both its ideas and implementation but was consistent in emphasizing personal freedoms and the uprooting of any vestige of militarism.

In the decades since 1945, nationalistic and historically revisionist manga explaining Japanese wartime history asserts the benignity of Japanese attempts to liberate their nation and the region's peoples from the yoke of Western imperialism. Several of these works have become bestsellers. Kobayashi Yoshinori's thick comic books in his *Gōmanism Sengen* series are arguably the best and most sophisticated representative of this genre. The series takes up prewar events in Taiwan, China, and Okinawa and considers, from a rightist position, the implications of that history of Japanese and international society today (Kobayashi 1998). The cartooning style is slickly modern, but the revisionist message harks back to World War II in asserting that the wartime Japanese nation was more victim than aggressor and always put the altruistic goal of liberating Asia from Western imperial domination before all others.

13.2 Post-1945 Developments: Florescence

Manga entered its golden age from the 1950s and especially during the "economic miracle" decades of the 1960s and 1970s. During this period, Tezuka Osamu emerged as a leading *manga-ka* or manga cartoonist through his widely popular *Astro Boy* series (actually *Atom Boy* would be a more accurate translation). Many followed in Tezuka's footsteps, focusing on robots, cyborgs, and dystopic futures. Unlike Tezuka's innocents, however, the characters depicted by artists who followed were often more explicitly sexualized types. Despite some differences in focus and tone, many of the basic changes that differentiate prewar and postwar manga can be seen in Tezuka's and his circle's work. During the first postwar decades, manga in large part moved from one-off serial cartoon strips in newspapers and magazines to multi-page, serial, manga-only stories in large, bound magazine formats. The new manga developed specialized narrative lines for specific audiences in illustrated serialized tales aimed at demographic groups such as children, young adults, women, and men.

During this transformative period, manga sales soared as did the fame and wealth of *manga-ka* and publishers. The publishing companies Kōdansha and its *Shōnen* magazine led the 1960s boom, registering sales of millions of copies monthly. The boom had as much to do with manga consumers as it did with the reconfigured product. A mass audience for the phonebook-size publications came with the Japanese public's growing prosperity and increased leisure time. Both factors helped provide a more diverse and older audience. Advances in printing technology that made for high-volume and high-speed production at a comparatively inexpensive cost provided the means to satisfy demand arising from additional disposable income and free time. Technological improvements in production also resulted in qualitative as well as quantitative ties between manga makers and marketers, and the public that consumed their output. Thanks to lower production costs, publishers could play to a wider variety of consumer tastes. Thematic foci diversified to satisfy ever more specialized demands for manga on topics ranging from the modern martial arts, samurai, gangsters, monsters, homoeroticism (the *bishōnen* of beautiful young boy stories in women's manga), and office politics.

Producers sensitive to opportunities in a growing market accordingly adjusted production to capture new customers. Manga publishers increasingly included women writers and illustrators who joined male counterparts in creating the more sexually explicit stories consumed by a growing audience, straight and gay. Sexualized stories and images also occasionally challenged the state's legal boundaries that banned depicting pubic hair, the penis, and a range of sexual acts. In getting around censorship the cartoonists used suggestively shaped and provocatively placed cartoon bubbles full of expressive utterances impossible to misunderstand. By camouflaging the action, however superficially, the *manga-ka* depicted all manner of explicit sexual acts, including rape (men on women and vice versa as well as by instrumentality).

Ero manga or erotic manga became and continues to be an important segment of the overall domestic market. The sub-genre caters to both women and men. Manga carrying images of extremely gruesome violence and thinly disguised sexual acts are also easily available to younger readers as products sold in unsupervised vending machines or as items discarded on trains and subways for recycling to the next reader. They can also be found among the waiting room magazines in restaurants and other commercial venues. Feminist groups and police authorities occasionally move to limit distribution and public accessibility to manga deemed to have crossed a boundary into excessive sexuality and violence. But a wider movement demonstrating concerted public pressure to crackdown on dissemination has never gained much momentum. The fundamental reason for this is that manga enjoy wide public acceptance as a variety of popular culture that many Japanese people deem legitimate and enjoyable.

13.3 Darkness and Light: Manga and the Ambivalent Social Acceptance of *Otaku* (Nerd) Culture

Since the early 1980s and continuing thereafter, manga has become a key element of what has become known as *otaku* culture. The term originated as Japanese slang meaning "nerd" or "geek," a usage overlay that grew atop its more generic meaning of simply "you." In its original slightly pejorative slangy usage, the word indicated the obsessive fan (compare "fan's" origins in "fanatic"). The object of the *otaku*'s obsession can be some form of popular entertainment of cultural activity. The range may vary from a deep interest in manga, animation, video games, cosplay, and electronic virtual reality relations – or, more commonly, a combination of this mix. The word *otaku* has grown in usage beyond slang just as *otaku* culture has grown from a subculture to occupy a more mainstream place in Japanese society and social awareness. Along the way, the term has also lost much of its negative meaning, particularly among the legions of fans who use it as a form of proud self-identification (compare the use of "queer" among members of the LGBTQ community).

Miyazaki Tsutomu, a serial murderer and manga/anime fanatic, severely dented the nerdy but largely innocuous *otaku* image in the 1980s. His actions – kidnapping, slaying, and partially cannibalizing four young girls in the late 1980s – transformed absorption in pop culture, personal quirkiness, shyness, and moderate social withdrawal into something far more pathologically dark and threatening. He blamed his actions on "rat man," a character that he obsessively sketched in cartoons during the long course of his trial. The Japanese press made much of his *otaku* lifestyle, typified by Miyazaki's existence as an unmarried, isolated loner in his forties, living alone in cramped quarters surrounded by countless anime videos. Miyazaki's extreme acts stimulated popular concerns with other aspects of *otaku*-ness, particularly the refusal of young *otaku* to attend school (*futōkō*) and the reclusive social withdrawal or *hikikomori* of *otaku* of all ages. The wider public increasingly condemned these behaviors as unhealthy to the individuals who practiced them and potentially threatening to the wider community. Japanese mass media described Miyazaki as conforming to this negative *otaku* profile on most of its mains points. His lifestyle at times was sensationally described as the rule, not the exception.

Despite the sometimes negative connotations that the word *otaku* suggests among the much-talked-about but largely mythical Japanese mainstream population, *otaku* culture's overall appeal has proven too broad, diverse, and economically valuable to be permanently damaged by Miyazaki's crimes. Manga has continued to be a mainstay of this culture as can be seen in the *Train Man* mega-enterprise that kicked off in 2004.

The Train Man of the title shares a lifestyle similar to Miyazaki's, living in isolation and shunning face-to-face contact in favor of disguised discussion online with a network of fellow *otaku*. But instead of being malevolent, Train Man protects a beautiful young woman who is being molested by an obnoxious drunk during the Train Man's return from his stomping grounds in Akihabara, the Tokyo neighborhood and Mecca of all that is *otaku*. The story, one that allegedly originated in a series of blog posts by the real "Train Man" and responses to them from his online correspondents, proceeds from this first unlikely act of chivalry as the hero attempts to win his love's heart. Eventually the serialized romance was transformed into four best-selling manga. It was also marketed in novelized, televised, and movie versions. Regardless of the medium, the story always focuses on the idiosyncratic character of an ostensibly unconventional *otaku*. But the main character's idiosyncrasy not only falls within the positive spectrum of acceptable social behavior, it also has an endearing, even sympathetic, quality. In the end, the tale is little more than a retelling of the pure-hearted albeit geeky boy-gets-girl story. The extremely profitable success of the *Train Man* manga and related formats attests that *otaku* culture is a highly commercialized phenomenon produced by big business and intended for mass consumption. The official use of manga to disseminate public information, promote partisan political campaigns, and display public service announcements (e.g. subway etiquette, AIDs prevention, etc.) also attests to its and *otaku* culture's central place in modern Japanese society.

13.4 International Dimensions

Manga and the word *"otaku"* have become popular and well understood far beyond Japan's borders. During the years after World War II, manga first made inroads into nearby countries in northeast Asia. In the 1960s and 1970s, Japan's role as an economic superpower and leader of the Asian "economic miracle" helped make the nation's popular culture appear chic and cool. This occurred despite attempts by the governments of Korea, Taiwan, and the People's Republic of China to restrict imports of Japanese movies, magazines, and other cultural materials. Consumers throughout Asia, however, to the degree that their governments allow and often in defiance of their governments' restrictions, appear to have separated Japanese popular cultural products from the wartime history of Japanese militaristic depredations in Korea, Taiwan, China, and Southeast Asia. This is partially explicable by a capacity to disassociate a product from its maker and an ever-present tendency toward local cultural appropriation or "glocalization" of imported material goods and ideas.

The dissemination of manga to the USA and Western Europe and regions outside of East Asia has gained momentum since the late 1980s down to today. The proliferation of graphic novels in countries outside of Japan reveals the strong influence of Japanese manga. In the USA, these novels have gone far beyond the thin comic books intended for a juvenile audience, the predictable *Superman* or *Archie* stories of thrilling super heroes vanquishing super villains or comically goofy adolescents in self-inflicted predicaments, to take up sophisticated stories of adult characters from many walks of life. The format of the graphic novel, thick collections of anthologized stories, also owes much to Japanese manga artistic presentation.

Since the early 1980s, Western academics have also paid serious attention to manga. This was stimulated by the publication of Frederik L. Schodt's, *Manga! Manga! The World of Japanese Comics* (Schodt 1983). Scholarly studies began even earlier in Japan and have culminated in several universities creating undergraduate departments and postgraduate degree programs dedicated to both the study of manga as literature and the fostering of manga production.

13.5 Manga in Japan Today: Fall and Rise?

Today, many commentators speak of a decline of manga and its sibling, Japanese animation. But the industry's scale, its success as an earner of foreign income, and steady popularity argue otherwise. Manga sales over the last few years account for approximately a full third of the Japanese book and magazine market and 40% of all books and magazines published annually (Hays 2013). Aside from full-length anime feature films, manga also are made into TV programs for domestic viewing and export. The toys, video games, character goods, and even food products spun off from manga also generate sales in the billions of dollars. The manga industry, despite advances in computer-assisted graphic productions, employs thousands of workers creating new characters and story lines. This generates a significant multiplier effect that engages employees at movie theaters, sales staff at manga specialty shops, and all the manga-related enterprises based in Akihabara, the aforementioned Mecca for Japanese *otaku*.

Manga's contribution to the Japanese economy is undeniable, but equally undeniable is a decline in manga production since 1995. This trend has paralleled a general slowing in the publishing sector overall as digital media replaces printed materials (Natsume 2003; Oricon 2010). Another factor in the decline is the demographic shift toward a "graying" Japanese population. Despite manga's variety and appeal to diverse tastes and age groups, it has long been associated with the *otaku* youth counter-culture. With Japan's population long having achieved zero population growth (ZPG), the youth-oriented market is clearly shrinking. Of course, graying *otaku*, similar to elderly hippies, may continue to consume manga regardless of their chronological age. In fact, manga fans such as former prime minister Asō Tarō, in his late seventies, continue to enthusiastically read and collect manga.

Yet, even if the fans' enthusiasm defies demographic gravity, production may also continue to decline because of virtual delivery of manga via cell phones and the proliferation of *dōjinshi* manga artists, who are great fans of the manga form, but produce for free for online distribution to fellow enthusiasts in rejecting and resisting the big business side of *otaku* culture. Piracy is also a growing problem, while competition from other nations making similar products – for example the boom in Korean wave manga, animation, movies, and music – may also increasingly erode Japanese manga production and profitability ("Death of Manga" 2015). Global economic downturns are an additional phenomenon that threaten to lower all manga boats regardless of national origins. This is true because manga and related cultural materials are, after all, luxury items subject to sacrifice for more essential commonplace items.

Despite a decline in printed manga output, some individual digital manga and anime spin-offs are still generating profits at home and abroad. Notwithstanding official Chinese government disapproval and largely ineffective attempts to restrict consumption of Japanese made or influenced anime and related products, the demand for such goods created an estimated $21 billion market in China in 2017 (Kodaka and Cho 2017). The success of these examples results from different strategies, including a new emphasis on marketing outside Japan and merging manga with gaming, as in the boom produced by *Pokémon Go*. The current success of manga that have gone beyond hard-copy production suggests that the predictions of manga's demise may be exaggerated. The ability of manga to adapt to new platforms and methods of delivery may enable the industry to evolve and thrive despite the many challenges it faces.

References

Bryce, M., Davis, J., and Barber, C. (2008). The cultural biographies and social lives of manga: lessons from the mangaverse. *Scan Journal* 5 (2): Retrieved from: http://scan.net.au/scan/journal/print.php?journal_id=114&j_id=14.

Death of Manga (27 April 2015). The Death of Manga: Failure to Adapt, Post-Bubble Culture: *Research on Contemporary Japan*. Retrieved from: http://postbubbleculture.blogs.wm.edu/201.

Dower, J.W. (1986). *War Without Mercy: Race and Power in the Pacific War*. New York: Pantheon Books.

Hays, J. (2013). Manga industry in Japan: Artists, schools and amateur Manga, *Facts and Details*. Retrieved from: http://factsanddetails.com/japan/cat20/sub135/item2891.html.

Kobayashi, Y. (1998). *Shin Gōmanzumu Special: Sensō-ron*. Tokyo: Gentosha.

Kodaka, W. and Cho, Y. (2017). Anime a $21 billion market—in China. *Nikkei Asian Review*, 2 May 2017, n.p. Retrieved from: https://asia.nikkei.com/Life-Arts/Arts/Anime-a-21bn-market-in-China.

Lewis, M. (2016). Kitazawa Rakuten as popular culture provocateur: modern *Manga* images and riotous democracy in early twentieth-century Japan. In: *Rewriting History in Manga: Stories for the Nation* (ed. N. Otmazgin), 29–55. New York: Palgrave Macmillan.

Natsume, F. (2003). Japanese manga: its expression and popularity. *ABD* 34 (1): 3–5. Retrieved from: http://www.accu.or.jp/appreb/09/pdf34-1/34-1P003-005.pdf.

Oricon (2010). Top-selling Manga in Japan by Series: 2010. *Anime News Network*. Retrieved from: http://www.animenewsnetwork.com/news/2010-11-30/top-selling-manga-in-japan-by-series/2010.

Schodt, F.L. (1983). *Manga! Manga! The world of Japanese comics*. Japan: Kodansha.

14

Bollywood

Aspirations of a Globalizing India
Suman Mishra

India produces the largest number of feature films in the world. According to an UNESCO 2018 report, in 2015 India produced approximately 1907 feature films, more than twice the number of films produced by the United States which produced 791 films in the same year (UNESCO 2018). India produces a large number of films partly because of its well-developed regional film industry. Each Indian state produces films in the particular state's language which makes up India's "regional cinema," a conglomeration characterized by movies in more than 20 different languages. The largest number of films are produced in four languages: Tamil, Telugu, Hindi, and Malayalam. Bollywood, situated in Bombay/Mumbai, produces the Hindi language cinema, which even though it is not the largest producers of films takes the lion's share of the revenues at the national box office.

The term "Bollywood" has become a globally recognized term which for many conjures up colorful and melodramatic cinema from India filled with singing and dancing. The term has served as a way to distinguish Indian cinema from Hollywood, but also to articulate its imitation of Hollywood. Bollywood has been inspired by Western cinema since its earliest beginnings but has also created its own indigenized and hybrid version of cinema that incorporates styles, forms, and esthetics from a wide variety of cultural influences (Desai and Dudrah 2008). The consequent richness has resulted in the creation of a cinematic experience that is appealing to a large audience in India and abroad.

In order to understand Bollywood and the Indian cinema, one needs to understand India's diversity in culture, language, region, and religion. This is the kind and degree of diversity that is usually found in a continent not in a country. One also needs to understand India's history, the intermixture of colonialism with nationalism, and the globalization that has shaped the country. In this international context, Indian cinema has developed in tandem with the development of a country that in 70 years has transformed itself from being a colonized nation to one poised to replace Britain and France and become the fifth largest economy in the world in 2018 (Reuters 2017). The domestic context is equally important, particularly the wide disparity in the Indian' population's income, education, and ability to access these. These social and economic factors make movies more central to many people's lives as an affordable means of entertainment and escapism. It is impossible to discuss all of India's complexity and nuances that give rise to its colorful cinema, so in this chapter I provide some basic information that can be a starting point for an exploration of Bollywood, India's vast dream factory.

Transnational Media: Concepts and Cases, First Edition. Edited by Suman Mishra and Rebecca Kern-Stone.
© 2019 John Wiley & Sons, Inc. Published 2019 by John Wiley & Sons, Inc.

14.1 A Brief History of Bollywood

Indian cinema has developed parallel to the Western cinema. Lumière Brothers film and technology arrived in India within a few months of its introduction in Paris in 1895. India at that time was under the British rule, but the colonial context did not stop Indian cinema from flourishing. In 1913, Dada Saheb Phalke, known as the father of Indian cinema, made the first full-length silent film *Raja Harishchandra* based on the story of a righteous Indian king. The actors in the film were all male as the medium was considered less respectable for women to work in at that time. The film received an overwhelming response from audiences who were mesmerized by its power to bring alive the tale's mythical characters.

Phalke's commercial success drew new investors to the business of movie-making, who established production houses in cities like Calcutta, Madras, Lahore (now part of Pakistan), and other parts of India thereby stimulating the growth of regional cinema. As more and more films were produced, the British colonial rulers became concerned about their content and the possible use of the medium in stirring protest against the British rule. These fears resulted in the introduction of The Cinematograph Act in 1918, which was soon followed by the creation of a Censorship Board to control the content of films. This act remained on the books until 1952, a full five years after Indian independence in 1947, when it was replaced by the Indian Cinematograph Act.

In 1931, Indian cinema reached a milestone with the production of its first feature-length talkie called *Alam Ara*, a love story of a prince and gypsy girl, directed by Ardeshir Irani. This was a few years after Hollywood produced its first full-length talkie/musical *The Jazz Singer* in 1927. *Alam Ara* featured seven songs that became very popular with the public. This film is credited with introducing song and dance to Bollywood films. The technological developments in more centrally produced films in Bombay were simultaneously adopted by regional cinema, which enjoyed its own commercial successes with talkies like *Bhakta Prahlada* in Telugu and *Kalidas* in Tamil.

The Indian film industry as whole, including the regional cinema, flourished post-independence, and the period between 1950 and 1960 became known as the golden era of Indian cinema. During this time, many films and film directors drew inspiration from the West, but also developed their own style to tell compelling stories of social conditions and social change. These black and white films, also referred to as "art-house films," touched upon social issues of human suffering, poverty, class struggles, caste issues, and changes from rural to urban life.

These films had prominent female protagonists. Waheeda Rehman, Nutan, Nargis, Vyjayanthimala, Sharmila Tagore, and Madhubala were among the notable actresses of this time who left an indelible mark on Indian cinema. Prominent directors and their films during this flourishing time included Satyajit Ray's *Pather Panchali* (*Song of the Little Road*, 1955), Raj Kapoor's *Awaara* (*Vagabond* 1951), Hrishikesh Mukherjee's *Anuradha* (1950), Guru Dutt's *Pyaasa* (*Thirsty* 1957), Mehboob Khan's *Mother India* (1957), Bimal Roy's *Do Bigha Zamin* (*A Small Plot of Land*, 1953), Ritwik Ghatak's *Meghe Dhaka Tara* (*The Cloud-Capped Star*, 1960), V. Shantaram's *Do Aankhen Barah Haath* (*Two Eyes Twelve Hands*, 1957), and K. Asif's *Mughal-e-Azam* (*The Great Mughal*, 1960). Many of these directors and their films found international audiences and fame. *Mother India* was nominated for the Academy Award for "Best Foreign Language Film." Raj Kapoor and his films *Awaara* and *Shree 420* became very popular in the former USSR where they were introduced as an alternative to Western cinema and became a symbol of hope and optimism (Shukla 2009). Satyajit Ray also received multiple awards for his films, including the Honorary Academy Award in 1992.

In the 1970s and 1980s, film production grew and the development of formulaic "Masala" (spice mixture) films began to gain popularity. These films had a little bit of everything: song, dance, melodrama, dramatic fight sequences, romance, and comedy. At this time, even though all genres of films were produced – including those focusing on romance which has been a staple of Bollywood films – the "angry young man" persona embodied in the characters played by popular Bollywood actor Amitabh Bachchan in films like *Zanjeer* (*Chain*, 1973), *Deewaar* (*A Wall*, 1975), and *Sholay* (*Embers*, 1975), became particularly popular. In this era, the softer images of men began to be replaced by tough and macho male characters. These characters took down the *goondas* (villains, mafia, or criminals) almost single-handedly in choreographed fight sequences. Many of these movies followed a formula where the hero and the villain would finally face each other, and the hero would fight the villain and ultimately prevail. This formula became well known to the audiences, but it did not affect their enjoyment, in fact many waited eagerly for the final showdown between the hero and the villain. The fight sequences were so popular with the kids, teenagers, and even some adults that they mimicked them as a part of their play, making the *"dhishum dhishum"* sound to resemble the sounds accompanying the fights sequences.

In the 1990s, after the period of the macho genre, the boy-meets-girl romance movies such as *Hum Aapke Hai Kaun* (*Who Am I to You*, 1994), *Dilwale Dulhania Le Jayenge* (*Bravehearts Shall Win the Bride*, 1995), *Dil To Pagal Hai* (*The Heart is Crazy*, 1997), and *Kuch Kuch Hota Hai* (*Something … Something Happens*, 1998) enjoyed renewed success. Many of these popular films included non-resident Indian (NRIs) characters and were shot in scenic foreign locales in Europe, America, or Australia. For many Indian viewers, these exotic settings provided them with an additional visual pleasure and a tourist gaze just at a time when India was liberalizing and opening its market to greater foreign trade, travel, and other exchanges. The inclusion of NRI characters and foreign locales was done to both provide novelty to the domestic audience and also draw the global, diasporic, and NRI audiences whose numbers were growing. For Indians living abroad, the NRI audiences, watching Bollywood movies had become one of the ways to remain connected with the motherland, and Bollywood producers were eager to entertain this as it significantly increased their profits.

Shooting in foreign locales was not new to Bollywood, which had provided audiences with a manufactured modernity dressed in Western clothing and set in "overseas" locations for a while. Movies made in the 1960s and 1970s such as *Sangam* (*Confluence*, 1964), *Love in Tokyo* (1966), *An Evening in Paris* (1967), *Purab aur Paschim* (*West or East*, 1970), and *Hare Rama Hare Krishna* (1971) are prime examples of films set in foreign locales. These older East-meets-West films focused on patriotic Indian ventures abroad, highlighted tensions between Indian and Western values, tradition, and modernity, and problematized Westernization, Western values, and lifestyles. This nationalistic conflict reduced over the years and, by the 1990s, Bollywood embraced hybridity, global cultures, individualism, Western ideals, and consumerism.

Bollywood films in the first two decades of the 2000s have continued to focus on young romance and NRI storylines. They have also focused on big budget productions with multi-star casting relying on star power to insure their success. Films such as *Mohabbatein* (*Love Stories*, 2000), *Dulhan Hum Le Jayenge* (*I'll Take the Bride*, 2000), and *Kaho Naa Pyaar Hai* (*Say You're in Love*, 2000) represent this trend. At the same time, Bollywood has also produced other genres of films such as "buddy road films" (*Dhoom* 2, 2006; *3 Idiots*, 2009; *Delhi Belly*, 2011, and *Zindagi Na Milegi Dobara* [*You Won't Get This Life Again*], 2011), "superhero films," films whose characters loosely resemble American comic book superheroes (e.g. *Krrish*, 2006, *Drona*, 2008, *Robot*, 2010, *Ra.One*, 2011, and *Krrish 3*, 2013), "macho films" (*Ghajini*, 2008 and *Dabangg*, 2010), and big budget "period dramas" with elaborate costumes and sets like *Jodhaa Akhbar* (2008), *Ashoka the Great* (2001), *Veer* (2010), and *Bajirao Mastani* (2015). Period films tend to focus on heroic historical characters and evoke pride and nationalist feelings among

Indians. They can also draw criticism for their story line or depiction of historical characters. Fringe nationalistic groups have taken to the streets to protest and call for boycott and censorship of the films when they have disliked a portrayal. *Padmavati* was one such recent film that's release was delayed because of fear of violence. This film was about a fourteenth-century Hindu Rajput queen known for her exceptional beauty who committed *jauhar*[1] by immolating herself to protect her honor from a Muslim invader Alauddin Khilji. The protest arose because of an alleged intimate scene between the two characters in a "dream sequence" where Khilji fantasizes about the Hindu queen. Director Sanjay Leela Bhansali repeatedly denied that there was any such "dream sequence" in the movie, but that did not stop Rajput Karni Sena and other Hindu right-wing nationalist groups from vandalizing theaters, threatening the actress, and calling for a ban (BBC 2017; *Hindustan Times* 2017). The film was finally released in 25 January 2018. It did not have the alleged scene. The film received rave reviews and performed extremely well at the worldwide box office.

Over the last two decades, Bollywood has also successfully adapted and produced William Shakespeare's plays. Films like *Maqbool* (2004) an adaptation of *Macbeth*, *Omkara* (2006), an adaptation of *Othello*, *Haider* (2014), an adaptation of *Hamlet*, and *Goliyon Ki Rasleela Ram-Leela* (2013), an adaptation of *Romeo and Juliet*, have enjoyed great commercial successes as well as critical acclaim.

Besides blockbuster films, Bollywood filmmakers have also produced low budget independent (Indie) films which have been described as "a hybrid juxtaposition of social realism and entertainment" and are marketed as an alternative to Bollywood to a wider audience (Davasundaram 2016, p. 25). Many of these films – such as the *Lunchbox* (2103), *Titli* (Butterfly, 2014), *Miss Lovely* (2012), *Margarita with a Straw* (2014), *Liar's Dice* (2013), and *Ship of Theseus* (2012) – have received critical praise in India and abroad.

Bollywood, like many other film industries around the world, continues to produce a wide variety of films, but song and dance remain Bollywood's most enduring characteristic.

14.2 Song and Dance in Bollywood Films

Song and dance play an important role in Indian culture, traditions, and everyday life. In many ways, their incorporation in Bollywood films is just a natural extension of cultural practice. Bollywood draws from traditional Indian culture as well as that of Africa and the West to create catchy hybrid sounds and rhythms. Song and dance, however, are not just superficial add-ons, but also help to forward a narrative, display a particular emotion, or just titillate the audience.

India is by and large still a traditional society with a conservative view on sex, sexuality, and public displays of intimacy. Thus, filmmakers have relied on symbols (e.g. birds and flowers coming together) to communicate messages of sex or have done so through displays of touch, facial expressions, and dance moves that simulate sex. This has helped the wider acceptability and distribution of the movies. Desai and Dudrah (2008, p. 11) explain, "the song and dance enable and incorporate multiple forms of performance and viewing within the film, for example non-normative or transgressive sexualities within the context of courtesan dance scenes or same-sex desire or intimacy."

In Bollywood films, there are many different types of songs and dances. One type that requires a special mention is the "item number" or "item song." Item numbers are provocative, sexy, and raunchy performances by actresses in skimpy clothes for a largely male gaze. These sexy dance numbers with sassy song lyrics are sometimes so popular that many watch the films just for these performances. This helps even mediocre films to make money and has thus encouraged more directors to include them in their films in order to increase the chances of success for their movies in the highly competitive market in India. In earlier movies, these types of songs and dances were performed by vamps or B-list supporting actresses like Helen in *Don* (1978). This reliance on back-ups was necessary in the eyes of producers and directors because leading performers could not be purveyors of activities, even imagined screen activities, considered too risqué and transgressive by Indian standards. This was especially true for lead actresses whose roles were often within the confines of a patriarchal notion of an "ideal woman." In recent movies, however, these "item numbers" are being performed by lead actresses because of their popularity with the public.

The songs and dances in Bollywood films have great economic and cultural significance. They are important commodities for the films themselves. Their portability, especially in the form of music and music videos, helps support other entertainment media like radio, television, cable, and live performances which rely heavily on content from Bollywood to fill the airtime. In addition, Indians are extremely fond of Bollywood songs and dances and incorporate them in their everyday life. Most people memorize and perform Bollywood songs and dances at weddings, house gatherings, parties, or clubs where they are popular form of entertainment and enjoyment.

14.3 Bollywood, a Rising Power in Global Film Production

In 2001, the Indian government granted Indian cinema an official industry status. This was a major shift for a commercial undertaking which for much of its history existed and flourished as a loosely organized industry with various independent players and with the financing source for the films varying from rich individuals to alleged criminal syndicates (Desai 2016). Before receiving the status of an official industry, movie-making was a far riskier business. With the newly designated industry status, Indian cinema is expected to grow through keeping pace with technological advances, skill development, better organization, professionalism, a stable source of financing through banks and other corporate sources, and co-production opportunities with production houses abroad (Ganti 2013; IBEF 2013). Even though this move has been applauded, critics are concerned that the corporatization of the industry will weaken creativity – make the industry "too legalistic" – and there will be a greater focus on the production of blockbuster formulaic movies to ensure the success of the films (Fuller 2000; TNN 2012).

In spite of these concerns and criticisms, Bollywood has begun to corporatize and formalize the co-production of films with several global players. Prominent global production houses are now operating in India and are producing films for Indian and international markets. The list of cooperative local and international ventures includes: Viacom18, a joint venture between Viacom and Network18; Fox Star Studios a joint venture between 20th Century Fox and Star; and UTV Motion Pictures, jointly owned by Walt Disney and UTV Software Communications. Sony has set up its own production house called Sony Pictures India. Walt Disney has also set up an independent unit in India called Walt Disney Pictures, as has Warner Brothers (Sharma 2014). These joint production houses have already produced successful films like *Slumdog Millionaire, My Name Is Khan, Roadside Romeo, We Are Family, Teree Sang (With You)*, and *Boss*.

Bollywood makes most of its profit in its domestic market, but its international revenue has been steadily rising with popularity of films like *Lagaan* (Taxation, 2001), *PK* (2014), *3 Idiots* (2009), *Dhoom3* (*Uproar*, 2013), and *Dangal* (*Wrestling Competition*, 2016). *Dangal*, the story of a father in rural India who teaches his two daughters to wrestle, made the highest revenue in the overseas markets including in China, which is a relatively new market for Bollywood films

(Raghunathan 2017). The USA, UK, Nigeria, South Africa, Pakistan, and the Gulf countries have been the main overseas markets for Bollywood. Even though Bollywood produces the largest number of films in the world, and sells the highest number of admission tickets, its profitability in dollar terms is quite modest compared to Hollywood. Hollywood's box office figure in 2017 was around $11.12 billion, compared to India's $1.6 billion (Box Office Mojo 2018; Statista 2017). This is partly because the ticket prices in India are quite low (ranging from 1 to 4 US dollars) compared to the United States and Europe. In addition, piracy and bootlegging, lack of quality content, lack of adequate screens, and a lack of a coherent global strategy have also hurt the industry's bottom line (*The Hindu* 2011).

In spite of these problems and challenges, Bollywood is steadily gaining popularity around the world. Bollywood's popularity can be seen not only in its growing revenue from overseas markets, but also in increased global partnerships. Today, well-known Bollywood actors (e.g. Priyanka Chopra and Irfan Khan) and other performers (e.g. musician A.R. Rehman and sound designer Resul Pookutty) are appearing in Hollywood productions with greater frequency. Western actors are also coming to Mumbai for parts in Bollywood films (BBC 2012). Many countries (Malaysia, Australia, Fiji, Italy, Germany, France, Czech Republic, Ireland, Turkey, South Africa, Mauritius, Canada, the UK, and the US) are offering Bollywood subsidies to shoot films in their country as it boosts their tourism industry (Deloitte 2016; Kapoor 2017). Tourism sites in Britain and Switzerland are providing information and interactive maps to tourists that list where popular Bollywood films were shot (Kapoor 2017). Bollywood Parks Dubai, a theme park with Bollywood sets, rides, stunt shows, and performances – similar to the Universal and Disney theme parks in the USA – has recently opened. Bollywood inspired dance studios can be seen in many cities all over the United States. Bollywood has also become quite popular in countries like Germany, where a German-language Bollywood magazine called *Ishq* (romance) has been launched (BBC 2012). Pestal, the author of a book *Faszination Bollywood* notes: "Hardcore filmy fans in Germany go for Bollywood dancing at night. They wear saris, bindis, bangles, and some even learn a bit of Hindi" (Ahmad 2014, para 8). Bollywood actors and musicians frequently tour overseas venues, drawing large crowds. In addition, a greater number of Hollywood and British films are being shot in India because of its attractive locations, low labor costs, and film infrastructure. Films such as *The Second Best Exotic Marigold Hotel, Million Dollar Arm, The Hundred Foot Journey, The Darjeeling Limited, Life of Pi, Mission Impossible IV, The Best Exotic Marigold Hotel*, and *Jobs* (Deloitte 2016) are all indicative of this new trend (Deloitte 2016).

The popularity of Bollywood abroad and the onsite involvement of major overseas film companies in India attest to Bollywood's growing global presence and impact. Bollywood is resonating with the global audience and is filling a niche in the global film market. This is captured well in the words of one of its German fans: "Let's say it's about passionate love, about romance, which is missing in Hollywood. It is strong on technology but a lot of feelings are gone. People want to cry, they want to laugh in this world. They are searching for these moments. Bollywood is filling these gaps" (BBC 2012).

Note

1 *Jauhar* was a mass suicide practice where widows in some Hindu communities would immolate themselves (voluntarily or through coercion) to show their devotion toward their husband and protect themselves from capture and enslavement after the death of their husbands during a war.

References

Ahmad, A. (26 April 2014). Bollywood goes global! Meet the fans of Indian cinema across the world who know their Shammi from their Ranbir. Retrieved from: www.dailymail.co.uk/indiahome/indianews/article-2613971/Bollywood-goes-global-Meet-fans-Indian-cinema-world-know-Shammi-Ranbir.html.

BBC (3 May 2012). Bollywood's expanding reach. Retrieved from: http://www.bbc.com/news/world-asia-india-17920845.

BBC (21 November 2017). *Padmavati: Why a Bollywood epic is facing fierce protests*. Retrieved from: http://www.bbc.com/news/world-asia-india-42048512.

Box Office Mojo (2018). Yearly Box Office. Retrieved from: http://www.boxofficemojo.com/yearly/?view2=mpaa&chart=byyear&yr=2017&view=releasedate&p=.htm.

Deloitte (2016). Indywood: The Indian Film Industry. Retrieved from: https://www2.deloitte.com/content/dam/Deloitte/in/Documents/technology-media-telecommunications/in-tmt-indywood-film-festival-noexp.pdf.

Desai, R.D. (3 March 2016). Bollywood's Affair with The Indian Mafia. Retrieved from https://www.forbes.com/sites/ronakdesai/2016/03/03/bollywoods-affair-with-the-indian-mafia/#7417b5884aa6.

Desai, J. and Dudrah, R. (2008). The essential Bollywood. In J. Desai & R. Dudrah (Eds.) *The Bollywood Reader* (pp.1–20). Berkshire: Open University Press, McGraw Hill.

Devasundaram, A.I. (2016). *India's New Independent Cinema: Rise of the Hybrid*. New York: Routledge.

Fuller, T. (2000). Financing films on a personal basis. Retrieved from: http://www.nytimes.com/2000/10/20/news/financing-films-on-a-personal-basis.html.

Ganti, T. (2013). Corporatization and the Hindi film industry. In: *Routledge Handbook of Indian Cinemas* (ed. K.M. Gokulsing and W. Dissanayake), 337–350. London: Routledge.

IBEF (November 2013). Corporatization of Indian film industry: A report on the progress of the Indian film industry and the impact of corporatization. Retrieved from: https://www.ibef.org/download/corporatisation-of-indian-film-industry.pdf.

Kapoor, A. (12 March 2017). How the Hindi film industry has found both fans and revenues in foreign shores. *The Economic Times*. Retrieved from: https://economictimes.indiatimes.com/magazines/panache/how-the-hindi-film-industry-has-found-both-fans-and-revenues-in-foreign-shores/articleshow/57600192.cms.

Ragunathan, A. (2017). Bollywood star Aamir Khan's Dangal is highest grossing Indian movie - spurred by China collection. *Forbes*. Retrieved from: https://www.forbes.com/sites/anuraghunathan/2017/06/27/bollywood-star-aamir-khans-dangal-is-highest-grossing-indian-movie-spurred-by-china-collection/#182a57e01880.

Reuters (26 December 2017). India Looks Set to Leapfrog the U.K. and France to Become the World's Fifth Largest Economy in 2018. *Fortune*. Retrieved from: http://fortune.com/2017/12/25/india-economy-uk-france-2018.

Sharma, N. (2014). 6 Hollywood Production Houses That Have Come To Bollywood. *Business Insider*. Retrieved from: https://www.businessinsider.in/6-hollywood-production-houses-that-have-come-to-bollywood/articleshow/34150721.cms.

Shukla, V. (5 October 2009). Why Raj Kapoor was popular in Russia: An old Russian lady said it was the optimism of the charismatic actor that inspired them to brave through hard times. *Hindustan Times*. Retrieved from: http://www.hindustantimes.com/entertainment/why-raj-kapoor-was-popular-in-russia/story-2IYoi7g6O0RLhF8kG04OCO.html.

Statista (2017). Leading box office markets worldwide in 2017, by revenue (in billion U.S. dollars). Retrieved from: https://www.statista.com/statistics/243180/leading-box-office-markets-worldwide-by-revenue.

The Hindu (22 April 2011). The Bollywood-Hollywood partnership. Retrieved from: http://www.thehindu.com/news/the-india-cables/the-cables/248355-The-Bollywood-Hollywood-partnership/article14691597.ece.

The Hindustan Times (19 November 2017). Padmavati controversy: Amid threats and protests, producers defer its release. *Hindustan Times*. Retrieved from http://www.hindustantimes.com/bollywood/padmavati-release-postponed-not-to-come-out-on-december-1/story-AAMT5dPtRloBAmSdqR4NRL.html.

TNN (2 December 2012). Corporatisation will kill art, says Shekhar Kapur. Retrieved from: https://timesofindia.indiatimes.com/entertainment/hindi/bollywood/news/Corporatisation-will-kill-art-says-Shekhar-Kapur/articleshow/17446649.cms.

UNESCO (2018). Reshaping cultural policies: Advancing creativity and development. Retrieved from: http://unesdoc.unesco.org/images/0026/002605/260592e.pdf.

15

The Korean Wave

Why It Swept the World

Shin Dong Kim

The "Korean wave" is a term coined by a Chinese newspaper that reported on the unexpected popularity of Korean-made media content, such as television dramas and dance music, in the mid and late 1990s in China. The Chinese public didn't have any access to Korean media and pop culture until some of the television stations began importing it and putting Korean programs on air in early 1990s. Interestingly, China was not alone in consuming the Korean media content around that time, other countries in East Asia joined as new consumers. Japan, Taiwan, Hong Kong, and Singapore became early importers, but the list grew quickly with the addition of members of Southeast Asian countries. Around a decade after the new millennium, Korean media content, or so-called K-pop culture, spread globally and established a firm visibility not only in Asia, but in the Americas, Europe, Africa, and Oceania. At the beginning of the tide, most people were unsure whether the wave of unexpected demand and consumption of Korea-originated content could be sustained.

Over the next two decades, however, the Korean wave grew to be a very subtle phenomenon with billions of fans around the world. Many reports and case studies have also been accumulating accordingly.[1] This short chapter will not repeat detail on how the Korean wave is victoriously pushing into new territory and gaining new fans. Instead, I will discuss some of the factors that might have significantly contributed to the rise of Korean media and pop culture. A short description on the development of the phenomenon will be unavoidable in the course of discussion, but my focus will be on the causes of the Korean wave and what made it possible.

15.1 Contributing Factors

Why the Korean wave? What made the media content and pop culture from Korea so successful in other societies globally? What are the reasons behind its popularity? Whenever I throw this question to my students or the audience of my lectures in China, Japan, Hong Kong, Vietnam, Philippines, or in Europe and the Americas, the most common answers are that they are fun, interesting, and the actors and actresses are handsome and beautiful. The music is new and different from both Western pop and their own domestic pops. K-pop easily grabs the soul of young fans and lets them jump on the wagon of global fan networks in which they feel membership and loyalty. Obviously, these do not qualify as whole answers to the question, though they may be true and enough reason to be in love with K-pop.

The success of Korean-made pop products must surely encompass these reasons. In the 1990s, the first wave began with television dramas and dance music. When the market seemed

Transnational Media: Concepts and Cases, First Edition. Edited by Suman Mishra and Rebecca Kern-Stone.
© 2019 John Wiley & Sons, Inc. Published 2019 by John Wiley & Sons, Inc.

saturated with those, the second wave followed with much bigger fandom for K-pop in the latter parts of the 2000s. That's when K-pop began replacing the term Korean wave or being used synonymously with it. K-pop initially meant Korean pop music uniquely, with its fast dance rhythm and group dance choreography, but later it began to loosely point to Korean pop culture in general depending on the context. In this chapter, I will also use the term both ways. Now people say K-pop is in its third stage of development, where its popularity not only covers dramas, music, film, but also includes fashion, food, tourism, etc.

So, what has made the Korean pop products popular among foreign consumers? Contributing factors come from far and near, with large and small impacts, on both long- and short-term time scales. I have divided them into two large groups: domestic factors and global factors.

15.1.1 Domestic Factors

It's easy to agree with the argument that the Korean wave began unexpectedly and had nothing to do with any kind of prepared plan. Indeed, there was no plan or vision that preceded the phenomenon. Not even a good expectation of success. Programs were cheap and the Korean government or any producer would give the programs away almost for free for the simple purpose of promoting the nation. This was the situation until the early 1990s. The pop culture market, including the television and film sectors, was not fully developed compared with the advanced markets. But in the early 1990s, the Korean media market was about to transform into a full-blown business and industry. A few domestic developments in the media market eventually contributed to the arrival of the Korean wave. First was the expansion of the television market with the introduction of the cable television system in the early 1990s – although the growth of the television industry was well on its way throughout the 1980s. Second, the accumulation of program production technologies and skills over a few decades upgraded the quality of the programs to a higher level, especially when the democratization of Korean society opened space for freedom of expression in the 1990s. Third, a new generation of creators and consumers of media and culture arrived in the 1990s. The mature and affluent mass of new cultural consumers was the true engine for the development of culture industries in general.

From its inception in 1960, television in Korea has remained under government control, and the government was a dictatorship until 1987. Television was a social and political institution rather than a business or industry during this period. But the continuing and remarkable growth of the Korean economy, which political economists later called a "development dicta-torship," throughout the period transformed the media system of the country into a somewhat grotesque giant. The two public television stations, Korean Broadcasting System (KBS) and Munhwa Broadcasting Corporation (MBC) have grown into big businesses under the protection of the state. It was a state-protected monopoly (or duopoly) system, where new entries were basically blocked from entering the system and, in return, the broadcasters were under the tight control of the authoritarian government. News and serial dramas were the two main genres in television programming that attracted most ratings. While news programs were busy churning out political propaganda for the dictators, drama production aimed much more to buy the viewers' affection. Quite a lot of air time was devoted to drama programming. All the stations aimed to win the ratings race in daily and weekly dramas. Competition among the producers became fierce, and their production skills and technologies in drama reached a high level after three decades of head-to-head competition.

This accumulation of the production technology didn't simply come from blind competition. Korean television drama production experienced a qualitative shift in the early 1990s when the society entered democracy following the fierce and successful democratization protests that overthrew the military government in 1987. Freedom of expression came to the media sector and the impact was immediately visible in the new films and dramas. Decades-long older formats of television drama gave way to more appealing and qualitatively refined ones. The young writer Song Jina, for instance, became a star overnight with her record-breaking drama *Sandglass*, which critically and retrospectively depicted the harsh years of dictatorship in a romance. Freedom of expression in the new democratic society paved the way for a new generation of creators to come up with improved productions in full capacity. In 1993, the first civil government in more than three decades was inaugurated under President Kim Young Sam, whose government opened the era of cable television in Korea. The age of three-channel television was closing and a new era was dawning. With the increased 20-plus channel capacity, the development of content was in high demand. The government also drafted a new law requiring that existing broadcasters allocate certain portions of their programming to outsourcing from independent production houses. This new law directly aimed to promote the development of independent production companies. Digitalization of television technology and business in the 1990s and the first decades of the new millennium principally removed the idea of scarce-resource discourse in television business and policy. Not only in Korea, but worldwide, channel capacity exploded with digital technologies and the demand for content grew accordingly.

The strong economic growth of the nation during the 1970s and 1980s propelled an explosion of advertising spending into the media market and prepared for the expansion of television with the introduction of cable. The government also promoted developing the platform businesses and content production through policies and laws. The media system of the country was no longer viewed as simply a social and cultural or political institution, but more as an industry and business. While these developments were doubtless all very significant steps toward the overall growth of the media and culture industries, the most fundamental source of media growth came from two origins. One was the unforeseen progress of digital technologies and the other was the rise of a new generation of cultural creators and consumers. The impact of digital technologies is not necessarily unique to Korean society. Korea Inc. was perhaps quicker and more aggressive in adopting and developing the digital technologies in full force, and it helped the nation to transform and advance its industrial structure from the manufacturing oriented 1970s style to the high-tech digital economy. Technological innovation was a buzzword in the 1980s and 1990s in Korean society, as evidenced by the fact that Korea began pouring money into R&D from the late 1980s, staying on top list of the R&D spending per capita income.

However, the most important but least noticed factor was the rise of a new generation of consumers as well as creators. Devastated by colonialism (1910–1945) and the Korean War (1950–1953), the country was impoverished until the end of the 1950s. The first Five Year Economic Development Plan (1961–1966) was successfully accomplished in the middle of the 1960s, and the nation began building up the public education system. This period was also the Korean "baby boomers'" (born between 1957 and 1963) schooling time. This generation, later called the 386 generation, became the first of the country's 5000 years of history that received systematic public education for the entire population. Illiteracy dropped and academic achievement became considered the most crucial condition for social mobility. Investment in education had expanded fast, both from public and private means. Traditional ties, such as blood ties and hometown ties – which had served as social capital for getting jobs and promotions – were gradually losing their importance to educational qualifications and alumni networks.

The growth of schools and investment in education has been astonishing since the 1960s. Many criticize that Koreans are overly investing in their offsprings' education. Korea is one of the top countries showing the highest rate of college education attainment out of Organisation for Economic Co-operation and Development (OECD) members. The college advancement rate since 2010 is over 70%, and it reached near 80% at one point. Needless to say, the intensive investment in education heightened the level of cultural capital in the general populace. It is not uncommon to bump into supermarket cashiers with college degrees in Korea. A high level of cultural capital among the general population creates a high demand for good quality products to satisfy their cultural appetite. Culture industries including television, film, and music since the 1990s have shown a sharp upward growth curve. The demand for cultural consumption is not only rising in the pop culture sector, but in highbrow art too. Classic concerts, musicals, books, and fine arts have sold well in the same period. In other words, the emergence of the Korean wave is not simply caused by and dependent on short-term government policies or industrial strategies and tactics. It has deep roots.

What, then, was the role of the state in developing the media and culture industries? Did the Korean government have a significant role in the rise of the Korean wave? My answer is no. But this is too much of an important issue to simply put to one side, since many observers think and argue that the Korean wave is much indebted to government initiative. Observers outside of Korea tend to lean to this view more than domestic scholars. This is probably because observers outside Korea rely more on government-issued materials or websites for information and data than those within the country. As far as I am aware, there was no policy or measure aimed at developing the Korean wave until it gained huge attention and recognition from both domestic and international media. Initially, the Korean government was more like a passive follower, though it later became an active participant once it saw the wave's success. The rise of the wave influenced the government deeply and they introduced policy supports in the next stage.

Kim Dae Jung's government from 1998 was probably the first administration that cared about culture and the culture industry in any true sense. The Ministry of Culture and Tourism of the Kim administration published a policy blueprint to promote the development of the creative industry under the slogan of "Creative Korea" for a while, but the actual contents of the policy were hard to evaluate in terms of their strength and effectiveness. The most significant measure that the Kim government introduced in the first year of their term was to lift the ban on Japanese pop culture. Since 1945, Japanese pop culture had not been allowed to be imported and was severely discouraged in the daily lives of Koreans. The colonial trauma against the Japanese ruling of Korea justified the ban for many years. At the time of the lifting of the ban, many people worried that the Korean culture industry would be washed away by the inroads of Japanese pop culture; this did not happen. On the contrary, the measure paved way for the Korean media to go to Japan. The legendry popularity of television actor Bae Yong June in Japan, which ignited the rise of the Korean wave in the country, was born from the television serial drama *Winter Sonata* in which he starred with a female actress Choi Jiwoo, who also became famous in Japan after its release. The drama was accidentally introduced by the NHK satellite channel, whose role as a public station is to cover the remote areas of the country. A producer of the station thought the Korean drama could be a nice filler for the mostly unwanted programming schedule in the morning and decided to buy and place the program there. To the surprise of almost everyone, it attracted a high viewership, and the station decided to rerun the program at a better time in the schedule – which garnered even higher ratings and news attention. Based upon this surprising result, the headquarters of NHK in Tokyo decided to put the program on its main terrestrial channel, only to see an explosive and tremendous success. The main channel had to schedule a rerun without dubbing but using subtitles, which was rare for foreign programs aired on the channel. This was upon the pressing requests of the viewers who wanted to listen the real voice of "Yon sama" (a respectful form of mentioning Bae Yong June by the fans). The Yon sama syndrome was enormous and significant part of the Korean wave in Japan in its early stages. People said that *Winter Sonata* played a more powerful role in improving the relationship of two countries than 60 years of official diplomacy did.

Government support for the growth of the Korean wave, and more broadly the development of media and culture industries in general, became more stable after a decade of trial and error. The government's role in relation to culture was very narrow and stayed within the spectrum of cultural conservation policy. The Ministry of Culture (and Tourism) largely focused on subsidizing the traditional and classical arts and artists, including literature. The ministry knew very little about the culture "industry" and related "economy." However, things changed and had to change further after the surge of the Korean wave. The government tried to understand the situation and created a new directorship of culture industry in the Ministry of Culture. The government's support and promotion of the culture industry materialized through state-backed institutions such as the Korean Creative Culture Agency (KOCCA), whose role since then has been significant.

15.1.2 Global Factors

The geopolitics of East Asian countries has had an impact on Korea. Many countries of the region remained intensely hostile after World War II. The Cold War in East Asia was probably the coldest around and after the division of the Korean peninsula. US troops were stationed in South Korea after the Korean War, which even now has not formally ended: an armistice was signed between the North and the USA, and technically the two Koreas and the US have been at war for over seven decades. China's alliance with the North, Japan's ambivalent position in the postcolonial era, and Russia also being seen as an enemy, resulted in a hostile environment for international politics, where South Korea became quite isolated at the eastern tip of Asian continent for half a century. The flow of information and culture during the Cold War era was basically negligible; if it was anything at all, it was an outright propaganda competition among the countries of East Asia. Political barriers were too high and firm for any kind of cultural globalization.

However, things started to change in the region when, in 1979, Deng Xiaoping declared reforms in Chinese socialism toward pragmatism and designated Shenzhen as a Special Economic Zone. China adopted an open-door policy and integrated the market system into its socialist political structure. China's development since then has been bumpy in many areas, including the media sector which has been under the strong control of the Chinese Communist Party. Media was at the core of the Communist Party oligarchy and still is, but the commercialization and industrialization of media was unavoidable following the reforms. In the 1990s, the Chinese government began expanding the television market and this created a huge demand for program content which led to the import of Korean programs into China. In the early 1990s, a few Chinese television stations imported dramas from Korea along with other imports from Japan and the West to meet the growing demand for programs in their expanding domestic media market.

The situation further changed after the fall of the socialist bloc along with the opening of China. It changed again drastically after the introduction of the internet. Until the 1980s, the so-called spill-over of broadcasting signals was considered, and condemned as, an invasion of cultural sovereignty. Countries were serious enough to organize meetings and issue declarations against the spill-over of foreign programs. The idea of consuming foreign content was viewed as dangerous and often invited suspicion but in the last three decades things have changed as the world has come together to watch programs on YouTube. Views and concepts relating to international communication have gone through paradigmatic changes from the nation-state-centered to a globalist perspective in which global flow and consumption of cultural content is taken for granted.

The platform revolution in media industries is worth highlighting here in relation to the successful penetration and consumption of the Korean wave in the 1990s. There is no doubt that the digitization of media technologies made it possible for consumers in other countries to watch and listen to Korean programs and music. Digital technology also made illegal reproduction extremely easy and costless. In early 2000, you could easily find street vendors with illegally copied movies and television dramas, including Korean made, on the streets of Beijing, Bangkok, Taipei, Manila, and so on. A decade later, the street vendors had almost disappeared, but the content went online and illegal downloads became even easier and cheaper if not without cost. Globalization of cultural content found its way through the global digital platforms. This was particularly true when we consider the fast expansion of the television market through the early 2000s worldwide. Taiwan, for example, saw the arrival of a 100+ channel era with the introduction of cable television. This created a massive demand for program content, and eventually became a powerful catalyst for program imports from Korea and other sources. This trend and situation were more or less the same in other countries. Korea's domestic television market also went through a similar phase.

The end of the Cold War, the spread of digital technologies, and economic growth in Asian countries helped usher in greater cooperation and cultural interaction among Asian countries. This interest grew through the popular acceptance and consumption of Japanese mass culture, such as J-pop, manga, anime, and dramas in the 1980s and 1990s by Asian consumers. Also noticeable was the cross-border cultural consumption of Hong Kong cinema and Canton pop in the 1980s and 1990s. In a sense, the Korean wave is another version of an inter-Asia cultural encounter that follows the footsteps of the Japanese and Hong Kong waves.

The successful spread of Japanese pop culture went beyond Asia and has now constructed firm bases globally, especially with manga and anime. Interestingly, however, Japanese television dramas and films thrived only for short time in the international market. It is unclear why this might be the case. Perhaps in real actor content, such as drama and films, it is less easy to de-emphasize their Japaneseness than in fictional manga and anime content. Koichi Iwabuchi uses the term "deodorization" of Japaneseness to explain this de-emphasis in Japanese culture commodities diluting the colonial trauma and facilitating consumption. Some observers note that the Japanese domestic market is already big enough to survive and thrive and suggest that this is the main reason why Japanese media industry has not sought global expansion. These and other reasons could be plausible explanations for why the Japanese television and film industry has not expanded beyond its borders.

Hong Kong presents a different case. Hong Kong used to be one of the most advanced and exotic places for many Asians in both imagination and reality. It was supposed to be a place of advanced Western culture in the East, and a city of affluence and prosperity. Romance films, Hong Kong noir, and martial art movies were immensely popular in Asian markets. Hong Kong films were the second largest after Hollywood in the Korean market for many decades. When Hong Kong was returned to China, the future of Hong Kong's film business looked fairly encouraging since the huge Chinese market seemed to be waiting for more from the Hong Kong image factory; the combination of Hong Kong technology in film making and Chinese money would push Hong Kong's film industry to become a global player. However, this did not happen; on the contrary, the Hong Kong film industry declined. No big stars, no big blockbuster films came out. Collaboration with Chinese money and Beijing's standard of censorship resulted in films with exaggerated fictional historical sagas. Growth and globalization of other Asian cities also made Hong Kong less central to Asian film production. Hong Kong eventually became a popular place for K-pop and K-drama.

People in the Korean culture industries are very sensitive to Chinese government policies on foreign cultural products since they directly affect their profitability in the Chinese market.

They ask the Korean government to negotiate well with the Chinese so that their businesses are protected and remain lucrative. Even though there have been fears related to business prospects in the Chinese market because of the communist regime's control over media, one can argue that the Chinese government's tight control on its domestic media and their content is actually helping the Korean producers to continue producing content to fulfill the demand of Chinese consumers. China has the resources to develop its culture industry but it will not advance yet because of the restrictions on freedom of expression. This is another paradoxical contributing factor to the sustained popularity of K-pop in China.

15.2 What is the Korean Wave to Koreans?

The Korean wave is the phenomenon of Korean-made pop content gaining popularity in foreign countries. So it is primarily a phenomenon happening not in Korea but outside Korea. But the Korean wave is still a critically important phenomenon to Koreans since the impact of the wave is long, deep, and in multiple directions. The Korean wave brought a few significant outcomes to Korea and Koreans. First, it had a huge psychological effect on the way Koreans perceive themselves and their country. Second, the economic impact of the Korean wave has been much bigger than just selling some dramas or films or music. Third, Korea's status and image in the international community has improved significantly.

For the majority of Korean people, the Korean wave is a huge psychological consolation. From colonial times to recent economic development, Koreans were pushed by themselves and by others to look up to the advanced societies and cultures. In the dominant paradigm of modernization, the West has been a model and goal to catch up with. Good things were almost always from outside the country. European classic cultures, American pop cultures, and Japanese technologies were the things that the Koreans were asked to emulate. Koreans were always busy importing foreign things. Export was something to be proud of, not only because it earned dollars but more significantly because it meant recognition of technologies and skills. The Korean films produced in the 1960s and 1970s often placed emphasis on Korean exports to the USA and Japan. The politics of recognition is hugely important for a postcolonial society in constructing identity and boosting self-esteem. The cultural significance of the Korean wave is immense to Koreans in this context. This recognition came along with the Korean achievements in other areas, such as the success of global corporations like Samsung, LG, Hyundai, and accomplishments of Korean artists and athletes. For most Koreans living today, this is a new thing that didn't exist before.

The economic impact of the Korean wave has also been more than great. Korean brands of all kinds, cosmetics, to food, fashion, electronics and cars, plus tourism have received high visibility in media and have been evaluated highly for their quality.

The Korean wave can be best explained through Joseph Nye's concept of "soft power." Soft power is the attractiveness of a country due to its cultural contents and quality. The importance of soft power was quickly linked to "nation brand" in early 2000. It's easy to agree that the images of nations are valuable assets after all.

15.2.1 Another Cultural Imperialism, or a Successful Counter Culture to the American Empire?

The spread of the Korean wave to many different cultures and the increasing consumption of Korean-made content has stimulated some arguments that the Korean wave is a new form of cultural imperialism in which Korean values are overstated and pose threats to the local culture and cultural industries. This is not a loud voice yet, but an opinion that the cultural creators and merchants need to take into consideration. Contrary to this argument, there's also an interesting line of thinking that sees the success of Korean pop culture in the regional and global market as a good example of a global counter-culture to Hollywood and Western domination. Booming Bollywood, telenovelas from Latin America, and the Korean wave are all suggesting that global culture industries in the twenty-first century are not necessarily dominated by Hollywood anymore.

These two theories are still very much at hypothetical stages. Both need more evidence and systematic presentation for the enrichment of studies in global communication. As mentioned before, the paradigm of international communication has changed. The thesis of cultural imperialism doesn't seem to be attracting much support. Cultural hybridization seems to be daily practiced but itself doesn't indicate either positive or negative results. Media consumers of the world are consuming common goods more and more and this may expand the common ground of cultural understanding.

15.3   Future Prospect

In this chapter, I have covered the rise of the Korean popular media and its roots both in the domestic and global arenas. The Korean wave did not happen overnight. It was also not a planned project. It is something that is still in progress; and nobody can predict whether it will keep growing bigger to challenge Hollywood's cultural factories or slowly fade away from the global scene like the Japanese and Hong Kong films. I would argue that the wave could stay for quite a while since its roots are deep and fandom has grown to a critical mass. One of the interesting things about cultural consumption is that the consuming process is embedded within the consumers' personal histories and memories. So, the cultural consumption becomes a part of the consumer's lived history. Once you become a fan of some music, film or drama, they stay with you for the rest of your life.

The production technology for cultural industries in Korea has reached a high enough level to attract both domestic and global consumers. At the time of writing, BTS, a Korean boyband, topped Billboard 200 after a series of successful appearances on global stages. At the root of the explosive rise of the Korean wave lies the complicated accumulation of cultural capital and technologies. Some of these will soon be transferred to other countries, as is already happening with China and some Southeast Asian societies. But the system won't lose its competitive edge soon, especially while the market is growing worldwide. The question is just how far the depth, variety, and richness of Korean-made content can grow. And this is the point to watch over the coming decades.

Note

1 This chapter does not review the existing scholarship on the Korean wave. Instead, I suggest a few good texts on the topic at the end of the chapter in place of references.

Further Reading

Choi, J. and Maliangkay, R. (eds.) (2015). *K-Pop: The International Rise of the Korean Music Industry.* New York: Routledge.
Chua, B.H. and Iwabuchi, K. (eds.) (2008). *East Asian Pop Culture: Analysing the Korean Wave.* Hong Kong: Hong Kong University Press.

Jin, D.Y. (2016). *New Korean Wave: Transnational Cultural Power in the Age of Social Media*. Urbana, IL: University of Illinois Press.

Kim, K. (2011). *Virtual Hallyu: Korean Cinema of the Global Era*. North Carolina: Duke University Press Books.

Kim, Y. (ed.) (2013). *The Korean Wave: Korean Media Go Global*. New York: Routledge.

Kim, K. and Choe, Y. (eds.) (2014). *The Korean Popular Culture Reader*. North Carolina: Duke University Press.

Lee, S.J. and Nornes, A. (eds.) (2015). *Hallyu 2.0: The Korean Wave in the Age of Social Media*, 31–52. Ann Arbor, MI: University of Michigan Press.

Yoon, T.-J. and Jin, D.Y. (2017). *The Korean Wave: Evolution, Fandom, and Transnationality*. Lanham & New York: Lexington Books.

16

Al Jazeera and Global News

Stages of Operation

Saba Bebawi

From its inception, audiences in the Arab world have paid attention to the Arabic-speaking Al Jazeera news network, which aimed to be different from the start. Journalism and media scholars, who have focused on Al Jazeera Arabic (AJA), have tended to present it as a democratizing influence in the mediated Arab public sphere. This is no surprise given the nature of the discourses it tackled that were not previously openly discussed on any Arab media platform. Since then, Al Jazeera (AJ), as an organization, has taken many twists and turns, but remains a controversial player in the region, as this chapter will discuss.

AJA was founded by the Emir of Qatar, began broadcasting in 1996 from Doha, Qatar, and has since launched a number of specialized television channels in addition to its English service Al Jazeera English (AJE), such as the Al Jazeera Sports Channel, Al Jazeera Sports Plus 1, and Al Jazeera Sports Plus 2. Al Jazeera also broadcasts an Arab channel called Al Jazeera Live which airs continuous live political, economic, or cultural events such as news conferences, discussions, or meetings. It has also set up a children's channel with the cooperation of the Qatar Foundation for Education, Science, and Community Development. In addition, Al Jazeera broadcasts a documentary channel in Arabic and runs two online websites: one in Arabic, aljazeera.net, and the other in English, http://www.english.aljazeera.net. The recent launch of its Facebook video platform, AJ+, has been very popular among Facebook users. Accordingly, AJ has sought to significantly expand its operations beyond the Middle East and has become an increasingly influential and profitable global player.

To better understand the various roles that AJ has played across time and across different platforms, three different stages in its historic development need to be discussed. In the first stage, AJA played a noted role within the Arab public sphere during the rise of pan-Arab satellite television. In the second stage, the post 9/11 period, AJA news reporting started to gain an international presence by focusing on discourses central to the Arab public sphere. Subsequently through AJE the organization entered the global public sphere. In the third stage, during and after the "Arab Spring" protests, AJ took on a notable role within Arab politics.

16.1 The Pan-Arab Stage

AJ's aim, in general, has always been to provide a distinct voice on social and political views that have not been voiced within the mediated public sphere before. AJA has explicitly attempted to present information from an Arab or Muslim perspective that challenges dominant Western perspectives from media organizations such as CNN International or BBC World. AJ came

Transnational Media: Concepts and Cases, First Edition. Edited by Suman Mishra and Rebecca Kern-Stone.
© 2019 John Wiley & Sons, Inc. Published 2019 by John Wiley & Sons, Inc.

after a time when Arab television stations were restricted to broadcasting within the boundaries of the state and were primarily government owned and controlled. At that time, Arab audiences could only access television stations that were operating within the nation-state they were residing in. Satellite technology was introduced to the Arab region with the launch of ARABSAT satellite in 1985. However, it was a couple of years later that this technology was put to use (Miles 2005), and it was after this that AJ was born.

The concept of *Al Jazeera* (which literally means "the island," referring to the Arabian Peninsula), was created by Qatar's Emir where a three-member committee was established with Sheikh Hamad bin Thamer Al Thani later becoming the director of the board of AJA (Zayani and Sahraoui 2007). AJA, Miles (2005, p. 29) notes, "never had a single owner, some of the company's shares being owned by the Qatari government, some by private citizens." The initial idea behind AJA was to create a democratic platform which promoted Qatar as a modern state. In a step toward realizing this, the Emir of Qatar eliminated the Ministry of Information in March 1998, thus putting an end to state media censorship. Accordingly, "[a]ll the media in Qatar, including Al-Jazeera, found their horizons dramatically broadened in terms of whom they could employ and what they could broadcast or publish" (Miles 2005, p. 29). In turn, AJA modeled itself on the forms of international reporting presented by BBC World and CNN.

It is also worth noting the significant timing of AJA's launch within the Arab world, as it came at a time when Arab audiences were skeptical about the coverage of state-run Arab media during the Iraq War in 1991, and the disappointment that loomed as a result of misleading coverage. In contrast to this, AJA brought to the average Arab home a variety of debates, topics, and views that were not openly discussed in society. This drew attention to the newly established channel. Hafez Al-Mirazi, chief of the AJA bureau in Washington, said at the time: "Al-Jazeera has a margin of freedom that no other Arab channel enjoys. Our motto is 'the view and the other point of view'" (quoted in El-Nawawy and Iskandar 2002a, p. 34), and as the Qatari Foreign Minister stated, "one opinion and the other opinion" (Rinnawi 2006, p. 55). The emergence of AJA was therefore seen by the Arab audience as a channel that allowed for open discussions within the Arab public sphere. This was despite the fact that many Arab governments regarded AJA as problematic due to its bold reporting. The above account of AJA has been prevalent and explains why AJA shot to fame within the Arab public sphere.

16.2 The Global Stage

From the time that AJA began providing the world with messages from Osama bin Laden, AJA became globally visible. AJA's role within the global public sphere was notable in challenging Western news reporting within the global public sphere. AJA's crisis reporting prior to that had always been problematic from certain Western and particularly American perspectives, as it was regarded as instigating hatred, encouraging resistance, and promoting "anti-American sentiments throughout the Middle East" (El-Nawawy and Iskandar 2002a, p. 180–181). Yet, it was after the attacks of 11 September, when bin Laden began using AJA as a platform for sending messages to the Western world (particularly the US administration), that the station gained global fame. Mixed with its reputation of being defiant to Arab regimes, AJA was categorized as an *alternative* channel that was perceived as not only controversial but, by many, as dangerously radical.

By contrast, others regard AJA as a positive contributor to democratization at both local and global levels. Volkmer (2007) considers AJA as a channel that plays an alternative role both within the Arab sphere and the global public sphere. She argues that AJA's role within the Arab sphere "can be seen as attempting to counterbalance conservative Arab state channels within this particular microsphere" (Volkmer 2007, p. 68). Consequently, Volkmer (2007) argues that this counterbalance entered the global public sphere during periods where there was a global focus on the Arab world. Iskandar (2005) has suggested that the question of how *radical* AJA is depends upon both its historical context and its reception. Indeed, Iskandar (2005) argues that AJA is now regarded as *mainstream* in the Arab world, whereas Western audiences regard it as alternative. Accordingly, El-Nawawy and Iskandar position AJE as practicing "contextual objectivity" (El-Nawawy and Iskandar 2002b, p. 54). What this means is that a media channel will try to balance itself between the notion of objective reporting and its target audience. This term, according to El-Nawawy and Iskandar, is intentionally oxymoronic since it reflects the tension which attempts to produce an objective message to a culturally sensitive audience (El-Nawawy and Iskandar 2002b).

In November 2006, and as a result of AJA's prominence at a global level, AJE was launched. Operating from Kuala Lumpur, London, and Washington, the inception of AJE came as a result of AJA's strategy to provide an Arab discursive angle on issues and events in the Middle East to a global audience, in addition to counter-balancing the coverage of dominant global media. The reason behind this, according to AJE, is to provide the global English-speaking audience with a better understanding of Arab conflicts by broadcasting Arab discourses that are not usually tackled by dominant global news media. AJE is regarded as the first English news network satellite television channel to broadcast from the Arab world at a global level. Although AJE caters to a Western audience rather than an Arab audience, it aimed to be perceived as an authority in the Middle East (Barkho 2007). Originally, AJE was intended to be called *Al Jazeera International* (AJI) but changed its name to *Al Jazeera English* (AJE). AJE shares its logo with AJA. This logo – which is an artistic calligraphy of the word *Al Jazeera* in Arabic – has become a visual global brand and one which AJE uses as a reinforcement and extension of that brand.

The creation of AJE led to a lot of public speculation regarding the sort of contribution an English language news network that stemmed from AJA might make to the field of global news. Given the reputation AJA had as a *radical* channel, particularly following various public criticisms that had been made of it that positioned it as the voice of terrorism (El Amrani 2006), an expectation arose that AJE might constitute both a source of radical perspectives that were previously unavailable to global audiences via high-profile, transnational satellite broadcasting, and serve to constitute an *Arab voice* that would present distinctive – and perhaps oppositional – perspectives on international news events.

Much of this expectation was fueled by AJE's own marketing and self-presentation, which sought to draw on AJA's reputation to position itself as offering a unique and important perspective. AJE was therefore active in promoting the channel through interviews, statements, and press releases. As part of its broadcasts, AJE featured a quote that promotes its aims in these terms: "Al Jazeera is about perspective. The Arab language channel was about presenting a new perspective. Now we're doing it in English" (Broadcast 18 March 2007). In this way, AJE explicitly positioned itself both as an extension of AJA and as a media channel that offered a different and alternative perspective. Accordingly, AJE attempted to promote itself as providing discourses that were not otherwise addressed in English language news media. Other examples of such positioning broadcast on AJE were the use of slogans such as: "Reversing the North to South flow of information," "Setting the News Agenda," "Every Angle/Every Side," and "All the News/All the Time."

With the establishment of the English satellite channel, AJE's audience reach was to include the global non-Arab speaking audience who were curious to know the discourses that AJA's coverage incorporated. AJE not only aimed to target the Western English-speaking world, but also those who sought a non-traditional perspective of the news. AJE promoted itself prior to its launch as a broadcaster explicitly in contrast to both BBC World and CNNI, citing differences in its coverage, its agenda, and its target audience. Despite AJE identifying the people on the street as a primary target audience, it also expressed interest in reaching influential segments of the world population.

16.3   Post "Arab-Spring" Stage

The "Arab Spring" protests marked the opening up of the Arab public sphere both on the streets and through media, specifically social media. Within such an environment, the need to question the role of AJ throughout these protests becomes vital, given how AJ has historically played a significant role in opening up the Arab communicative space. The protests began in December 2010 and were instigated by a Tunisian street vendor by the name of Mohamed Bouazizi who eventually ended his life through self-immolation. On the 17 December 2010, Bouazizi poured gasoline on himself and set himself on fire in front of the governor's office, an hour after his wares were confiscated by a female municipal inspector. The Tunisian Revolution, or the *Basta* Revolution as it was called in the Arab world in reference to the fruit cart that Bouazizi used, marked the start of protests which spread through Tunisia and which lead to the ousting of the Tunisian President Zine El Abidine Ben Ali who fled to Saudi Arabia. The protests on the Tunisian streets spilled over to other Arab countries and ultimately led to the cessation of other leaderships such as Egypt's Hosni Mubarak, Libya's Muammar Ghaddafi, and Yemen's Ali Abdullah Saleh.

To understand the role of AJ during the Arab Spring protests and the discourses surrounding its involvement, it is necessary to gain an idea of Qatar's political involvement in the region during this time. During the events of the Arab Spring, Qatar played an active political role reflecting "a drastic shift away from its previous focus on diplomatic mediation in favor of actual intervention and picking sides in regional conflicts" (Ulrichsen 2012, p. 12). Examples of Qatar's active role in the region include: joining NATO forces during the Libyan uprising "to dilute concerns of another Western intervention in the region" (Ulrichsen 2012, p. 13); championing the Muslim brotherhood rule during the Egyptian elections; and supporting the Syrian opposition, calling for Syria's president, Hafez Al Assad, to step down during sessions at the Arab League and United Nations (Ulrichsen 2012). As a result of this involvement, AJ was banned in many Arab countries during the uprisings, such as in Libya where their office was closed immediately after the start of the revolution, and in Egypt where its satellite signal covering Egypt was dropped from NileSat (Khanfar 2012). According to Figenschou, AJE's role in the Arab Spring protests was subject to "structural limitations and contradictions" that have shaped the channel itself; she argues that "the channel's resource-intensive production strategies make it highly dependent on its Qatari sponsor" (Figenschou 2013, p. 161). This explains the direction AJE adopted in its reporting on the protests, where the channel itself took a political part. This, in turn, enhanced its political power through its mediated discourses.

As a result of AJ's direct involvement in the political framing of the events post-Mubarak regime in Egypt, several AJ reporters were imprisoned. These journalists included Australian Correspondent Peter Greste, and producers Mohammed Fahmy and Baher Mohamed, who were arrested in Cairo on 29 December 2013, and who were accused of spreading pro-Muslim brotherhood news. In an interview with Wadah Khanfar, who was Director General of AJ from 2003 to 2011, Khanfar said "We are journalists; we are not political activists!" – yet he did acknowledge that they were "participating in creating the environment for the Arab Spring" (Edwards 2011). What this means is that AJ journalists were not just mediators but actors in the conflict, which emphasizes the media power a news network can hold in shaping the political uprisings and the aftermath. As a result of this, many prominent staff members left AJ following the Arab Spring protests. One correspondent said the reason behind his resignation was that "Al-Jazeera takes a clear position in every country from which it reports – not based on journalistic priorities, but rather on the interests of the Foreign Ministry of Qatar" (Kühn et al. 2013). Examples of AJ's political reporting during the Arab Spring include its role in shaping discourses on Libya where, at the start of the protests against Ghaddafi, the station began to use the rebel's tricolor flag instead of Libya's official green flag (Baker 2011). The political role of Al Jazeera was also noted during the Syrian crisis, where AJ staff were reported as being very close to the rebels, which in turn was also reflected in AJ's reporting (Kühn et al. 2013). When the Arab league submitted a proposal to the Syrian government in November 2011 to address the crisis, the Syrian foreign minister replied "that the deal should include a stipulation requiring 'certain television channels' stop their 'poisonous' reporting" (Souaiaia 2011). Such examples note the power that news networks have in not only shaping public opinion, and in turn social reality, but also in becoming political players themselves in the conflict.

In 2017, AJ was once again in the midst of political tension when on the 5 June 2017, the Gulf Crisis arose as a result of Saudi Arabia, the United Arab Emirates (UAE), and Bahrain initiating an ongoing ban on Qatar on the basis that Qatar was supporting terrorism. Qatari citizens were given 14 days to evacuate these Gulf states, and their own citizens were banned from traveling or residing in Qatar. They were also joined by Egypt, which did not impose the ban on its citizens but did impose restrictions. The restrictions included closing off airspace to Qatari aircrafts. In return for lifting the restrictions imposed, which included a 13-point list, Qatar was asked to "shut down Al Jazeera and other Qatar-funded news outlets" (BBC 2017). Demands to close off Al Jazeera are evidence of how powerful news organizations can be within the political landscape. Al Jazeera is fully aware of this, as can be seen in a quote taken from its Listening Post program broadcast on Al Jazeera English on 25 February 2007: "The media are the most powerful institutions on earth – more powerful than any bomb, more powerful than any missile." Whatever political role Al Jazeera has played in the Middle East, it can certainly be said that it has played an influential role. AJ, as a phenomenon, is testament to the power that media organizations hold, making AJ's role in the Arab media landscape worthy of study.

References

Baker, A. (24 May 2011). Bahrain's voiceless: How Al-Jazeera's coverage of the Arab Spring is uneven, *Time*. Retrieved from: http://world.time.com/2011/05/24/bahrains-voiceless-how-al-jazeeras-coverage-of-the-arab-spring-is-uneven.

Barkho, L. (2007). Unpacking the discursive and social links in BBC, CNN and Al-Jazeera's Middle East reporting. *Journal of Arab and Muslim Media Research* 1 (1): 11–29.

BBC (19 July 2017). *Qatar crisis: what you need to know*. Retrieved from: http://www.bbc.com/news/world-middle-east-40173757.

Edwards, H.S. (30 September 2011). Former Al Jazeera head on quitting, the Arab Spring, and Qatar's role, *The Atlantic*. Retrieved from: http://www.theatlantic.com/international/archive/2011/09/former-al-jazeera-head-on-quitting-the-arab-spring-and-qatars-role/245932.

El Amrani, I. (2006). In US, a cold welcome for Al Jazeera International. *Arabian Business*. Retrieved from http://www.arabianbusiness.com/a-cold-welcome-for-al-jazeera-international-217444.html

El-Nawawy, M. and Iskandar, A. (2002a). *Al-Jazeera: How the Free Arab News Network Scooped the World and Changed the Middle East*. Cambridge, MA: Westview Press.

El-Nawawy, M. and Iskandar, A. (2002b). The minotaur of 'contextual objectivity': war coverage and the pursuit of accuracy with appeal. *Transnational Broadcasting Studies* 9 (Fall/Winter): Retrieved from: https://web.archive.org/web/20120211102357/http://www.tbsjournal.com/Archives/Fall02/Iskandar.html.

Figenschou, T.U. (2013). *Al Jazeera and the Global Media Landscape: The South is Talking Back.* Hoboken: Taylor & Francis.

Iskandar, A. (2005). Is Al Jazeera alternative? Mainstreaming alterity and assimilating discourses and dissent. In: *Real (Arab) World: Is Reality TV Democratizing the Middle East? and other studies in satellite broadcasting in the Arab and Islamic worlds* (ed. Cairo: Adham Center for Electronic Journalism, The American University in Cairo and Oxford: Middle East Centre, St. Antony's College, University of Oxford), 249–261. Oxford: Oxford University Press.

Khanfar, W. (2012). *Al Jazeera and the Arab Spring,* Talk at Chatham House, London, 19 January.

Kühn, A., Reuter, C., and Schmitz, G. P. (15 February 2013). After the Arab Spring: Al Jazeera losing battle for independence, *Spiegel Online.* Retrieved from: http://www.spiegel.de/international/world/al-jazeera-criticized-for-lack-of-independence-after-arab-spring-a-883343.html.

Miles, H. (2005). *Al-Jazeera: The Inside Story of the Arab News Channel that is Challenging the West.* New York: Grove Press.

Rinnawi, K. (2006). *Instant Nationalism: McArabism, Al-Jazeera and Transnational Media in the Arab World.* Oxford: University Press of America.

Souaiaia, A.E. (17 November 2011). Qatar, Al Jazeera, and the Arab Spring, *MRZine.* Retrieved from: http://mrzine.monthlyreview.org/2011/souaiaia171111.html.

Ulrichsen, K.C. (October 2012). *Small states with a big role: Qatar and the United Arab Emirates in the wake of the Arab Spring,* Discussion paper 3, Retrieved from: http://dro.dur.ac.uk/10011/1/10011.pdf?DDD35.

Volkmer, I. (2007). Governing the "spatial reach"? Spheres of influence and challenges to global media policy. *International Journal of Communication* 1 (1): 56–73. Retrieved from: http://ijoc.org/index.php/ijoc/article/viewFile/17/18.

Zayani, M. and Sahraoui, S. (2007). *The Culture of Al Jazeera: Inside an Arab Media Giant.* Jefferson: McFarland & Co.

Part V

Europe

Transnational Media: Concepts and Cases, First Edition. Edited by Suman Mishra and Rebecca Kern-Stone.
© 2019 John Wiley & Sons, Inc. Published 2019 by John Wiley & Sons, Inc.

Figure V.1 Map of Europe.

Europe (Figure V.1) is frequently discussed as having two halves: West and East. The latter shares its borders with Asia, and many countries along this eastern edge may be socio-politically less associated with the rest of Europe. Overall, Europe has a population of approximately 742 billion, of which 60% lives in Western Europe and 40% in Eastern Europe (UN, World Population Prospects 2017). Europe is important as a transnational focus due to the large number of country-specific immigrant migrations in recent years as well as for the production of global media brands.

Europe is home to a number of transnational media brands and companies, among the most notable are Bertelsmann, SKY, and Vivendi. Bertelsmann, which is based in Germany, owns and operates television, radio, and content production throughout Western and Eastern Europe, Southern and Eastern Asia, and in the Americas. In addition, as a part of Penguin-Random house they also have publishing houses on every continent. SKY, currently a subsidiary of News Corp. and based in Britain, has television across Western Europe and Southern and Eastern Asia. Vivendi, a French based company, has television in Western Europe, as well as in over 25 countries in Western and Central Africa, six Caribbean nations, two countries in Southeast Asia, and a number of French-speaking overseas territories. In addition, Vivendi is the owner of StudioCanal that provides and produces television and movies throughout Europe, the United States, and China. Also, a number of countries in Europe import media from around the globe, including Portugal from Brazil, Scandinavian countries from the United States, and many satellite programs from Asia and Africa.

PV.1 European Union

The European Union (EU) consists of 28 member countries, including Germany, Italy, Lithuania, Hungary, and Sweden, among others. At present, the United Kingdom is still a part of the EU, but after Brexit the UK will no longer be included. It has an overall population of 512.6 million people, with Germany, France, the United Kingdom, and Italy comprising 54% of the total (Eurostat 2018). The EU has an overall GDP of 16.5 trillion in USD (World Bank 2016a).

Not all countries in Europe belong to the EU, namely Norway, Iceland, Russia, and Ukraine among others. Norway, for example, chose not to join for economic reasons. In order for a country to join the EU they must adhere to EU laws, have a stable democracy, and have a free market economy (European Union 2018). Currently, there are five countries – Turkey, Albania, Montenegro, the Republic of Northern Macedonia, and Serbia – in the process of becoming member countries, but to do so they must fully implement EU rules into their national law (European Union 2018). One interesting point to be made is the creation of the Schengen border free area, which comprises 26 EU and non-EU nations who have allowed their borders to be open to business, tourists, nationals, and non-nationals with limited border checks. However, concerns about external and internal border controls have been an increasing topic of debate among citizens living in the EU.

Television is the most used medium in Europe (82%), with the highest viewership in Romania, Portugal, Bulgaria, and Belgium. Internet is the second most widely used medium (60%), and radio is third (Statista 2018a). Radio, however, has the highest level of trust, especially for news, and is most popular in Germany, Ireland, Slovenia, and Austria (Statista 2018a).

As noted, television is the medium with the highest use across Europe. Countries throughout the EU have both a commercial television sector as well as a public broadcasting sector. The strength of each varies from country to country. The EU has specific audiovisual directives aimed at protecting children and media pluralism, reducing hatred, and encouraging cultural diversity (European Union 2018). The EU is therefore permitted to limit film imports but also subsidizes strong public broadcasting sectors in EU countries as a way to promote diversity not otherwise seen or heard in commercial television and radio. The history of public service media, as well as how different they can be across the EU in various countries, is discussed in Chapter 17.

Internet usage is high in Europe, where 85% of the population has access from home (Eurostat 2017). The highest access is in Luxembourg and the Netherlands (97%), but all other Northern European countries have access above 90%. The lowest penetration rates are in Bulgaria (64%) and Greece (69%) (Eurostat 2017). EU candidate countries have penetration percentages in the mid to upper 60s (Internet World Stats 2017b).

European countries overall promote a free press. According to Freedom House (2017), Norway currently has the freest press in the world, followed by Sweden, the Netherlands, Finland, Denmark, Switzerland, Belgium, Iceland, Luxembourg, Liechtenstein, and Estonia. Notably, all of these countries are situated in Northern Europe. In Norway, for example, freedom of expression and the right to access government documentation is evenly and strongly protected by the constitution and upheld by the courts, and censorship is very low. Estonia also supports Russian-language media, which despite concerns over "politically motivated journalism by Russian pro-government outlets" (Freedom House 2017a, para. 7) has only strengthened Russian media offerings to a large Russian minority in the country. Other countries in Europe, while lower on the list for having more divisive political and legal environments, do support a free press and free expression. Spain, France, and Slovenia, for example, while all politically pluralist, have seen new security and gag laws which have undermined elements of a free media environment (Freedom House 2017b). Countries within Europe that maintain only a partly free press include Italy, Poland, Bosnia-Herzegovina, Greece, and Hungary. This is primarily due to lack of support for freedom of expression, despite its declaration in many country's constitutions (Freedom House 2017c), and pluralism of views is on the decline due to political pressure and government intervention (Reporters Without Borders 2018a, b, c).

Freedom House (2017) designates some countries within Eastern Europe – specifically Moldova, Ukraine, and Belarus, as well as Russia – as Eurasian countries and separates them from the rest of Europe and Asia. None of these countries currently enjoy a free press; however, Moldova and Ukraine are working to increase democratization and "European integration" (Freedom House 2017) and are at least partly free. Both countries are being supported by the EU in their efforts, and these two countries may apply for candidacy in coming years.

PV.2   Sweden

A country in Northern Europe, more specifically in what is considered the Nordic region, Sweden has a population of 10.2 million people, which has increased by 1.2% in the past year (Statistics Sweden 2018). Situated between Norway and Finland, Sweden is essentially divided into three sections. The capital, Stockholm, is in the central portion of the country along the eastern coast, while Malmö and Göteborg, the other two largest cities, are in the southern region along the western coast. Malmö's population is comprised of one third immigrants. The country has a GDP of 514.46 billion in USD (World Bank 2016b). Their primary religion is evangelical Lutheran.

The country has a constitutional monarchy, but the monarchy has no real governing authority and instead the Riksdag – the parliament – is the official governing body. Swedish is only one of five official languages in Sweden, although it is the most spoken. In a 2000 charter aimed at protecting Swedish cultural minorities, Sweden established policies to enhance cultural understanding and languages of the Sami people, Torrendal-Finns, the Roma, and Jews. As a result, besides Swedish, Sami, Meänkieli/Finnish, Romany Chib, and Yiddish are all official languages. It is also mandated that cultural education of these groups happens in schools, each group has representation in the parliament, and media programming is offered. Many of these minority groups have been producing their own media for quite some time. The Sami, of which approximately 20 000 reside in the northern regions of Sweden, have their own parliament and news stations.

Sweden strongly promotes freedom of the press and freedom of expression, and continually has one of the best press freedom scores. Currently, Sweden ranks 2/180 according to Reporters Without Borders (2018d). It encourages strong media pluralism, professionalization, and a right to information for all people. Journalists, who have never worried about censorship or concerns over reporting news and events, have begun to self-censor on issues such as immigration and Islam for fear of appearing bigoted or offensive (Reporters Without Borders 2018d). Newspaper readership is still higher in Northern European countries as compared to Eastern and Southern Europe (Hallin 2005), according to Statista (2018b) in 2016 62% of the population read a daily morning paper. As expected, those who are younger tend to read the newspaper online. There are also over 200 minority newspapers in dozens of languages, representing the multicultural population of Sweden.

Television and radio are the platforms used most by Swedes. Eighty-one percent of Swedes watch television on an average day, and 62% listen to the radio (Nordicom 2018). Just like many other countries in the EU, Sweden has a strong public broadcasting sector, although it also contends with a large commercial sector. While once there was a public service monopoly, commercial television was slowly introduced in the 1980s (Wadbring and Ohlsson 2018). Since then, both public service radio and television have grown. SVT is the public service broadcaster and runs three television channels and four radio stations. Radio is dominated by the public service sector and is funded through the government and licensing fees. Of note is the SVT charter that stipulates that not only should there be focus on Sweden and Swedish life, but programming should also "reflect the many different cultures and cultural manifestations in Sweden" as well as take special care with "linguistic and ethnic minorities" (SVT 2018), including recent refugees from Syria, Afghanistan, and Iraq. Three commercial companies, Bonnier, MTG, and Discovery Communications, operate the many commercial television stations. While the first two are Swedish corporations, Discovery Communications is a US company that airs shows to over 220 countries worldwide. Sweden has one of the most concentrated media markets in all of Europe (Wadbring and Ohlsson 2018).

Internet is a growing medium in Sweden as more and more people get online. On average, 65% of Swedes use social media daily, and 51% use traditional internet daily (Nordicom 2018). Younger people are more likely to use social media and to stream television online. Overall, Sweden has a 93% penetration rate, among the highest in the world. There have been concerns over what appears to be more government intervention in online practice. In recent years there have been a number of laws allowing for surveillance of internet traffic content and copyright infringement. Other issues include net neutrality. Chapter 18 discusses how issues surrounding internet file-sharing created a new political party in 2006: the Pirate Party – a political party that now exists in countries all over the world.

PV.3 Germany

Germany is the most populous and industrialized country in Europe. Situated in central Europe, it has more neighbors than any other European country. It has a population of 82.8 million, of which 10.6 million are foreign born (Destatis Statistiches Bundesamt 2018). Of the foreign-born population, 72% are from countries in Europe. Of these, 43% are from EU countries, namely Poland, and 19% from EU candidate countries, namely Turkey. Twenty percent are from Asia, namely Syria and Iraq. In 2016, 1.6 million people sought protection in Germany, primarily from Syria, Afghanistan, and Iraq (Destatis Statistiches Bundesamt 2018). Germany has a GDP of 3.5 trillion in USD (World Bank 2016c).

Established as a federation after World War II, the country was divided into states. After East and West Germany unified in 1990, a total of 16 states emerged. These 16 states have localized governing power. The current government is a parliamentary democracy and the country has a strong welfare state, just like Sweden. Four culturally ethnic minority groups have special protection in Germany: the Danish minority, the Friesians, the Lusatian Sorbs, and the Sinti and Roma (Facts About Germany 2018). Germany has no official language or religion. Most people do speak German or English, but there are lots of languages that represent the multicultural population. There are also 16 dialects throughout country. Germany also supports religious neutrality. While 59% of the population practices Christianity, 34% do not have a religious affiliation.

Like other northern European countries, Germany also guarantees a free press and free expression constitutionally. However, their press freedom ranking of 15/180 according to Reporters Without Borders (2018e) is lower than some of its neighbors. Decreasing media pluralism due to economic closures of print media venues, data blocking on the internet, and recent laws allowing for penalties against whistleblowers and media who use leaked information (Reporters Without Borders 2018e) have influenced this.

In a 2010 survey of European media systems, news media was considered the most credible in Northern Europe (Popescu 2011). Germany has a long and important relationship with the press, and has some of the highest newspaper circulation in the world. The country encourages media pluralism. Print outlets are all private, and rely on advertising for funding. There are over 1528 dailies in circulation (Thomaß and Horz 2018), with many aimed at the international population. *Frankfuter Allgemeine Zeitung* and *Bild* are two important mass circulation dailies.

Radio is the most trusted medium in Germany, but television is the most used. There are over 70 public stations, which are primarily regional, and 283 commercial stations (Thomaß and Horz 2018). Public stations are funded through license fees and advertising, while the commercial stations, which are private, are only funded through advertising. ARD is the organization that handles public radio and television, both regional stations and national. Deutsche Welle, a foreign radio and television service, broadcasts in 30 different languages throughout Germany and internationally, particularly in Africa and Asia. Its television channel – DWtv – broadcasts in English, German, Spanish, and Arabic. There are over 400 television channels, including Pay-TV. Public broadcasting has the largest audience share at 45%, with the commercial RTL Group at 23%, and Pro7Sat1 at 19%.

As noted earlier, Bertelsmann is the largest media owner in Germany, followed by AxelSpringer and ProSiebenSat1. Bertelsmann owns multiple types of media platforms and many media outlets within those platforms. It owns the largest book publisher in the world, Penguin-Random House; the fourth largest music publisher, BMG; Europe's largest magazine, Gruner + Jahr; and Europe's largest broadcast and production company, RTLGroup. RTL broadcasts throughout Europe and produces content globally through Freemantle media. Penguin-Random House has publication houses on every continent. An in-depth look at Bertelsmann can be found in Chapter 18.

The third most used medium in Germany, the internet, has a penetration of 89.6% (internetworldstats.com) and 78% of people visit the internet daily (Statista 2018c); 51% of the population regularly visits online newspaper sites (Thomaß and Horz 2018). According to Destatis Statistiches Bundesamt (2018), 55% of online individuals are there to create messages in social networks or blogs, 90% use it to search for goods and services, and 57% use it for online banking.

PV.4   Russia

The largest country in the world, half is considered a part of Europe and the other half part of Asia. Russia has a total population of 144 million, with most people living within major cities (Statista 2018d). The population is also concentrated in the European side of the country. Russia is over 80% ethnic Russians, with Tatars and Ukrainians the next two largest ethnic groups (RT 2018). There are over 160 ethnicities in Russia. It has a GDP of 1.3 trillion in USD (World Bank 2016d).

The Russian Federation was created in 1991 after the collapse of the United Soviet Socialist Republics (USSR). All of the republics became independent nations. The Russian Federation consists of Russia and Crimea, which was annexed from Ukraine in 2014 despite international condemnation. Currently, Russia is a presidential republic with a multiparty representative democracy: Russia has both a president and a prime minister. The country is divided into 83 federal states, each with varying degrees of state autonomy. Within the 83 states, there are 22 republics that were specifically created for non-Russian ethnic minorities (RT 2018). The foreign-born population is primarily from former Soviet countries, namely Ukraine, Uzbekistan, and Armenia (Chudinovskikh and Denisenko 2017). There are over 100 different languages in Russia, but Russian is the state language. There are four recognized religions: Orthodox Christianity, Islam, Buddhism, and Judaism. Many within the country state that they are atheists (RT 2018).

Despite a constitutional provision for free press and speech, Russia does not have a free press and it currently ranks 148/180 on the World Press Freedom index (Reporters Without Borders 2018e). Censorship is high, and journalists are quickly punished for reporting anything that goes against ruling party doctrine. Government entities continually block access to information and regulate media content (Freedom House 2017e). Television is also a vehicle for propagandist Russian nationalism. Russian media is either owned by the state or is private, but controlled by corporations with strong government ties.

According to a 2010 survey of European media, news is the least credible in Southern and Eastern Europe – Russia included (Popescu 2011). This may be because political, business, and special interest influences are highest in Russia and Eastern Europe, and lowest in Northern Europe (Popescu 2011). Popescu also notes that agenda setting of political issues by news media is prominent across Europe but is lowest in Russia. The internet has made journalists more responsive to the public, especially in Russia (Popescu 2011). Newspaper circulation has been dropping in Russia, much like other places in the world. There are three types of newspapers: national, regional, and local. The first two are housed in either Moscow or important regional areas. The last, the local press, while published less frequently, is where most Russians get their print news (Vartanova 2018). At the national level there is more readership of general interest dailies.

Television is where most Russians get their news and entertainment. According to Vartanova (2018), television is the main source of news for 86% of the population, and is trusted by more than half of the population. Terrestrial television is available across the country, but there are initiatives by the Russian government to bring digital to all homes. Satellite and cable are available in large urban centers. There are three primary media companies that bring television as well as other media to Russia. VGTRK is a state-owned television and radio broadcaster. National Media Group (NMG) has television – terrestrial and satellite – print, and digital properties. Their television channels reach former Soviet states, and satellite channels import global media. Of particular interest is Media Alliance, which is a joint effort between NMG and Discovery Communications. In addition, NMG has partnered with Sony Entertainment, a Japanese based conglomerate, as well as airing Hollywood and European entertainment through Viasat. NMG also owns the Russian arm of *Metro* newspapers, advertising opportunities, and digital analytics. Gazprom Media is owned by Russia's largest energy corporation. It too has similar media platforms as NMG, but also has a number of radio stations and magazines. Gazprom Media is both state and privately owned.

Of particular note is the independent broadcaster RT, which receives funding from the Russian Federation. RT broadcasts to over 100 countries globally and has broadcast centers in the USA, the UK, France, and Russia. Shows are aired in English, Arabic, Russian, and Spanish. Its aim is to bring a Russian perspective to global news (RT 2018). More on RT can be found in Chapter 20, which examines not only RT but its political and cultural role in the global news market.

Lastly, Russia has an internet penetration of 76% (Internet World Stats 2017a). The internet has offered different views from traditional media and has expanded cultural pluralism (Vartanova 2018). As with most places in the world, the internet is used by younger audiences to get news. About 56% of individuals connected via mobile phones in 2017 (Vartanova 2018). VKontakte (VK) is the largest social media network, however Instagram is also very popular.

References

Chudinovskikh, O. & Denisenko, M. (2017). Russia: A migration system with Soviet roots. *Migration Policy Institute*. Retrieved from: https://www.migrationpolicy.org/article/russia-migration-system-soviet-roots.

Destatis Statistiches Bundesamt (2018). Facts and figures. Retrieved from: https://www.destatis.de/EN/FactsFigures/FactsFigures.html.

European Union (2018). European Union. Retrieved from: https://europa.eu/european-union/about-eu/countries_en#others.

Eurostat (2017). Internet access and usage statistics - households and individuals. *Eurostat*. Retrieved from: http://ec.europa.eu/eurostat/statistics-explained/index.php/Internet_access_and_use_statistics_-_households_and_individuals.

Eurostat (2018). First population estimates. EU population up to nearly 513 million on 1 January 2018. Increase driven by migration. Eurostat. Retrieved from: http://ec.europa.eu/eurostat/documents/2995521/9063738/3-10072018-BP-EN.pdf/ccdfc838-d909-4fd8-b3f9-db0d65ea457f.

Facts About Germany (2018). Demographics. Retrieved from https://www.tatsachen-ueber-deutschland.de/en/demographics

Freedom House (2017). Press freedom. *Freedom House*. Retrieved from: https://freedomhouse.org/report/freedom-press/freedom-press-2017.

Freedom House (2017a). Estonia. *Freedom House*. Retrieved from: https://freedomhouse.org/report/freedom-press/2015/estonia.

Freedom House (2017b) Spain. *Freedom House*. Retrieved from: https://freedomhouse.org/report/freedom-press/2017/spain.

Freedom House (2017c). Hungary. *Freedom House*. Retrieved from: https://freedomhouse.org/report/freedom-press/2017/hungary.

Freedom House (2017d). Ukraine. *Freedom House*. Retrieved from: https://freedomhouse.org/report/freedom-press/2017/ukraine.

Freedom House (2017e). Russia. *Freedom House*. Retrieved from: https://freedomhouse.org/report/freedom-press/2017/russia.

Hallin, D. (2005). Comparing mass media in Europe and the United States. *Insights in Law and Society* 5 (3): 1–4.

Internet World Stats (2017a). *Europe*. Retrieved from: https://www.internetworldstats.com/europa2.htm.

Internet World Stats (2017b). European Union. Retrieved from: https://www.internetworldstats.com/stats9.htm.

Nordicom (2018). Media Barometer 2017 – Sweden. Retrieved from: www.nordicom.gu.se/en/latest/news/some-results-media-barometer-2017.

Popescu, M. (2011). Survey of European media systems. *Media Systems in* Europe.org. Retrieved from: http://www.mediasystemsineurope.org/files/EMSS2010_Report.pdf.

Reporters Without Borders (2018a). Poland. *Reporters Without Borders*. Retrieved from: https://rsf.org/en/poland.

Reporters Without Borders (2018b). Italy. *Reporters Without Borders*. Retrieved from: https://rsf.org/en/italy.

Reporters Without Borders (2018c). Bosnia-Herzegovina. *Reporters Without Borders*. Retrieved from: https://rsf.org/en/bosnia-herzegovina.

Reporters Without Borders (2018d). Sweden. *Reporters Without Borders*. Retrieved from: https://rsf.org/en/sweden.

Reporters Without Borders (2018e). Russia. *Reporters Without Borders*. Retrieved from: https://rsf.org/en/russia.

RT (2018). About us. *RT*. Retrieved from: https://www.rt.com/about-us.

Statista (2018a). Media usage in Europe. *Statista*. Retrieved from: https://www.statista.com/topics/4039/media-usage-in-europe.

Statista (2018b). Share of individuals who read daily newspapers in Sweden. *Statista*. Retrieved from: https://www.statista.com/statistics/543316/share-of-individuals-who-read-daily-newspapers-in-sweden.

Statista (2018c). Internet frequency among individuals in Germany. *Statista*. Retrieved from: https://www.statista.com/statistics/379036/internet-usage-at-home-germany.

Statista (2018d). Russia total population: 2012–2022. *Statista*. Retrieved from: https://www.statista.com/statistics/263767/total-population-of-russia.

Statistics Sweden (2018). Population statistics. Retrieved from: http://www.scb.se/en/finding-statistics/statistics-by-subject-area/population/population-composition/population-statistics/pong/tables-and-graphs/monthly-statistics--the-whole-country/preliminary-population-statistics.

SVT (2018). The broadcasting charter. *Sveriges Television*. Retrieved from: https://www.svt.se/aboutsvt/the-broadcasting-charter.

Thomaß, B. & Horz, C. (2018). Media landscapes – Germany. *European Journalism Centre*. Retrieved from: https://medialandscapes.org/country/germany.

United Nations (2017). World population prospects. Retrieved from: https://esa.un.org/unpd/wpp/Publications/Files/WPP2017_KeyFindings.pdf.

Vartanova, E. (2018). Media landscapes – Russia. *European Journalism Centre*. Retrieved from: https://medialandscapes.org/country/russia/media/television.

Wadbring, I. & Ohlsson, J. (2018). Media landscape – Sweden. *European Journalism Centre*. Retrieved from: https://medialandscapes.org/country/sweden.

World Bank (2016a). European Union. Retrieved from: https://data.worldbank.org/region/european-union.

World Bank (2016b). Sweden – country profile. Retrieved from: http://databank.worldbank.org/data/views/reports/reportwidget.aspx?Report_Name=CountryProfile&Id=b450fd57&tbar=y&dd=y&inf=n&zm=n&country=SWE.

World Bank (2016c). Germany – country profile. Retrieved from: http://databank.worldbank.org/
data/views/reports/reportwidget.aspx?Report_Name–CountryProfile&Id–b450fd57&tbar–y&d
d=y&inf=n&zm=n&country=DEU.

World Bank (2016d). Russia – country profile. Retrieved from: http://databank.worldbank.org/
data/views/reports/reportwidget.aspx?Report_Name=CountryProfile&Id=b450fd57&tbar=
y&dd=y&inf=n&zm=n&country=RUS.

17

Public Service Media in Europe

Common Values, Different Political Contexts, and a Variety of Practices

Karen Donders

Public service broadcasting, meaning the delivery of radio and television services in the public interest, has traditionally been catered for by public broadcasters. These institutions held a monopoly position in most Western and Northern European countries from the 1930s until the 1970s, or even 1980s. The most well-known European public broadcaster, the BBC, was founded in 1927 (Crisell 2002, p. 28; Regal 2005, p. 75). Its functioning has been steered by the Reithian philosophy "to inform, to educate and to entertain." This adage, formulated first by the BBC's first director-general John Reith (Cody et al. 2003), became a guiding principle for most public broadcasters in Western and Northern Europe. Their task was to emancipate citizens. As said by Murdock (2005), "public service broadcasting was 'educational' in the original Latin sense of 'leading out,' opening up new horizons and experiences for those who would otherwise be denied them" (p. 178). Public broadcasters' initial status of monopolist in the 1930s was, however, not so much caused by this elevated objective, but rather by the aspiration of politicians to control the broadcast medium in an era of spectrum scarcity (Burgelman 1990). Monopoly came to an end throughout the 1970s and 1980s. The United Kingdom and Italy had already introduced competition in their broadcasting markets in the 1950s and 1960s; Luxembourg never had a public broadcaster (Iosifidis 2008, p. 305). In Southern and Central and Eastern Europe public broadcasting is relatively new and became a legal phenomenon only after fascism or communism came to an end. In practice, we can see that several member states of the European Union ("EU") have difficulties, in practice, embracing the idea of an independent public, instead of a state, broadcaster (Levitsky and Way 2010).

Whereas public service broadcasting is considered a European phenomenon, its transposition in practice varies and is very much intertwined with the political, historical, economic, societal, and cultural context in which it is embedded (Katsirea 2008). It is fair to say that some common values underlie the ideal of public service broadcasting and its organization through public broadcasters. Universality, quality, social cohesion, etc. are typical examples of such values. These are considered valid on all platforms. In other words: public service broadcasting is no longer exclusively about radio and television, but evolves into the technology agnostic concept of public service media. In this chapter, these common values are discussed first. Subsequently, attention is devoted to the different political contexts in which public broadcasters work. In some parts of Europe there is an evolution toward a libertarian "free market place of ideas" ideology, putting pressure on a holistic public broadcaster servicing all groups in society (Donders 2012). In other parts of Europe, the social democratic or even media welfare state (Syvertsen et al. 2014) seems to be fairly resistant. In another group of countries, scholars refer to the emergence of competitive authoritarianism, combining the features of neo-liberal with authoritarian ideologies (Vladisavljević 2016). These "models" in turn cover

Transnational Media: Concepts and Cases, First Edition. Edited by Suman Mishra and Rebecca Kern-Stone.
© 2019 John Wiley & Sons, Inc. Published 2019 by John Wiley & Sons, Inc.

an even bigger variety of public service media practice in Europe. Public broadcasters relate differently with their audiences, other public institutions, competitors, politicians, and with themselves, depending on what EU Member State we are talking about. This chapter mostly aims to illustrate that public service media and public broadcasters are far from a homogeneous thing, but are in fact – for better or worse – a perfect example of the diversity that characterizes the EU. This and other conclusions are outlined in the final section of the chapter.

17.1 Common Values: From Public Service Broadcasting to Public Service Media

Following the idea of empowerment and believing firmly in the fundamental role of public service broadcasting in contributing to a democratic public sphere (Habermas 1991), pluralism and universality were central elements of the value set underlying public broadcasters. Public broadcasters were entrusted with the realization of the task to educate, inform, and entertain the audience (Price and Raboy 2003). They had to perform these tasks for all people in society, providing objective news and depicting the variety of opinions in society. There was of course pressure on both the idea of public service broadcasting and the organization through public broadcasters, and this was largely due to the upsurge of neo-liberalism in the 1980s (Blumler 1991; Garnham 1990, pp. 127–128). Nevertheless, the public broadcaster "axis" remained firmly rooted in most Western and Northern European countries. Admittedly, the distinctiveness of public broadcasters' offerings versus commercial media services became more important. Nevertheless, from the 1930s onwards a series of shared values that underpinned the essence of public service broadcasting (Donders and Pauwels 2012; Donders and Van den Bulck 2016) has been placed central in policy frameworks and has steered – at least in theory – the functioning of public broadcasters across the whole of Europe. Reference can be made to the following values:

- Universality: Public broadcasters' content should be available and accessible to all citizens, regardless of their geographical location, their ability/willingness to pay, their gender, ethnical background, and so on (Garnham 1990).
- Quality and distinctiveness: Public broadcasters should distinguish themselves through the quality of their services; they should be distinctive from what others offer. Although commercial media companies, some policy makers, and a few scholars advocate a complementary, gap-filling role for public broadcasters, most scholars agree on the need for a holistic, full-portfolio approach (Bardoel and d'Haenens 2008, p. 344).
- Identity construction and diversity: The identity-building aspect of public service broadcasting largely refers to a process of unification around a nation, language, and/or culture (Van den Bulck 2001), while the diversity aspect is concerned with reflecting the growing cultural and ethnic fragmentation occurring within national boundaries, with catering to minority interests, and with celebrating the diversity of cultures on a global scale (Horsti and Hultén 2011).
- Creativity and innovation: Public broadcasters should offer creative services, provide a safe harbor for experiment, and engage in innovation in service and technology (Cunningham 2009, p. 85), particularly in internationalizing media markets where innovation is under pressure (Cunningham 2015).
- Accountability: Editorial independence is key to public broadcasters' functioning (Council of Europe 2009), so is accountability to citizens and legislators. Accountability relates both to the existence of formal control (through independent monitoring bodies or self-regulatory agencies) and to an attitude of transparency and responsiveness to society (Baldi 2007, pp. 17–19).

Although public service broadcasting and public broadcasters have appeared to be more resilient than perhaps expected (Collins et al. 2001), several trends have put the policy project under pressure. First, late modernity questions the emancipatory and, some would say, paternalist project of public service broadcasting. Its core values, mostly defined by academics and policy makers, are often transposed in ways that do not appeal to younger, more diverse and fragmented audiences (Jakubowicz 2010). The research of Just et al. (2017) shows that media users younger than 40 identify values for public service broadcasting that are currently not included in the mission statements of public broadcasters nor in most scholarly work, such as self-direction. Second, some remain convinced that, especially in a digital era, the free market can deliver public value to citizens in a more efficient manner than public broadcasters (Elstein 2008). Third, public broadcasters are imperfect institutions. While scholars defend them fiercely, these institutions are legacy players that often lack flexibility, transparency, and efficiency required to anticipate market dynamics while still holding true to their core task (Born 2003; Donders 2012). Within such a context, several scholars have advanced adapted versions of public service broadcasting and/or of the organizational form through which the project should be realized. Proponents of a more economic approach, less well-represented in academic research, predominantly advocate for a market failure rationale as the basis for government intervention. In other words: governments should intervene only in those areas where the market is under-providing services with positive externalities (e.g. information and historical documentaries and not talent shows or soap operas) and where government failure is lower than market failure.

Intervention is also not necessarily tied to one particular institution (Armstrong and Weeds 2007). Some have for that reason proposed to limit the scope of existing public broadcasters' activities, turning them into providers of niche services. This is basically a public service light scenario (Peacock 2004). Others argue that market mechanisms should be introduced in the provision of public services as well. That means that all companies can apply for government funding to provide public interest-driven media services (Elstein et al. 2004). The social responsibility approach in media and communication sciences, on the other hand, supports the expansion of public service broadcasting beyond broadcasting (Donders 2012). First, it is assumed that public service broadcasting is at the core of democracy and the fulfillment of democratic values. Hence, the justification for public broadcasters lies not in market failure or in scarcity of airwaves, but in its non-commercial role in society (Garnham 1990, p. 120). As such, technological evolutions do not invalidate the legitimacy of public service broadcasting. Spectrum scarcity was not the sole, nor most important, reason for having public broadcasters either (Hoffmann-Riem 1995, p. 82). Second, public broadcasters are considered the most optimal means to realize the public interest in media. There is refusal to disconnect the idea from the organization historically entrusted with the execution of the idea, claiming the choice of an institution in charge of public service broadcasting has, even though not always optimally, delivered value to citizens. In that sense, one chooses to be pragmatic, refusing to go for more market-oriented options that are at best unproven (Barnett 2006). Third, the assumption is that public service broadcasting should evolve into public service media, meaning radio and television are not the only means to deliver the public interest in media. The task of public broadcasters should reach beyond these technologies and entail basically everything that allows public broadcasters to reach their audience, in a more interactive manner too (Moe 2008). Public service media is nowadays used as the most dominant concept to describe this new form of public service broadcasting. For example, the European Broadcasting Union, representing public broadcasters in Europe, consistently talks about public service media when referring to both project and organization at the same time.

17.2   Different Political Contexts and a Variety of Practices: Evolution Toward a Libertarian or Competitive Authoritarianism Model

The actual status of public service media organizations in Europe can be quite different, though, and is highly dependent on the political economic context. Hallin and Mancini (2004) distinguish between three types of European media models. In each of these types, public broadcasters take a different position. First, there are the liberal systems such as the USA, the United Kingdom, Ireland, and Luxembourg. These set out from a free market ideology, assuming competitive markets will deliver most value to consumers. The latter are considered rational human beings, choosing consciously to watch or read a particular broadcaster or newspaper. Intervention from government in the media sector is limited to market failure only. Second, countries such as Germany, Belgium, Austria, Norway, and the Netherlands are part of the democratic corporatist model. There is extensive state intervention, but largely with an eye on safeguarding pluralism and diversity of the media. Independence of the media is constitutionally protected. The historical coexistence of public and commercial media is deemed to be the optimal scenario for diverse and pluralistic media. Third, countries with weak commercial media and highly politicized public service media organizations are part of the polarized pluralist model. The state takes an active role in both the private and public media sector, not so much with an eye on furthering some of the values of public service media discussed above, but more so with the aim to instrumentalize the media to further the government's political agenda. Typically, that model can be observed in previously fascist countries such as Portugal and Spain. Obviously, there is criticism of these models for being too reductionist (Humphreys 2012). Is the United Kingdom with its big public broadcaster, the BBC, actually part of the liberal model? Can Scandinavian countries be classified within the democratic corporatist model or do they represent a separate model, referred to as the "media welfare state" (Syvertsen et al. 2014)?

Models can clarify the main differences between European countries. They are not static though. Most scholars would agree on a convergence between the liberal and democratic corporatist model. As a consequence of the rising popularity of neo-liberal ideology (Dyson 1985; Regourd 1999) and national and European deregulation policies in the media sector (Humphreys 2008; Noam 1991), several of the democratic corporatist countries are moving toward the liberal model. Having said that, they still stick to a strong public broadcaster, even if regulated more strictly in the online realm, and spend considerable amounts of subsidies on the production of film, domestic TV production, documentary, etc.

Besides the pressure on the democratic corporatist model, several scholars have claimed the polarized pluralist model does not capture fully the complexity of media in post-communist countries. Hallin and Mancini (2004) did not include these countries in their typology. Terzis (2007) added a fourth category of post-communist countries to Hallin and Mancini's model. However, this addition was largely ignorant of the diversity in this group of countries as well. Several previously communist countries could be said to have moved toward the democratic corporatist or liberal models. For example, Latvia has adopted a discourse of open markets, liberalization, and digitization in its policies. Its media market is competitive and, at the same time, shows significant tendencies toward media concentration. It ranks 28th on the World Press Freedom Index (compared to the 71th place for Hungary and the 54th position for Poland). Issues concerning independence of the media relate mainly to the media serving the Russian-speaking community in Latvia. These media are known to be pro-Kremlin. Other countries such as Poland and Hungary have adopted recipes for the media sector that show a marked resemblance to the authoritarian view of media as a tool of government to defend the status quo (Siebert et al. 1956). In Hungary, the media law adopted in 2014 has provoked massive outcry in the country itself and within the EU. It is said to increase the government's influence over the media, particularly when deciding on the appropriateness of content and on granting licenses to broadcasters. The public broadcaster is considered a state broad-caster by most observers. Its programming policies are reported to be influenced by the lead party in government and tough questioning of its politicians is being actively discouraged (Dunai 2014). In Poland, the government has strengthened its control over the public broad-caster, gaining decision-making power over management appointments (Greenslade 2016). Several scholars (e.g. Levitsky and Way 2010; Vladisavljevic 2016) have classified such coun-tries in the model of competitive authoritarianism, meaning they have become a part of the EU's internal market and, hence, accepted a capitalist organization of the media. However, at the same time, the intervention of government in the media has intensified and freedom of speech is being curbed significantly (Metykova and Waschková Císarová 2009). Whereas the trend toward more liberal ideologies puts pressure on public broadcasters' online activities, the crystallization of competitive authoritarianism presents us with an admittedly more fundamental issue. The essence of independent media as part of European democracies is being questioned. Whereas free media exist from an economic point of view, the same cannot be said from a political, societal, and cultural perspective. Not surprisingly, public broadcasters in countries that are moving toward or have adopted a competitive authoritarian view on media and society can better be considered state broadcasters (Hanretty 2011). The question then is whether in these countries the existence of a public/state broadcaster con-tributes to the set of common values that is part of theories on public service broadcasting and public service media.

It would be wrong to assume that media models or typologies explain fully the state of play of public service media in Europe. They still cover a range of practices. Public broadcasters transpose the common values of public service media within the wider context of more strin-gent policies (whether market oriented or steered by an increasing desire of governments to control public broadcasters) in a variety of ways. When relating to audiences, other public institutions, competitors, politicians, and themselves as an organization, public broadcasters show vastly different behaviors. Audience ratings are more important for some than for others. There is also a noteworthy difference in audience ratings, with public broadcasters such as those operating in Iceland, Germany, Finland, the United Kingdom, Norway, Denmark, Italy, Sweden, the Netherlands, etc. having high market shares with over 35% of the audiences watching their TV channels. On the other side are the public broadcasters from Lithuania, Bulgaria, Greece, Macedonia, Romania, Ukraine, etc. These have difficulties attracting 10% of the viewers (EBU 2017, p. 5). Most public broadcasters offer online services such as simulcast or catch-up video. However, only 34% of public broadcasters offer full episodes of programmes on Youtube, and a mere 35% is active on radio streaming services such as Spotify. The duration of online offers differs significantly as well. Seventy-four percent of European public broadcasters offer content online up to one month after initial broadcast. Others go beyond that period (EBU 2017, pp. 30–31), especially for content types such as culture, historical programming, documentary, etc. Some public broadcasters are more active when it comes to online media. For example, the BBC is known to invest heavily in its websites and dedicated content for online. In 2017, it announced it was strengthening its online content offering for children. Other public broadcasters – such as the German, Swiss, and Irish – are more reluctant to enter this area or face more restrictions doing so. The Swiss and German public broadcasters are exemplary cases of how public broadcasters' online expansion can be curbed through the adoption of lists of new media services they cannot offer, a word limit in text articles, the requirement that new services must be related to existing radio and television services, etc. Whereas in most markets tensions between public broadcasters and commercial media can be quite high, some witness the emergence of collaborations between both parties to further joint interests in an internationalizing media landscape. In Belgium, but also in Sweden, you see the emergence of such initiatives. Some public broadcasters spend a lot of money on external production. The United Kingdom and Belgium are examples of countries that impose rather ambitious quotas on their public broadcasters in this respect. They invest up to 20% of their programming budget on independent production. In other countries, such as Ireland, Sweden, Denmark, and France, this figure does not exceed 10% and most production budgets are spent in-house. In terms of funding, the variety across Europe is enormous, with the Scandinavian public broadcasters, the Swiss, Austrian, British, and German ones being funded rather generously. Not surprisingly, Central and Eastern European public broadcasters receive less money from the state. This also shows when looking at employment numbers. Swiss public broadcasters, for example, employ 5022 people (which amounts to 628 per million inhabitants). France Télévisions provides work to 15 261 people, which is in absolute figures much more, but only 240 people per million inhabitants (Van den Bulck et al. 2016). This is only a snapshot of what public broadcasters do or don't do, how much money they get, audience ratings, budget expenditure, etc. An in-depth comparative perspective would show an even greater diversity.

17.3 Conclusions: Unity in Diversity?

Whereas a shared set of values underlies public service media across Europe, the practices of what public broadcasters do and the contexts within which they work are in fact very diverse. That is in itself not problematic as public broadcasters, in contributing to social cohesion, national identity, the provision of high-quality content, independent journalism, etc. are necessarily a phenomenon that is embedded within a specific historical, economic, political, and socio-cultural setting. What might be more challenging is the observation that the highly utopian idea of what public broadcasters ought to be does not necessarily correspond with what is happening in practice. Aspirational goals can in such cases be (ab)used to pretend that all is well with public service media in Europe. As illustrated above, this is certainly not the case.

More European action is needed to strengthen public service media. So far, the EU's most active role in this area is situated in the field of competition law. The European Commission checks that the state aid (subsidies, license fee) given to public broadcasters by EU member states is not market distortive. In so doing, the European Commission has asked countries to be more specific about what it is they expect their public broadcasters to do, to install independent monitoring of performance, and to ensure funding does not exceed the amount of money necessary to deliver the entrusted services (Donders 2012). Whereas the role of the European Commission has had positive effects on public broadcasters' governance, its goal is essentially to limit public broadcasters' activities. There is no balancing act from parts in the European Commission that are more concerned with strengthening democracy, journalism that informs citizens, and independence of the media in general. That is a major weakness, largely caused by member states' opposition to European interference in this arena.

References

Armstrong, M. and Weeds, H. (2007). Public service broadcasting in the digital world. In: *The Economic Regulation of Broadcasting Markets: Evolving Technology and Challenges for Policy* (ed. P. Seabright and J. von Hagen), 81–149. Cambridge: Cambridge University Press.

Baldi, P. (2007). Media accountability in Europe: a fragmented picture. In: *Broadcasters and Citizens in Europe: Trends in Media Accountability and Viewer Participation* (ed. P. Baldi and U. Hasebrink), 17–32. Bristol: Intellect.

Bardoel, J. and D'Haenens, L. (2008). Reinventing public service broadcasting in Europe: prospects, promises and problems. *Media, Culture and Society*, 30 (3): 337–355.

Barnett, S. (2006). Public service broadcasting: a manifesto for survival in the multimedia age (a case study of the BBC's new charter). Paper presented at the RIPE Conference, Amsterdam, 2–6 October.

Blumler, J.G. (1991). *Broadcasting Finance in Transition: A Comparative Handbook*. Oxford: Oxford University Press.

Born, G. (2003). From Reithian ethic to managerial discourse: accountability and audit at the BBC. *Javnost The Public*, 10 (2): 63–80.

Burgelman, J.-C. (1990). Omroep en politiek in België. Het Belgisch audio-visuele bestel als inzet en resultante van de naoorlogse partijpolitieke machtsstrategieën (1940–1960). Brussels: BRT. [Broadcaster and politics in Belgium. The Belgian audiovisual set-up as the stake and outcome of post-war party-political power strategies (1940–1960)]

Cody, M.J., Fernandes, S., and Wilkin, H. (2003). Entertainment-education programs of the BBC and the BBC world service trust. In: *Entertainment-Education and Social Change: History, Reach and Practice* (ed. A. Singhal, M.J. Cody, E.M. Rogers and M. Sabido), 243–260. London: Routledge.

Collins, R., Finn, A., McFayden, S., and Hoskins, C. (2001). Public service broadcasting beyond 2000: is there a future for public service broadcasting? *Canadian Journal of Communication*, 26 (1): Retrieved from: http://www.ecj-online.ca/viewarticle.php?id=615.

Council of Europe (25 June 2009) Recommendation 1878 (2009) on the funding of public service broadcasting.

Crisell, A. (2002). *An Introductory History to British Broadcasting*, 2e. London: Routledge.

Cunningham, S. (2009). Reinventing television: the work of the "innovation" unit. In: *Television Studies After TV: Understanding Television in the Post-Broadcast Era* (ed. G. Turner and J. Tay), 83–92. London: Routledge.

Cunningham, S. (2015). Repositioning the innovation rationale for public service media. *International Journal of Digital Television* 6 (2): 203–220.

Donders, K. (2012). *Public Service Media and Policy in Europe*. Basingstoke: Palgrave Macmillan.

Donders, K. and Pauwels, C. (2012). Ex ante tests: a means to an end or the end for public service media. In: *Regaining the Initiative for Public Service Media* (ed. G. Lowe and J. Steemers), 79–96. Gothenburg: Nordicom.

Donders, K. and Van den Bulck, H. (2016). Decline and fall of public service media values in the international content acquisition market: an analysis of small public broadcasters acquiring BBC worldwide content. *European Journal of Communication* 31 (3): 299–316.

Dunai, M. (2014) How Hungary's government shaped public media to its mould. *Reuters*. Retrieved from: https://www.reuters.com/article/us-hungary-media-insight/how-hungarys-government-shaped-public-media-to-its-mould-idUSBREA1I08C20140219.

Dyson, K. (1985). The politics of cable and satellite broadcasting: some West European comparisons. In: *Broadcasting and Politics in Western Europe* (ed. R. Kuhn), 152–171. London: Routledge.

EBU (2017). *PSM Barometer*. Geneva: EBU.

Elstein, D. (2008). How to fund public service content in the digital age. In: *The Price of Plurality: Choice, Diversity and Broadcasting Institutions in the Digital Age* (ed. T. Gardam and D.A. Levy), 86–90. Oxford: Reuters Institute for the Study of Journalism.

Elstein, D., Cox, D., Donoghue, B. et al. (2004). *Beyond the Charter: The BBC After 2006*. London: The Broadcasting Policy Group.

Garnham, N. (1990). *Capitalism and Communication: Global Culture and the Economics of Information*. London: Sage.

Greenslade, R. (11 January 2016). Polish journalists protest at state control of public broadcasting. *The Guardian*. Retrieved from: https://www.theguardian.com/media/greenslade/2016/jan/11/polish-journalists-protest-at-states-control-of-public-broadcasting.

Habermas, J. (1991). *The Structural Transformation of the Public Sphere*. Cambridge, MA: MIT Press.

Hallin, D.C. and Mancini, P. (2004). *Comparing Media Systems: Three Models of Media and Politics*. Cambridge: Cambridge University Press.

Hanretty, C. (2011). *Public Broadcasting and Political Interference*. London: Routledge.

Hoffmann-Riem, W. (1995). Germany: the regulation of broadcasting. In: *Public Broadcasting for the 21st Century* (ed. M. Raboy), 64–86. London: John Libbey.

Horsti, K. and Hultén, G. (2011). Directing diversity: managing cultural diversity media policies in Finnish and Swedish public service broadcasting. *International Journal of Cultural Studies* 14 (2): 209–227.

Humphreys, P. (2008). The principal axes of the European Union's audiovisual policy. In: *Communication and Cultural Policies in Europe* (ed. I. Fernandez Alonson and M. de Moragasi Spà), 151–184. Barcelona: Government of Catalonia, Catedra Unesco de Communicacio and Autonomous University of Barcelona.

Humphreys, P. (2012). A political scientist's contribution to the comparative study of media systems in Europe: a response to Hallin and Mancini. In: *Trends in Communications Policy Research* (ed. N. Just and M. Puppis), 157–176. Bristol: Intellect.

Iosifidis, P. (2008). Public television policies in Europe: the cases of France and Greece. *International Journal of Media and Cultural Politics*, 4 (3): 349–367.

Jakubowicz, K. (2010). PSB 3.0: reinventing European PSB. In: *Reinventing Public Service Communication: European Broadcasters and Beyond* (ed. P. Iosifidis), 9–22. New York: Pallgrave Macmillan.

Just, N., Büchi, M., and Latzer, M. (2017). A blind spot in public broadcasters' discovery of the public: how the public values public service. *International Journal of Communication* 11: 20.

Katsirea, I. (2008). *Public Broadcasting and European Law: A Comparative Examination of Public Service Obligations in Six Member States*. New York: Wolters Kluwer International.

Levitsky, S. and Way, L. (2010). *Competitive Authoritarianism: Hybrid Regimes After the Cold War*. Cambridge: Cambridge University Press.

Metykova, M. and Waschková Císarová, L. (2009). Changing journalistic practices in Eastern Europe. *Journalism*, 10 (5): 719–736.

Moe, H. (2008). Discussion forums, games and second life: exploring the value of public broadcasters' marginal online activities. *Convergence: The International Journal of Research into New Media Technologies* 14 (3): 261–276.

Murdock, G. (2005). Public broadcasting and democratic culture. In: *A Companion to Television* (ed. J. Wasko), 174–198. Oxford: Blackwell.

Noam, E. (1991). *Television in Europe*. New York: Oxford University Press.

Peacock, A. (2004). Public service broadcasting without the BBC? In: *Public Service Broadcasting Without the BBC?* (ed. A. Peacock), 33–53. London: Institute for Economic Affairs.

Price, M. and Raboy, M. (2003). *Public Service Broadcasting in Transition: A Documentary Reader*. The Hague: Kluwer Law International.

Regal, B. (2005). *Radio: The Life Story of a Technology*. Westport: Greenwood Publishing Group.

Regourd, S. (1999). Two conflicting notions of audiovisual liberalisation. In: *Television Broadcasting in Contemporary France and Britain* (ed. M. Scriven and M. Lecomte), 29–45. New York: Berghahn Books.

Siebert, F.S., Peterson, T., and Schramm, W. (1956). *Four Theories of the Press: Authoritarian, Libertarian, Social Responsibility, Soviet Communist: Concepts of What the Press Should Be and Do*. Chicago: University of Illinois Press.

Syvertsen, T., Enli, G., Ole, M., and Moe, H. (2014). *The Media Welfare State: Nordic Media in the Digital Era*. Michigan: University of Michigan Press.

Terzis, G. (2007). *European Media Governance: National and Regional Dimensions*. Bristol: Intellect.

Van den Bulck, H. (2001). Public service television and national identity as a project of modernity: the example of Flemish television. *Media, Culture & Society* 23 (1): 53–69.

Van den Bulck, H., Raats, T., and D'Haenens, L. (2016). De VRT gebenchmarkt. Organisatie, aanbod, financiering en bereik. In: *Een VRT voor Morgen of Morgen geen VRT Meer?* (ed. T. Raats, D. Van den Bulck and L. D'Haenens), 107–132. Kalmthout: Pelckmans Pro.

Vladisavljević, N. (2016). Competitive authoritarianism and popular protest: evidence from Serbia under Milošević. *International Political Science Review* 37 (1): 36–50.

18

Sweden and Beyond

The Pirate Party and Non-Media-Centric Media Politics

Martin Fredriksson

On 17 March 2006, Dan Eliasson, secretary of state at the Swedish Department of Law, received a letter from the Motion Picture Alliance of America (MPAA) asking the Swedish authorities to take action against the Swedish filesharing site The Pirate Bay. Representatives of the MPAA argued that if the authorities did not act forcefully against the infamous site, Sweden could face trade sanctions for insufficient protection of intellectual property rights (IPR). Two months later, the Swedish police conducted a raid against The Pirate Bay's server hall outside Stockholm. The raid did little to stop The Pirate Bay – the site was soon up and running again – but it set an example and saved Sweden's good relations with the United States. It also fueled a political mobilization of ideological filesharers, and self-proclaimed pirates, protesting against the harsh methods of the so-called copyright industry (Burkart 2013; Özdemirci 2014).

These issues had been on the agenda for some time, not least in America. In the late 1990s, a wave of court cases against filesharers and filesharing sites across the USA had begun to draw attention to the problem of an expanding copyright regime. This critique grew with the passing of the Sonny Bono Copyright Term Extension Act (CTEA) in 1998, which extended the copyright term from 50 to 70 years after the death of the author, and the Digital Millennium Copyright Act from the same year, which prohibited circumvention of Digital Rights Management (DRM) protection (Mitchell 2005). Protests were widespread and CTEA was even challenged in the USA's Supreme Court; by now "a new skepticism about copyright was," as Henry Mitchell (2005) puts it, "finally beginning to leave the pages of the law reviews and take on political shape" (p. 41).

One of the most active debaters in Sweden was the so-called Pirate Bureau, a hybrid between a think-tank, an activist group, and an art collective that was also partly aligned with The Pirate Bay (Burkart 2013). When the MPAA and the Swedish authorities launched a campaign against The Pirate Bay, they thus opened fire against a flagship of a global, ideological pirate movement, ready to be mobilized on a wider scale. One consequence of this politicization of the filesharing question was the formation and growth of the Pirate Party.

This chapter will try to map the development of the Pirate Party in Sweden and internationally and situate it ideologically and politically. Relying on a series of interviews I carried out with Pirate Party members in Europe, the USA, and Australia between 2011 and 2014,[1] I will show how the defense of a Swedish filesharing site came to have political implications far beyond its original geographic and political sphere and contribute to a recontextualization of the concept of media politics. David Morley (2009) and others (Krajina et al. 2014) have argued

Transnational Media: Concepts and Cases, First Edition. Edited by Suman Mishra and Rebecca Kern-Stone.
© 2019 John Wiley & Sons, Inc. Published 2019 by John Wiley & Sons, Inc.

for a new way of doing non-media-centric media studies that approaches media not primarily as a set of representations but acknowledges it as embedded in a range of different social, technological, and political practices. By applying a non-media-centric media studies approach to the Pirate Party, I will show how their political platform reflects a wider understanding of what media politics can be in a mediatized society.

18.1 The Birth of the Pirate Party

A couple of months before the Pirate Bay raid, on 1 January 2006, Richard Falkvinge, a then 36-year-old IT engineer without any significant political experience, launched a website announcing a plan to form what he called a "Pirate Party," dedicated to legalizing filesharing. His initiative had an immediate impact. The website had three million visitors in the first two days and he soon met the initial goal to collect the 1500 signatures required to register a political party in Sweden. Initially, the Pirate Party was a response to the implementation of the EU's Information Society Directive of 2001 (2001/29/EC) that harmonized and strengthened the rights of copyright holders within the European Union. When the directive was implemented in Sweden in 2005 it was heavily criticized for imposing more restrictive copyright regulations that, among other things, prohibited copying of protected works for private use (Fredriksson 2015a; Svensson and Larsson 2009, p. 17).

When the Swedish police raided the server halls of the Pirate Bay, it sparked the mobilization of the newly formed Pirate Party. As the prosecution of the Pirate Bay continued, so did the growth of the Pirate Party, and when the three owners of the Pirate Bay – Gottfrid Svartholm Warg, Fredrik Neij, and Peter Sunde – were sentenced to one year in prison and fined 30 million SEK (approximately 3.6 million USD) in an infamous trial in March 2009, the Swedish Pirate Party was at its peak, winning 7.1% of the votes in the EU election which earned them two seats in the European Parliament (*The Economist* 2009).

This was possibly the first time in European political history, and certainly the first time in Swedish history, that a political party had been successfully established on a program predominantly focusing on media politics. This was not just about the Pirate Bay: between 2006 and 2009 a number of other laws with potentially severe implications for the new media landscape had been passed in Sweden and elsewhere. In 2004, the European Parliament passed another copyright directive called the Intellectual Property Rights Enforcement Directive (IPRED) (2004/48/EC). This complemented the Information Society Directive and enhanced copyright enforcement by giving media companies and copyright organizations extensive rights to monitor individual internet users in order to uncover copyright violations. The directive was implemented in Sweden under heavy protest in April 2009, one month after the closing of the Pirate Bay trial and three months before the EU election (Svensson and Larsson 2009, p. 17). Yet another contributing factor was the passing of a set of anti-terrorist laws in 2008 that gave military authorities extensive rights to monitor and intercept digital communication between citizens.[2] This offered the Pirate Party an opportunity to take a strong position on privacy rights (Erlingsson and Persson 2011; Rydell and Sundberg 2010).

To some extent, these factors were specific to Sweden's political development in those years. In other regards they were part of an international media development, as most of them concerned the implementation of international copyright regimes in national law and politics. On that level, the early history of the Swedish Pirate Party merely tapped into an international resistance against how copyright had been used to impede the sharing of culture and information between users and to maintain the dominance of the media industry at the expense of free speech (Arvanitakis and Fredriksson 2016; Fredriksson 2012, 2014).

18.2   The Pirate Parties International

The Pirate Party was barely ever an exclusively Swedish concern as it very soon turned into an international movement. The international mobilization of pirate parties began almost immediately after the Swedish party was announced: by the end of 2006 an international organization for coordination and exchange of information – Pirate Parties International (PPI) – had been initiated and over the following year national parties were formed in a number of different countries (Rydell and Sundberg 2010, p. 160). Even though the first pirate parties were European, they soon spread to other continents. At an early stage, pirate parties were formed in Australia and North America and by 2012 they had also, according to the PPI, been initiated in a number of South American, Asian, and African countries (Pirate Parties International 2012; cf. "The Stream" 2012). The most unexpected impact of the Pirate Party might be the fact that Tunisia came to be the first country where the Pirate Party acquired national political representation when the blogger and Pirate Party activist Slim Amamou was appointed secretary of state in the new government that took over after the Ben Ali Regime was taken down in October 2011 ("Tunisian Blogger ..." 2011; "Who are ..." 2011).

Since 2006, the Pirate Party has had its ups and downs and different national parties have taken turns keeping the party on the political map. The rapid growth of the Swedish Pirate Party halted after 2009 and they lost both seats in the EU Parliament in the EU election of 2014. But at this point the German Pirates, conversely, won one seat in the parliament. The German Pirate Party had existed since 2006 and made a big impact in regional elections across Germany in the fall of 2011. After 2012, their support began to shrink and their impact in the EU election of 2014 was far below their expectations. However, from the time it was founded in 2012, the Icelandic Pirate Party had been growing steadily and in the national election in Iceland, on 29 October 2016, they got 14.5% of the votes, making them the third party with 10 out of 63 seats in the parliament (Helgadóttir 2016). More recently, the Czech Pirate Party got 10.6% of the votes in the parliamentary election in the Czech Republic in October 2017, making it the third largest party with 22 seats in the parliament (Cobain and Henley 2017). Although the impact of national pirate parties tends to be short lived, they seem to be persistent as an international movement, showing up in different and more or less unexpected places.

In many regards, the mobilization of pirate parties across the world ran parallel to that of the Swedish Pirate Party. Andrew Norton, who was active in forming both the PPI and the United States Pirate Party, confirms that the internationally recognized and widely infamous raid and trial against the Pirate Bay strongly contributed to this rapid mobilization of pirate parties (Interview, Norton). On a more fundamental level, all these different parties reacted against the same development toward a global harmonization of copyright legislation, through international copyright treatises, that threatened to limit the growth and freedom not only of filesharing networks, but of many forms of new social and digital media networks that relied on the freedom to share and remix existing works (Burkart 2013; Fredriksson 2015a).

Yet, one of the strengths of the Pirate Party was that it could also adapt and respond to local conditions. After the EU elections of 2009, many Pirate parties actively and deliberately expanded their agendas to include a range of issues beyond their initial focus on copyright and filesharing (Cammaerts 2015; Fredriksson and Arvanitakis 2015; Jääsari and Hildén 2015). In many cases, democracy issues were emphasized in these new Pirate agendas. Many of the American Pirate Party members describe their work with the Pirate Party as a response to the lack of transparency and democratic participation in American politics

(Fredriksson 2013, 2015a; Fredriksson and Arvanitakis 2015; Fuller 2017). The UK Pirate Party took a similar position when it opened its party program by declaring:

> Democracy is in crisis in the United Kingdom. Whether it is online or on the doorstep, people are telling us that they feel alienated, ignored, that they have given up voting as it changes nothing. (Pirate Party UK 2012, p. 2)

The Tunisian and the Icelandic cases are more dramatic examples where the party interfered directly in a national political crisis. Slim Amamou was a well-known blogger and activist who earned his political position by publicly opposing the Ben Ali dictatorship. Along with other Pirate Party members, he objected to internet censorship and general restrictions of free speech, which resulted in him being jailed and tortured by the old regime in early January 2011. When the Ben Ali regime was overthrown shortly thereafter, Amamou was appointed minister of youth and sport in the new interim government where he served until May 2011 (Christafis 2011a, b; "Tunisian Blogger..." 2011; "Who are..." 2011). Amomou was thus never publicly elected as a representative of the Pirate Party, but rather was put in the center of the revolution though his personal commitment to freedom of speech and digital liberties. These values were, however, central to the Pirate ideology, and his involvement with the Pirate Party was symbolically important for Pirate Party members in other parts of the world. Jay Emerson from the US Pirate Party has, for instance, described how he closely followed the fate of Amamou and contacted the embassy to get his incarcerated Tunisian party comrade released (Interview, Emerson; Fredriksson Almqvist 2016b).

Iceland was suffering from its own political turmoil that began with the Icelandic banking crisis of 2008, when the Icelandic banks bankrupted the country through the misuse of short-term credits and high-risk investments (Sigurjonsson 2010). The political establishment's reluctance to interfere and the lack of critical voices in the established media created what Birgitta Jonsdottir, one of the Pirate Party's members of the Icelandic Parliament, has described as a collapse of the political institutions that the Icelandic people had put their trust in (Jonsdottir, Pers comm). Although the Icelandic Pirate Party was formed in 2012, it traces its origins back to a movement that helped uncover the dealings behind the bank crisis. In August 2009, Wikileaks published leaked documents revealing that Kaupthing had issued large and insecure loans to companies owned by some of its largest shareholders. When a court order prohibited Icelandic news media from reporting on Kaupthing's corrupt affairs, state TV referred the viewers to Wikileaks, making Wikileaks the main source of information for the Icelandic people (Sigurjonsson 2010). At that stage, Birgitta Jonsdottir acted as Wikileaks' spokesperson in Iceland, which made her one of the few who publicly spoke out against the corruption (Knight 2013; Withnal 2016). The Icelandic Pirate Party thus drew its genealogy directly from a movement that exposed a corrupt economic and political establishment (Fredriksson Almqvist 2016b).

18.3   From Media Piracy to New Communication Politics

All of these cases – from government transparency in the USA to the Icelandic banking crisis and the Tunisian revolution – seem alien to the party's original focus on copyright and filesharing. Yet they touch on two very important aspects of the pirate agenda: freedom of information and government transparency. At the heart of this lies a communicative ethos that is sometimes hard to tell apart from mere self-gratification.

The first wave of mobilization largely took place on online forums that attracted people interested in filesharing and digital rights (Burkart 2013; Erlingsson and Persson 2011;

Fredriksson Almqvist 2016a, b; Fredriksson and Arvanitakis 2016; Fredriksson 2013, 2015). Significant for this mobilization is the fact that it often centers on apparently mundane acts of media consumption. Although some Pirate Party activists see filesharing as "a form of civil disobedience in itself" (Interview, Brunner and Adams Green; Interview, Emerson; Fredriksson 2015; Fredriksson and Arvanitakis 2015), the bulk of filesharers are more likely to be seeking cheap and accessible entertainment than looking to make a political statement (Andersson Schwarz 2014; Da Rimini and Marshall 2014). The Pirate Party's own statistics suggest that the takedown of major filesharing sites remained one of the strongest factors mobilizing supporters long after the Pirate Bay trial. One of the most obvious expressions of this is the takedown of the filesharing site TankaFetast in October 2012, when a link to the Swedish Pirate Party was posted on the closed torrent site, causing an intense growth of members. This is one example of how a mundane act of filesharing, which in most cases surely lacked political intention, caused a large number of people to make a political commitment when they realized that their habits of media consumption were threatened (Fredriksson Almqvist 2016a).

The case of TankaFetast would suggest that the Pirate ideology is merely a pretext to claim access to free entertainment. That is probably also the case for many of the party's less active supporters. The Pirate Party interventions in Tunisia and Iceland, however, tell an apparently different story, where the Pirates step up as defenders of fundamental liberal and democratic values. So, how did the Pirates get from the takedown of a Swedish filesharing site to the Icelandic banking crisis and the Tunisian revolution? If we acknowledge that what from the outside appeared to be a single-issue agenda around copyright and filesharing was actually a much more coherent communication policy platform, then the struggles in Sweden, Iceland, and Tunisia are not as disparate as they seem. These struggles essentially circle around common questions of freedom of information and its different limitations and implications. The fact that the initial intervention into new media policies turned into a much wider democracy movement does not necessarily signify a loss of political focus, but rather implies a more comprehensive application of the party's communication policy perspective. The focus on media and communication issue remains at the core of Pirate Party agendas but is contextualized in relation democratic participation and transparency rather than to culture and entertainment.

The Pirate Party's ability to address filesharing and the Arab Spring within one platform challenges the borders of media politics, but also reflects a changing relation between media and society. Many have expressed concerns over the mediatization of politics and envisioned how the emergence of media as the fourth estate threatens to corrupt the independence and integrity of politics. The examples from Iceland and Tunisia, however, highlight that we cannot really make a distinction between politics and media in an age of global mediatization. Instead, we need a more holistic perspective on media politics that addresses what Mazzoleni and Schulz (1999) describe as a "mediatized democracy" where mass media "construct the public sphere of information and opinion and control the terms of their exchange" (p. 250).

The Pirate Party's intervention in the political landscape can thus be seen as an example of a non-media-centered information politics that not only addresses media as a sphere of symbolic, mediated representations but also sees communication as a technologically and politically situated social practice. In a society that is essentially mediatized, media cannot be isolated as an object for research or politics. This implies a new kind of information politics that can be about free speech in a dictatorship, or about speaking up against corruption in a compromised democracy, or simply about sharing the latest music and movies with friends and strangers. This is not to say that all of these causes are equally worthy or equally urgent, but they all speak to the same demand for freedom of information. And, not least, they show that media politics in a mediatized society has to address not only how society is represented, but also how it is governed.

Notes

1 This text relies on empirical material collected for the project "Globalization of Copyright and the Ideology of Piracy": Funded by the Swedish Foundation for Humanities and Social Sciences (Riksbankens jubileumsforn).
2 A piece of legislation generally known as the FRA Law, named after Sweden's military agency for radio surveillance: "Försvarets Radioanstalt."

References

Andersson Schwarz, J. (2014). *Online File Sharing: Innovations in Media Consumption*, Routledge. New York.

Arvanitakis, J. and Fredriksson, M. (2016). Commons, piracy and the crisis of property. *Triple C* 14: 132–144.

Burkart, P. (2013). *Pirate Politics*. Cambridge, MA: MIT Press.

Cammaerts, B. (2015). *Pirates on the Liquid Shores of Liberal Democracy: Movement Frames of European Pirate Parties*, vol. 22, 19–26. Javnost – The Public.

Christafis, A. (2011a). Tunisian Dissident Blogger Takes job as Minister. *The Guardian*, 19 January 2011. Retrieved from: https://www.theguardian.com/world/2011/jan/18/tunisia-dissident-blogger-minister.

Christafis, A. (2011b). Tunisian Dissident Blogger Quits Ministerial Post. *The Guardian*, 27 May 2011. Retrieved from: https://www.theguardian.com/world/2011/may/25/tunisian-dissident-blogger-minister-quits.

Cobain, I. and J. Henley (2017). Anti-establishment billionaire Andrej Babiš to be named Czech MP. *The Guardian*, 24 October 2017. Retrieved from: https://www.theguardian.com/world/2017/oct/22/anti-establishment-billionaire-andrej-babis-to-be-named-czech-pm.

Da Rimini, F. and Marshall, J. (2014). Piracy is normal, piracy is boring: systemic disruption as everyday life. In: *Piracy: Leakages from Modernity* (ed. M. Fredriksson and J. Arvanitakis), 323–344. Sacramento: Litwin Books.

Erlingsson, G.O. and Persson, M. (2011). The Swedish pirate party and the 2009 European parliament election: protest or issue voting? *Politics* 31: 121–128.

Fredriksson, M. (2012). Piracy, globalisation and the colonisation of the commons. *Global Media Journal: Australian Edition* 6 (1): 1–10.

Fredriksson, M. (2013). An open source project for politics: visions of democracy and citizenship in American pirate parties. In: *The Citizen in the 21st Century* (ed. J. Arvanitakis and I. Matthews), 201–213. Witney: Inter Disciplinary Press.

Fredriksson, M. (2014). Copyright culture and pirate politics. *Cultural Studies* 28 (5–6): 1022–1047.

Fredriksson, M. (2015). The pirate party and the politics of communication. *International Journal of Communication* 9: 909–924.

Fredriksson Almqvist, M. (2016a). Pirate politics between protest movement and the parliament. *Ephemera* 16: 99–116.

Fredriksson Almqvist, M. (2016b). Piracy and the politics of social media. *Social Science,* 5 (3): https://doi.org/10.3390/socsci5030041.

Fredriksson, M. and Arvanitakis, J. (2015). Piracy, property and the crisis of democracy. *Journal of Democracy and Open Government* 7: 135–150.

Fuller, R. (7 November 2017). Pirates, democracy and the digital revolution. *Los Angeles Review of Books*. Retrieved from: https://lareviewofbooks.org/article/pirates-democracy-and-the-digital-revolution#.

Helgadóttir, O. (30 October 2016). No, the Pirates didn't win Iceland's election. Here's what happened instead. *The Washington Post*. Retrieved from: https://www.washingtonpost.com/news/monkey-cage/wp/2016/10/30/no-the-HYPERLINK, https://www.washingtonpost.com/news/monkey-cage/wp/2016/10/30/no-the-pirates-didnt-win-icelands-elections-heres-what-happened-instead/?utm_term=.334594fceb12pirates-didnt-win-icelands-elections-heres-what-happened-instead/?utm_term=.334594fceb12.

Jääsaari, J. and Hildén, J. (2015). From file sharing to free culture. The evolving agenda of European Pirate Parties. *International Journal of Communication* 9: 879–889.

Knight, S. (7 October 2013). Icelandic activist Birgitta Jónsdóttir explains how Wikileaks changed her country forever. *Take Part*. Retrieved from: http://dev.takepart.com/article/2013/10/17/how-wikileaks-changed-my-country-forever/index.html.

Krajina, Z., Moores, S., and Morley, D. (2014). Non-media centric media studies: a cross generational conversation. *European Journal of Cultural Studies* 17 (6): 682–700.

Mazzoleni, G. and Schulz, W. (1999). "Mediatization" of politics: a challenge for democracy? *Political Communication* 16 (3): 247–261. https://doi.org/10.1080/105846099198613.

Mitchell, H.C. (2005). *The Intellectual Commons: Towards an Ecology of Intellectual Property*. Lanham, MD: Lexington Books.

Morley, D. (2009). For a materialist, non-media-centric media studies. *Television & New Media* 10 (1): 114–116.

Özdemirci, E.G. (2014). BitTorrent: stealing or sharing culture? A discussion of the Pirate Bay case and the documentaries "steal this film I & II". In: *Piracy: Leakages from Modernity* (ed. M. Fredriksson and J. Arvanitakis), 157–176. Sacramento: Litwin Books.

Pirate Parties International (2012). Retrieved from: http://pp-international.net.

Pirate Party UK (2012). *Manifesto*. Retrieved from: www.pirateparty.org.uk/media/uploads/Manifesto2012.pdf.

Rydell, A. and Sundberg, S. (eds.) (2010). *Piraterna: Historien the Pirate Bay, Piratpartiet Och Piratbyrån*. Stockholm: Ordfront.

Sigurjonsson, T.O. (2010). The Icelandic bank collapse: challenges to governance and risk management. *Corporate Governance: The International Journal of Business in Society* 10: 33–45.

Svensson, M. and Larsson, S. (2009). *Social Norms and Intellectual Property: Online Norms and the European Legal Development*. Lund: Lund University.

The Economist (5 September 2009). Keeping pirates at bay. Retrieved from: http://www.economist.com/node/14299558.

The Stream (9 April 2012). Can Pirates shake up European politics?. *Al Jazeera*. Retrieved from: http://stream.aljazeera.com/episode/22166.

Tunisian Blogger Appointed Minister (19 January 2011). *Al Jazeera*. Retrieved from: http://www.aljazeera.com/news/africa/2011/01/201111992639946635.html.

Who are Tunisia's Political Parties? (27 October 2011). *Al Jazeera*. Retrieved from: http://www.aljazeera.com/indepth/features/2011/10/201110614579390256.html.

Withnal, A. (26 January 2016). Iceland's Pirate Party takes big lead in polls ahead of election next year. *The Independent*, 2016. Retrieved from: http://www.independent.co.uk/news/world/europe/iceland-pirate-party-takes-big-lead-in-polls-ahead-of-election-next-year-a6834366.html.

19

Bertelsmann SE & Co. KGaA

Scott Fitzgerald

Bertelsmann is the largest European-based multinational media corporation in the world. Headquartered in the small northern German city of Gütersloh, the corporation operates in approximately 50 countries around the world, although its primary markets are in Western Europe (especially Germany, France, and the United Kingdom) and the United States. As well as being the world's largest commercial publisher of "trade" books (books aimed at a general readership), Bertelsmann's media operations include television and radio broadcasting, video content, and magazines. A conglomerate, it describes itself as a "media, services and education company," and indeed its operations in the service industries make a large contribution to the overall corporation. The corporation traces its history back over 180 years and it is still owned and controlled by the billionaire Mohn family, descendants of the founder, Carl Bertelsmann.

From the late 1980s it ranked as one of the largest media corporations in world. However, it was surpassed by the formation of major US media conglomerates in the 1990s and, more recently, by the rise of the so-called tech corporations (Google, Facebook, Amazon, Apple). According to the German Institute of Media and Communications Policy's 2017 ranking, Bertelsmann's revenues place it as the 16th-largest media corporation in the world (this list does not include pure telecom or technology providers). In 2017, it had about 119 000 employees and produced revenues of over €17 billion (USD 21 billion). Such figures always need to be put in perspective. In the same year, Germany's largest corporation, Volkswagen, the world's largest automotive manufacturer, had 642 300 employees and produced revenues of over €220 billion.

Bertelsmann has large businesses in national, regional (television and radio broadcasting and magazines), and international markets (book publishing and television content). Adopting a political economic lens, this chapter will first provide an overview of the history of this privately owned and controlled company and place its development within the wider media landscape of Germany. In the next section it reviews the company's principal media operations and assesses their significance in terms of expanse of operations and dominance in particular media markets.

19.1   Bertelsmann's History

The history of Bertelsmann reflects an interesting relationship between media nationalism and transnationalism. Although a transnational media corporation, it is indelibly marked by the history of media in Germany, and specifically the relationship between concentrated media power and fascism in that country (Fitzgerald 2012).

Transnational Media: Concepts and Cases, First Edition. Edited by Suman Mishra and Rebecca Kern-Stone.
© 2019 John Wiley & Sons, Inc. Published 2019 by John Wiley & Sons, Inc.

For nearly a century after its founding in 1835 as a publisher of Protestant hymnals and religious books, C. Bertelsmann Verlag, as it was known, remained a relatively small publishing house. By the 1920s the company had diversified into popular novels and non-fiction texts, but it only turned itself into a mass-market publisher with national operations through cooperation with the National Socialist (Nazi) regime in the early 1930s. The company continued to expand in the years before World War II, but once hostilities started it rapidly developed into the most important supplier of books for frontline German soldiers. Between 1935 and 1943, Bertelsmann's revenues grew by 2000%. Due to "total war" conditions, the company ceased operations in 1944, but in 1946 was able to recommence its business in the Allied occupied zone with its printing operations and management structure largely intact. Drawing on its organizational strength, Bertelsmann began buying smaller competitors in the traditional book business and in 1950 pursued this strategy of horizontal integration (i.e. buying up businesses in the same industry or sector) in the re-emerging book club business in the new West Germany. It then diversified into recorded music clubs in 1956. As with its book operations, it quickly pursued vertical integration (i.e. buying businesses that span different stages of production and distribution) in its music operations, buying a music publishing company and establishing a record printing company to support the distribution of its recorded music clubs.

Just as World War II had originally provided the foundations for Bertelsmann's rapid corporate expansion, the corporation's postwar development was significantly shaped by the media policy and regulation that emerged in West Germany. Given the Nazi Party's use of the press, film, and radio as propaganda instruments, the country's postwar media policy was designed to limit state control; yet, it was also shaped by a desire to prevent the re-emergence of the sort of media mogulism displayed by German industrialist Alfred Hugenberg who, in the Weimar period (1919–1933), used his large newspaper and film operations to shape public opinion in favor of Hitler. It was in this context that Reinhard Mohn (1921–2009), the great, great grandson of Carl Bertelsmann, took over the company from his father in 1947, and to clearly mark a break with the company's past he began to present Bertelsmann as a unique form of a private family company, one that sought to adopt modern forms of decentralized, hierarchical management.

In the 1960s, Bertelsmann purchased other West German publishers but, given the country's strict anti-cartel laws, its further domestic expansion was limited. Thus, beginning in 1962, the company began to internationalize its operations, establishing book and record clubs across Western Europe and Latin America throughout the 1960s. By the end of that decade, Bertelsmann had fully established itself as a diversified media multinational corporation. Between 1969 and 1976 it reinforced its position as a central player in the Western German media industry through the gradual acquisition of a majority stake in Gruner + Jahr, West Germany's fourth-largest magazine publisher. By this time, Bertelsmann ranked alongside the Axel Springer newspaper empire as the largest media company in West Germany.

Reflecting broader concerns about the concentration of ownership in the media industry, in 1976 the West German Federal Government introduced stringent new anti-cartel laws that specifically focused on the already highly regulated media landscape. Bertelsmann made one more publishing acquisition in West Germany, the Goldman paperback publishing company; however, by then Bertelsmann's strategy was firmly focused on international acquisitions, in particular in the United States. Although the corporation had extensive international operations in the German and Spanish geo-cultural markets (markets that span nation-state boundaries based on common cultural and linguistic understandings), the United States was not only the largest single cultural market but also produced English-language cultural commodities that were consumed globally. Having purchased a majority of Bantam Books in 1977, Bertelsmann made significant investments in the US media market in 1986, acquiring Doubleday, the

New York-based publishing house, and the RCA record company. Bertelsmann merged its US publishers into the Bantam Doubleday Dell Publishing Group (BDD) and RCA Records and Bertelsmann's other record labels into the Bertelsmann Music Group (BMG), one of the handful of global record label "majors."

Controlling distribution is a key business strategy in the cultural industries and, with global distribution networks in music and books, Bertelsmann was now one of the largest transnational media corporations in the world. Yet it had not given up on new opportunities in the German market. In the early 1980s, Federal Court rulings signaled that private television channels would be permitted into West Germany. In preparation for this "broadcasting revolution," Bertelsmann acquired a 38.9% stake in Compagnie Luxembourgeoise de Télédifussion (CLT), a Luxembourg-based broadcasting company which began broadcasting a German language channel, RTL Plus, into West Germany. Over the ensuing decade, RTL Plus surpassed the West German public broadcasters ARD and ZDF in both ratings and advertising revenue.

In the 1990s, Bertelsmann's growth was marked by a number of major developments. It quickly expanded into the former East Germany after German reunification; it created Europe's largest commercial broadcaster through a 1997 merger with the Luxembourg broadcaster CLT, and reinforced this status in 2000 with a merger with the UK-based Pearson TV, forming the RTL Group; and in 1998 it acquired the New York publishing company Random House which, when combined with BDD, made Bertelsmann the world's largest English-language trade book publisher.

Yet Bertelsmann faced two major challenges. First, the pace of international media ownership concentration had increased dramatically and competing US-based corporations, such as Time Warner, News Corporation, and Viacom, all owned Hollywood film and television production studios which formed a central component of their vertical integration strategies. Bertelsmann's management refused to either take on massive debt or dilute the Mohns' ownership to acquire such assets. Second, Bertelsmann was confronted by the emergence of new forms of digital distribution and the rise of corporations such as Amazon and Apple, which destabilized its global distribution networks in music and books (Fitzgerald 2015). Its attempts at gaining a foothold in online books via a share of Barnes & Noble's online bookstore and its own Books Online (BOL) and online music (Napster) proved to be variously unsuccessful and disastrous. After merging its music operations with Sony (Sony-BMG) in 2003, it sold its half share in 2006. In 2011, it began to close its Direct Group division, which had housed its book club operations, and completed the process in 2015. As compared to the previous bold steps toward internationalization, for Bertelsmann the first decades of the twenty-first century have largely been marked by a focus on organic growth, cost-cutting, and reinforcing its strength in its established markets. A key example of the latter was the 2013 merger of its Random House book publishing division with Pearson Media Group's Penguin Group to form Penguin Random House (PRH), viewed by many analysts as a response Amazon's growing influence in the book publishing industry. As one publishing consultancy executive noted, "Amazon couldn't play rough with PRH because it's such a behemoth ... It can't go after them if it wants to have good relations with the book market" (Chazan 2017).

Although Bertelsmann had become a less diversified corporation in the first decades of the twenty-first century, a corporate restructure in 2016 signaled a renewed focus on diversification as a means to drive growth. At the beginning of that financial year, the BMG re-emerged as a separate division reflecting the corporation's relatively small but growing investment in music rights (as opposed to earlier operations in music recordings). The Bertelsmann Education Group was also established as a provider of education services. Both divisions were designated as "strategic growth segments." Through the Bertelsmann Investments division, the corporation has also indicated other areas it is seeking growth from: Bertelsmann Digital Media Investments (BDMI), Bertelsmann Asia Investments (BAI), Bertelsmann Brazil Investments (BBI), and Bertelsmann India Investments (BII).

As noted, the Mohn family (Reinhard Mohn's wife Liz and their children Brigitte and Christoph) remains firmly in charge of Bertelsmann. Indeed, the corporation's retreat from some of its more aggressive expansion strategies in the first years of the twenty-first century in part reflected the desire of the Mohn family to cement its control after Reinhard Mohn died. Family control is in itself not unusual in the international media industry; most of the top media content companies have a major individual owner (Noam and The International Media Concentration Collaboration 2016). However, the form through which the Mohns have maintained control is somewhat different, being achieved through a non-profit foundation that received the majority ownership (80.9%) of Bertelsmann in 1993. The Mohn family, in turn, maintain control over the Bertelsmann Foundation and have built it into the largest and most influential think-tank in Germany. The policy causes championed by the Bertelsmann Foundation are often viewed as favoring the media and more general business interests of the corporation. These operations are detailed in the next section.

The 380 employees at the Bertelsmann Foundation are currently working on around 70 projects with the simple stated goal of contributing to "social reform." These projects include "Discovering Music," designed to sponsor music's promotion of "tolerance, participation and equitable opportunities in society" (Bertelsmann Foundation 2017, p. 25). The Foundation is also influential in policy areas such as education (particularly higher education), health care, social and labor market polices, European governance, and political reform. While its main offices are in Gütersloh, it has established a branch in Washington, DC to advance transatlantic economic integration and free trade. According to its critics, the fundamental "political motivation behind the Bertelsmann Foundation is to diminish state control of any kind" (Becker 2016, p. 152). This does not merely reflect a broad ranging commitment to the advancement of economic liberalism; rather, its advocacy of "reform" of local government, for instance, through outsourcing and privatization, promotes the interests of its service industry division (Arvato), which has substantial business in the area of outsourced public services. Furthermore, critics point to the growing privatization of politics: despite its extensive lobbying operations and connections with officials across various levels of government in Germany, the "shadow government in Gutersloh" is argued to lack democratic legitimacy.

19.2 Bertelsmann's Media Operations

As Table 19.1 indicates, Bertelsmann is currently structured into eight divisions: RTL Group (broadcasting and television content), Arvato (services), Penguin Random House (book publishing), Bertelsmann Printing Group (printing), Gruner + Jahr (magazines), BMG (music rights), Bertelsmann Education Group (education), and Bertelsmann Investments (an international network of funds). The latter two divisions are comparably very small, producing negligible revenues (see Figure 19.1). Although the corporation has announced a renewed focus on international expansion, Germany remains the central location for the majority of its operations (see Table 19.1).

Bertelsmann holds 75.1% of the RTL Group, the Luxembourg-based company which is the largest private television and radio company in Europe. The RTL Group produces over half of Bertelsmann's operating income. Through RTL, Bertelsmann controls varying ownership stakes in 57 television channels and 31 radio stations and engages in content production

Table 19.1 Bertelsmann's divisions: revenue 2015–2017 (€ millions).

	2017 (Germany %)	2016 (Germany %)	2015 Germany %
RTL Group	**6373** (35.6)	**6237** (35.4)	**6029** (35.7)
Arvato	**3823** (39.8)	**3838** (42.5)	**3783** (58.3)
Penguin Random House	**3359** (7.4)	**3361** (7.9)	**3717** (7.6)
Bertelsmann Printing Group	**1681** (56.9)	**1624** (55.9)	**1744** (55.8)
Gruner + Jahr	**1513** (63.7)	**1580** (60.7)	**1611** (56.5)
BMG	**507** (6.5)	**416** (7.5)	**371** (10)
Bertelsmann Education Group	**189** (0.5)	**142** (0)	**110** (0)
Bertelsmann Investments	–	–	**1** (100)
Total	**17 190** (34)	**16 950** (34.6)	**17 141** (33.9)

Source: Bertelsmann Annual Report (2017).

Figure 19.1 Bertelsmann (2017) revenue. *Source:* Bertelsmann Annual Report (2017).

throughout the world. In Europe, the RTL Group's TV channels are either the number one or number two in audience share in eight countries. These channels include:

- RTL (RTL Germany)
- M6 (Groupe M6, France)
- RTL 4 (RTL Nederland)
- RTL-TVI (RTL Belgium)
- RTL Klub (RTL Hungary)
- RTL Televizija (RTL Croatia)
- Télé Lëtzebuerg (RTL Luxembourg)
- Antena 3 (Atresmedia, Spain).

According to research conducted by Noam and The International Media Concentration Collaboration (2016), Bertelsmann's RTL ranked 8th in terms of revenue share among the world's television broadcasters (with 2.9%), yet it is distinctive in its control of networks in several European countries, whereas most terrestrial broadcasters limit their activities to their home countries. Reflecting the size of the markets, Germany (Mediengruppe RTL Deutschland) and France (Groupe M6) together produce over half (56%) of RTL's revenues; these two countries also account for 79% of the group's profits.

While advertising produces the bulk of RTL's revenues (television 48% and radio 4.1%), a sizable proportion of the revenue is produced from content production (21.2%). This is via RTL's FremantleMedia, one of a small number of international TV production super-groups, and one of the largest outside the US. FremantleMedia has a global network of around 50 production companies located in 31 countries, which produce and distribute over 400 programs and over 60 TV formats. FremantleMedia produces almost 12 000 hours of broadcast programming a year including shows such as *American Idol, Family Feud, Britain's Got Talent, The X Factor*, and *The Eureka Moment* for CCTV in China. Adding to its scripted programming, FremantleMedia recently produced the series *American Gods,* which was distributed by US pay-TV channel Starz and outside the US on Amazon's Prime Video platform. FremantleMedia also produced *The Young Pope* for HBO, Sky, and Canal Plus. Primarily through Google's YouTube platform, RTL Group has the most online video "views" among European media companies. Analysis of the combined TV content industry – broadcasting and video channels (Noam and The International Media Concentration Collaboration 2016) – ranked Bertelsmann 6th in terms of revenue share among the world's television content producers (behind the BBC with 3.2% world revenues). Although Bertelsmann's RTL once led the European TV production super-groups, US media groups such as Time Warner and News Corporation have more recently been acquiring leading European independent television production companies and changing the balance of the industry.

As noted, through its Penguin Random House (PRH) division, Bertelsmann is the world market leader in general or trade book publishing and according to estimates accounts for one in four trade books sold, or 25% of the world market. PRH comprises nearly 250 imprints and brands on five continents, with more than 15 000 new titles and 800 million print, audio, and e-books sold annually. With worldwide revenue of more than $4 billion, Penguin Random House is ranked 4th among the world's 10 largest publishers (behind educational and professional publishers, Pearson, Reed Elsevier's RELX Group, and ThomsonReuters). In this broader publishing market, PRH's world market share is estimated be around 9% (Noam and The International Media Concentration Collaboration 2016). However, its revenues dwarf the other four big trade book publishers, HarperCollins, Hachette, Macmillan, and Simon & Schuster; for instance, its revenues are twice as large as HarperCollins, the world's second largest trade publisher, and almost five times as large as Simon & Schuster, the world's fifth largest trade publisher. Penguin Random House's chief market is the United States, where over half of its revenues are generated. PRH only controls 7–9% of the entire US book publishing market but some estimates give it as high as 37% of the trade book market. It also obtains significant sales from the United Kingdom, Germany, and the rest of Europe. Attempts to increase its share of the German publishing market have been blocked by regulators. In 2017, Bertelsmann paid $780 million to increase its stake in PRH to 75% (Pearson retains a 25% stake in PRH). As Bertelsmann has expended its presence in the international book publishing industry it has focused on increasing its profitability or operating margin above 15%, a rate not commonly achieved in publishing. Presently PRH's operating margin is 15.5%, compared with 23.2% for RTL. A key strategy it has pursued is concentrating on best-sellers such as *Camino Island* and *The Whistler* by John Grisham.

Based in Germany's northern city of Hamburg, Gruner + Jahr (G + J) is the second largest magazine publishing company in Europe behind the Bauer Media group, also based in

Hamburg. G + J publishes around 500 printed and digital media products across approximately 20 countries. Unlike other international competitors, such as Time Warner and Lagadère which have sold their large magazines operations, in 2014 Bertelsmann signaled its commitment to the magazine publishing industry by expanding its control of G + J to 100%. However, this has been accompanied by a renewed focus on the publisher's two principal markets: Germany and France (where respectively 63.2 and 23.3% of 2017's revenues were generated). Having been the first German magazine company to expand into other markets in Europe and the United States in the late 1970s, G + J has since sold its US magazine operations (in 2005) and more recently sold its businesses in the Netherlands, China, and India and discontinued the international businesses of some of its German operations. It has also embarked on a cost-cutting and restructuring drive. This, together with recent acquisitions, has increased the publisher's focus on digital publishing, which now makes up one quarter of G+J's sales.

The other major segments of Bertelsmann are outside of its traditional media operations, although they are in some instances connected, as with the Bertelsmann Printing Group's book printing operations. The employees of Arvato division, which offers business process outsourcing (BPO) services, make up almost 59% of Bertelsmann's workforce or 70 000 employees. This division contributes 22% of Bertelsmann's revenue. While its sales have slowly increased, its contribution to Bertelsmann's operating income has slowly declined, now representing less than 12% of the corporation's profits. Operating in more than 40 countries, Arvato's operations include Customer Relationship Management (CRM), Supply Chain Management (SCM), Financial Solutions, and IT Services. Arvato's revenues can be broken down by region: 38.9% in Germany, 10.1% in France, 5.5% in the United Kingdom, 29.2% in the rest of Europe, and 8.7% in the United States. The Bertelsmann Printing Group comprises all of Bertelsmann's offset and gravure printing activities in Germany, the United Kingdom, the United States and France. As Table 19.1 indicates, the majority of the Printing Group's revenues are produced in Germany. As with Arvato, it is facing intense competition in many of its operations and large sections of its business are viewed as being in structural decline. Nonetheless the divisions play an important role in generating the capital required for Bertelsmann's media operations.

19.3 Conclusion

Outside Germany few people may have heard of Bertelsmann. Its operating segments, such as Penguin Random House, FremantleMedia, or BMG, have more international "brand recognition" and this is in large part an intentional outcome of the discreet, decentralized approach it has adopted to media ownership. Yet, despite competitive challenges in the twenty-first century media environment, Bertelsmann remains one of the world's largest multinational media corporations, with leading European television assets and internationally dominant book publishing operations. Its sway on political discourse in Germany, and the European Union, arises not just from its media operations but also from the powerful Bertelsmann Foundation.

References

Becker, J. (2016). Bertelsmann SE. In: *Global Media Giants* (ed. B. Birkinbine, R. Gomez and J. Wasko), 144–162. London: Routledge.

Bertelsmann (2017). Annual Report. Retrieved from: https://www.bertelsmann.com/media/investor-relations/annual-reports/annual-report-2017-financial-information-2.pdf (Accessed 12 March 2018).

Bertelsmann Foundation (2017). Annual Report. Retrieved from: https://www.bertelsmann-stiftung.de/fileadmin/files/BSt/Publikationen/Infomaterialien/IN_Annual_Report_2017_EN_2018-03-08.pdf (Accessed 12 March 2018).

Chazan, G. (2017). "Bertelsmann benefits from print's resilient popularity", *Financial Times*, 31 January 2017.

Fitzgerald, S. (2012). *Corporations and Cultural Industries*. New York: Rowman & Littlefield.

Fitzgerald, S. (2015). Structure of the cultural industries – global corporations to SMEs. In: *Routledge Companion to the Cultural Industries* (ed. J. O'Connor and K. Oakley), 70–85. London: Routledge.

Institute of Media and Communications Policy (2017). "Media Database – International Media Corporations 2017". Retrieved from: http://www.mediadb.eu/en.html (Accessed 12 March 2018).

Noam, E. and The International Media Concentration Collaboration (2016). *Who Owns the World's Media? Media Concentration and Ownership Around the World*. Oxford: Oxford University Press.

20

Broadcasting Against the Grain

The Contradictory Roles of RT in a Global Media Age

Liudmila Voronova and Andreas Widholm

RT (formerly Russia Today) is a transnational television news broadcaster launched in 2005 by the Russian government. It is one of the most controversial global news actors, often associated with misinformation and propaganda. In this capacity, the channel can also be seen as an instance of an increasingly pluralized global information space where traditional legacy media meet competition from alternative news outlets. This chapter takes a broad view on RT and delves into its roles and objectives as have been addressed by media scholars, NGOs, other news media institutions, and not least RT itself. We begin by discussing RT's activities and competitors on the global news market, after which we discuss these activities from the perspectives of soft power, public diplomacy, propaganda, and nation branding. The chapter ends with concluding remarks and suggestions for future research in this area.

20.1   RT and Its Competitors in a Global Media Environment

There are several examples of transnational information initiatives throughout history that have taken the form of news journalism. The BBC, for example, started transnational radio broadcasting across the states of the British Empire in the 1930s as a way of "helping Britain retain its influence in the wider world" by promoting a transnational "Britannic community" (Potter 2012, pp. 4–5). Other influential examples are Voice of America and Radio Free Europe/ Radio liberty, all US government-sponsored radio networks launched in the 1940s and which are still on air (Puddington 2000; Xie and Boyd-Barrett 2015). The increasingly globalized television news environment that media consumers witness today, however, is largely a product of the rapid development of international satellite technology that took place from the 1980s onward; a new cross-border information space that in its early stages was dominated by one single news broadcaster: American CNN. CNN revolutionized the television business by launching 24-hour rolling news, a format that became widely influential during the 1991 Gulf War, and the channel continued thereafter to expand its activities toward international audiences (McPhail 2010; Volkmer 1999). CNN's success sparked reactions among various new actors, yet it was not only commercial companies that saw the strong potential in transnational news broadcasting, but also nation-states who feared a consolidation of an American news hegemony in the global public sphere. Hence, from the mid 1990s and onward, channels such as BBC World News, Euronews, France 24, Al-Jazeera, and Russia Today were launched, each with their own national or regional outlook on the world (Robertson 2015). To this, we can add the plethora of more traditional news formats that later were made available on a much larger

Transnational Media: Concepts and Cases, First Edition. Edited by Suman Mishra and Rebecca Kern-Stone.
© 2019 John Wiley & Sons, Inc. Published 2019 by John Wiley & Sons, Inc.

scale through the internet. Strukov (2014) has defined three categories of "multinational" TV-channels: *pan-continental channels* that primarily serve audiences of a large entity of several states, *international ethnic TV-channels* that focus on emigrants and diaspora communities, and broadcasters with a more *global approach* that seek audiences in several languages at once (pp. 239–242). RT belongs to the third group, with its multi-platform broadcasting, multilingual content, and global audience orientation.

When Russia Today was launched in 2005, it was first and foremost aimed at improving the image of Russia abroad. However, the channel gradually changed character, and in conjunction with the 2009 rebranding of its name to the more distinct abbreviation RT, it started to focus more exclusively on world events, presenting news from a Russian perspective. It was also during this time that RT's counter-hegemonic strategies took their current form, with a more confrontational approach vis-à-vis Western so-called "mainstream media" through the official broadcasting motto "Question more." As to content, RT provides a broad range of news and current affairs programs, including traditional news bulletins as well as debates, talk shows, and documentaries.

The channel has also recruited television and Hollywood celebrities such as Larry King and Stephen Baldwin in order to attract large audiences. Other examples include the international football profiles José Mourinho and Stan Collymore, who were hired as experts in conjunction with Russia's hosting of the 2018 FIFA World Cup. Using celebrities can, as Joseph Nye (2011) argues, help make ideas and practices appear more "palatable, acceptable, and colourful" (p. 83). However, the use of well-known faces does not mean that the content provided is unoriginal or predictable. A distinctive feature of RT is rather a sort of "unconventionalism"; a search for stories and perspectives that break with the narratives of the mainstream. One of the most telling examples of this approach was the "Julian Assange Show" broadcast in 2012 where the highly controversial Wikileaks' founder talked to politicians and activists across the globe.

Today, RT has more than 20 bureaus across the globe and a yearly budget of more than $300 million, exceeding the budgets of both Voice of America and Radio Free Europe/Radio Liberty ("Comparing Russian and American ..." 2017). It also claims to reach more than 700 million people in over 100 countries. In terms of audience reach, there are few real success examples of transnational news broadcasting, although CNN, Sky News, and BBC World often are described as the top brands of the genre. In comparison with these global news brands, RT has still a long way to go – at least when considering the viewing figures in Europe which are relatively low (Widholm 2016). RT is more successful on digital platforms; often referred to as the largest global news broadcaster on YouTube in terms of video views (Hutchings et al. 2015), at the time of writing it had 4.97 million likes on Facebook and 2.68 million followers on the official Twitter account. How many of those are bots, fake accounts, or actual people is, however, far from clear.

20.2 RT, Soft Power and Public Diplomacy

As noted above, a typical feature of RT is its claim to offer news stories that are different from those provided by Western media. This function is often referred to as "counter-hegemonic," given that the channel very openly wants to challenge public discourse outside its borders (Miazhevich 2018; Robertson 2015). A typical example of this strategy was seen in connection with RT's news coverage of the conflict in Ukraine in 2014 (Widholm 2016). After Russia's annexation of Crimea, heavy sanctions against Russia were imposed by the EU and the USA. However, RT's answer to this imposition was not to depict their consequences in Russia, as most Western journalism institutions did. Instead, the channel informed viewers about a European Union in crisis, suffering from its own misdirected sanctions, while a Russian trade ban directed toward the EU was about to destroy German businesses. Other counter-narratives could be seen during the MH17 investigation, where Western news media such as the BBC and *The New York Times* were severely criticized for biased reporting, propaganda, and fabrication of evidence. Both cases were also characterized by a discursive one-sidedness.

In the constantly expanding transnational public sphere, news media institutions are dependent on credibility in order to maintain their audience and their trust (Nye, 2011). However, as noted by Widholm (2016), while Western news media institutions acquire credibility through senses of objectivity and professionalism, the selling point of RT's news is rather ideological transparency. Partiality, especially in relation to the West, is thus a central and constitutive part of RT's public identity and, from that perspective, it can accuse Western mainstream media of biased reporting and fake news while still acquiring credibility. As Miazhevich (2018) has noted, RT's broadcasting motto "Question more" is both a journalistic mode and a means of reaching audiences who already have an "anti-establishment, anti-corporation and anti-western (anti-American) predisposition" (p. 5).

Despite RT's distinctive position in the global television market, it is important to note that it has several aspects in common with many of its competitors. Broadcasters such as BBC World News, France 24, and Euronews rely on governmental funding, most often in combination with commercial revenues. Such funding is often bound to certain public diplomacy efforts, which typically include communication of values and perspectives that can have a positive impact on a country's so-called "soft power" internationally and globally (Nye 2011; Snow 2010). Soft power has been a popular theoretical concept in media studies and international relations that aims at encircling how states act strategically through communication of cultural narratives, political ideals, and policies in such a way that they are considered attractive and appealing among people in other countries. Soft power is thus related to the formation of collective attitudes and beliefs which cannot be achieved by "hard" power, such as the use of military force or economic sanctions. The development of international broadcasting, hosting of global mega events, and proliferation of a variety of cross-border partnerships and exchanges are all examples of attempts to put soft power into practice (Roselle et al. 2014, p. 71). On the policy level, soft power can be understood as a central goal of what has come to be known as "public diplomacy," e.g. global communication efforts to inform influence and engage foreign publics in support of national interests (Snow 2010, p. 87). As Nye has noted, politics in the information age is ultimately about whose story wins, and thus "narratives become the currency of soft power" (Nye 2011, p. 83). Soft power depends at the same time on credibility, meaning that governments do not want to be associated with misinformation or propaganda. RT is, thus, somewhat of anomaly as an agent of soft power, given that it often is associated with propaganda – something we discuss in more detail below.

20.3 RT As a Propaganda Channel and "Foreign Agent"

RT is often accused of being a propaganda channel by Western media analysts and politicians. According to Hutchings et al. (2015), RT's transformation toward a "semi-militarized propaganda" tool took place in connection with the conflict in Ukraine (p. 646). In October 2017, the US Department of Justice (DOJ) required that a Washington, DC corporation, T&R Productions, LLC should register as an "Agent for the Russian Government Entity [ANO TV-Novosti] Responsible for Broadcasting RT," under the Foreign Agents Registration Act (FARA) (Department of Justice 2017). Enacted in 1938 as a reaction to attempts by Nazi Germany to spread propaganda inside the USA, FARA "is a disclosure statute that requires persons acting as agents of foreign principals in a political or quasi-political capacity to make periodic public disclosure of their relationship with the foreign principal" (Foreign Agents Registration Act, 1938/2017). RT argued that as a bona fide media organization they should be exempted from FARA and planned to challenge the decision in court ("String of brain-dead slogans" 2017). Yet, for the exemption to be received, RT "would need to disclose its finances, board members and show evidence of editorial independence from the Russian government" (Pisnia 2017). According to the special report by the Atlantic Council, the channel would not qualify to be exempt from registration, as "RT advances Russia's interests abroad and uses communication channels to influence US domestic and foreign policy" (Postnikova 2017, p.16).

On 13 November 2017, RT registered as a "foreign agent," meaning that all of RT's US material should be labeled as "on behalf of" the Russian government (Pisnia 2017). In addition, the channel should every half year report on both receipt and expenditure of funds. Despite the prognosis that "RT would be able to continue operating in the US without restriction" (Postnikova 2017, p. 16), the USA withdrew the Congressional press credentials of RT due to the channel's new status. This situation allowed RT to once again question the existence of freedom of speech in the Western countries, and their hegemony in defining what propaganda is (see also Hutchings et al. 2015). The channel used a variety of sources and references to criticize the DOJ decision and to suggest that actions against RT represent a "backdoor censorship" ("US used 'backdoor censorship'" 2017). Lee Camp, host of RT America's "Redacted Tonight," blamed what he labeled as "the corporatocracy" for failing to recognize that the channel offers its audience "the undiluted, stone-cold reality about the corporate state in which we live" ("Meet 'foreign agent'" 2017). Margarita Simonyan, the editor-in-chief of RT, shared a picture of herself in a T-shirt with the phrase "freedom of speech" being transliterated to Cyrillic alphabet on a green background, thus suggesting that RT is a legitimate guardian of #фридомофспич (Simonyan 2017). RT's treatment in the USA finally led to similar countermeasures to US propaganda in Russia, where media outlets such as Voice of America and Radio Free Europe/Radio Liberty were listed as foreign agents and all denied access to the Russian Parliament.

20.4 Beyond Propaganda: RT As a Brand and An Instrument of Branding

While the discussion of RT as the "Kremlin's mouthpiece" has been colorful, some media scholars suggest that viewing RT purely as propaganda is a simplification. According to Saunders (2016), RT's pro-Russian bias is essentially comparable with CNN International's relationship with Washington, or the BBC, which he argues is distinctly pro-British in its international coverage (p. 222). It is true that news media institutions, national and global, tend to reproduce the foreign policy orientation of their home country (Riegert 2011), but in the US domestic context, CNN's depictions of the current presidency have been anything but pro-Trump. In fact, in the spring of 2017, CNN's and the BBC's relationship with the White House was so poisoned that the two networks were banned from attending the daily press briefings ("White house blocks" 2017). Thus, there are similarities but also profound differences between RT and its global competitors. Hutchings and Tolz (2017) call RT a "mixed bag", comprising misleading stories, alternative perspectives on events, but also narratives that contradict the Kremlin's positions.

Some media scholars look at RT as a brand and as a tool of nation branding. As such, the channel positions itself as a "cool" media source for rebellious audiences, and a "counter-hegemonic" brand of broadcasting (Miazhevich 2018). Simultaneously, RT still aims to promote a positive image of Russia and Russians, where the "state brand 'Russia' is evoked as an authority of fairness in the 'unfair' Western world" (Strukov 2016, p. 199). By doing this, RT maintains a national attachment and shows that "international media can be patriotic in the era of global journalism" (ibid., p. 191). According to Miazhevich (2018), RT reiterates "the image of Russia as a bearer of conservative values" in contrast to the liberal values reigning in the West. RT participates in the branding of the Russian state by, for example, promoting international media events such as the military-technical forum "Army of Russia" or the International Tank Biathlon (Pilbeam 2015). Broadcast to transnational audiences, such media events can show Russia as a powerful country in the international arena.

RT's messages can also be understood as an invitation to the symbolic space of the Russian world (cf. Voronova 2017). From the beginning, the "Russian world" signified a community of Russian speakers and compatriots in various geographical settings, but it has recently acquired a changed and largely politicized meaning as it moved to the frontline of the Russian cultural foreign policy (Suslov 2016; Yagodin 2017). The Russian world is promoted not only as an invitation to investors and tourists, which is typical for nation branding, but also as a space welcoming the public to become a *part* of it by identifying with the official Russian State ideology. By participating in the interactive projects of RT and accepting the challenge to "question more," one can feel part of the Russian world imagined community.

20.5   Concluding Remarks

This chapter has addressed the contradictory roles played by RT in the increasingly pluralized landscape of transnational television news. We have highlighted RT as a counter-hegemonic actor, and the channel's capacity as state vehicle for propaganda, nation branding, public diplomacy, and as a contributor with "alternative" perspectives on world events. According to Hutchings et al. (2015), these also come with a certain "democratizing potential" as RT to an increasing extent draws on participatory elements on new platforms. Yet, each of these roles can be questioned further in future research. The "alternative" aspect of RT can be discussed in the US context, given its similarity to, for example, Fox News: both tend to highlight conservative ideals and the dangers of migration in general and Islam in particular. This also relates to its "propagandistic" character, which is by no means unique to RT in the current post-truth age where alternative media outlets have become increasingly influential. The "democratizing" potential could furthermore be addressed in relation to possibilities/limitations of professional autonomy among the staff at RT. Moreover, researchers should look more closely at consumption and online interaction with actors like RT in order to fully understand their significance in the digital age.

References

Comparing Russian and American government "propaganda" (2017). *Meduza* (14 September). Retrieved from: https://meduza.io/en/short/2017/09/14/comparing-russian-and-american-government-propaganda (accessed 21 January 2018).

Department of Justice (2017). Production Company Registers Under the Foreign Agent Registration Act as Agent for the Russian Government Entity Responsible for Broadcasting RT. Retrieved from: https://www.justice.gov/opa/pr/production-company-registers-under-foreign-agent-registration-act-agent-russian-government (accessed 21 January 2018).

Foreign Agents Registration Act of 1938 (1938). 22 U.S.C. § 611–621. Retrieved from: www.fara.gov (accessed 21 January 2018).

Hutchings, S., Gillespie, M., Yablokov, I. et al. (2015). Staging the Sochi winter Olympics 2014 on Russia today and BBC world news: from soft power to geopolitical crisis. *Participations: Journal of Audience & Reception Studies* 12 (1): 630–658.

Hutchings, S. and Tolz, V. (2017). Will Alex Salmond's RT show make him a Kremlin tool? *The Conversation* (November 14). Retrieved from: https://theconversation.com/will-alex-salmonds-rt-show-make-him-a-kremlin-tool-87410 (accessed 22 December 2017).

McPhail, T.L. (2010). *Global Communication: Theories, Stakeholders, and Trends*. Chichester.: Wiley-Blackwell.

Meet "foreign agent": Americans in America covering American news for Americans (2017). *RT* (20 November). Retrieved from: https://www.rt.com/usa/410452-rt-foreign-agent-redacted-tonight (accessed 21 January 2018).

Miazhevich, G. (2018). Nation branding in the post-broadcast era: the case of RT. *European Journal of Cultural Studies* https://doi.org/10.1177/1367549417751228.

Nye, J.S. (2011). *The Future of Power*. New York: Public Affairs.

Pilbeam, K. (2015). Clash of titans: Tank biathlon starts 2015 International Military Games near Moscow. *RT* (1 August). Retrieved from: https://www.rt.com/news/311344-tank-biathlon-russia-military (accessed 5 November 2015).

Pisnia, N. (2017). Why has RT registered as a foreign agent with the US? *BBC* (15 November). Retrieved from: http://www.bbc.com/news/world-us-canada-41991683 (accessed 21 January 2018).

Postnikova, E. (2017). Agent of Influence: Should Russia's RT Register as a Foreign Agent? Atlantic Council Report. Retrieved from: http://www.atlanticcouncil.org/images/publications/RT_Foreign_Agent_web_0831.pdf (accessed 21 January 2018).

Potter, S.J. (2012). *Broadcasting Empire: The BBC and the British world, 1922–1970*. Oxford: Oxford University Press.

Puddington, A. (2000). *Broadcasting Freedom: the Cold War Triumph of Radio Free Europe and Radio Liberty*. University Press of Kentucky.

Riegert, K. (2011). Pondering the future for foreign news on national television. *International Journal of Communication* 5 (19): 1567–1585.

Robertson, A. (2015). *Global News: Reporting Conflicts and Cosmopolitanism*. New York: Peter Lang.

Roselle, L., Miskimmon, A., and O'Loughlin, B. (2014). Strategic narrative: a new means to understand soft power. *Media, War & Conflict* 7 (1): 70–84.

Saunders, R.A. (2016). *Popular Geopolitics and Nation Branding in the Post-Soviet Realm*. New York, NY: Routledge.

Simonyan, M. (2017). Twitter account. Retrieved from: https://twitter.com/m_simonyan?lang=en (accessed 21 January 2018) (in Russian).

Snow, N. (2010). Public diplomacy: new dimensions and implications. In: *Global Communication: Theories, Stakeholders and Trends* (ed. T. McPhail), 84–102. Chichester: Wiley-Blackwell.

"String of brain-dead slogans" – Social media reactions to RT's foreign agent registration (2017). *RT* (10 November). Retrieved from: https://www.rt.com/usa/409511-twitter-reactions-rt-fara (accessed 21 January 2018).

Strukov, V. (2014). "Russia today": (national) self-representation and transnational television. In: *From Central to Digital: Television in Russia* (ed. V. Strukov and V. Zvereva), 231–265. Voronezh: Nauka Press in Russian.

Strukov, V. (2016). Digital conservatism: framing patriotism in the era of global journalism. In: *Eurasia 2.0: Russian Geopolitics in the Age of New Media* (ed. M. Suslov and M. Bassin), 185–208. Lanham: Lexington.

Suslov, M. (2016). The "Russian world" concept in online debate during the Ukrainian crisis. In: *Eurasia 2.0: Russian Geopolitics in the Age of New Media* (ed. M. Suslov and M. Bassin), 295–316. Lanham: Lexington.

US used "backdoor censorship", attacked RT "like a weasel" – journalism prof (2017). *RT* (14 November). Retrieved from: https://www.rt.com/usa/409792-rt-fara-foreign-agent-censorship (accessed 21 January 2018).

Volkmer, I. (1999). *News in the Global Sphere: A Study of CNN and Its Impact on Global Communication.* Luton: University of Luton Press.

Voronova, L. (2017). Gender politics of the "war of narratives": Russian TV-news in the times of conflict in Ukraine. *Catalan Journal of Communication & Cultural Studies* 9 (2): 217–235.

White House blocks CNN, BBC, New York Times, LA Times from media briefing (2017). *Independent* (24 February). Retrieved from: www.independent.co.uk/news/world/americas/white-house-blocks-news-outlets-from-media-briefing-a7598641.html (accessed 21 January 2018).

Widholm, A. (2016). Global online news from a Russian viewpoint: RT and the conflict in Ukraine. In: *Media and the Ukraine Crisis: Hybrid Media Practices and Narratives of Conflict* (ed. M. Pantti), 107–122. New York: Peter Lang.

Xie, S. and Boyd-Barrett, O. (2015). External-national TV news networks' way to America: is the United States losing the global "information war"? *International Journal of Communication* 9 (18): 66–83.

Yagodin, D. (2017). The Social Media Networks of Russia's Cultural Statecraft. 7th Annual Aleksanteri Conference, 25–27 October, Helsinki, Finland.

Part VI

Oceania

Transnational Media: Concepts and Cases, First Edition. Edited by Suman Mishra and Rebecca Kern-Stone.
© 2019 John Wiley & Sons, Inc. Published 2019 by John Wiley & Sons, Inc.

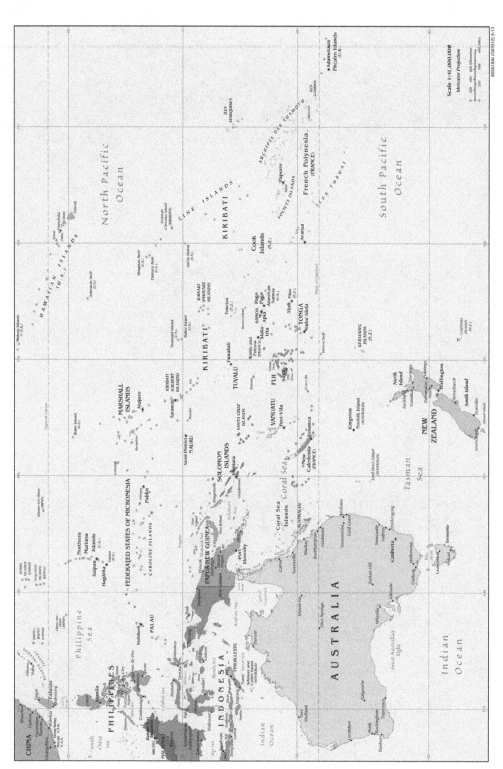

Figure VI.1 Map of Oceania.

The Oceania region consists of Australia and New Zealand, Melanesia, Micronesia, and Polynesia (Figure VI.1). The history of the Oceanic region is filled with familiar colonial scripts: European settlers, discovery of gold, a conflict between the European settlers and the indigenous people, spread of diseases on contact, and significant decline in the indigenous population. However, the region has developed and made many progresses in social, political, and economic arena.

In this section, a brief introduction to two of the larger areas within the Oceania region – the island continent of Australia and the country of New Zealand – are discussed along with brief introductions to their media landscape.

PVI.1   Australia

Australia is the sixth largest country in the world with a relatively small but diverse population of 23.4 million inhabitants (ABS 2016). It is a developed country with a GDP of 1204.62 billion USD and an annual growth rate of 2.8% (World Bank 2016a). Australia ranks as one of the best countries in the world to live in by international comparisons of wealth, education, health, and quality of life (BBC 2018, para 1). The framework within which Australia's political system is constituted is called the federal parliamentary constitutional monarchy, which has three parts: the monarch, the Senate, and the House of Representatives. Australians select their parliamentary representatives through a *compulsory* voting system. Australia's current prime minister Malcolm Turnbull and his party have focused on liberal progressive issues such as climate change and same-sex marriage – which was legalized in December 2017.

The majority of Australians are Christians (57.7%), though 29.6% of the population do not identify themselves with any religion (AUS 2016 Census). English is the primary language spoken at home by a majority of Australians (72.7%) and Mandarin, Arabic, Cantonese, Vietnamese, and Italian are spoken at home by 22.2% of the population (AUS 2016 Census). These are largely the immigrant population. Today, like many countries, Australia is dealing with immigration issues, and migration once again has become a hotly debated and contentious issue among Australians as refugees from the Middle East, Africa, and other countries arrive at its shores. The government has taken tough measures to deal with refugees and asylum seekers, creating a crisis. Australia's offshore refugee detention centers (Nauru and Manus), away from the mainland, have drawn widespread condemnation from the international community for indefinite detention of refugees in camps where many suffered psychological harm and physical and sexual assaults. Australia for a long time had an immigration policy that excluded non-Whites and favored white Europeans. The "White Australia Policy" ended in early 1970s, allowing more non-Whites to become Australian citizens (Commonwealth of Australia 2017). Australia today faces many challenges related to the assimilation and integration of multicultural groups in its society. However, it is also one of the most diverse countries in the world. In addition, the society also continues to wrestle with the issues and conditions of its indigenous population. Aboriginal and Torres Strait Islander peoples are recognized as Australia's First Peoples and have distinctive rights. Their population today is rising, and conditions have improved, but this group remains one of most vulnerable groups in Australia (Australian Human Rights Commission 2014).

Media in Australia is said to be "creatively, technologically and economically advanced. There is a tradition of public broadcasting, but privately-owned TV and radio have the biggest audience share" (BBC 2016, para 1). The Australian Broadcasting Corporation (ABC) and

Special Broadcasting Service (SBS), which has multilingual services, are two public broadcasters (television and radio). SBS is governed under the Special Broadcasting Services Charter of 1991, which states that, "The principal function of the SBS is to provide multilingual and multicultural radio, television and digital media services that inform, educate and entertain all Australians, and, in doing so, reflect Australia's multicultural society" (Australian Government 1991, Section 6). This includes indigenous populations as well as immigrant populations, and broadcasts are done in various languages. ABC broadcasts globally via media partnerships to promote the national identity of Australia. Until recently, it also offered short wave radio stations, such as Radio Australia, but these were cut due to funding. These stations were of particular importance to many areas of Melanesia, Micronesia, and Polynesia, as they provided outside news and helped promote media freedom (Sitigata 2018). Commercially, Rupert Murdoch, owner of News Corp Australia, and Fairfax Media are the two private media giants that control most (85%) of print and broadcast media (BBC 2018) in the country. They too export media via media partnerships with Netflix, BBC, and CBC, among others.

Australia ranks high on 2018 World Press Freedom Index (19/180); however, some of its recent restrictions on news coverage of the refugee detention centers, its whistleblower protection, and a telecommunication law that has the potential to compromise confidentiality of news sources, have raised concerns (Reporters Without Borders 2018a). The Australian film and television industry are well developed and receive funding and subsidies from the government. They also benefit tremendously from rules that restrict foreign media imports in the country. However, these industries are undergoing challenges with cuts to their funding and proposals to lift restrictions on foreign media. A debate has been brewing over continued protectionism versus internationalism of these industries for their future viability. Broinowski (2018, para 3) writes, "It's a multiplayer battlefield, with billions of dollars at stake. Should foreign productions get bigger tax breaks? Should Australian content quotas be removed? Should funding to the public broadcasters be cut?" are at the heart of the debate.

In terms of the digital media landscape, in 2017 Australia had approximately 14.2 million internet subscribers and 26.7 million mobile handset subscribers (ABS 2018). Australians are active users of Facebook, YouTube, FB Messenger, and Instagram (Hootsuite 2018). While the Australian mainstream media remains prolific and dominant, over the years indigenous people have developed their own forms of media – which include community newspapers, radio and television, and interactive technologies – to preserve their local language and culture and challenge mainstream perceptions and representations of their peoples and communities, which they perceive is "at best inappropriate, and at worst racist" (Meadows 1995, para 1). Australian indigenous media are covered in more detail in Chapter 21.

PVI.2 New Zealand

New Zealand is a developed country with an estimated population of approximately 4.9 million (Stats NZ 2018a). Its economy is based largely on agriculture, mining, and tourism. The New Zealand government reports about 3.82 million annual visitors to the country, roughly 80% of its population (Stats NZ 2018b). It has a GDP of approximately 185 billion USD and an annual growth of 3.1% (World Bank 2016b). It is a democratic country with a constitutional monarchy and parliamentary democracy. England's Queen Elizabeth II is ceremonial head of state, represented in the country by the Governor-General. Local government in New Zealand has only the powers conferred upon it by Parliament. There are five parliamentary parties in the 52nd Parliament: The Act Party, Green Party, Labour Party, National Party, and the New Zealand

First Party. Its current prime minister, Jacinda Ardern, is from the Labour Party. New Zealand's 2013 census shows the following demographic make-up: Europeans (74%), Māori (15%), Asian (12%), Pacific Peoples (7%), and Middle East/African/Latin American (1%) (Stats NZ 2015). English is the most common language spoken in New Zealand (96.1%), followed by te reo Māori (3.7%), Samoan (2.2%), Hindi (1.7%), Northern Chinese (including Mandarin) (1.3%), and French (1.2%) (Stats NZ 2014). Christianity is the most prominent religion in the country. Social and economic inequality, relations between white (Pākehā) and Māoris, environmental issues such as dealing with global warming, are some of the challenges facing this scenic country. Earthquakes and tsunami are common in the region. The 2011 Christchurch earthquake had a major impact on the country.

New Zealand ranks high (8/180) on 2018 World Press Freedom Index. Reporters without Borders (2018b, para 1) reports: "Media freedom thrives in New Zealand but is not entirely exempt from pressure, especially economic pressure. Media pluralism and independence are constantly under threat from moves to concentrate media ownership in ever fewer hands." However, New Zealand does have five locally-owned privately-held media companies. In terms of broadcasting, it has state-owned Television New Zealand (TVNZ) and privately-owned TV3 and TVNZ. Paid TV, Sky TV, and public Māori Television are also in the mix. Various radio stations, both private (e.g. The Rock, The Edge) and public (e.g. Radio New Zealand, Niu FM aimed at Pacific Islanders), and Māori-owned radio Ruia Mai in the Māori-language are available. The *New Zealand Herald* is the largest circulated newspaper, but many other newspapers serve the region. On 8 June 2018, a Māori media industry group was established to help expand Māori content globally, such as through Netflix and Amazon (Boynton 2018).

In 2017, New Zealand had 3.8 million mobile phones with active internet connections (Stats NZ 2018c). Leading social networks are YouTube, followed by Facebook, Instagram, and Pinterest (Statista 2018). New Zealand has a dynamic film industry that caters to both national and international audiences. It has the drawn attention of international audiences thorough films such as Roger Donaldson's *Sleeping Dogs* (1977) and later through films like the *Lord of The Rings* and *Hobbit* film franchises in the 2000s by director Peter Jackson – who is discussed in Chapter 22. Jackson's technologically advanced movies have often incorporated New Zealand's beautiful landscapes, helping the city of Wellington, where his production studio is, and the country become a prime tourist destination. Other New Zealand film directors like Andrew Adamson have also done the same through his film *The Chronicles of Narnia: The Lion, the Witch and the Wardrobe*.

References

ABS (2016). 2016 Quick Facts. Retrieved from: http://www.censusdata.abs.gov.au/census_services/getproduct/census/2016/quickstat/036.

ABS (2018). Internet Activity, Australia, December 2017. Retrieved from: www.abs.gov.au/ausstats/abs@.nsf/mf/8153.0.

Australian Government (1991). Federal Register of Legislation - Special Broadcasting Service Act - 1991. Retrieved from: www.legislation.gov.au/Details/C2014C00736.

Australian Human Rights Commission (2014). Face the facts: Aboriginal and Torres Strait Islander Peoples. Retrieved from: www.humanrights.gov.au/education/face-facts/face-facts-aboriginal-and-torres-strait-islander-peoples.

BBC (2016). Australia profile – Media. Retrieved from: http://www.bbc.com/news/world-asia-15675260.

BBC (2018). Australia country profile. Retrieved from: http://www.bbc.com/news/world-asia-15674351.

Boynton, J. (8 June 2018). Māori content could shine in new media landscape. *RNZ*. Retrieved from: www.radionz.co.nz/news/te-manu-korihi/359171/Māori-content-could-shine-in-new-media-landscape.

Broinowski, A. (29 April 2018). The industry will be gutted': why Australian film and TV is fighting for its life. *The Guardian*, Retrieved from: https://www.theguardian.com/culture/2018/apr/29/the-whole-industry-will-be-gutted-why-australias-film-and-tv-industry-is-fighting-for-its-life.

Commonwealth of Australia (2017). A history of the department of immigration: Managing Migration to Australia. Retrieved from: www.homeaffairs.gov.au/CorporateInformation/Documents/immigration-history.pdf.

Hootsuite (2018). 2018 Digital Report: Retrieved from: https://wearesocial.com/au/blog/2018/02/2018-digital-report-australia.

Meadows, M. (1995). Ideas from the bush: indigenous television in Australia and Canada. *Canadian Journal of Communication* 20 (2): https://doi.org/10.22230/cjc.1995v20n2a866.

Reporters Without Borders (2018a). Threats to investigative journalism and whistleblowers. Retrieved from: https://rsf.org/en/australia.

Reporters Without Borders (2018b). Difficult politicians. Retrieved from: https://rsf.org/en/new-zealand.

Sitigata, L. (9 August 2018). Australia: ABC's short-wave cutback 'weakens thin link' for Pacific, says PMC. *Pacific Media Centre*. Retrieved from: http://www.pmc.aut.ac.nz/pacific-media-watch/australia-abc-s-shortwave-cutback-weakens-thin-link-pacific-says-pmc-10207.

Statista (2018). Active social media users as percentage of the total population in New Zealand from 2015 to 2018. Retrieved from: https://www.statista.com/statistics/680698/new-zealand-social-media-penetration.

Stats NZ (15 April 2014). 2013 Census QuickStats about culture and identity. Retrieved from: http://archive.stats.govt.nz/Census/2013-census/profile-and-summary-reports/quickstats-culture-identity/languages.aspx.

Stats NZ (28 January 2015). Major ethnic groups in New Zealand. Retrieved from: https://www.stats.govt.nz/infographics/major-ethnic-groups-in-new-zealand.

Stats NZ (2018a). Population Clock. Retrieved from: 2018http://archive.stats.govt.nz/tools_and_services/population_clock.aspx?url=/tools_and_services/population_clock.aspx.

Stats NZ (23 April 2018b). International travel and migration: March 2018. Retrieved from: https://www.stats.govt.nz/information-releases/international-travel-and-migration-march-2018.

Stats NZ (2018c). New Zealand internet is going mobile. Retrieved from: http://archive.stats.govt.nz/browse_for_stats/industry_sectors/information_technology_and_communications/isp-2017-mobile-connections-story.aspx.

World Bank (2016a). Australia profile: Retrieved from: http://databank.worldbank.org/data/views/reports/reportwidget.aspx?Report_Name=CountryProfile&Id=b450fd57&tbar=y&dd=y&inf=n&zm=n&country=AUS

World Bank (2016b). New Zealand country profile: Retrieved from: http://databank.worldbank.org/data/views/reports/reportwidget.aspx?Report_Name=CountryProfile&Id=b450fd57&tbar=y&dd=y&inf=n&zm=n&country=NZL.

21

Indigenous Media in Australia
Lisa Waller

21.1   Introduction: Talking Back to Mainstream Media

Australia's Indigenous media sector is unique, prolific, mature, and evolving. Diversity and differences of purpose, as well as uncertainty, are part of its nature – offering space for a wide range of opinion and methods of delivery. Media that is owned and/or created by Indigenous people serves the news, information, and entertainment needs of the nation's Aboriginal and Torres Strait Islander people, who represent 2.8% of Australia's population according to the Australian Bureau of Statistics. Contrary to what many people think, the majority of Aboriginal people live in cities in Australia's eastern states and not in the remote desert regions of the continent; although, as we will see later in this chapter, the media services in these remote areas are arguably among the most innovative and distinctive. Digital technologies have made Indigenous news and information services increasingly accessible throughout the land for both Indigenous participation and "mainstream" interaction.

Australia's Indigenous media can be understood as a product of the nation's colonial past and its complex political and policy history (McCallum and Waller 2017b). When white colonizers arrived in 1788, Australia was declared *terra nullius* (no one's land) and this fiction formed the basis of colonizing policies and practices that robbed Australia's Aboriginal and Torres Strait Island people of their lands. This injustice was reinforced by racist policies that resulted in discrimination and disadvantage. As a consequence, today Indigenous people are over-represented in Australia's criminal justice system, and there is a significant gap in a number of outcomes between Indigenous and non-Indigenous people. In particular, Indigenous people have worse health, higher mortality, as well as lower literacy and numeracy (see Australian Government 2016).

In an overview of the scholarship on mainstream media representations of Indigenous people and issues, McCallum and Waller (2017b) note that the majority of research has provided a critique of "media racism." Such work has focused critically and analytically on how media coverage and reporting practices serve to sustain racist ideologies, and has repeatedly found that routine journalistic practices result in portrayals of Indigenous people and issues as a source of conflict, blame, and deficit (see for e.g. Due and Riggs 2011; Jakubowicz et al. 1994; Meadows 2001). Such representations contribute to an environment that produces negative social and health outcomes for Indigenous people, both directly and in their contribution to the process of developing and implementing policy (Paradies et al. 2008;

Transnational Media: Concepts and Cases, First Edition. Edited by Suman Mishra and Rebecca Kern-Stone.
© 2019 John Wiley & Sons, Inc. Published 2019 by John Wiley & Sons, Inc.

Stoneham et al. 2014). In summarizing the findings of a wide range of relevant studies McCallum and Waller (2017a) conclude:

> ... [mainstream] news reporting overwhelmingly represents Indigenous Australians as a source of societal risk and as problematic for the mainstream; Indigenous policy is generally only of interest when it meets a narrow range of news values – most importantly conflict and proximity to political elites, and the media construct Indigeneity as deviance and privilege news values of conflict and otherness. (p. 54)

In response, Indigenous peoples have developed their own media to provide news and information about, and relevant to, their communities. Indigenous media advance agendas including self-determination, sovereignty, cultural representation, and talking back to those in power. The development of a dynamic community broadcasting sector and the flourishing of Indigenous digital media have provided Aboriginal and Torres Strait Islander people with spaces that have enabled them to deliberate together, as well as tools for identity building, creative and political expression, for revealing and contesting Australian colonialism, sharing of news and entertainment, and participation in the wider political sphere (McCallum et al. 2012, Meadows 2005). From early newspapers, community broadcasting, and National Indigenous Television (NITV), to what we have termed "Indigenous participatory media" to describe Indigenous innovations in digital and social media (Waller et al. 2015), Indigenous-led media has responded, reacted to, and challenged Aboriginal and Torres Strait Islander peoples' representation in dominant Australian media.

The information presented in this chapter on the histories and aims of a range of Indigenous news and information outlets confirms the pivotal role they play as conduits of community information, in Indigenous activism, as mechanisms for debate and development of public opinion, in language sharing, and as tools of resilience and education – all of which have long been recognized (Forde et al. 2009; Hartley 2003; Hartley and McKee 1996, 2000). The brief overview provided in the following sections provides a picture of the rich history, proliferation, and variety within Australia's Indigenous media sphere across cities and rural and remote settings, as well as community, public broadcasting, and commercial contexts, and legacy and digital media.

21.2 Indigenous Media Overview: Pages, Channels and Platforms

21.2.1 Print Media

Indigenous newspapers have provided a wide range of perspectives on Aboriginal rights and other debates across the Australian political and social landscape since early colonial times. The long, proud, and continuing Indigenous print tradition dates back to the first Aboriginal community newspaper, *The Flinders Island Chronicle*. The inaugural edition dated 10September 1836, was written at Wybalenna Aboriginal settlement, Flinders Island, Tasmania. The last known edition was dated January 1838 (Burrows 2014; Meadows 2002). Its aim is set out in its first sentences: "the object of this journal is to promote Christian civilization and learning to the Aborigines, inhabitants at Flinders Island" (Burrows 2014). The purpose of Aboriginal newspapers changed dramatically in the twentieth century to become organs for political discussion and mobilization. *Abo Call: The Voice of Aborigines* was possibly the first "advancement movement" newsletter to be published, and it lasted six months from 1938.

It was followed by many small, community-based publications promoting Aboriginal causes (Meadows 2002). There is not space here to explore this history, but scholars have examined the roles played by Indigenous newspapers and found that these publications have not only kept communities informed about Indigenous organizations and perspectives on issues, but have also been "tools of resistance, empowerment and motivation" (Burrows 2010, p. 37).

The land rights movement that succeeded in having the doctrine of *terra nullius* over-turned through the landmark Mabo High Court case in 1992 has been the key Indigenous political movement in Australia. This is reflected by the fact that the land rights struggle has been an enduring and prominent theme throughout Indigenous newspaper content, and from the 1970s onwards newspapers were published with the specific purpose of informing, educating, and influencing about the land rights movement. *Land Rights News* was first printed in 1976, is owned by the Central and the Northern Land Councils, and is Australia's longest-running Aboriginal newspaper. It produces two print editions. One is centered on the capital, Darwin, in the tropical north. The other is based in Alice Springs and serves the people of the desert regions. *Land Rights News* provides a wide range of Indigenous political commentary and breaks local news across the vast Northern Territory, which has the highest proportion of its population who are Aboriginal (30%, compared with 4.7% or less for all other states and territories). Approximately 80% of Aboriginal people in the Northern Territory live in remote communities.

Published fortnightly since 1991, the *Koori Mail* is a 100%-owned Aboriginal commercial operation, published in hard copy weekly and online. It is distributed Australia wide and has a readership of more than 100 000 (Parker 2011) It prides itself on adhering to traditional jour-nalism values, including objectivity, and provides news, views, advertisements, and other material of relevance to Indigenous and non-Indigenous Australians interested in Indigenous affairs. The *National Indigenous Times* began publishing fortnightly in 2002, went weekly in 2011, and changed ownership in 2016, when it went wholly online (www.nit.com.au). It focuses on politics, and part of its content is reprinted from mainstream media. The battle to attract enough independent or government funding to continue publishing is a problem faced by most Indigenous publications.

21.2.2   Broadcasting

Aboriginal community broadcasting is seen as crucial for the promotion of Aboriginal culture and languages and the communication needs of Indigenous communities (Forde et al. 2009). In 1972, 50 years after the first radio broadcast in Australia, the first Indigenous-produced com-munity radio programs went on air. The sector enjoyed solid growth throughout the 1970s and 1980s and since then has expanded to include television and more than 130 community radio stations, establishing its own unique space in the Australian communications sphere.

The vibrant and innovative Indigenous community broadcasting tradition is reflected in the history and reach of well-established community-owned organizations, such as the National Indigenous Radio Service Limited (NIRS), which was set up in 1996 and delivers four radio channels of content. It takes program feeds from Aboriginal and Torres Strait Islander media associations from around Australia to provide 24/7 content to Indigenous media organizations that do not have the staff or resources to provide their own around-the-clock programming. NIRS is part of a much bigger story about the network of tiny media operations that are the bedrock of Aboriginal broadcasting. In remote areas, Indigenous people were provided with basic broadcasting and media production equipment in 1987 through the Federal Government's Broadcasting for Remote Aboriginal Communities scheme (BRACS), which was designed to give access to, and control of, their own media at a community level. The scheme had very limited funding, so basic domestic audio and video equipment was provided. The scheme ended years ago but laid the foundations for the innovative and important community media work done today in studios at the community level. This includes broadcasts in various languages and music styles that reflect the diversity of each audience and coverage area.

Indigenous involvement in the production and broadcasting of television, particularly for Indigenous audiences, has grown significantly since the first Indigenous television went on air. It was 1988, the 200-year anniversary of the arrival of British settlement, when Imparja Television was established in Alice Springs in the Northern Territory. There is now one national, state-sponsored television station, NITV, and Imparja continues to operate as a commercial satellite licensee. The community satellite TV network Indigenous Community Television (ICTV) was set up in 2001 and there are now three terrestrial open narrowcasting services (GTV in Broome, in the north of Western Australia; Ngarda TV in Roeburn, located in Western Australia's Pilbara region; and Larrakia TV in the Northern Territory capital of Darwin). An online initiative, Indigitube (run by ICTV), collects remote community content and makes it accessible on the internet for free. NITV's move in 2012 from a pay-TV subscription service to a free-to-air broadcaster marked a decisive moment: Indigenous voices and stories from across the country – and the world – have become readily available in the Australian media landscape. The channel now reaches more than two million unique viewers a month (Sheppard 2016). In urban areas, content produced by Indigenous media groups is broadcast through the regional arm of the national public broadcaster, the Australian Broadcasting Corporation (ABC), or community radio stations.

21.2.3 Digital and Social Media

The internet has enabled Indigenous people to participate more vigorously than ever before in forms of "mainstream" media, especially social media such as Twitter and Facebook. Sites such as the Koori History website (www.kooriweb.org), which dates back to 1994, not only amplify broad Indigenous concerns, but also enable diverse and dissenting Indigenous voices – which, as Indigenous blogger Celeste Liddle (2014) points out, is crucial for a healthy democracy.

The enthusiasm for new media technologies is no surprise, given the long history of Indigenous media innovation and adapting media to culture (see for e.g. Batty 1993; Michaels 1986). In addition, the commercial, distribution, and esthetic parameters of internet-based media are still relatively flexible, offering a field for renegotiation of Indigenous representation. Many major Indigenous institutions, including land councils and health organizations, are active online. Some provide specialized digital news and information sources. For example, the peak body for the network of 140 Aboriginal Medical Services across Australia, the National Aboriginal Community Controlled Health Organization (NACCHO), runs a daily online health news service, produces the newspaper *NACCHO News*, and uses social media to publish, circulate, and connect with others interested in Indigenous health-related news.

There are now scores of Indigenous multimedia hubs celebrating music, language, and culture across the country, from Ngaanyatjarra Media, in the Western Desert of Western Australia, to Gadigal Information Service's Kooris in Space based in the heart of Australia's biggest city, Sydney. They share the aim of creating greater appreciation and understanding of their cultures and provide opportunities for speaking and self-representations through uploading stories, sounds, and images. Other exciting developments include Indigenous digital media innovators aggregating Web 2.0 content in projects such as @Indigenous X and Deadly Bloggers, a network that operates across the internet and social media. Its founder, Leesa Wattego, says it feels good to have a place to "speak in my own voice" and provide a media platform for all Indigenous people who want to use the space. Others share this goal. Just a hashtag away in the Twittersphere,

@IndigenousX has attracted a strong national following of those willing to listen out for Indigenous voice (Sweet et al. 2013). Founded by activist Luke Pearson, @IndigenousX is a rotating Twitter account that features a different Indigenous commentator on a new topic each week. It is an example of user-driven innovation and of how Indigenous voices are emerging strongly in the rapidly evolving digital landscape. Pearson's foundational aim was to share the platform he had established on Twitter for storytelling to an attentive audience. Sweet et al. (2013) argue that its effectiveness now ranges from it providing the means to "both scale and tear down barriers to participation" (p. 108) to fostering cultural, emotional, and social wellbeing, and as both a journalistic innovation and a community development intervention.

But critical scholars including Dreher et al. (2016) warn against assuming that the proliferation of Indigenous and other minority voices enabled through the affordances of digital media guarantees democratic participation. They argue that in order to effect full participation, marginalized peoples must be listened to by the powerful (Dreher et al. 2016). This brings us back to the role of mainstream media in representing Indigenous people, and research findings that its narrow sourcing practices and sensationalist coverage persist, despite the proliferation of Indigenous media content and its wide availability via digital platforms (Dreher et al. 2018)

21.3 Conclusions: Looking to the Future

The Australian media landscape is undergoing seismic technological and industrial transformation. Mainstream news media institutions face revenue, audience, and staffing pressures, and journalists' and audiences' practices are changing with the move to digital platforms. At the same time, Indigenous people have succeeded in creating what is arguably one of the largest, strongest, and most distinctive alternative media subcultures in Australia (Waller et al. 2015). Five dimensions of Indigenous journalism culture have been identified in an international survey conducted by Hanusch (2014). These are: empowerment, counter-narrative, language revitalization, appropriate environment, and the watchdog function – which are all evident in the brief overview provided here. According to Hanusch (2014), "Indigenous media are almost always a response to the dominant culture's media treatment of Indigenous people" (p. 953. See Hokowhitu 2013, for a critical analysis of this position). The histories and aims of just a few of the wide range of Indigenous media outlets we have touched on here confirm the pivotal role they have played in Indigenous activism and as mechanisms for debate and development of public opinion.

Looking to the future, as with the challenges faced by news media more broadly, Indigenous outlets are adversely affected by audience fragmentation which makes it harder to gather a large audience for any one piece of media content. As Latimore et al. (2017) have argued, the challenge faced by Indigenous news media is to find a "centralized" or "aggregated" audience, and also "bridge" Indigenous perspectives and stories into mainstream news media more directly – in order to achieve the amplification of its intervention, on which full participation in terms of impact and influence relies. (Latimore et al. 2017, p. 9).

References

Australian Government (2016). Overcoming Indigenous disadvantage: Key indicators 2016. Retrieved from: www.pc.gov.au/research/ongoing/overcoming-indigenous-disadvantage/2016.
Batty, P. (1993). Singing the electric: Aboriginal television in Australia. In: *Channels of Resistance: Global Television and Local Empowerment* (ed. T. Dowmunt), 106–125. London: British Film Institute.

Burrows, E. (2010). Tools of resistance: the roles of two Indigenous newspapers in building an Indigenous public sphere. *Australian Journalism Review* 32 (2): 33–46.

Burrows, E. (2014). Resisting oppression: the use of Aboriginal writing to influence public opinion and public policy in Van Diemen's land from 1836–1847. *Media History* 20 (3): 221–238.

Dreher, T., McCallum, K., and Waller, L. (2016). Indigenous voices and mediatized policymaking in the digital age. *Information, Communication and Society* 19 (1): 23–39.

Dreher, T., Waller, L., and McCallum, K. (2018). Disruption or transformation? Indigenous voices contesting policy in the digital age. In: *Global Cultures of Contestation* (ed. E. Peeren, R. Celikates, J. de Kloet and T. Poell), 215–240. London: Palgrave Macmillan.

Due, C. and Riggs, D. (2011). *Representations of Indigenous Australians in the Mainstream News Media*. Brisbane: Post Pressed.

Forde, S., Foxwell, K., and Meadows, M. (2009). *Developing Dialogues: Indigenous and Ethnic Community Broadcasting in Australia*. Bristol: Intellect.

Hanusch, F. (2014). Dimensions of Indigenous journalism culture: exploring Maori newsmaking in Aotearoa New Zealand. *Journalism* 15 (8): 951–967.

Hartley, J. (2003). Their own media in their own language. In: *Remote Control: New Media, New Ethics* (ed. C. Lumby and E. Probyn), 42–66. Cambridge: Cambridge University Press.

Hartley, J. and McKee, A. (1996). *Telling Both Stories: Aboriginal Australia and the Media*. Perth: Arts Enterprise, Edith Cowan University.

Hartley, J. and McKee, A. (2000). *The Indigenous Public Sphere: The Reporting and Reception of Aboriginal Issues in the Australian Media*. Oxford: Oxford University Press.

Hokowhitu, B. (2013). Theorizing Indigenous media. In: *The Fourth Eye: Maori Media in Aotearoa New Zealand* (ed. B. Hokowhitu and V. Devadas), 101–123. Minneapolis: University of Minnesota Press.

Jakubowicz, A., Goodall, H., Martin, J.A. et al. (1994). *Racism, Ethnicity and the Media*. Sydney: Allen & Unwin.

Latimore, J., Nolan, D., Simons, M., and Khan, E. (2017). Reassembling the Indigenous public sphere. *Australasian Journal of Information Systems* 21: 1–15.

Liddle, C. (2014). On diverse views of constitutional recognition. *Rantings of an Aboriginal Feminist*. Retrieved from: blackfeministranter.blogspot.com.au.

McCallum, K. and Waller, L. (2017a). *The Dynamics of News and Indigenous Policy in Australia*. Bristol: Intellect.

McCallum, K. and Waller, L. (2017b). Indigenous media in Australia: Traditions, theories and contemporary practices. In: *Minorities and the Media in Australia* (ed. J. Buderick and G.S. Han), 134–161. London: Palgrave Macmillan.

McCallum, K., Waller, L., and Meadows, M. (2012). Raising the volume: indigenous voices in news media and policy. *Media International Australia* 142: 101–115.

Meadows, M. (2001). *Voices in the Wilderness: Images of Aboriginal People in the Australian Media*. Westport: Greenwood.

Meadows, M. (2002). Bridging the gaps: towards a history of Indigenous media in Australia. *Media History* 8: 9–20.

Meadows, M. (2005). Journalism and Indigenous public spheres. *Pacific Journalism Review* 11 (1): 36–41.

Michaels, E. (1986). *The Aboriginal Invention of Television*. Canberra: AIATSIS.

Paradies, Y., Harris, R., and Anderson, I. (2008). *The impact of racism on Indigenous health in Australia and Aotearoa: Towards a research agenda*. Discussion Paper 4, Darwin: Cooperative Research Centre for Aboriginal Health.

Parker, K. (2011). Indigenous people in the media: telling it like it is and how it could be. In: *Unsettling the Settler State: Creativity and Resistance in Indigenous Settler-State Governance* (ed. S. Maddison and M. Brigg), 51–67. Sydney: The Federation Press.

Sheppard, H. (2016). Indigenous radio and television. Retrieved from: www.australia.gov.au/about-australia/australian-story/indigenous-radio-and-television.

Stoneham, M.J., Goodman, J., and Daube, M. (2014). The portrayal of Indigenous health in selected Australian media. *The International Indigenous Policy Journal*, 5(1), 1–13. Retrieved from: http://ir.lib.uwo.ca/iipj/vol5/iss1/5.

Sweet, M., Pearson, L., and Dudgeon, P. (2013). @IndigenousX: a case study of community-led innovation in digital media. *Media International Australia* 149: 104–111.

Waller, L., Dreher, T., and McCallum, K. (2015). The listening key: unlocking the democratic potential of Indigenous participatory media. *Media International Australia* 154: 57–66.

22

The Story of Wellywood

How Director Peter Jackson Conquered the World While Remaining in New Zealand

Grant Hannis

It is one of the most remarkable stories in cinema history. In New Zealand, an isolated country in the south Pacific with a tiny population (about 5 million in 2018), some of the biggest and most successful Hollywood blockbusters of the last 20 years have been made. They cost hundreds of millions of dollars to make and have generated billions in revenue.

The movies' director, Peter Jackson, steadfastly refused to move to the US. Instead, Hollywood came to him, with actors and technicians traveling to New Zealand to make the movies alongside New Zealanders. Jackson's studios are based in the country's capital, Wellington, thereby earning the city the nickname "Wellywood."

This chapter considers Jackson's career, focusing on how he was able to pull off this extraordinary feat.

22.1   A Kiwi Boy

For many years, New Zealand's isolation and small population conspired to constrain the country's film industry. There were some tenacious New Zealand filmmakers early in the twentieth century, but by the 1970s the industry was largely moribund. The government stepped in, establishing the New Zealand Film Commission to help fund New Zealand movies, on the basis that such films would help promote New Zealand's cultural and economic life.

Even so, those who succeeded in the New Zealand film industry typically went overseas to further their careers. Directors like Roger Donaldson, Lee Tamahori, and Taika Waititi all built careers in Hollywood, as did actors such as Sam Neill and Temuera Morrison. The big exception has been Peter Jackson.

Jackson was born in 1961 and grew up in Pukerua Bay, a coastal settlement not far from Wellington. An only child, the young Jackson fell in love with the movies, including *King Kong* (1933) and *Jason and the Argonauts* (1963), fantasy films that combined stop-motion animated models with live actors. He also developed a liking for horror movies, particularly comedy gore as found in the material of British comedy troupe Monty Python and movies such as *The Evil Dead* (1981) and *Re-Animator* (1985). His adult career began with the production of similar material, and throughout his career his movies have featured many visual effects.

On leaving school at 17, Jackson worked for a short time as a photo-engraver at a local newspaper. At the weekends, Jackson and some friends began making his first movie, *Bad Taste* (1987). The film was a comical, albeit highly bloody, account of aliens rampaging through

Transnational Media: Concepts and Cases, First Edition. Edited by Suman Mishra and Rebecca Kern-Stone.
© 2019 John Wiley & Sons, Inc. Published 2019 by John Wiley & Sons, Inc.

a small New Zealand town. Jackson learnt from fan magazines such as *Famous Monsters of Movieland* how to make the latex masks for his aliens, baking the masks in his mother's oven.

After four years of filming and at a cost of $37 000[1] (mostly Jackson's own money), *Bad Taste* was still unfinished. Jackson eventually obtained about $355 000 in Film Commission funding to complete the movie. The Commission's paperwork required Jackson to have a name for his then notional, filmmaking company. He came up with WingNut, the name of a friend's pet rabbit. *Bad Taste* received limited overseas distribution, but mostly favorable reviews.

22.2 Important Meetings

Around this time, Jackson forged relationships with a range of people who would have a profound effect on his career. One was Jim Booth, a leading figure at the Film Commission. Recognizing Jackson's talent, Booth left the Commission to become an independent producer, working with Jackson on his next three movies. Jackson felt vindicated by having Booth, a film-industry professional, support him. Sadly, Booth died before Jackson's career went stellar. "He was there for me at just the right time," Jackson later said of Booth. "Had he lived I'm certain we'd still be partners today" (Jackson, quoted in Sibley 2006, p. 272).

Around the same time he met Booth, Jackson met a young couple: Richard Taylor and Tania Rodger. They were trying to launch a visual effects business and had already made puppets for a New Zealand television show. Taylor and Rodger would go on to run the visual effects departments on all of Jackson's subsequent movies. Jackson also met Fran Walsh, with whom he would write the screenplays for all his subsequent movies. Walsh later became Jackson's partner and together they are the parents of two children.

Jackson joined forces with Booth, Taylor, Rodger, and Walsh to produce his second feature, the gory and sexually explicit puppet comedy *Meet the Feebles* (1989). The movie relied largely on New Zealand Film Commission funding for its $980 000 budget. The team's next collaboration was yet another comedy horror movie, *Braindead* (1992), renamed *Dead Alive* in the US. This film's $3.7 million budget was mostly funded by the Film Commission too. The movie was a blood-soaked homage to zombie films. Jackson defended the gore, likening it to Monty Python. "You go so totally over the top that people will have to laugh" (quoted in Pryor 2003, p. 97).

Although Jackson's movies had only limited releases in the US and were not major hits, his talents were starting to be noticed in Hollywood. Mark Ordesky at film company New Line Cinema had seen and liked *Bad Taste*. On the strength of this, New Line commissioned Jackson to write an (ultimately unused) script for a horror film. The Disney company also approached Jackson to direct a teen-zombie romance. Jackson declined, preferring to work on his own projects back in New Zealand. Jackson later explained: "Staying in New Zealand and making low-budget, independently financed movies allowed me to control my career path and make my own decisions in a way that would have been impossible in Hollywood" (quoted in Sibley 2006, pp. 233–234). Nevertheless, Jackson hired a US agent, Ken Kamins, to represent his interests in Hollywood.

22.3 No More Gore

Jackson's fourth movie marked a change of tone, as he abandoned comedy gore. *Heavenly Creatures* (1994), again funded by the Film Commision, was based on an actual 1950s murder in New Zealand. Two teenagers, Juliet Hulme and Pauline Parker, had formed an intense friendship, including creating their own fantasy world. Tragically, their delusions saw them eventually murder Parker's mother.

Heavenly Creatures was a major step forward, showing that Jackson could produce a sensitive movie of emotional depth. The visual effects in the movie marked the first use of computer technology in a Jackson movie. Impressed by the film, US film company Miramax distributed *Heavenly Creatures* in America, where it was a moderately successful arthouse movie.

Around this time, Jackson, Taylor, and Rodger – along with another long-time Jackson colleague, editor and producer Jamie Selkirk – formed Weta, a company designed to produce visual effects for Jackson's and others' films. Jackson would later recall: "It was scary – none of us had a clue about running a company, but it felt the right thing to do" (quoted in Hawker 2014, p. 8). Weta could produce top-quality visual effects at a fraction of the cost US competitors charged, largely because of lower labor costs in New Zealand. For instance, it was estimated that if George Lucas' Industrial Light and Magic had been used on the *Heavenly Creatures*, a single shot would have consumed the movie's entire visual effects budget.

Jackson's reputation in the US continued to grow. Indicative of this, Jackson's next project, *Forgotten Silver* (1995) – a mockumentary about a pioneering New Zealand filmmaker – featured some of Jackson's high-powered American friends, including film reviewer Leonard Maltin and, long before his fall from grace, then Miramax head Harvey Weinstein. First shown on New Zealand television, *Forgotten Silver* was funded by New Zealand On Air, a government-owned institution that finances local television productions, and the Film Commission.

22.4 Hollywood Movies

Through Kamins, Jackson met Robert Zemeckis, a movie producer and director at Universal Pictures. Zemeckis was best known for the enormously popular *Back to the Future* trilogy. Zemeckis was interested in commissioning Jackson and Walsh to write a horror film. This morphed into Jackson also directing the movie, titled *The Frighteners* (1996). This was Jackson's first Hollywood-backed movie, although, true to form, he made it in New Zealand. The movie sported many visual effects and a bona fide movie star – Michael J. Fox – in the lead role. Fox was keen to work with Jackson after seeing *Heavenly Creatures* at a Canadian film festival.

Weta continued to grow, providing the many digital and other visual effects for *The Frighteners*. As well as local staff, Weta imported designers from overseas. This led to some tensions when it became clear the effects people from the US were often paid considerably more than their local counterparts.

The Frighteners was strongly promoted in the US but was not a box office success. Against a budget of $50 million, it generated about $40 million in revenue internationally. Perhaps its offbeat tone did not connect with audiences. Nevertheless, the movie signaled that Jackson was now a Hollywood player.

At this juncture, Universal commissioned Jackson to produce a remake of *King Kong*, the movie that had so influenced Jackson as a child. Millions of dollars were spent on pre-production, but, with the release of competing movies *Godzilla* (1998) and *Mighty Joe Young* (1998), Universal canceled the project. Jackson and his team were devastated, but the cancelation proved a blessing in disguise.

Jackson moved onto his next proposed project, filming J. R. R. Tolkien's book *The Lord of the Rings*. He settled on pitching a two-movie version of the Tolkien classic, believing digital technology could portray Tolkien's fantastical world convincingly. To minimize the production cost, Jackson proposed that both movies be made simultaneously in New Zealand.

Jackson approached Harvey Weinstein, who was prepared to allow Jackson to undertake the project in New Zealand but would only bankroll one movie. Jackson declined, feeling it was impossible to do justice to the book in one film. It seemed that, as far as Jackson's involvement was concerned, the project was dead. But following Ken Kamins' intercession, Weinstein agreed to give Jackson four weeks to find another studio prepared to produce two movies, in which case Weinstein would enter into a partnership with that studio to make the films.

Jackson and his team took up the offer and approached New Line. Jackson's old friend Mark Ordesky was keen to help – he had long been a fan of *The Lord of the Rings*. To Jackson's pleasant surprise, New Line was prepared to produce *three* movies, Jackson's preferred option. The project got the green light.

Always adept at publicity, Jackson was able to mobilize the New Zealand population and authorities to support the production. Indeed, the country became one giant studio, with filming taking place across New Zealand. Jackson imported actors from the US, Great Britain, and Australia for the major roles. The core cast resided in New Zealand for nearly two years to make the movies. New Zealand actors filled out many of the lesser roles. Likewise, Weta imported an army of technical staff from overseas, who lived and worked alongside talented locals. Initially, New Line had been skeptical that Weta could handle the massive technical work involved in making the movies but was eventually convinced – no doubt in part because Weta could produce its visual effects at a cost far less than US alternatives.

Shooting in New Zealand was not a radical idea for US studios. Since the 1990s, facing rising costs at home, Hollywood studios had been making movies and television shows in other countries, such as Canada and Australia. This often allowed the studios to use advantageous exchange rates, lower labor costs and government-backed incentive schemes to make the productions more cheaply than in the US (US National Archives and Records Administation 2001). These factors applied in New Zealand too. Major US television series were made in New Zealand, including *Hercules: The Legendary Journeys* (1995–1999) and *Xena: Warrior Princess* (1995–2001). Between 1999 and 2011, the main production period of the *Rings* trilogy and its prequel, *The Hobbit*, the New Zealand dollar was on average worth 60% the value of the US dollar, so the US studios' budgets went further when the money was spent in New Zealand (figures derived from Reserve Bank of New Zealand 2018). We have already seen how Weta undercut US competitors like Industrial Light and Magic. The *Rings* production also benefited from millions of dollars in tax breaks offered by the New Zealand government (at least partially offset by the boost in tourism and employment the movies generated). The *Rings* movies (2001–2003) were still expensive to make – about $400 million – but making them in the US would have cost far more.

The *Rings* movies were a massive success, generating about $4 billion internationally and catapulting Jackson to the top rungs of the directorial ladder. He now had the clout to raise Hollywood money relatively easily to make films in New Zealand. He returned to *King Kong* (2005), financed by Universal. The cost was high – $250 million – but the resulting film was another major financial success, generating more than half a billion dollars worldwide.

Jackson's next movie, financed by a consortium of US studios, was a change of pace. *The Lovely Bones* (2009) told the grim story of a raped and murdered teenage girl observing her family from the after-life. The movie was not a great commercial success, no doubt in part because of its subject matter.

22.5 Diversification

Jackson began to diversify into production. He had earlier co-produced a low-budget New Zealand film, *Jack Brown Genius* (1997), but now worked on major projects. The first was *District 9* (2009), a science-fiction film set in South Africa. The next was *The Adventures of*

Tintin (2011), a film about the Belgian comic-book hero, directed by Steven Spielberg. Jackson followed this with the documentary *West of Memphis* (2012).

Weta also diversified, supplying visual effects for a myriad other movies and television shows, including some of the biggest films of the time. Many were made in New Zealand. This strategy had begun as long ago as 1993, when Taylor and Rodger had provided creature effects for Stephen King's *Tommyknockers* television series. Weta worked on the *Narnia* (2005–2010) movies, James Cameron's *Avatar* (2009), and the *Planet of the Apes* (2011–2017) franchise. Taylor said that when the original *Kong* project collapsed, diversification saved Weta. In particular, working on Zemeckis' movie *Contact* (1997) was "the project that saved our bacon" (quoted in Sibley 2006, p. 340).

Although Jackson had originally intended only to produce and co-write the *Rings* prequel trilogy, *The Hobbit* (2012–2014), events led to him directing the movies as well. Delays in preproduction caused the original director, Guillermo del Toro, to leave the project and Jackson took over. He had limited time to prepare to direct the films, but pressed on regardless. The *Hobbit* movies were funded by another consortium of US studios and were massively expensive, costing about $800 million. The New Zealand government gave the *Hobbit* producers about $110 million in tax breaks to help sweeten the deal.

But the government went even further. In the New Zealand film industry, actors are typically hired as contractors and therefore have fewer workers' rights than do employees (employees' rights include the right to paid vacations, receive redundancy, unionize, etc.). An industrial dispute arose, with some actors demanding the *Hobbit* production treat actors as employees. The studios involved in financing the film, Warner Brothers and New Line, threatened to take the production to another country if the issue was not settled to their satisfaction. In response, the New Zealand government passed a law that confirmed that those who work in the local film industry are contractors, not employees. That legislation is now known colloquially in New Zealand as the "Hobbit law." A recently elected new government announced in late 2017 that it intends to repeal the legislation because, as it only applies to the film industry, it is regarded as discriminatory. Despite the problems, the *Hobbit* movies proved another massive commercial success, earning about $3 billion worldwide.

Jackson's most recent project was *They Shall Not Grow Old* (2018), a feature-length documentary about British soldiers' experiences in World War I. The documentary included digitally restored and colorized archive footage. He also co-produced and co-wrote *Mortal Engines*, a science-fiction blockbuster, made in New Zealand and financed by US studios. The film, directed by Jackson protégé Christian Rivers, was released in late 2018. In the future, Jackson hopes to produce a long-delayed remake of *The Dam Busters* movie, as well as making some smaller films telling New Zealand stories (Croot 2018; Exeter College 2015).

22.6 Conclusions

While remaining in the small, isolated country of his birth, Peter Jackson has made some of the most expensive, technically sophisticated, and commercially successful movies ever. How has he managed this?

In part, it is because of his innate talent. Without attending film school or serving any kind of apprenticeship in the industry, Jackson has instinctively been able to create massively popular movies. It seems he was born to make films, learning his craft as he went along.

He coupled his natural talent with tenacity. Despite lacking money, time, and professional actors, over the course of four years he made his first movie. He successfully accepted the challenge to find within four weeks another backer for the multimillion-dollar *Rings* trilogy. When the *Hobbit* project hung in the balance, and with little time to prepare, he stepped in to direct the movies.

And he benefited from the input of vital colleagues, including Jim Booth, Richard Taylor, Tania Rodger, and Fran Walsh. By some lucky chance, all these remarkable New Zealanders happened to be living in Wellington in the late 1980s and met each other. His contacts in the US – including Ken Kamis and Mark Ordesky – also played key roles at critical stages in his career. And his steady output of films was proof of his abilities and work ethic.

Another compelling reason for Jackson's success was economics. In his early years, the Film Commission's financial support helped Jackson establish himself. And when he graduated to blockbusters, although they cost hundreds of millions to make, they were still *relatively* inexpensive. Lower labor costs, an advantageous exchange rate, and government assistance (including tax breaks and the Hobbit law) meant Jackson could make blockbusters more cheaply in New Zealand than if they had been made in the US. Coupled with this, Weta's diversification strategy strengthened the company's finances, helping the company to survive, flourish, and continue to support Jackson.

Jackson's approach of making three movies simultaneously, which he did for both the *Rings* and *Hobbit* trilogies, further reduced the cost of each film. That is because the production team needed to convene just the once to make each trilogy. But this approach was risky for the studios. Should the first movie of a trilogy fail, the money had already been spent making the second and third movies, now also likely to fail. The studios could not cut their losses by canceling production of the second and third movies. Indeed, Jackson has said that if the *Rings* trilogy had failed, the consequences for New Line would have been "disastrous" (Jackson 2016).

But, of course, the *Rings* movies succeeded, and this encouraged everyone to stick with a winning formula. Jackson had proven he could deliver, so US studios were happy for him to continue making blockbuster films in New Zealand.

Could such a feat be replicated elsewhere? The combination of talent, hard work, luck, and economics that produced Jackson seems so remarkable as to suggest not. But who knows? Perhaps in some other remote, small part of the world is the next Jackson – a child eagerly watching the *Rings* and *Hobbit* films, who will grow up to make world-beating movies without leaving home.

Note

1 To allow comparisons over time, all dollar figures are adjusted for inflation and expressed in 2017 US dollars.

References

Croot, J. (12 November 2018). *Sir Peter Jackson hasn't given up hope of making The Dam Busters.* Retrieved from: https://www.stuff.co.nz/entertainment/celebrities/108520139/sir-peter-jackson-hasnt-given-up-hope-of-making-the-dam-busters

Exeter College (30 July 2015). Sir Peter Jackson in conversation [YouTube video]. Retrieved from https://www.youtube.com/watch?v=9XDsSr3sGSI.

Hawker, L. (2014). *Weta workshop: celebrating 20 years of creativity.* New York: HarperCollins.

Jackson, P. (16 November 2016). Peter Jackson interview on "The Lord of the Rings" (2002) [YouTube video]. Retrieved from: https://www.youtubc.com/watch?v= ggVDYcvNxg.

Pryor, I. (2003). *Peter Jackson: From Prince of Splatter to Lord of the Rings.* Auckland: Random House.

Reserve Bank of New Zealand (2018). *Exchange rates and TWI.* Retrieved from:https://www.rbnz.govt.nz/statistics/b1.

Sibley, B. (2006). *Peter Jackson: A film-Maker's Journey.* Sydney: HarperCollins.

U.S. National Archives and Records Administration (2001). *The Migration of U.S. Film & Television Production: The Impact of 'Runaways' on Workers and Small Business in the U.S. Film Industry.* Washington, DC.: U.S. National Archives and Records Administration.

Index

Note: Page numbers in *italics* refer to figures, those in **bold** refer to tables.

Transnational Media: Concepts and Cases, First Edition. Edited by Suman Mishra and Rebecca Kern-Stone.
© 2019 John Wiley & Sons, Inc. Published 2019 by John Wiley & Sons, Inc.

CPSIA information can be obtained
at www.ICGtesting.com
Printed in the USA
LVHW020708180723
752586LV00012B/1357

9 781119 394